CONTENTS

KIDS ACROSS THE SPECTRUMS

KIDS ACROSS
THE SPECTRUMS

GROWING UP AUTISTIC IN THE DIGITAL AGE

MERYL ALPER

The MIT Press
Cambridge, Massachusetts
London, England

The MIT Press would like to thank the anonymous peer reviewers who provided comments on drafts of this book. The generous work of academic experts is essential for establishing the authority and quality of our publications. We acknowledge with gratitude the contributions of these otherwise uncredited readers.

This book was set in Stone Serif and Stone Sans by Westchester Publishing Services, Danbury, CT. Printed and bound in the United States of America.

Library of Congress Cataloging-in-Publication Data

Names: Alper, Meryl, author.
Title: Kids across the spectrums : growing up autistic in the digital age / Meryl Alper.
Description: Cambridge, Massachusetts : The MIT Press, [2023] | Includes bibliographical references and index.
Identifiers: LCCN 2022033238 (print) | LCCN 2022033239 (ebook) | ISBN 9780262545365 (paperback) | ISBN 9780262373999 (epub) | ISBN 9780262374002 (pdf)
Subjects: LCSH: Mass media and youth. | Technology and youth. | Autistic children. | Youth with disabilities.
Classification: LCC HQ799.2.M352 A47 2023 (print) | LCC HQ799.2.M352 (ebook) | DDC 302.23083—dc23/eng/20221212
LC record available at https://lccn.loc.gov/2022033238
LC ebook record available at https://lccn.loc.gov/2022033239

10 9 8 7 6 5 4 3 2 1

ACKNOWLEDGMENTS

Writing this book primarily during the COVID-19 pandemic has been a solitary process in some ways, but I have never been alone. I mentally revisited past conversations with research participants as I reread their words. I shared chapter drafts with friends via email and enjoyed looking over their thoughtful notes in the margins. And I tried to spend as much precious time as possible with the loved ones in front of me instead of staring at a screen.

Many people have helped me to realize this book from start to finish. First, I want to thank all of the children and parents who allowed me into their homes and shared a part of their world with me. There would be no book without them. I am also indebted to the nonprofit groups and advocacy organizations that circulated my recruitment materials among families, including TILL (Toward Independent Living and Learning, Inc.) and the Autism Program at Boston Medical Center.

I am very appreciative of those at Northeastern University who provided funding for the project on which this work is based, including the Al Khalifa family and the Latifa Al Khalifa Grant, the College of Arts, Media, and Design (CAMD) Dean's Office, and Northeastern's Institute for Health Equity and Social Justice Research. I am also grateful to research assistants Adesewa Adelekun, Madison Irons, and Erika Christiansen for their invaluable help with fieldwork, memo writing, transcription, and data analysis.

Thank you to everyone at the MIT Press, especially my editor, Susan Buckley, for her steady guidance and encouragement over the many years that we have had the pleasure of working together. I immensely appreciate the anonymous reviewers' feedback on the book prospectus and manuscript.

Various scholars generously provided me with comments on research materials, chapter drafts, and other work and ideas that appear in this book, including Morgan Ames, Linda Blum, Kristen Bottema-Beutel, Elizabeth Ellcessor, Elizabeth Fein, Kristen Harrison, Os Keyes, Paul Lichterman, Melissa Morgenlander, Dylan Mulvin, Jeff Nagy, Matt Rafalow, Kate Ringland, Beth Semel, and Olga Solomon. Over the years, I have also learned a great deal from autism advocates and autistic writers who shared their resources and insights, both on social media and in person. Thank you especially to Lydia X. Z. Brown, Alyssa Hillary, and M. Remi Yergeau.

I have had the honor of presenting in-progress work from this book at several conferences and workshops, including annual meetings of the International Communication Association (ICA), the Society for Social Studies of Science (4S), and the Association of Internet Researchers (AoIR). Thank you to the attendees of those presentations and my copanelists. I would also like to thank the organizers and attendees of the Communicating Universal Design workshop at Lund University, particularly Aimi Hamraie and Bess Williamson.

This book has additionally been enriched by my participation in several fellowship programs. Thank you to the Northeastern Humanities Center Faculty Fellows Program and the 2018–19 "Cultures of Ability" cohort, led by Sari Altschuler and Lori Lefkovitz; the CAMD Dean's Fellows Program and Dean Elizabeth Hudson; and Northeastern's Institute for Health Equity and Social Justice Research Faculty Fellows group, especially Alisa Lincoln and Suzanne Garverich.

At Northeastern, it has been a great privilege to work, collaborate with, and teach among stellar colleagues in the Department of Communication Studies over the past several years, including Ryan Ellis, Dale Herbeck, Susan Mello, and Brooke Foucault Welles, and to have the departmental support of Angela Chin.

I am tremendously lucky to have wonderful friends in Boston, Los Angeles, New York, and beyond who have always been there to support me in my successes and cheer me on during challenging times. I am beyond blessed to have the family that I do, whose unconditional love and pride in me is a constant source of encouragement. And last, but never least, thank you to Glen for being my PPE (Pandemic Partner Extraordinaire).

1 INTRODUCTION

In 1959, an article titled "Joey: A 'Mechanical Boy'" appeared in the popular science magazine *Scientific American*.[1] It was written by the influential child psychologist Bruno Bettelheim, who at the time was the director of the Orthogenic School of the University of Chicago. Bettelheim's career and reputation were built on his work with children at the school who, like Joey, were on the autism spectrum, which was known in the scientific community at the time as childhood schizophrenia. In his *Scientific American* piece, Bettelheim frames the story of Joey as a cautionary tale: "a case history of a schizophrenic child who converted himself into a 'machine' because he did not dare be human."[2] Bettelheim claims that in his daily life, Joey adopted the persona of a robot that rejected human feelings and that his pathology was caused by his supposedly unloving parents. Joey also drew pictures of himself, featured in the piece, full of wireless controls and electrical circuits. Using these self-portraits and his notes on Joey's treatment, Bettelheim crafts a therapeutic narrative in which Joey "ceased to be a mechanical boy and became a human child" by the end of his treatment with Bettelheim; the psychologist treated Joey when he was between 9 and 12 years old.[3]

Bettelheim would later come to prominence as a public intellectual for his 1976 book *The Uses of Enchantment*, which argued that fairy tales were important for children's development because the dark and fantastical stories allowed them to grapple with complex emotions.[4] In the years since his passing in 1990, however, Bettelheim's work has received significant rebuke. The criticism includes claims that his academic credentials were fraudulent, that he abused patients under his care, and that his theories of the causes of autism were wrong.[5] Yet the dominant and dehumanizing image of the autistic mechanical boy persists in the public eye and in popular culture. Through his own fantastical, dark telling of Joey's story, Bettelheim perpetuated the idea that autistic children are inherently mechanical in their thinking and behavior, functioning "as if by remote control."[6]

The notion that kids on the spectrum prefer technology over human interaction has taken many shapes in mass media. News reports falsely imply a link between autism, violent video games, and school shootings, as well as associate people on the spectrum with criminality.[7] In a much milder version of the mechanical-boy stereotype, autistic youth are assumed to have a natural affinity for technology. This belief underpins investments in social therapy robots and in workforce training programs in the high-tech sector, which are designed primarily to capitalize on autistic children's purported penchant for detail and preference for repetition.[8] The trope of mechanized children is also reflected in anxieties that mobile devices and new media rewire the brains of neurotypical young people (i.e., those whose intellectual and cognitive development is considered normative), allegedly reducing empathy, causing the avoidance of eye contact, and rendering them unable to handle spontaneous social interactions.[9] At its most alarmist and panic-stricken, such rhetoric warns of screens inducing an "epidemic of cultural autism."[10]

Since the publication of "Joey," other forms of misinformation about autism have proliferated, including the dangerous claim that it is caused by childhood vaccination.[11] Though the exact neurological and genetic basis of the condition is unknown, autism is, in the broadest possible terms, a cognitive, biological, and behavioral phenomenon that influences how people move, think, and perceive the world around them.[12] Some people on the autism spectrum are very talkative, while others may be unable to reliably communicate through oral speech. Some are intellectually gifted, while others have significant cognitive challenges. Some autistic individuals are highly sociable, while others prefer greater solitude.[13] These qualities and abilities are variable and can fluctuate over the years or depending on the day. People are born autistic and remain so throughout their lives, though there is far more research on children than on adults. Individuals today are far more likely to personally know someone who is on the spectrum than they did when "Joey" was first published. This is for a multitude of reasons, including disability activism in the late twentieth century that pushed for the closure of inhumane institutions housing disabled people and for their fuller community integration.[14]

This book invites a retelling of history that centers on Joey's story instead of Bettelheim's version. The reductive and overly simplistic characterizations of young people on the spectrum, their technology use, and associations between autism and media present a paradox because, in actuality, there is very little real-life research on the media environment that surrounds autistic children into which any new technological innovation or intervention would presumably enter. Nor has much work chronicled the digital experiences of children on the spectrum who might otherwise contend with major opportunity barriers to social and digital inclusion based on their race, ethnicity, class, or gender.[15] Beyond Joey's beloved circuits and controls, the persuasive and appealing design of new media may also uniquely interact with the social, behavioral, and communicative characteristics of autism and neurodivergence in both positive and negative ways.[16] I set about working on this book to reconcile how neurotypical people could talk with such authority about the relationship between autism, children, and technology without a strong empirical basis to their claims, and to remediate some of the harms done to autistic people by the perpetuation of these myths.

Kids Across the Spectrums critiques and complicates stereotypes about "mechanical boys" by presenting the first book-length study of autistic young people and their everyday uses of media and technology. From 2013 through the beginning of the coronavirus pandemic in 2020, I conducted in-depth qualitative research in the homes of more than sixty children, ages 3 to 13, in Boston and Los Angeles. This diverse group comprised young people of many races, ethnicities, socioeconomic classes, and genders, for there are "Joeys," but there are also "Josephines" and "Josefinas." The work was informed by the multiple ethical, communicative, and practical considerations of conducting ethnographic fieldwork with speaking and nonspeaking autistic young people.[17] I interviewed adolescents about their media likes and dislikes, consulted with caregivers about their hopes and concerns about screens, and observed autistic children at home engaging in their favorite media activities. This included playing video games with their parents, chatting with their friends on FaceTime, and making YouTube videos with their siblings. Executing this research over the past decade, I focused less on passing technological trends and more on patterns that consistently emerged in the narrative accounts of autistic children and their loved ones.[18]

I found that what kids on the spectrum are doing with media is not necessarily radically different from what the nonautistic population of young people are doing. Indeed, prior research has shown that autistic children's overall time spent with media on average may be on par with the time spent by neurotypical school-age kids.[19] However, the experiences that children on the autism spectrum have with technology are less explained by their diagnoses alone and more by the intersections of their disability with other aspects of their identity and the modern conditions of childhood. They differentially face significant social and health inequalities—including limited recreational programs, poor neighborhood safety, and challenges receiving appropriate therapeutic services—and I argue that these disparities spill directly over into autistic children's media habits.

Employing a grounded theory approach, in which participant data is used to develop explanatory insights from the bottom up,[20] I identified three overlapping areas of autistic children's successes and struggles with technology that I explore in this book: *cultural belonging, social relationships*, and *physical embodiment*. This project documents the marginalization that technology can compound while highlighting the strengths that autistic young people bring to digital media and the unique opportunities that they find there for social connection, communication, and creativity.

THE SOCIOTECHNICAL SHAPING OF SOCIALITY

While this book chronicles the mediated lives of individual autistic children, the stories of these young people are linked together. Furthermore, how their stories are connected has to do with much more than just their or their family members' singular experiences. Sociologist C. Wright Mills used the term "sociological imagination" to describe the ability to identify relationships between personal biography and larger social realities.[21] Social science theories help us explain those associations, identify specific phenomena, and enhance public understanding. In this book, I draw on a range of theories from several relevant academic fields, such as sociology, child development, and science and technology studies (STS). I critically reimagine these ideas in new and practically useful ways based on my conversations and observations, and additionally through the lenses of disability and autism.

Research in the field of communication studies—my primary academic discipline—increasingly explores the role of new media in the lives of marginalized groups and how technology can both ameliorate and contribute to their invisibility, exclusion, and misrepresentation. Disability and its connections to social, cultural, and political life though are little understood, with notable exceptions.[22] This omission not only masks the multifaceted ways that disability intersects with other dimensions of human difference, but also dislocates disabled people from important theoretical and conceptual debates. For, as historian Katherine Ott writes, "Disability is unique in the extent to which it is bonded with technology, tools, and machines as a medium of social interaction."[23] This book extends an analysis of technology and marginality that I examined in my last book, *Giving Voice*.[24] That project centered on how nonspeaking children with disabilities (primarily autism) used Apple iPads as assistive speech aids, otherwise known as augmentative and alternative communication (AAC) devices, and the extent to which those technologies gave them a metaphorical and literal voice.

Considering the multimedia potential of the iPad, I became interested in everything else that autistic kids were doing with digital devices. Ethnographers have illustrated the value of media in children's lives and how racially and ethnically marginalized youth navigate this landscape,[25] but they have rarely focused on disabled children.[26] While their preferences for media platforms and activities do not diverge significantly from those of their nonautistic peers (e.g., television, YouTube), autistic children's motivations for seeking out certain content can vary; for example, they may be seeking sensory stimulation or emotional comfort.[27] Children on the spectrum are also reportedly more likely than nonautistic youth to engage in excessive media use, with possible negative health effects including sleep disruption, increased sedentary activity, and decreased exercise—all of which has been exacerbated by the COVID-19 pandemic.[28] Yet the evidence for these outcomes is often incomplete and decontextualized from daily life. Most published research is based on parent surveys, focus groups, or phone interviews that oversample White, educated, upper-middle-class mothers of boys.[29] Reflecting other sociological work on the geographies of youth,[30] this book fills a gap by directly engaging diverse autistic children in conversations about their media use from within in their home environments, where they spend the most time with technology.

This book also builds upon theories from the academic field of STS, which looks to examine the historical, sociocultural, and political context of the development and impacts of science, technology, and their entwinement (i.e., the sociotechnical). Since the beginnings of the field's existence, there has been an awareness of how disability and disabled people complicate linear, progress-oriented narratives of technological innovation and scientific discovery.[31] With respect to autism, there is a burgeoning scholarly space in STS for examining how biomedical discourses construct the condition as a social category.[32] Autism, for instance, has long been employed as a cultural metaphor to describe self-isolation and a personal tendency toward aloneness.[33] This pathologized framing is rooted in a prescriptive, neurotypical understanding of what ideal sociality and communication should be like. Less attention has been paid, though, as to how ideas about autism shape popular technological discourse itself, or as disability studies scholars David Mitchell and Sharon Snyder note, how "disability underwrites the cultural study of technology *writ large*."[34]

In this book, I argue that the technological experiences of autistic children underscore the intricacies, anomalies, and expectations of the socially mediated world, or what I term "the sociotechnical shaping of sociality" (STSS). Sociologist John Law notes that "the social is not purely social at all" because society is also structured by technology.[35] But what it means to *be* social—to possess social skills, interact socially, and have meaningful relationships—also does not exist outside of the affordances and constraints of technologies for enacting sociality, nor is it beyond social stigmatization and the boundaries of society more broadly. For instance, as part of the iOS 14 software update in 2020, Apple added the Eye Contact function to its FaceTime video chat app. According to the company, the new feature "uses machine learning to subtly adjust the position of your eyes and face to make video calling more natural even when you're looking at the screen instead of the camera."[36] The fact that Eye Contact is enabled by default on the iPhone highlights the subtle ways in which neurotypical social norms become embedded in design. While a non-autistic person might not notice any differences in their communication as a result of Eye Contact being turned on, autistic people commonly report that making eye contact feels unnatural to them and that forced eye contact with others is painful and anxiety inducing.[37]

In my development of STSS, I draw on what cultural anthropologists Elinor Ochs and Olga Solomon term "autistic sociality" to convey how the set of social repertoires that autistic people work from, like preferring to avoid direct eye contact in conversation, is one of many valid, not lesser, possibilities for being social.[38] Implicating autism in the complexity of that which is sociotechnical disrupts the use of autism as a symbol through which rigid and oppressive normativity is reinforced.[39] Even to Bettelheim, Joey's case was about more than any one child. "His story," Bettelheim wrote, "has a general relevance to the understanding of emotional development in a machine age. . . . [Our] society of mechanized plenty often makes for [difficulties] in a child's learning to relate."[40] The tale of Joey, Bettelheim writes, is one of humanity triumphing over machines.

It is a tale, I contend, that needs to be retold, and by people besides just myself. The more that researchers and lay individuals learn about autism, the more challenging it becomes to summarize or universalize. One reason for this is that the story of disability has historically been told by those without disabilities.[41] People on the spectrum (who themselves vary vastly in their opinions and beliefs) are increasingly taking discursive ownership through autistic autobiography, or what rhetorician M. Remi Yergeau terms "autie-biography."[42] Because of this, it is important to note early on that I do not identify as autistic, nor do I have a close family member on the spectrum. I rigorously approach critical questions of disability and communication technology through the theoretical lens of an academic committed to equity, and in applied contexts as an educational researcher who has worked over the past 20 years to make inclusive and accessible learning products with media organizations such as Sesame Workshop, Nickelodeon, and PBS KIDS. Considering my focus on inequalities, it is also relevant to share that I am an upper-middle class, White-appearing, English-speaking, straight, and cisgender woman who has benefitted from privileges produced by these distinctions in a contemporary US context.[43] In *Kids Across the Spectrums*, I incorporate the research of autistic scholars who address autism and neurodiversity from a variety of disciplinary, theoretical, and methodological perspectives, as well as the writings of a diverse group of disability activists, journalists, and youth regarding their experiences with media, technology, and marginalization.[44]

In the following pages, I build a case for STSS, first by reviewing the literature on autism and the contested framing of autistic people's sociality—and effectively, their humanity. I then discuss how the power to deem certain technologies or technological usage "social" and the conditions under which this is done is rarely in the hands of autistic people, although these dynamics are gradually shifting, especially for youth as they employ digital and social media to share their unique viewpoints.[45] Next, I turn toward young people on the autism spectrum and the varied ways in which "social technologies" shape their lives. Lastly, I detail the complexity of "the spectrum" in the context of autism, media, race, and socioeconomic status, and conclude with an overview of this book and a summary of subsequent chapters. I begin now with a discussion of how media, technology, and sociality can take on a range of domain-specific meanings for autistic young people, illustrated by Adrian's story in the next section—which I should note for readers contains discussion of physical victimization and emotional trauma, all too frequent occurrences for autistic individuals (see also the beginning of chapter 7).[46]

"IT'S TURNED INTO MORE OF A SOCIAL MEDIA WEBSITE FOR ME"

I interviewed 13-year-old Adrian, a White autistic boy, in his dimly lit living room in the Boston suburbs while he nestled into an overstuffed chair, his auburn curls peeking out from the sweatshirt hood that he kept up for much of interview.[47] His mom, Brianna, referred to Adrian as "an Aspie," referencing an Asperger's syndrome diagnosis that he had received before it fell under the umbrella of autism in the fifth edition of the American Psychiatric Association's *Diagnostic and Statistical Manual of Mental Disorders* (DSM-5), which is used by clinicians to diagnose the condition. Brianna noted that her husband, Adrian's father, Stewart, "would say he has Aspie-like qualities" as well. When I asked Adrian what he most liked to do on the computer, he brought up Scratch, a kid-friendly computer programming website and online community developed by researchers at the Massachusetts Institute of Technology for children to share and remix projects that they code and design. I was perplexed, however, when Adrian referred to the website as "social media," a label that seemed more fitting for the mobile apps Instagram or Snapchat, neither of which he used. "Scratch was originally meant to be a 'share what you have learned' type of thing, but people have turned it into a really active social media page," he said.

Adrian had started using Scratch at age 7 and enjoyed making "slightly buggy, really large, fun games." Lately though, he had been using the studios feature on the website (i.e., collaborative pages where different users can put multiple coding projects) to engage in a role-playing game in which players use the Comments section to discuss characters that they and others create. "It's turned into more of a social media website for me instead of just a normal coding website," Adrian said of this activity. He described a constant flow of users commenting on one another's content and receiving notifications that he would sometimes check on his phone during class if he finished a test early. "People have learned how to turn this into like pretty much automatic chatting where you can keep up with people almost instantly," he said. Outside of Scratch, Adrian rarely texted people and preferred to talk on the phone with friends from school or his weekly Pokémon League gaming meetup. He did belong to Amino, a social networking app for anime fans, but used it more for consuming content than receiving follows and comments. Said Adrian, "I still check [Amino] every day just to see what new art there is, but I don't use it as social media anymore."

Adrian's reflections on the social adaptability of Scratch and his selective use of social media for interpersonal purposes reminded me of a long history of the co-optation of new communication technologies, personal definitions of the "social" in social media, and instances of platforms being appropriated for uses beyond those intended by their original designers.[48] Consider those on Tinder who use the dating app in an "off-label" way to professionally network instead of meeting romantic partners.[49] The landline telephone was eventually used as means of social connection and conversation, but only after it was initially advertised for business and household management.[50] Scratch already invites such ambiguity of use[51] as both a computer programming tool and online community. Adrian and his fellow users had turned the message boards of a website dedicated to designing games into a role-playing game itself.

His engagement with Scratch also speaks to larger issues of cultural norms, social power, and technological agency. Adrian's digital media use occurred against the offline backdrop of peer bullying, which started for him in fifth grade, the year he began attending the same arts-focused charter school as his older brother, Marco. Brianna and Stewart hoped the more creative environment would be a better fit for Adrian than the sports-oriented public schools in their town. The charter school, however, did not provide him with any of the support services for his autism, anxiety, and dyslexia that were detailed in his Individualized Education Program (or Plan) (IEP), a legal document outlining how a child's specific learning needs will be met in the US education system. The school's failure to adhere to the IEP came to a head one day when Adrian placed his hands on a desk near another girl in his class. She asked him to move and when he did not, she responded by stabbing him with a pencil, to which he reacted by hitting her.

While the girl was not punished—an outcome perhaps less likely if her victim had not been autistic—Adrian was suspended from school for two days. Though Adrian was only 10 years old at the time, the girl's father also decided to press charges with the police. To make matters worse, when Adrian returned to school, a group of older boys cornered him on the playground and told him to "fight like a man." Brianna worried that if the abuse continued, Adrian would end up in a residential treatment program or harming himself. After the incident, the girl's parents said that they would drop the charges if Brianna and Stewart pulled Adrian out of school, which gave them the impetus to leave. She and her husband subsequently enrolled him in a private school for students with learning disabilities. His tuition was funded under Massachusetts's Chapter 766 law, which guarantees the rights of all young people with disabilities to an educational program best suited to their needs.[52]

Throughout Adrian's traumatic and turbulent experience, he was systematically isolated while simultaneously denied the opportunity to build social and emotional competencies. What he underwent emphasizes how disability and impairment are intertwined,[53] as it is difficult to disentangle the social traumas that intensified Adrian's autism-related challenges from the impact of being stripped of his entire social world because he was autistic. In programs at his new private school and through counseling outside of school, Adrian worked on social pragmatics (i.e., the language one uses in social situations) or what his family referred to as "keeping your shit together." He put significant effort into emotional regulation and managing his frustration. The training that Adrian received was bound up with his desire to connect with others around him and through media. Brianna noted how playing video games at home with Marco and his friends motivated Adrian to keep himself levelheaded as to not embarrass himself in front of the older boys. "If he gets frustrated playing a game, he has learned that he can't slam the door to his room and throw stuff around because people will hear that," said Brianna, "so he will quietly walk up the stairs and lay in bed and read if he's had enough."

Technological and creative play were central to Adrian's forging of social bonds. Referencing his reading challenges, he said that Scratch was "great for me and many other kids because it usually says outright what the block does ... it's a way easier type of code for me to understand." He had "lots of story ideas" for Scratch and showed me one such animated clip he had made that reminded me of an artsy indie film, in which an elevator door opened and closed on different scenes. Adrian's technical skills were also opening doors for him professionally, so to speak. After attending a Scratch camp where he excelled at helping younger campers, he got offered a part-time job mentoring kids at a different computer camp with their projects on Minecraft, another digital game space for creative worldbuilding. "I'm really glad that I'm starting now," Adrian said about the job, "because I was getting concerned like oh, you know, I'm starting slow," reflecting a pressure commonly felt by US teens to start their professional advancement early. Far from retreating into the digital world, Adrian's rich involvements with Scratch and Minecraft were an important social bridge to new participatory prospects.

DEFINING AUTISM

It is important to contextualize Adrian's choice of words to socially classify networked technologies. He was someone who not only eschewed what might traditionally be thought of as social media, but a person who was clinically characterized as lacking sociality by virtue of his diagnosis. No test like blood samples or a brain scan can diagnose autism; doctors instead rely on behavioral observations and caregiver reports. "Infantile autism" was first recognized as a clinical diagnosis in the United States in the third edition of the DSM within a class of several "pervasive developmental disorders."[54] Along with the World Health Organization's International Classification of Diseases (ICD-11), released in 2018, the revised DSM-5 outlines various criteria for making an autism diagnosis.[55] It defines the condition as a spectrum of closely related disorders that present as "persistent deficits" in an individual's development of social relationships, as well as "restrictive, repetitive" patterns of behavior, interests, or activities. However, diagnostic manuals are not politically neutral tools, as they have historically been wielded in unjust ways.[56] For example, homosexuality was pathologized in earlier editions of the DSM.[57] Childhood schizophrenia was phased out as a diagnosis—a change though that was motivated by a racist and racialized desire to distinguish White "autistic children" from Black "childhood schizophrenics."[58]

Defining autism exclusively through the lens of diagnostic manuals like the DSM fits into what is known as a medical model of disability, in which disability is located biologically within the individual.[59] The aim of therapeutic interventions and research supported by this model is to prevent, diminish, or correct for a disability. In the case of autism, this medicalization regularly manifests in language used to describe increasing rates of autism diagnoses as a "crisis" or as a "disease" in need of a "cure."[60] Many in the autism community find this rhetoric and media coverage harmful because it characterizes autistic people as a burden and rationalizes violence against them.[61] This perspective may have also contributed to the ableism that Adrian experienced in school. The material and symbolic environment around an autistic person (e.g., the laws and policies shaping Adrian's education) can also significantly restrict and limit their abilities, reflecting a social model of disability that shifts emphasis away from the individual and toward the stigmatizing effects of society. Another formulation, the political/relational model of disability,[62] recognizes gaps in both models for overlooking the collective strengths and pleasures of being disabled.[63] For example, Scratch hosts several animated videos made by autistic children discussing and explaining proudly what their autism means to them.[64]

In their everyday lives, kids on the spectrum encounter challenges across their individual, social, and political contexts, and these obstacles are shaped by the fact that neurotypical communication and movement is the dominant cultural standard. In terms of interaction with nonautistic people,[65] these challenges can include back-and-forth conversation, understanding emotional intention and nonverbal communication, and expressing oneself with language.[66] Behaviorally, autistic children may have difficulties with executive functioning, including planning ahead, handling changes to routines and transitions between activities, and dealing with sensory input sensitivities.[67] Autistic children are regularly victims of bullying and social exclusion.[68] But life is not always a struggle, and there are unique assets that autistic children may have as well. For example, some learn to read at an early age (or what is known as hyperlexia).[69] Cognitively, strengths can include visual pattern recognition, attention to detail, rule-based thinking, and rote memory. Some have a keen sense of humor, especially when it comes to jokes that defy logic and expected setups.[70]

The terms for referencing autism are also far from straightforward. The medical field largely uses "autism spectrum condition" (ASC) or "autism spectrum disorder" (ASD), and accordingly, "person with autism/ASC/ASD." Parents and clinicians tend to prefer using "person with autism," which in disability parlance is known as "person-first" language, over "autistic" or "autistic person," which is referred to as "identity-first" language. Some would argue, however, that the phrase "person-first" has more to do with word order than necessarily putting people first in the sense of prioritization. Autistic adults generally favor "identity-first" language, reflecting the idea that their autism is an inseparable part of who they are, though this varies culturally.[71] Using "person with an autism diagnosis" as an alternative is complicated because not everyone who would meet the criteria for a diagnosis is able to get one. Being diagnosed is distinct from culturally identifying with autism, as in the shared rituals, language, and art that produce common meanings among autistic people.[72] This is particularly true for autistic adults, many of whom did not receive formal diagnoses as children or for various reasons have not sought one out as an adult, such as Adrian's father.

Another common and perhaps more neutral diagnostic term is being "on the autism spectrum," a concept introduced by Lorna Wing, a medical researcher and parent of an autistic child.[73] The word "spectrum" is meant to symbolize many things: that autism is more like multiple related conditions than a single one; that these conditions can be expressed in myriad ways; and that there are many possible life trajectories for a person with an autism diagnosis. However, as continuums have beginning and end points, this language may also reinforce the idea of a hierarchy of abilities, whereby some are deemed "low" or "high" functioning.[74] These terms are controversial within the autism community because they create a binary and can end up minimizing the struggles of people considered high functioning and minimizing the strengths of people considered low functioning. Science journalist Steve Silberman points to multiple clusters instead of a single linear spectrum, noting that autism "[produces] a distinctive constellation of behavior and needs that [manifest] in different ways at various stages of an individual's development,"[75] a perspective that I adopt in this book.

AUTISM AND SOCIALITY

Clinical autism research focuses primarily on evaluating an autistic individual's one-on-one social competencies, and less so on the effects of social life and cultural expectations in their groups and communities.[76] Cognitive theories have dominated autism research with little attention paid to how social contexts shape understandings and experiences of autism; hence, ethnographies like this book are quite rare. The prefix "aut" in autism comes from the Greek word *autós*, meaning "self." The term "autism" was coined in 1911 by German psychiatrist Eugen Bleuler to describe people who he believed had an inner life not readily accessible to others.[77] In the early 1940s, Leo Kanner was the first scientist to publish research on infantile autism,[78] which had a significant impact on the development of the DSM. The DSM-5 includes diagnostic criteria such as "deficits in social-emotional reciprocity" (i.e., social interaction), "deficits in nonverbal communicative behaviors used for social interaction" (i.e., social communication), and "deficits in developing, maintaining, and understanding relationships" (i.e., social imagination).[79]

The wide assumption of preferred solitude among those on the autism spectrum is currently undergoing resistance and revision by psychologists, anthropologists, and autism self-advocates.[80] They contend that the social motivations of autistic people do not rest solely within the diagnosed individual but arise from dynamic interactions and relationships in specific contexts over time.[81] For example, in a much commented-upon 2019 article in the academic journal *Behavioral and Brain Sciences*, psychologists Vikram Jaswal and Nameera Akhtar argue that people on the spectrum *appearing* socially uninterested is not the same as them actually *being* socially uninterested.[82] Perceptions of autistic people's social behaviors are influenced by how others (particularly those who are nonautistic) interpret their expressions of social interest.[83] Being understood as having strong interpersonal abilities depends on how both society and technologies designate someone as a social person, subjective determinations that are influenced by perceptions of disability as well as race, ethnicity, class, gender, and sexuality.[84]

Proponents of neurodiversity, a term coined by sociologist Judy Singer and popularized by journalist Harvey Blume,[85] argue that neurological differences impacting learning, attention, and other cognitive functions are authentic forms of human diversity (conditions including but not limited to autism, such as attention-deficit/hyperactivity disorder [ADHD]). They challenge the idea that neurodivergent people should be forced to socially conform to a neurotypical ideal.[86] Neurodiversity is both a philosophy centered on acceptance and a movement focused on access to needed supports and accommodations. Through the lens of neurodiversity, autistic education scholar Damian Milton contends that instead of individuals on the spectrum not being able to see the perspectives of others, it is neurotypical people who have a "double empathy problem" by being unwilling to empathize with those who are autistic.[87] Far from isolated in their own worlds, autistic people often have a deep sense of morality and are finely attuned to various forms of social injustice.

Within the fields of sociology and anthropology, flexible interpretations of social interactions have only recently been extended to individuals on the spectrum. Georg Simmel, one of the first sociologists to study sociality, described sociability as the urge to associate with others for the sake of associating and as an essential part of society.[88] However, the impulse to engage in small talk, for example, is not universal. Ochs and Solomon offer autistic sociality as a concept that describes a form of sociality shared by autistic individuals that is not quantitatively less social than the form preferred among nonautistic people, but instead qualitatively different.[89] Human sociality encompasses a range of possibilities for social coordination shaped by situational contexts, materials, and the dynamics of groups and individuals, with autistic sociality being one such permutation. For instance, people on the spectrum report that they find very satisfying companionship in nonhuman entities like animals, objects, and even their own bodies.[90] In his memoir, penned when he was 12 years old, the autistic author Ido Kedar writes that he treats self-stimulatory behaviors such as flapping his hands "like a welcomed friend because they are really with me all the time."[91]

Ochs and Solomon distinguish between the social that is interpersonal and the social that is sociocultural, while recognizing their co-constitution. For example, the ability of autistic people to navigate conversational rules and norms of social behavior depends a great deal on the normative and neurotypical structures of society. Anthropologist Ben Belek, in his ethnographic study of autistic university students, draws attention to "the creative technologies people design when typical responses to social rules remain out of their reach."[92] Marginalized social groups may internally develop "alternative techniques of social proficiency" when expected social rules are "inherently inaccessible"[93] to them. For example, when autistic people began to organize Autreat, a retreat-style conference, in the 1990s, they developed a color-coded communication system using red, yellow, and green badges to indicate personal willingness to be approached for conversation.[94] In his use of the term "creative technologies," Belek refers to *techne*, which is the Greek root of "technology" and means the capacity for humans to transform their abilities and the world.[95] Remaking the social world through code and craft is essentially something that autistic people and individuals with disabilities are well equipped to do.[96]

AUTISM AND THE SOCIOTECHNICAL SHAPING OF SOCIALITY

Autistic people provide at once unique and undervalued insights into research on technology and society that speak to both specific and broad experiences of marginalization. They have much to add as a group whose interpersonal relations have long been mediated by the internet because of stigma, bias, and discrimination.[97] New media—for example, social media hashtags on Twitter such as #ActuallyAutistic, #AskingAutistics, and #BlackAutisticLivesMatter—have made visible a wider range of social identities and intersectionality that exist around being autistic and has helped connect people on the spectrum with one another despite the physical distance between them.[98] Online spaces have certain affordances—such as the removal of facial cues, asynchronous conversation, and the ability to pause for breaks—that allow many on the spectrum to communicate with both neurotypical and neurodivergent individuals in a more natural and pleasurable way.[99] That autistic people develop community online runs counter to the asocial diagnostic classification of autism. Social norms and perceptions of sociability are both created and contested by autistic people through digital technology.

This negotiation illustrates the sociotechnical shaping of sociality, or, in more formal terms, the interrelation of technology, society, and social norms across mutually dependent macro-level institutions and micro-level interactions. Feminist approaches to STS have critiqued histories of technological development that lend too much power to scientific and technical experts when marginalized social groups, including disabled people, are actively excluded from participation in those processes.[100] STS has also inadequately accounted for autism and neurodiversity in theorizing the relationship between human and technological trajectories, with some perpetuating the claim that autistic people are "are born without socialness."[101] In recent years, this has been contested by feminist STS scholars such as Jessica Rauchberg, who call for neurodivergence and neuroqueer technoscience to more richly inform the development of information and communication technologies. These scholars draw on the concept of "crip technoscience," proposed by disability scholars Aimi Hamraie and Kelly Fritsch, in order to center disabled knowledge production within the social study of technology.[102] STSS is most directly derived from the social shaping of technology approach in STS,[103] which deconstructs how technology enables certain societal opportunities while society and social actors (e.g., developers, users) generate different technological options, with neither being predetermined.[104] For autistic young people, this means that the living, socializing, and coping mechanisms available to them and their families are shaped by the media platforms at their disposal, which children like Adrian also fluidly co-opt for different social purposes.

STSS generates broader questions beyond autism about how both interpersonal and sociocultural dynamics shape and are shaped by technology, with particular attention paid to those individuals who find dominant social rules to be uninterpretable or social spaces to be inaccessible. For example, Sara, mom of 8-year-old Isaac (a nonspeaking White boy with communication and sensory processing challenges) noted that "he watches YouTube all the time. I feel like socially he gets this whole other aspect of this whole other world that maybe he wouldn't be able to access." Experiencing sociotechnical inaccessibility can itself generate meaningful social processes and new technological possibilities. By centering autism and the perspectives of autistic people in the study of technology, society, and sociality, STSS responds to Mara Mills and Jonathan Sterne's call for "dismediation," which prompts a rethinking of media theory through disability theory, or, in other words, understanding "disability as a constituting dimension of media, and media as a constituting dimension of disability."[105]

Additionally, STSS builds upon work in communication studies and media sociology that challenges the presumed superiority of physical, face-to-face contact,[106] as well as questions the taken-for-grantedness of "social" behaviors on social media platforms, such as liking or sharing.[107] Such presumptions underlie much psychological work on autistic youth media use. For example, in their study "Prevalence and Correlates of Screen-Based Media Use Among Youths with Autism Spectrum Disorders," clinical psychologist Micah Mazurek and her colleagues write that a majority of autistic 13- to 17-year-olds in the United States "spent most of their free time using non-social media (television, video games)" while less than a quarter of them "spent time on social media (email, internet chatting)."[108] Compared to children with intellectual disabilities, learning disabilities, and speech and language impairments, autistic children used social media less and non-social media more.

While it may be a clear-cut distinction from the purview of clinical psychology, deeming one type of media social and another nonsocial is difficult to do within media and cultural studies, where it is understood that people make all kinds of media—including television and video games—socially meaningful through their shared practices and experiences.[109] Communication scholar James Lull, for example, highlights how TV has structural uses, in that it can shape the flow and organization of human behavior in various settings, as well as relational uses, in that it may facilitate or curb communication, social learning, and interaction.[110] Video game play is often presumed to be solitary and separate from social engagement with friends and family, but this is rarely the case, especially for autistic children.[111] The claim that young people on the spectrum choose less immediately socially interactive media due to their supposed social impairment is problematic because it makes an essentialist argument about the relationship between autism and sociality that somehow exists outside of technology. Instead of starting from the socially determinist assumption that autistic people are asocial or antisocial, or the technologically determinist idea that television or any other kind of media is inherently social or antisocial, STSS asks how media and technology directly and indirectly impact how people learn to participate in and contribute to society and the meaning of sociality itself.

MODERN AUTISTIC CHILDHOODS

Autistic children are rarely understood to be social actors or recognized as engaging in social activities, which in turn impacts how they express themselves socially through media and technology. For kids on the spectrum, the failure to follow unwritten implicit social codes of the neurotypical majority has psychosocial consequences. Frustration arising from unsuccessful social exchanges, pressure to conform to neurotypical expectations, and peer victimization can all lead to negative mental health outcomes, such as depression and anxiety.[112] When young people on the autism spectrum enter the complicated landscape of adolescence, research has shown that they express a desire to connect with their peers but end up infrequently participating in social activities or hanging out with friends outside of school.[113] Self-help books with titles like *The Asperkid's (Secret) Book of Social Rules* are written with the aims of helping autistic adolescent audiences master etiquette in order to prevent future harms.[114] Many participate in school-based intervention programs that are focused on social skills.[115] Some researchers have argued, however, that these programs center the neurotypical communication preferences of therapists and that social programs built around shared interests are more effective.[116]

The social challenges that autistic children face occur among the broader conditions of contemporary childhood, within which media and technology are increasingly central. Today's young people on the spectrum might have much in common with past generations of autistic individuals who are now adults in terms of their social, emotional, and sensory needs. It is important to recognize, though, the differential influence of growing up in the hypermediated twenty-first century. There are important distinctions between the experiences of older autistic adults and autistic children today that are borne of the latter coming of age following passage of the Americans with Disabilities Act (ADA) of 1990. The ADA resulted in legal and cultural shifts toward greater (yet not full) inclusion, leading disability rights activist Rebecca Cokley to coin the term "the ADA generation."[117]

Modern communication technologies also impact multiple interconnected layers of children's lives inside and outside their homes. This encompasses, for example, a child's use of a Google Chromebook for homework, Google's data policies in school districts, and a lack of legal regulation of Alphabet, Google's parent company.[118] Dynamic understandings of the relationship between society and technology also extend to the level of the individual, meaning that children and adolescents both act on and are acted upon by sociological and technological forces. For instance, machine learning algorithms embedded in search engines and recommendation systems for streaming video content on YouTube or Netflix may have a disproportionately negative impact on autistic children, and in more than one way. These technological features could make it difficult for those who have challenges with top-down executive functioning to set their own time limits on media use; those with cognitive challenges might have difficulty understanding the persuasive intent of digital advertising, marketing content, and political propaganda.[119] The STSS approach incorporates transactional and ecological system perspectives on autism and human development,[120] which emphasize how autism is not a static entity and that the social influences on any one autistic person are multilayered across their immediate social environments and the wider sociocultural context.[121]

AUTISTIC CHILDREN AND "SOCIAL" TECHNOLOGIES

Children on the spectrum reportedly spend more time with screen-based media than any other leisure activity, averaging about four and a half hours per day.[122] Research on their media use is largely clinically oriented and centered on correcting deficits in the individual child, framing their social expression as more biomedically determined than contextually dependent.[123] However, when applied to autistic young people and their use of technology, being social has multiple meanings. This includes research on how media purportedly promote harmful *antisocial* behavior and exacerbate *asocial* self-isolation, the development and deployment of instructional technologies intended *to socialize* autistic children, and media that autistic children adopt and appropriate for their own *socializing*.[124] What makes a technology a "social technology" is negotiated across these different categories. The STSS perspective highlights how these varied framings of sociotechnical dynamics shape one another as well.

A focus on asocial behavior is reflected in work on curbing improper screen use and problematic addiction.[125] Negative media effects measured in such studies include autistic children's diminished ability to read facial expressions, lower friendship trust, and feelings of alienation.[126] Some research suggests that children on the spectrum prefer interactive media because it is more predictable and easier to control than social or environmental stimuli, which are often unpredictable.[127] Far less work has examined media's positive psychosocial effects on them.[128] The majority of published research on the harms of screen and interactive media for autistic children has been on television and video games. Autistic adolescents report a preference for video games over other leisure activities[129] and spend on average one hour more per day playing them than their typically developing peers.[130] Little of that time with video games is reportedly spent on social interaction.[131] Even within games that contain some opportunity to interact with others, online exchanges can lead to negative social consequences like cyberbullying and online harassment, which are further exacerbated by challenges that autistic children may encounter in registering emotional cues.[132] These reports on overall media use also reflect the gendered skew of autism research and higher rates of video game use among boys.[133]

When autistic children are encouraged to use technology by teachers, therapists, and counselors, it is often with the purpose of having them more fully adapt into neurotypical society. Apps, robots, and other socialization tools encourage social learning and imitation, with the goal of assisting autistic children by reducing anxiety or uncertainty when encountering novel social situations.[134] These digital media emphasize specific goals such as teaching children turn-taking in play, rules in games, and reciprocity in face-to-face conversation. However helpful they might be, these technologies are often implicitly or explicitly designed to make children appear "less autistic" in their communication and behavior.[135] They are rarely designed to support nonautistic young people in how they communicate and socialize with their autistic peers or the interdependence between people with and without disabilities.[136]

Socialization technologies span a wide range of philosophical intentions. Virtual reality has been used to teach autistic children to recognize body language, register facial expressions, and gauge emotional environments in a customizable digital simulation. Studies have shown that virtual reality can aid autistic children in adapting to pretend play situations with a peer.[137] Robots programmed to predictably perform simple social interactions, based on the principles of cognitive behavioral therapy and applied behavior analysis,[138] have similarly been used to practice joint attention, reading facial expressions, and initiating conversations.[139] Wearable devices like Google Glass are also being deployed with autistic children. Through speech recognition algorithms, spoken words can be translated into text and paired with a social response, then projected onto the lens of the glasses in the user's line of sight.[140]

Educational, therapeutic, and medical technologies for autistic socialization come with a host of limitations, including a lack of empirical support even if one accepts their rationale.[141] Critics contend that some of these technologies treat autistic children like machines and perpetuate Bettelheim's framing of them as robotic and inflexible in their movement, language, and emotions.[142] It should be noted that some autistic people, most famously the animal behaviorist Temple Grandin, describe their thought processes in technological terms or "thinking in pictures," the title of Grandin's 1995 book.[143] The focus on autistic minds as computers, though, can overshadow other helpful interventions. There is strong evidence that art, nature, and animal-based therapies are enjoyed by autistic children and can similarly support social interactions by reducing anxiety.[144] Yet funding for "innovative" research tends to go toward new gadgets.[145] Therapeutic technologies are generally geared toward a particular kind of sociality, which does not necessarily include the kinds of social activities, interactions, and relationships that autistic individuals indicate that they desire.[146] Teaching children that sociality can be followed like a script also raises ethical issues regarding compliance and agency.[147]

Taken together, the asocial, antisocial, and digital socialization framings of autistic children and their media use underpin the pervasive belief that screens must be educationally or therapeutically beneficial in order for them to be worthwhile. This imbalance is reflected in the lack of research on autistic youth's digital socializing, which takes place in physical and virtual social spaces where there is a digital presence. It involves digital tools designed for and by autistic people as well as those that youth on the spectrum like Adrian adapt for social purposes.[148] For example, autistic tweens, teens, and young adults like influencer Chloé Hayden have taken to the musical social media platform TikTok to change public perceptions of autism, partly in reaction to the ableism perpetuated on the app.[149] Through their digital ethnographic work, Kathryn Ringland and colleagues have studied Autcraft, a private Minecraft server that provides a supportive space for autistic children to play in the virtual world.[150] The Autcraft community works with the strengths that autistic children have while also being responsive to realistic challenges. Young people with disabilities ought to be able to enjoy the pleasurable aspects of digital play and performance regardless of any measurable clinical benefit.[151]

ACROSS THE (AUTISM, MEDIA, AND SOCIOECONOMIC) SPECTRUMS

Besides engaging with a full range of media in this book, I center the stories of children who not only are on the autism spectrum, but who also come from vastly different socioeconomic, racial, and ethnic backgrounds along with other aspects of human difference. The STSS perspective attends to the different ways in which social groups are historically marginalized in society. The study of autism is inherently incomplete based on who does and does not have access to a diagnosis. This book is no different, as illustrated by the story of Monisha and her three sons Orion (age 4), Kahlil (age 7), and Clayton (age 8). Monisha is a single Black mother without a college degree who, when I met her in the summer of 2019, was trying to find work as a home health aide. She and her sons lived in an apartment subsided through the Section 8 rental assistance program for low-income households.

I first interviewed Monisha on a hot June day in Boston. She wore a black tank top, and I immediately noticed, on her upper right arm, a large tattoo of three interlocking puzzle pieces, each containing the name of one of her sons. Puzzles are an object of children's play, but puzzle pieces have also become a ubiquitous symbol of autism.[152] Monisha verified that her tattoo was "kind of autism inspired." What primarily interested me about the tattoo, though, was that only two of her children, Orion and Kahlil, were diagnosed with autism. Older brother Clayton was part of Monisha's tattoo but not technically eligible for my study because he did not (yet) have an autism diagnosis. The reason for his exclusion reveals how autism is never one spectrum, but multiple.[153] Race, class, and ableism work in tandem; in the United States, more than half (56 percent) of autistic children live in poverty, whereas, of the children not on the spectrum, the rate is 42–47 percent.[154]

What we know about autism and autistic children is heavily influenced by who gets counted in the first place.[155] In the United States and other industrialized countries, the number of children with a diagnosis has been on the rise since researchers first began systematically tracking autism in the early 2000s. Among children, the Centers for Disease Control and Prevention (CDC) estimates that one in forty-four 8-year-olds had an autism diagnosis in 2018, up from an estimated one in 166 in 2005.[156] The National Center for Education Statistics reports that autistic children ages 3 to 21 comprised 11 percent of disabled school children in the United States in 2019–2020 but 1.5 percent in 2000–2001.[157] However, scientists are largely in consensus that the overall prevalence of autism has risen due to greater awareness, improved monitoring, and changes to diagnostic criteria. For instance, it was only in 2006 that the American Academy of Pediatrics began to recommend screening all children for autism during routine pediatrician visits at 18 and 24 months.[158]

If anything, official counts of autism diagnoses are underestimations. Diagnosis rates in the Global South are low due to cultural stigma and gaps in the recognition, interpretation, and reporting of autism.[159] In the United States, significant disparities remain even though widespread screening has led to improved detection among underrepresented groups.[160] CDC data shows that Latino children are identified with autism at lower rates than are Black or White children. This is due to several factors, including culturally and linguistically inappropriate clinical care.[161] White children regularly stand in for all children in autism research because many studies fail to even report the race or ethnicity of research participants, rendering non-White kids doubly invisible.[162] Boys are four times more likely than girls to receive an autism diagnosis, reflecting historical gender biases in the construction and delivery of autism assessments.[163] Children who live in urban geographic areas with a higher concentration of clinical services are also more likely to receive a diagnosis than those in underresourced rural regions.[164]

At the moment, Clayton did have a diagnosis—but of "emotional behavioral disorder." Monisha thought that he had been misdiagnosed and was trying to make a doctor's appointment to get him reevaluated. "They don't want to diagnose him with [autism] because they felt like he was on the border with it," Monisha shared, "but some of the similarities [between Clayton and his brothers] I see too." In the United States, Black boys like Clayton are statistically more likely to be misdiagnosed prior to receiving an autism diagnosis and are disproportionally diagnosed with emotional disturbance.[165] Black children also receive autism evaluations and resulting support services at older ages than White children.[166] Those like Clayton who do not have an intellectual disability are diagnosed with autism at lower rates than are White children.[167] Labels like emotional disturbance have also long been used to pathologize the trauma produced by racism that Black people endure.[168] Autism has historically been the domain of White, upper-middle class boys ever since it was first studied in the United States and Europe at the turn of the twentieth century.[169]

While Adrian's mom, Brianna, had access to a set of vocabulary from which she could comfortably refer to Adrian as an "Aspie," Monisha's tattoo was an indelible claim to the same for Clayton, written in ink on her arm instead of with a pen on a clinician's notepad. Parents—especially mothers—contend with major challenges in managing the complex bureaucracies of health care and education that present difficulties for children with often "invisible disabilities" like ADHD and autism.[170] Clinical and diagnostic uncertainty means that children and adults may receive multiple diagnoses that shift over time. In some cases, additional disabilities may accompany autism (such as intellectual disability, language delay, and anxiety), which complicates how autism is treated as well as singled out to be diagnosed.[171] Receiving one or more diagnostic labels can also unlock services like occupational and sensory integration therapy for those who know to advocate for them. The structural inequalities embedded in these systems are compounded for single mothers and for caregivers raising children of color, and acutely so for those in both groups like Monisha.

My inability to formally count Clayton in this study because, unlike all of the other children, he did not have a diagnosis at the time, speaks to the complex racial inequalities around autism and how multiple forms of marginalization, stigmatization, and discrimination underpin all discussions of social institutions. Clayton was struggling socially, emotionally, and behaviorally, and an autism diagnosis might lead to him getting the right kind of support—the kind that Adrian was receiving with a significant investment of energy, advocacy, and money from his parents. "When he tries to make friends," Monisha said of Clayton, "I notice a lot of kids just sitting back observing because he's real loud [and] he doesn't really get the pitch in his voice," an auditory processing issue that can be a sign of autism.[172] Like Adrian, Clayton could get overwhelmed by small stressors like homework, leading to tears and anger. His social and emotional challenges were also compounded by physical bullying that was largely ignored by staff at his school, which prompted Monisha to move to a better school district just outside of Boston.

As did Adrian, Clayton showed a real aptitude for art and an interest in the complexities of the Pokémon universe and media franchise. While we sat in his living room during my observational visit, Clayton made multiple trips to his bedroom to retrieve and show me one highly detailed Pokémon illustration after another. "I'm trying to draw all the 151 Pokémon from Gen 1," he said, proudly laying his colorful Bulbasaur, Ivysaur, and Venusaur character drawings out on the sofa (figure 1.1). Clayton said that he had learned how to draw Pokémon by studying YouTube tutorials. "When I grow up," he stated matter-of-factly, "I'm going to be a very social artist." At the moment though, Clayton's ability to become "a very social artist" was limited by educators and clinical professionals who could not piece together that he was likely a Black child on the autism spectrum.

While Clayton and Adrian illustrate differences between families of autistic children, Clayton and his two brothers demonstrate the variations that can exists within the autism spectrum. Their neurodivergent profiles and media interests were similar yet dissimilar. Clayton and Orion enjoyed playing together on the video game platform Roblox from their respective tablet computers. Kahlil liked to listen to music on Monisha's old phone, holding the speaker to his ear while walking around the apartment on the periphery of his brothers' play. Clayton was very talkative, Orion was just starting to gain more confidence speaking after receiving in-school speech therapy, and minimally speaking Kahlil was recently issued an AAC device to communicate with in class, though Monisha said that he would sometimes sing

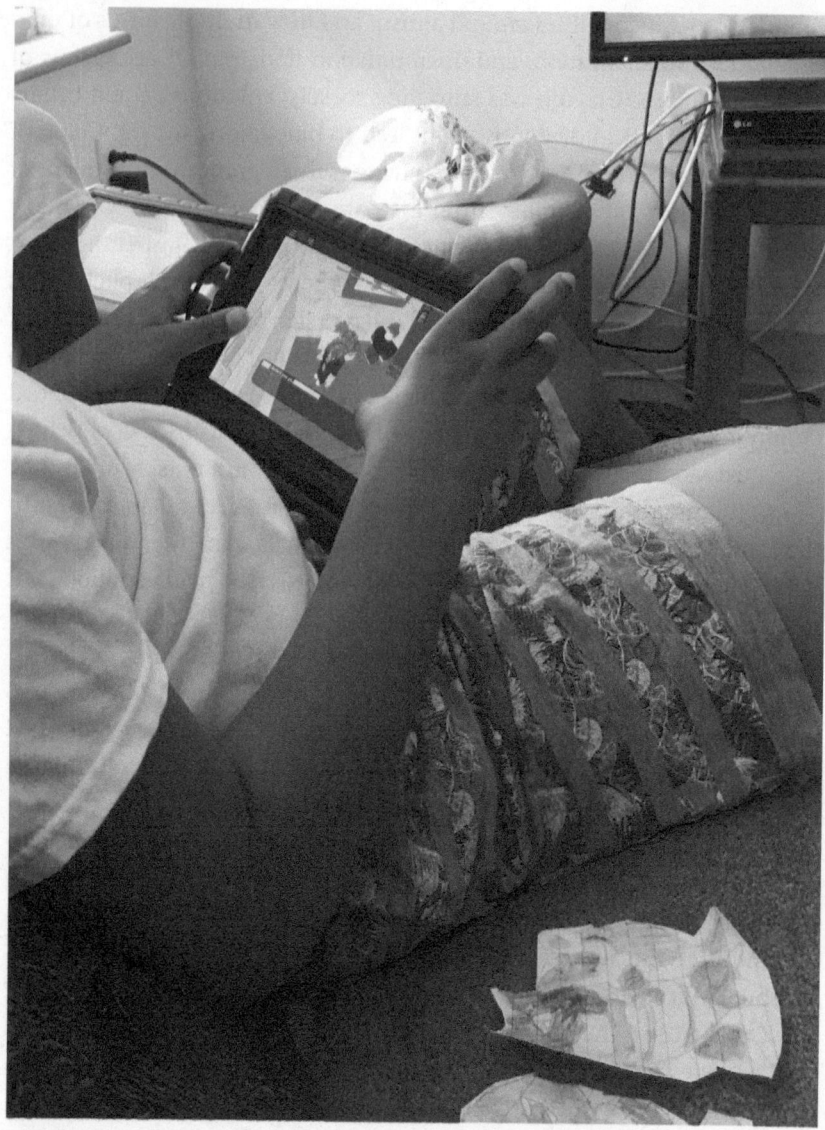

FIGURE 1.1
Clayton (*front*) and Orion sit side by side on the sofa, playing video games on their respective tablets with a movie on the television set in the background. Clayton's Pokémon drawings are beside him. *Source*: Meryl Alper.

to himself or along with YouTube music videos. The story of Clayton and his brothers illustrates how being autistic does not explain everything that a child does with media—in fact, it might only account for a small portion.

STUDY OVERVIEW

For this book, I employed a range of research methods that allowed for deep inquiry with autistic children and their families (see the Appendix for a further explanation). Fifty-eight households took part; in total, there were sixty-two children, including four sets of autistic brothers. I interviewed parents—mostly mothers, but sometimes fathers and couples—about their family life and the benefits and challenges of their autistic child's media use. The average child was approximately 7 years old at the time of the initial parent interview. With this background information, I returned to the homes of fifty-three kids to observe them engaging in a favored media activity, sometimes solo or with family members. Because they are rarely considered experts on their own lives,[173] I interviewed eighteen speaking autistic children between the ages of 6 and 13 years as part of my return visit. I also reinterviewed and reobserved a handful of children and parents a year later and, in one case, five and a half years later, in order to gain longer-term perspectives.[174] This recontact work stretched into the start of the COVID-19 pandemic in April 2020, though my fieldwork did not continue further into that tumultuous year. Twenty-six children in the study, or a little over 40%, had a communication impairment. I was able to conduct a remote asynchronous interview with one nonspeaking child in which their parent wrote down and sent back responses to my questions that the child answered by pointing to letters on a letterboard. Many were too young to be interviewed, did not use their AAC device regularly at home (if they had one to begin with), or were not receiving adequate speech-language therapy services to support their ability to be interviewed.

The most upsetting example of this was 8-year-old Saaida, who did not speak, who had no assistive communication system, and whose development was severely impaired due to lead poisoning from paint chips in the apartment that her family first rented when they moved to Boston from Bangladesh. While Saaida's father had mentioned in our initial interview that they did not keep paper of any kind in the home because Saaida liked to eat it, I made the mistake of bringing a small notebook with me to the follow-up observation. When I would not give her the book after she lunged for it, she yanked my hair and bit my arm, forcing me to end the observation early. Being able to be interviewed for this book—be it through spoken, written, or symbolic language—is in some ways more a marker of privilege than the absolute ability of an autistic child. It was important to include children like Saaida—nonspeaking, non-White girls from the Global South—because they rarely make an appearance in autism research.

In recruiting families for the study, I employed what Lindlof and Taylor term "maximum variation sampling" in order to study children and families from many possible angles.[175] Through a variety of methods, I purposively recruited more children of color and those from poorer and lower income families than are generally included in autism research. A little more than half were from families that earned less than $100,000 annually ($n=33$) and a little less than half earned more ($n=29$). Ten were from families earning less than $25,000 a year. Some children lived in spacious houses, others lived in small apartments, and yet others were housing insecure. Half were non-White ($n=31$) and half were White ($n=31$). The sample skewed more toward children who identified as boys ($n=44$) than those who identified as girls ($n=18$), but it is still more gender balanced than the available distribution data on autism. The study enrolled at least one transgender child and one parent who identified as genderqueer.

These young people had much in common besides an autism diagnosis. They lived in Los Angeles or Boston—progressive coastal cities and industry hubs that were resource rich but deeply segregated. Both cities were near sites of world-class medical care yet also grappling with severe income inequality. Media and technology were also a clear commonality among them. Many parents allowed their children to watch YouTube with minimal restrictions, and most did not know of or chose not to use the supposedly more age-appropriate YouTube Kids app. Streaming video sites like Netflix were readily adopted, though less well-off families were more likely to gain access through accounts shared with friends. Young children consumed a lot of educational PBS KIDS programming, while older children were drawn to YouTube personalities. Across households, nearly all children and parents had their own personal mobile devices, be it a phone or tablet, a broken hand-me-down or the latest model.

BOOK OVERVIEW

In the pages that follow, I detail how autistic children's experiences with media converge and diverge with those of neurotypical children and of each other in three main ways: (1) *cultural belonging* through their identity development and learning (chapters 2 and 3), (2) *social relationships* among their family and friends (chapters 4 and 5), and (3) *physical embodiment* in terms of their sensory and emotional processing (chapters 6 and 7). These themes and topics touch upon concerns for all children and adolescents in the digital age, namely the relationship of social-emotional development to other developmental domains (e.g., physiology, cognition) and the myriad cultural, political, and historical factors shaping childhood.[176] These themes also overlap, such as in how autistic children's use of media for emotional expression is influenced by their interactions with peers and family members.

Chapter 2 looks at how children on the spectrum come to understand themselves, their autism, and its intersections with their race, ethnicity, and gender *identity* through the media content they create, consume, and share. Some autistic kids find their identities reflected in popular media characters that are implicitly and explicitly disabled, and others create opportunities for identification through the avatars they design and the comics they illustrate. Parents can be a critical part of their child's identity formation and sense of belonging cultivated through their media use. Autistic parents and other adult role models on the spectrum may be especially useful by providing valuable guidance.

Chapter 3 addresses the potential for autistic children's informal *learning* with media at home against the backdrop of struggles to access a fair and appropriate public education, particularly in under-resourced schools. Much has been made of using flashy gadgets to teach autistic children social skills, but little work explores their families' preexisting values, routines, habits, and beliefs about media, technology, and learning.[177] Outside the classroom, digital media allows many autistic children to pursue their interests and hobbies as well as to engage in self-directed and self-paced learning in areas like reading and math, social and communication skills, and creative expression. However, these very platforms also put autistic children at a heightened risk for privacy and safety violations.

Chapter 4 focuses on the ways that media and technology become central to relationships, bonds, and intimacies between autistic children and their parents, siblings, and extended *family* members. Parents make constant tradeoffs to promote benefits and prevent harms to their children in the long and short term. Media is central to this negotiation, with the outcomes more or less successful not only because of the decisions that individual parents make, but also because of infrastructural and institutional issues like poverty and social media platform policies beyond their immediate control. The extreme uncertainties facing households disproportionately impact families of children with disabilities.[178] These pressures manifest in the outsized role that media plays in many of these young people's lives, as well as those of their family members.

Chapter 5 extends the discussion of relationships to autistic children's mediated *friendships* with neurodivergent and neurotypical peers. This chapter looks at the positive and negative aspects of social interactions between autistic kids, their classmates, and online friends, and how those connections and tensions are shaped by popular culture, media, and technology. Autistic children's friendships are co-constructed by the normative social affordances of communication technologies, as well as by broader societal forces that often limit the physical and digital spaces available to these young people.

Chapter 6 draws attention to how embodiment and *sensory* processing shape autistic children's social interactions through and around media and technology. Media is often thought of as stimulating external senses, like sight, hearing, and touch, but internal ones, like body awareness and movement, are less often considered in that context. This chapter takes an integrated approach to how autistic children experience a full range of pleasurable and painful sensory stimuli and how their experiences shape domestic spaces, intimate relationships, and family practices during media use. Autistic children and their caregivers often alter the immediate media environment around a child to meet their sensory needs, but families with less financial resources have diminished control over the built world in general.

Chapter 7 examines the ways that mass media and communication technology impact how autistic kids recognize their own internal states, specifically the ways that their *emotions* and behaviors are read by their social partners, and how technologies come to interpret their feelings and actions. Digital technologies used to treat and identify signs of autism (e.g., algorithms, apps) operate from a very simple notion of emotion, namely that autistic people cannot identify the emotional states of others or their own.[179] This chapter illustrates the depth and complexity of autistic children's affective states and examines how media technologies could better account for these expressions and interpretations. Also discussed are the wider ethical and design implications for emotion and behavioral recognition technologies.

Lastly, chapter 8 concludes by pointing toward new directions for understanding sociality and social technologies and for supporting autistic children and adolescents in the digital era. This chapter incorporates the reflections of young people on the spectrum and their parents at the beginning of the COVID-19 pandemic. I discuss implications of the book's findings for the education, health-care, and technology sectors, offered with the goal of guiding more effective efforts toward equity, access, and justice for autistic kids at home, at school, and in their communities.

Broad-stroke discussions about autism, technology, and kids look very different up close if you pay attention to what seems like minor details in the aggregate. Nondisabled and neurotypical people have much to learn if we are to build a more resilient and compassionate world. There is an adage that goes, "If you've met one person with autism . . . you've met one person with autism," which is a twist on the pejorative phrase, "If you've met one person [insert description], you've met them all." The revised phrasing is meant to highlight the complexity of autism, but even the more inclusive version can be too focused on the level of the individual. "One person with autism" is also someone shaped by their physical environment, social context, and historical factors, and is an individual who inhabits a body that is seen by others as having a race, ethnicity, gender, and sexuality. If you've met only one autistic person, you really should meet more, starting with the next chapter.

Belonging

2 IDENTITY

Casey, a 6-year-old White girl, sat perched on her bed with her mom, Jennifer, both of them facing a propped-up iPad as they watched *Free to Be . . . You and Me* for the umpteenth time. *Free to Be* premiered in 1974 as an hour-long televised special in the United States, starring actress Marlo Thomas and a multicultural cast of children and celebrities who sang, danced, and performed sketches promoting gender equality. The moment with Casey and Jennifer was bathed in color: awash with the lime green walls of Casey's bedroom, light shining through the pastel stained-glass window above her bed, the rainbow striped leggings she wore, and the faded pink streaks in her long brown wavy hair (figure 2.1). Both mother and daughter had a strong affinity for *Free to Be*. "I had that on ever since [Casey] was little and never turned it off because I loved it so much," Jennifer shared.[1] Considering the educational element of *Free to Be*, I asked Casey if she had learned anything from watching it. "That we're all free to be ourselves. You and me, free to be," she replied, echoing the title song's lyrics.

Casey and Jennifer exemplify the gender freedoms championed by *Free to Be*, while extending its titular meaning to the realm of neurodiversity. In addition to being autistic, Casey is transgender. The former was verified by clinicians through a lengthy process when Casey was two and a half years old, and the latter confirmed in a short talk between mother and child a year later. Jennifer explained that one day, she had asked Casey, "'Oh, how's my sweet boy?' and she's like 'Mom, I'm a girl.' I'm like, 'Okay, how's my sweet girl?' and that was the entire conversation." Jennifer thought, however, that Casey being male presenting when they sought an autism diagnosis had

FIGURE 2.1

Sitting on her bed, Casey selects *Free to Be . . . You and Me* to watch on her iPad. *Source*: Meryl Alper.

advantaged her within the health-care system. "More boys are diagnosed than girls," Jennifer said, "so her, at the time, presenting as a boy, she was able to receive her diagnosis. [Otherwise] it would've been a lot harder." The underlying reasons why are unclear, but a growing body of research suggests that autistic people may be more likely than the general population to identify as LGBTQ.[2] Jennifer herself identifies outside normative categorizations of gender, sexuality, and disability; specifically, Jennifer said, as "genderqueer around to femme" and "autistic but undiagnosed."

The particular words that Casey and Jennifer each use to refer to themselves matter. Some of the identities that they claim, as child and adult, are marginalized in different but intersecting ways. Their stories are also important because they highlight various features of identity—a complex sociocultural and psychological construct that concerns the traits and characteristics that one assigns to the self. Identity has many components. It spans the role of self-concept and self-awareness in a child's personal development and how people on the spectrum come to see themselves and others like them as autistic. It includes the ways that media enables people to understand who they are, who they have been, and who they want to be, as well as how technologies identify, classify, and sort groups and individuals.[3] Questions of identity are also core to the sociotechnical shaping of sociality. The ways that we associate with others are tied to how we understand ourselves and also to the tools and materials at our disposal to develop and maintain a sense of self.[4]

In this chapter, I explore how autistic kids like Casey develop their identities in relation to and sometimes in tension with neurotypical social expectations and norms. I also look at the everyday role of technology and media in this continually evolving process of becoming within their families, among their peers, and in their communities. While some research has explored how mass media representations of disability impact the identity of disabled adults, the same cannot be said for children.[5] I focus primarily on how school-age young people on the spectrum (ages 6–13) co-construct their idea of what it means to be autistic alongside other aspects of themselves (e.g., gender identity) as well as part of the disability community through their creation, circulation, and consumption of media content. Among younger autistic children (ages 3–8), for whom the cognitive, social, and emotional aspects of individuation and identity development are still nascent, the discussion centers on their parents' interpretations of popular autistic characters and individuals featured in mass media and how this impact the identities that they imagine and enact for their child.

As I detail in the pages that follow, children on the autism spectrum have limited opportunities to see autistic people positively and accurately represented in mainstream media. Only a limited range of autistic traits are reflected in media tropes (e.g., "quirky" girls and "robotic" boys). Despite these constraints, they find ways to learn more about themselves through a media universe that includes online platforms, books, and movies, as well as media characters that are not explicitly autistic. This exploration is significantly shaped by having parents, friends, teachers, and other social partners who facilitate and enable such play and curiosity. Better understanding the role of media and technology in autistic children's personal and social identity formation may ultimately help inform programs and services that support their mental health and well-being. Though we do not currently live in a world in which all of us are truly "free to be you and me" without repercussions of stigmatization and discrimination, we can still learn a lot from autistic kids like Casey—and autistic parents like Jennifer—about recognizing and honoring more expansive claims of personhood and dignity.

FRAMING IDENTITY DEVELOPMENT THROUGH THE LENSES OF MEDIA AND AUTISM

For the purposes of this chapter, identity formation can be divided broadly into two interdisciplinary areas: the development of identity in childhood and the role of media and technology in a child's evolving sense of self. Autism, and the experiences of autistic youth, offer important insights into each, specifically the development of autistic identity across the lifespan, as well as how different forms of media play a part in identity development for young people on the spectrum.

IDENTITY AND HUMAN DEVELOPMENT

Identity development occurs over our entire lives. It begins at an early age when, according to psychologist Jean Piaget, children use their senses to gather information about the world, including their own bodies.[6] Most kids can recognize their reflection in a mirror by their first birthday and identify themselves in photographs by age 2. Over time, children become increasingly more sophisticated in their understanding of distinctions between the "self" and "other." Throughout the toddler and preschool years, they learn labels and terms that represent themselves (e.g., their names). At around age 7, kids can think more abstractly about social categories (i.e., race, gender, disability), their identification with them, what these categories mean, and why they matter.

There is no single unifying theory that explains identity development. The fields of social psychology and sociology do offer a number of useful insights. Psychologist Erik Erikson, for instance, considered the end of adolescence to be the completion of a critical process of becoming who we are for the rest of our lives.[7] It is in adolescence, Erikson argued, that one solidifies their identity through personal exploration and builds a cohesive sense of self that guides future actions, beliefs, and behaviors.[8] Psychologist Carl Rogers theorized that self-concept is our overall conception of who we are as people, which comprises self-image (how we see ourselves), self-esteem (how much we value ourselves), and the ideal self (who we wish we could be).[9]

Psychological theories of identity development can be understood not only in terms of personal identity, but also who we are in relation to others.

James Marcia's identity status theory explains that adolescence is a critical time for exploring and committing to particular identities and ideologies (e.g., religion, political beliefs), and that this process involves questioning and potentially distancing oneself from the values and expectations passed down from parents and authority figures.[10] Besides individual identities (i.e., "Who am I?"), we also develop collective identities (i.e., "Who are we?").[11] Social identity theory, proposed by psychologist Henri Tajfel and colleagues, posits that humans have a propensity to define themselves based on group membership, and that the positive feelings that one derives from such affiliation results in a greater sense of well-being and self-esteem.[12]

While psychologists are generally focused on how the mind influences identity development, sociologists and those in allied fields (e.g., sociolinguistics) concentrate more centrally on the role of society and social interactions.[13] Sociologist Erving Goffman, for example, argued that there is no stable self, only the identities that we present to others in the moment (using a theater metaphor, on the "frontstage" of our lives) and the identities that we draw upon depending on the social context (from the "backstage.")[14] Sociological theorist Anthony Giddens contends, however, that in order to have an identity, there must be a self to begin with.[15] Our ability to maintain a stable sense of self is anchored in our relationships and resulting feelings of trust and safety, or what Giddens termed "ontological security." Without that secure attachment, we are more likely to "play to the crowd" in order to seek acceptance.

AUTISTIC IDENTITY

We can apply this dual psychological and sociological framing to how autistic people incorporate autism into their identity and sense of self. "Autistic identity" means very different things among autistic people and with respect to their individual, social, and political identities. Disabled people may perceive their disability as both positively and negatively affecting their identity and see being disabled as more or less central to their self-concept.[16] As a disability category, autism is inherently unstable; how it is defined and diagnosed has changed significantly over time. These fluctuations have a direct influence on those who have been identified or who identify with autism.[17] Philosopher Ian Hacking refers to this mutual shaping of category and identity as a "looping effect."[18] Part of the challenge of grappling with the complexity of autism as a category is that it is difficult to say anything definitive about it.

The life stage at which a person receives an autism diagnosis impacts their autistic identity formation. Some individuals get diagnosed as children, and others, much later in life. Diagnoses are often difficult to receive once a person has aged out of formal schooling.[19] An official diagnosis has both material and symbolic effects for an autistic person. It is generally required to gain access to support services and can also authenticate one's identity, or what feminist disability scholar Ellen Samuels terms "biocertification."[20] Without official documentation, a self-diagnosis of autism may still be part of a process of identity formation and reconciliation for autistic adults, resulting in improved well-being and quality of life.[21] Sociologist Catherine Tan refers to this process of developing an enriched sense of self, one that is reconciled through clinical explanation as "biological illumination," which inverts a narrative of diagnosis as loss or disruption.[22]

Beyond the individual, an autistic person's identification with autism shapes and is shaped by their social interactions. Having a positive collective identity can buffer some of the negative psychological impacts of ableism.[23] Research has found, for example, that the more positive attributes an autistic adult associates with autism (e.g., unique problem-solving skills), the more likely they are to identify with other autistic people.[24] Stigmatization, however, can be a negative social influence on an autistic person's self-concept. Pressure to appear more neurotypical to nonautistic people, known as "camouflaging" or "masking," requires a significant psychological effort and can take a toll on mental health.[25] Autistic girls and women are more likely to camouflage than boys and men because they are socialized to "fit in."[26] This performativity echoes, but also complicates, Goffman's "frontstage/backstage" metaphor. As one autistic YouTuber notes about her proficiency in masking, "Life is a stage, yeah? To me it really is, and I'm a really good actress."[27]

Lastly, autistic identity is also political. It allows people on the spectrum to build coalitions and enact change.[28] Neurodiversity, as both a social paradigm and political movement, has provided many autistic people with a cultural identity outside of a purely medical model of autism focused on deficits.[29] Autism can be understood as a "neuroidentity," or an identity based on distinct, though not fully defined, neurological differences.[30] The politics of autistic identity also play out across complex intersections with racial, gender, and sexual identity.[31] Intersectionality theory, rooted in Black feminism,[32] explains how the various identity categories that a person inhabits never combine in a purely additive way.[33] For instance, some autistic people embrace their "neuroqueerness," a term encompassing neurodivergence and sexual and gender variance.[34] Ultimately, it may be helpful to think about identification with autism in the plural, as in multiple autistic identities.[35]

IDENTIFYING WITH AUTISM IN AND THROUGH MEDIA

In developing their sense of identity, individuals on the spectrum have to navigate a media landscape populated by more stereotypes about autistic people than autistic people themselves.[36] As a social institution, media plays a powerful role in organizing society. It represents a version of reality that is at once reproduced and contested by users and audiences.[37] The characters, plots, and lessons depicted in mass media are not automatically understood in the ways that producers intend. The meanings that audiences infer depend on their own lived experiences, or what cultural theorist Stuart Hall termed the encoding/decoding model of communication.[38] Popular presentations of people on the spectrum in media are largely inconsistent with autistic people's sense of self and their identification with autism because they are created and intended to be consumed by nonautistic people.[39] People with disabilities live in a world that perceives what Samuels calls "fantasies of identification" as reality, in that media (e.g., literature, movies, news) have heavily shaped societal ideas about disability, but these schema have little relation to actual disabled people and their identities.[40]

As a case in point, the majority of autistic roles in mass media are not developed or portrayed by people on the spectrum.[41] The media production with the largest and most enduring impact on popular conceptions of autism is the 1988 film *Rain Man*, in which the lead character of Raymond Babbitt, an autistic man, is played by nonautistic actor Dustin Hoffman. At the 1989 Academy Awards, *Rain Man* was awarded Best Picture and Hoffman won Best Actor. Thirty years later, musical artist Sia, who is not autistic, generated controversy in the autism community for jokingly describing her 2020 movie *Music* as "*Rain Man* the Musical, but with girls" in an interview with *Variety*.[42] Sia was seemingly unaware of the damage that *Rain Man* has done over the years by perpetuating the misconception that all autistic people are savants (as Babbitt was portrayed) and by insinuating that those on the autism spectrum are better off institutionalized (as happens to Babbitt in the film) than living in their own communities.[43]

Putting *Music* aside, there have been some positive shifts in the entertainment industry in recent years with respect to autism representation.

Characters are being developed alongside autistic self-advocacy groups and portrayed by actors on the autism spectrum, such as Madison Bandy, a nonspeaking autistic girl of color who voices the lead character Renee in Pixar's 2020 animated short film *Loop*. Black autistic boys are superheroes in the educational TV show *Hero Elementary* and the 2017 film reboot of the *Power Rangers* franchise. Queer autistic media figures like comedian Hannah Gadsby have gained prominence and acclaim not despite their autism, but by centering their specific disabled experience in their creative work.

Besides autistic media characters and entertainment figures, individuals on the spectrum may identify with fictional characters who are "autistic coded."[44] One such example is Abed Nadir on the TV sitcom *Community*, who possesses traits associated with autism that are recognizable to mass audiences, including a tendency to fidget, difficulty picking up social cues, and a love of routine.[45] This interpretive flexibility, which members of other marginalized groups also engage in, allows autistic people to see themselves more fully represented in a media text. These readings are also known as "autistic headcanons," in that people on the spectrum create their own interpretations outside of what is official or canonical, such as fan fiction. As autistic writer Sarah Kurchak argues, "Headcanon after headcanon, autistic people are demanding—and envisioning—more from an industry that's increasingly profiting from our lives."[46] Such interpretations are not met without resistance though. Media creators of autistic coded characters may distance themselves from an obligation to portray autism in a fully fleshed out manner.[47] Autistic fans who claim existing characters as their own sometimes encounter vocal opposition among other fans who associate autism with stigma and resist coupling beloved characters to what Goffman termed a "spoiled identity."[48]

Beyond mass media, the internet has been central to many speaking and nonspeaking autistic adults' identity development as a space to reclaim the power to identify with autism, confront stereotypes, manage their visibility, engage in activism, and circulate new narratives.[49] Despite claims by some autism researchers that "in a sense, everyone is autistic online" (due to the lack of nonverbal social cues in online environments),[50] the relationship between being autistic and being online is far more complex, including challenges in performing disability "authentically" in relation to the social and communicative affordances of digital platforms.[51] Self-representations and expressions of autistic culture are created, consumed, and shared through social media and online platforms like YouTube, TikTok, and Twitter.[52] As artists and media makers, autistic people may use online tools and platforms to express creativity in a manner that defies neurotypical conceptions of originality (e.g., employing repetition). There is no universal way in which autistic people encode and decode messages about autism in media or employ communication technology as a means of self-expression and identification.

IDENTITY DEVELOPMENT AMONG AUTISTIC YOUTH

Thus far in this chapter, the research presented on autistic identity development and how it is articulated through media has tended to focus on adults more than on young people.[53] Not a great deal is known about how children and adolescents who are diagnosed with autism develop their own sense of autistic identity and selfhood.[54] The work that does exist primarily focuses on older cisgender White boys on the spectrum without communication and intellectual disabilities, and less so on younger kids, girls and gender nonbinary youth, non-White children, and those who are nonspeaking or minimally speaking.[55] In some ways, how diverse autistic children and adolescents learn to think about themselves may have much in common with their neurotypical peers,[56] but there are also specific considerations for how they understand autism as a part of their identity.

Identity development can be particularly challenging for autistic youth because of the multiplicity of autism's meanings.[57] For example, adolescents on the spectrum report being unsure if autism is a disability.[58] The ways that children of different ages understand their diagnosis is not straightforward either.[59] Some autistic children's comprehension of autism may be basic, while others are self-aware and recognize how their behaviors distinguish them from others in various social contexts (e.g., compared to siblings or classmates). They may struggle with what to make of how autistic people are perceived negatively within society.[60] Some express ambivalence and work to reconcile their challenges with the strengths and assets that are also part of autism.[61] They might ultimately embrace, contest, or reject the use of autism as an identity marker.[62] Recent research with autistic college students in the United States suggests, though, that learning one is autistic at a younger age is associated with heightened well-being and quality of life.[63]

There are a number of social factors shaping autistic children's overall identity development, including parental acceptance of a child's autism diagnosis and if or how they share that diagnosis with their child.[64] Nonautistic parents of autistic children sometimes struggle with how to explain autism, and few report receiving advice for how to do so.[65] The language, terminology, and approach that they use can directly impact their child's self-image and self-knowledge.[66] The voluntary disclosure of a diagnosis by parents influences if an autistic child sees their autism in a positive or negative light.[67] Some caregivers may not initially make an autistic child aware of their diagnosis due to challenges in processing their own emotions about their child's disability.[68] Parental disclosure avoidance can lead to internal confusion for autistic children in the long-term about the reasons for their differences.[69] In discussing an autism diagnosis with their child, the experiences of autistic parents and nonautistic parents are similar yet different. Both groups of parents think it important to individualize the discussion to their specific child. Parents who are themselves on the spectrum, though, are less likely to think that telling their child that they are autistic will have a negative effect on them, and these parents feel more equipped to discuss autism with their autistic child without the help of professionals.[70]

Beyond the family context, the level of autism acceptance in an autistic child's classroom, out-of-school activities, and community also impacts their self-esteem.[71] Peer groups for autistic kids that are centered around shared interests can cultivate a positive sense of individual and collective identity.[72] In Australia, for example, nonprofit organization Yellow Ladybugs runs informal social events for autistic girls and gender diverse children ages 5–16 in order to foster belonging, connection, and pride in being autistic.[73] Children whose autism goes undetected in the early years, which is more likely to be girls and children of color, may miss out on developing a positive sense of autistic identity.[74] It is important for all kids to learn to be comfortable with who they are, but for young people on the spectrum, developing an autistic identity can help them especially to feel understood, supported, and included.[75]

AUTISTIC YOUTH, IDENTITY, AND MEDIA

Print, screen, and interactive media provide kids in general with endless materials and tools for developing their own self-concept, and emerging research suggests that this is also true for young people on the autism spectrum.[76] Examples of media shaping children's identity development include the fictional characters that preschoolers adopt in their pretend play, the virtual spaces and digital games that school-age children use to explore their interests and talents, and the online communities in which teens take part to find people who are like them.[77] Digital media have significant implications for how kids develop self-image and cultivate self-esteem throughout childhood, particularly for youth who might feel uncomfortable expressing themselves in offline spaces due to pervasive ableism, racism, xenophobia, and homophobia.[78] The role of media in the identity development of autistic children may or may not be congruent with the way it is for young people from other socially and culturally marginalized groups, including those with other disabilities.[79]

Autistic children encounter both unique barriers and opportunities to using media and technology to develop a stable, coherent, and meaningful sense of self. The dominant media messages about autism that autistic children and their peers absorb are largely negative and harmful to their mental health, well-being, and self-esteem. These messages include inaccurate and incomplete fictional portrayals of autistic people.[80] A 2019 report from the Geena Davis Institute on Gender and Media found that 1–8 percent of leading characters in popular shows and movies for children had a disability, and that such characters were more likely than nondisabled characters to be depicted as violent or helpless or to ultimately die.[81] Driven by the momentum of the disability rights movement over the past decade and the passage of landmark legislation like the Americans with Disabilities Act in 1990, literature has at least been one main source for children and adolescents to find accurate stories about disability and neurodivergence.[82] Speaking and nonspeaking autistic authors have written picture books and young adult novels addressing pertinent topics such as sensory processing challenges and bullying.[83] Informational handbooks like *The Spectrum Girl's Survival Guide: How to Grow Up Awesome and Autistic* speak directly to youth autistic audiences from the vantage point of a peer.[84]

Digital media, social media, and video games can also provide important networked spaces for autistic young people to find autism acceptance, challenge mischaracterizations of disabled people, and further develop their autistic identities.[85] For example, children on the spectrum may cultivate an enriched sense of self through traditional digital identity markers such as avatars.[86] Autistic youth also use an array of media artifacts including YouTube videos and blogs to spread cultural acceptance of autistic people.[87] Social media provides a space for communicating their unique experiences.[88] Instagram and TikTok creators like Paige Layle have used the platforms to document themselves stimming (e.g., flapping hands, twirling fingers) alongside the catchy, rhythmic music that is popular as a soundtrack to user-generated videos on the apps.[89] As it pertains to justice broadly, autistic teens like Greta Thunberg and Dara McAnulty have used

Twitter to great effect to lead and organize other activists, young and old, around a global movement for environmentalism,[90] though doing so also opens them up to ableist harassment online.[91]

Media and sociality are each central to autistic children's self-descriptions. They may internalize messages about autism being the "geek syndrome" and related to nerdiness or having deep knowledge of popular culture.[92] Shared interests around media can become part of how they identify with others and learn to conceptualize autism itself.[93] Recent work surveying autistic children ages 7–14 about their self-identified strengths, interests, and positive attributes found that when asked "What do you enjoy most?," a majority responded with "technology and gaming" (a little over 50 percent) followed by "social interaction" (almost 35 percent).[94] The everyday dynamics, however, between self-identification, media, and sociality are underexplored in the literature on autism and child development. The next section provides deeper insight into how mass, digital, and social media afford identity formation and expression for diverse autistic youth.

MEDIA AND AUTISTIC CHILDREN'S IDENTITY FORMATION

Among the children that I spent time with for this book, there was great variation in terms of autism diagnosis disclosure by their parents. Factors shaping these conversations include the child's age, their level of cognition, and their parents' comfort level. But even children who did not have these talks with their parents were able to articulate feeling different or identifying with disability in some manner. Media plays a key role in how they make sense of this part of themselves, though the effectiveness and utility of media are limited by a family's access to essential resources like appropriate mental health support. To this end, I identified three main themes: (1) autistic children as audience members for mass-produced media featuring disabled, autistic, and autistic coded characters; (2) kids on the spectrum producing, making, and sharing media as a means of working through their identification with autism; and (3) girls exploring gender and its intersections with autistic identity through their engagement with media.

AUTISTIC YOUTH AS DISABILITY MEDIA AUDIENCES
Several autistic children consumed mass media such as movies, television shows, and books that allowed them to recognize and name certain characteristics about themselves. Some of this media was explicitly about autism,

while others pertained to disability more broadly. Children also tried to understand their autism through autistic-coded media characters. In all of these cases, their media reception was shaped by social and cultural factors including school curriculum, peers, and family members.

MEDIA ABOUT DISABILITY   One media text that multiple autistic children ages 8 to 13 discussed as a favorite was *Wonder*, a 2012 *New York Times* best-selling children's novel by R. J. Palacio (with subsequent spinoff books) that was made into a 2017 movie starring Julia Roberts. *Wonder* is about a young boy named Auggie who has a significant congenital facial abnormality and his turbulent transition from homeschooling to a new school in fifth grade. Through Auggie's story, *Wonder* tackles difficult issues such as bullying and prejudice, as well as friendship and self-acceptance. While Auggie is not autistic, a number of children on the spectrum found his encounters with ableism and discrimination to be compelling and relatable.

Eleven-year-old son Jackson (White, boy) did not really know what autism meant, according to his mom, Linda, but he was developing a relationship to disability through his consumption of all things *Wonder*. When I sat down for my interview with Linda at the family's home in a working-class neighborhood in Boston, I noticed a library copy of *Auggie & Me: Three Wonder Stories*, one of the *Wonder* spin-off books, on the dining room table. "They're reading that in school," Linda said. Jackson's class had also read the original *Wonder* book and watched the movie in class. "Whatever he's into at school, he looks for when we go to the library because he likes to read them here with me," Linda said. She speculated that the reason Jackson was attracted to *Wonder* specifically was "because it talks so much about how different the kids are, and he talks about that. Like how different Auggie was to other people and how the kids didn't want to interact with him." The experience was close to Jackson, as he had been bullied repeatedly in school too. Linda said, "I feel like sometimes he feels like that himself because the kids don't interact with him, or he feels like he's different."

Though Jackson mumbled and had difficulty expressing himself through oral speech, he was clearer and more resolute when talking about Auggie than during the rest of our interview. When I asked him what his favorite movie was, he chose *Wonder*. Not only had he seen it, he said, but he was also reading the *Wonder* books. "I read the number one *Wonder*," Jackson said, "It has a lot of narrators: Auggie; Via, Justin's sister; Justin; Jack Will." I asked him what he liked about *Wonder*, to which he replied, "It shows Auggie. When he had that thing on the back of his head and also he got bullied by Julian and he got a friend, Jack Will. And he had a sister, Via. That was all." "What do you like about Auggie?" I inquired further. Discussing a final scene in the book, he replied, "It shows that he's a wonder. At the end part. Whispering to his mom. And she said, 'He's actually a wonder.'" Jackson seemed excited to talk about Auggie, so I asked, "And what does that mean, to be 'a wonder'?" "Because, uh . . . so people know that they're wonders as well," he said. "Hm, I like that," I replied, "Did it make you feel like you're a wonder, too?" "Oh, yeah," he responded. Jackson explained the appeal of *Wonder* by listing its many narrators and orienting me to its central relationships. In Auggie, Jackson recognized someone else who had been treated like an outcast because of his disability, and wishfully identified with how Auggie maintained a strong sense of self despite great adversity.

Like Jackson, 8-year-old Karim (Middle Eastern/Algerian, boy) also did not yet have a full grasp on the meaning of autism, but he had latched on to something personally resonant about Auggie. Karim's mom, Nour, along with Karim's therapists, had decided until middle school to avoid talking about autism by name with him, instead focusing on language about difference. "We approached that with his CBT [cognitive behavioral therapist] and with his [therapy] providers in a way where, 'Everybody has his strengths and weaknesses. Everybody is different,'" she said. Interestingly, Nour said that language from *Wonder* was one of Karim's preferred "scripts." A common part of autistic people's vocal repertoires, scripting is the act of repeating lines, phrases, and sounds from the speech of others, particularly from movies, television shows, and other media. Nour said that Karim would specifically script about "what Auggie went through." Scripts can provide a scaffold, or form of support, for autistic children to master semantics as well as a shorthand for articulating their feelings and state of mind.[95] While he was not yet able to name or speak about autism, Karim was employing mass media content to share something about his disabled experience.

MEDIA ABOUT AUTISM   When explicitly autistic characters were featured in movies, TV shows, and books, children on the spectrum had various reactions, including being curious about and critical of their portrayal. Books about autism were bound up with 9-year-old Cody's (White, boy) initial understandings of his diagnosis. As Cody told it, "We went to the beach and then we were going to the library after. So, Mom tells me that I have autism, so we just checked out a bunch of books about it." The books "helped me learn about people with autism," Cody said. His mom, Meg, explained that they picked ones "that were geared toward his age and a little bit older because he can read and understand at a much higher level. To read those was really helpful to him." There was one fictional book written from the point of view of an autistic adolescent that included descriptions of what precipitated the character's meltdowns, or a temporary loss of behavioral control in response to overwhelming emotional situations or sensory stimuli. "That was a good tool," said Meg, "because Cody would come to us with certain sections and say, 'I understand what he's feeling' and we could read it and kind of understand what was in his brain." Another book, *The Survival Guide for Kids with Autism Spectrum Disorders (And Their Parents)* by Elizabeth Verdick and Elizabeth Reeve, offered an age-appropriate overview of autism. Meg said of the book, "It was written to a kid's level. You know, 'You might be scared. You might be excited.' A little bit of everything. I think it was well-written that way."

Cody and Meg talked about how books not only helped Cody understand autism but aided his peers' and younger brother's understanding as well. Cody lived in a wealthy Boston suburb and was in a mainstream, public school classroom in which autism was openly talked about. He got to lead a conversation in his class about their reading of the book *Rules* by Cynthia Lord, which is about a nondisabled preteen girl struggling to accept her autistic brother. While the book has generated criticism in disability circles for centering on a nonautistic protagonist,[96] Cody nonetheless was thrilled to have a chance to educate his classmates. Cody said, "Well, everyone in my class knows [I have autism]. Like, we're reading a book called *Rules* and a character in it has autism." Meg chimed in, "Yeah, you were pretty excited about that. And you got a chance to talk about it." Meg said that another book for slightly younger kids, *All My Stripes: A Story for Children with Autism* by Danielle Royer and Shaina Rudolph, was additionally helpful for Cody's little brother, Mason, to understand the diagnosis.

The outcomes of these conversations and information were very positive for Cody. Prior to using the autism label, Meg and her husband had talked with Cody "about how his brain worked differently." After they told Cody about his diagnosis and he got to read about autism, "he was excited to put a name to it and understand it. It was a relief to him to know that there's nothing wrong with him." Providing him with books about autism set him on a path toward self-acceptance and open communication. "He's expressed [that] having that diagnosis has freed him up to express to us some of his social frustrations and that he wishes he could talk more easily," said Meg, "Like when he gets excited in his brain, to be able to express that to a friend or talk with a friend about a topic." Based on their positive experience, Meg encouraged other parents to use media "to help their child, as much as they can, [to] understand [about autism]." Cody viewed his relationship to autism and receiving an autism diagnosis in a healthy light, thanks in part to his family and classmates' support and enthusiasm, as well as to kid-friendly books about autism that gave him a sense of clarity about himself and autonomy over his own story.

In contrast to Cody, fictional depictions of autistic people generated dissonance for Raul. For a number of reasons, Raul's mom, Nina, had not shown him episodes of popular TV shows like ABC's *The Good Doctor* and Netflix's *Atypical* with autistic lead characters (though played by nonautistic actors). For one, she was not a frequent viewer herself and thought that the topics covered in the shows were a bit mature for an 11-year-old like Raul. But the main reason Nina did not share them was because of the shows' one-dimensional portrayals of autism and lack of nonspeaking autistic characters. Raul "isn't *The Good Doctor*, he isn't Sheldon [Cooper from the TV sitcom *The Big Bang Theory*], he isn't the guy from *Atypical*," she said. Unlike those White and autistic or autistic-coded characters, Raul is Latino, nonspeaking, and uses augmentative and alternative communication (AAC) technology to express himself.

Raul's identity was not only tied to his diagnosis of autism but also how he communicated, which I will detail later in this chapter. He regularly sported T-shirts with slogans like "AAC is My Jam," in reference to his use of assistive communication technology. Because of this, a different TV show—the ABC sitcom *Speechless*—was more compelling to Raul because it starred a nonspeaking lead character, even though the character's speech disability was due to cerebral palsy and not autism.[97] "We did tell Raul about [*Speechless*]," said Nina, "We would watch it and he would kind of come in and out of the living room [to watch]. So for me, I found that to be fulfilling and empowering." Raul's lack of singular focus on the stationary screen was less a sign of disinterest in the TV show and more indicative of his sensory need for vestibular movement. Echoing the earlier discussion of disabled media characters, it was more compelling for Nina, if not her son too, to watch someone on TV who communicated like Raul than who shared the exact same clinical diagnosis.

MEDIA ABOUT AUTISTIC-CODED CHARACTERS   Even though Raul did not identify with the autistic-coded character of Sheldon Cooper, the tremendous global popularity of *The Big Bang Theory* provided some autistic children with a well-known character with which to identify. Jamie said that her 10-year-old son Levi (Latino and White, boy) had noticed similarities between himself and Sheldon, who appears in both *The Big Bang Theory* and a spinoff, *Young Sheldon*. Jamie noted that while "it hasn't even come out on the show that [Sheldon is] on the spectrum . . . , [Levi] just finds him very funny and seems to relate to him." Besides Sheldon's brand of humor, Jamie suspected that Levi found something kindred in their shared interests. He picked up on the fact that Sheldon also "wears a lot of the superhero shirts" and that he and his friends "play [the board game *Settlers of*] *Catan*" too.

Unlike Meg, Jamie struggled with how to disclose her son's autism diagnosis to him. "Would it help him to understand who he is and how he functions, or would he fixate on that and make it worse?" she wondered. The decision was complicated by Jamie's lack of a local support network and an itinerant lifestyle due to her husband's job as a traveling church youth pastor. "Maybe [we'll have] that conversation with one of the specialists who gets to know him, about how we can go about doing that and what would be the benefits," she said. Jamie was also unsure just how much Levi understood about his diagnosis. "I don't think he knows it yet," she said, but "what he will say is he has 'anger issues' or has 'trouble controlling his temper.'"

For that aspect of his inner life, Jamie turned to a Disney movie. "We watched *Beauty and the Beast* somewhat recently and we were like, 'You have trouble controlling your temper like the Beast,'" she said. Though the character was a familiar touchstone, Jamie also worried that using media in this way also ran the risk of oversimplifying Levi's experience. "I wonder if [telling him about his diagnosis] would make him feel better," she shared, as if to say, "'It's not just you. You're not a bad boy.'" In the absence of a more robust support system, characters that were not definitively labeled as disabled or autistic helped Levi understand his social and emotional states. At the same time, relying on fictional characters to explain significant psychological challenges, especially a monstrous and villainous (although ultimately lovable) character like the Beast, was no replacement for high-quality clinical and therapeutic care.

PRODUCING, MAKING, AND SHARING AUTISTIC IDENTITY

Children on the spectrum were not limited to consuming media that helped them to reconcile aspects of their identity as an autistic person. They also used online platforms to create and distribute media as a means of expressing their identity, one linked both explicitly and implicitly to being autistic as well as to different ways of being autistic.

ONLINE COMMUNITIES When I asked 13-year-old Adrian (White, boy) if there was a mass media character with whom he most closely identified, he explained that he did not have one—*but* he had "a thing called an OC, which is . . . I made a character that I cleverly named after myself because I'm super creative and it's not like anyone else did that." Without missing a beat, he added, "I'm being sarcastic. Literally everyone does that." By "OC," Adrian was referring to a term used within anime and fan fiction culture to describe an "original character" that does not already exist or is only mentioned in passing within a media property.[98] Designed and invented by fans, sometimes in their own likenesses, OCs inspire creative practices, including fan art and cosplay, offline and on social media platforms like Tumblr and Amino.[99]

The website Scratch was Adrian's primary site for identity play and creative practice through his OC (also named Adrian), though he also drew upon and incorporated multiple social and cultural references into his creations. As an online community and digital programming platform, Scratch is a rich site for fan culture and interest-driven creative pursuits among adolescents.[100] Scratch community members regularly use the platform to generate animation, interactive stories, and games about their OCs. The website is also a space for difficult conversations and negotiations around identity and marginality. Young people, for example, have used the platform and their OCs to engage in discussions around race, media representation, and the lack of racial diversity within the Scratch community itself.[101]

As a means of self-expression, Adrian modeled his OC after himself in several ways. With shoulder-length brown hair, pale skin, and a hoodie sweatshirt, "Adrian" physically looked like him. Adrian's OC was additionally accessorized with a long stick with blue duct tape wrapped around the middle. Adrian showed me the actual stick as he walked me through the sunroom of his house. The room was packed with Rubbermaid bins and Ziplock bags full of costumes and props that his whole family used for taking part in live-action role playing games, including a giant foam sword nearly as tall as me. "I've got so many cool things and my favorite is this stick with duct tape on it," Adrian chuckled. When he gave me a tour of his bedroom (with his mom within earshot), he asked, "Does this look familiar?" picking up a small LEGO set and figurine, "There's a sweatshirt and a staff?" "Oh, it's your character!" I responded, immediately recognizing that he had built a replica of his OC out of LEGO bricks.

Besides bearing a physical resemblance to Adrian, his OC was also a way for him to work through his own personal narrative and emotional journey. In the hands of Adrian's OC, the duct-taped stick transformed into a magic staff that held symbolic meaning for him. "So honestly," Adrian said, "I think I've told like several people that this is what I consider a 'comfort item.' I think, yeah I pretty much have fallen in love with this thing," he said of the stick. From talking with his mother, Brianna, I knew that Adrian could use a consistent and reliable source of comfort, as the bullying and victimization he dealt with at school, discussed in chapter 1, had been intensely traumatizing. Because of the subject's sensitivity, I did not pry further when Adrian shared, "I'd say I made this character because, I think—I actually, I'm not going to go into my story because that's kind of a personal thing for me." Adrian drew a boundary at this moment, marked out a space for privacy, and felt comfortable enough to assert his autonomy.

Personality-wise, Adrian's OC was not only a reflection of himself, but also of media characters with whom he identified. The one he connected to the most was Leo in the *Percy Jackson and the Olympians* fantasy adventure book series by Rick Riordan. Leo's witty commentary on relationships struck a chord with Adrian. "I personally love his sense of humor," he said, "and that's what I try to build into my OC." Adrian did not explicitly say that Leo was on the spectrum, but he gestured toward it in his description of the character. Adrian's favorite line of Leo's in the book had to do with the fact that the character was the son of the Greek god Hephaestus. News of Leo's paternity was relayed to him by a Roman, whose civilization referred to the same god by the name of Vulcan. Adrian said, "My favorite line [of Leo's] was, 'Vulcan, why son of Vulcan? I don't even watch *Star Trek*.' And after, there was this other paragraph where he was referred to as Mr. Spock. I think honestly that's when I'm like, 'Okay, this character is great.'" Adrian's favorite lines from Leo were ones that referenced the cultural phenomenon of *Star Trek*'s Spock, a media character commonly read as autistic-coded both outside and within the autism community.[102]

In Scratch, Adrian built a fictional world to experiment with storytelling and code. He crafted animated interactive storylines featuring his OC in a Scratch Studio that he called "Geekdom." The studio was a central webpage collection of all of the Scratch projects that he had made with the multiple Geekdom characters that he had invented.[103] His projects included one inspired by the fantasy role-playing game *Dungeons & Dragons*. In another, Adrian embedded his OC within his own interactive version of the multiplayer first person shooter video game *Overwatch*. Adrian had made an animated introduction to all of the Geekdom characters in a sort of programmed slide show, or what is known as a "character sheet" in role-playing games.[104] The one for Adrian's OC's read, "a mix of things. depends on whats going on. logical thinker."[105] For Adrian, applying logic to a situation was central to his conception of and relationship to autism. When I asked Adrian what autism meant to him, he summed it up by saying, "Overall, it's basically my ability to think logically and just work with my mind better. It's not really got an actual definition to me." Using the multimedia capabilities of Scratch, Adrian was able to combine and remix media properties in order to build a character in his likeness and a virtual world that accommodated the workings of his mind.

NETWORKED PUBLISHING   On account of his dyslexia, writing was not Adrian's self-identified strength. He was able to express himself, however, using the block-based code of Scratch and its simplified tools for making interactive stories. For Raul, words, writing, and literature were central to his self-concept, not only as an autistic person, but a nonspeaking person on the spectrum who communicates using a combination of an AAC app, a letterboard (i.e., a physical board with letters to manually point to), and a keyboard. When I asked Raul, through a written interview, if there was something that he was really interested in or loved to talk about, he said, "I am very interested in writing" and he shared that technology "opens a world of learning without assistance." Back in 2013, when I first met Raul at age 5 and interviewed his mom, Nina, a college professor, she was supporting his authorship and helping him to develop a sense of autistic pride. At their dining room table, she showed me "a photo book" that she and Raul had put together to share with his classmates to "help normalize this idea of him communicating with an iPad."

Raul's intertwined identity as a writer and autistic person continued to develop over his childhood. By the time I interviewed Nina in 2019, she said of her son, "I think that his autistic identity is pretty strong. When he was 6 years old, he referred to himself as 'Autistic Raul.'" At age 11, he enjoyed watching cartoons on YouTube and said that he liked to "go on my bed, listen to music, and document stories." When asked if there was something that he did not like about media and technology, he shared that "I don't like apps that influence people to perceive themselves a certain way," highlighting how he valued authenticity online. Raul said that his favorite movies were either from the *Lord of the Rings* or the *Harry Potter* series because "they both have mythical characters that have mythical abilities like myself." Raul's abilities, much like those of other nonspeaking people, were often shortchanged. Individuals with communication disabilities face rampant discrimination, including being denied self-determination and equal opportunities to meaningfully participate in all aspects of life. The perspectives of AAC users are also marginalized within the autism community and underrepresented in autism research.[106]

Raul channeled his frustrations with being misunderstood into his writing. In third grade, his teacher had tasked each student with writing a short nonfiction book, and he chose to write about being autistic and nonspeaking. Raul's teacher encouraged him and his parents to self-publish the book online. In it, Raul writes about the challenges and struggles he faces, particularly difficulties in coordinating his brain, sensory system, and motor control to communicate in a way that is easily interpreted by others. "The book basically is his experience with autism," said Nina, "So it's all about his identity." Raul writes about "the things that make him unique and cool as an autistic child," she said. That message about identity had resonated with other kids on the spectrum, who read the book and left messages for Raul through email and social media. Nina said, "We've gotten nothing but positive feedback from those kids and just saying thank you. Kind of like 'I don't feel alone when I read your work.'" Being able to write about his point of view, as well as share his story widely with others, allowed Raul to come into his own as an autistic writer, with both autism and authorship as key components of his identity.

MEDIATED EXPLORATIONS OF GENDER, GIRLHOOD, AND AUTISM

Raul's vantage point as a nonspeaking Latino person speaks to the multiplicity of autistic identities and the intersections of autism with various aspects of identity. Seeing as autism was originally clinically defined largely through its presentation in White cisgender males,[107] autistic girls and gender-nonconforming children, particularly those of color, also contend with a relative invisibility that extends to media and popular culture. Some autistic girls and their parents noted this absence and remarked upon its impact on identity development. Identity exploration and experiences of autistic girlhood were informed not only by media but also by other gender norms and gendered institutions as well, such as the family.

REPRESENTATIONS OF AUTISTIC GIRLS IN MEDIA Over the course of my fieldwork, an autistic girl character was introduced on the US version of one of the most popular TV shows in the world, *Sesame Street*. Sesame Workshop, the nonprofit behind the program, sought input from autism organizations and researchers, feedback that led to the Workshop's deliberate choice to make the character a girl in order to "make it clear that girls can be on the spectrum, too."[108] The result was Julia, a 4-year-old girl Muppet first introduced in 2015 as part of the Workshop's "*Sesame Street* and Autism: See Amazing in All Children" initiative aimed at reducing autism stigma.[109] Julia's unveiling garnered significant publicity, including a television debut on the news program *60 Minutes* in the weeks leading up to her arrival on *Sesame Street* in 2017.[110] Because the Workshop launched Julia gradually during my years in the field, I was able to notice emerging awareness of her among parents, and to some extent, autistic children. Parent reactions were largely positive in terms of the similarities they saw between their children and Julia, but some also expressed ambivalence around the choice to make the first autistic Muppet a girl.

Several caregivers of preschool-age autistic girls had an emotional reaction to seeing Julia on screen. I talked to 3-year-old Emma's (White, girl) mom, Nikki, the day after the airing of the *60 Minutes* segment that served as Julia's public debut, which both Nikki and Emma's maternal grandma, Sue Ellen, had watched. Nikki mentioned how Julia reflected Emma in a way that she had never see on TV. "They talk about how she flaps, [the way] Emma sometimes does," Nikki said. "I'm thrilled that they're gonna have a character like that." Sue Ellen also chimed in to say that she had already browsed Amazon to see if there were any Julia books to buy. Angelica, mother of 4-year-old Bella (Cape Verdean, girl), was similarly touched by Julia. She said, "When I was watching it by myself, because getting to know the character, I cried because I'm like, 'This girl is my daughter.'" Angelica had hoped that Bella would connect with Julia too and was disappointed that was not the case. "I wanted my daughter so much to like [Julia], want to watch it and be engaged, but she had no desire," Angelica said.

Though Bella may not have been enthralled, 8-year-old Amaya (Black, Latina, and White; girl) had innately recognized something of herself in Julia. At the end of my home observation of her media use, her mom, Kimberly, shared with me that she had told Amaya beforehand that I "worked at *Sesame Street* and she got excited." I suddenly remembered that before our first interview, I had shared with Kimberly that I had interned during college with *Sesame Street* when explaining some of my professional background. Feeling slightly put on the spot, I realized that I had some photos on my phone taken at a recent Sesame Workshop alumni event with a few of the Muppet puppets, including Julia. "So that one's Julia," I said, showing Amaya the photo. "A big Julia?" Amaya inquired, remarking on the relative size of the puppet. Yes, I replied, and showed her another photo that I had taken of some Julia toys, including a plush figurine. "Julia doll? You like Julia?" Amaya asked, to which I replied affirmatively.

Amaya, as it turned out, was a big fan of Julia. She was more animated and conversational talking about the character with me than about any other topic, though this may have been related to the visual prompting from my photos. Kimberly said that when Amaya watched Julia on *Sesame Street* and observed her "doing stims just like her" such as hand flapping, she saw "someone like her on TV." This was important, considering that while Kimberly had told other people that her daughter was autistic, she had not relayed that information to Amaya because she said that she did not want Amaya to think that "anything is wrong with her." As with Karim earlier, despite her mother's reluctance to talk about her diagnosis, Amaya had identified with a disabled character long before she was given the language to describe her own disability and identity as an autistic person.

Other parent reactions, though, were less positive and raised questions over to what extent Julia was, or even should be held up as, representative of all autistic children. Bailey, mother of 6-year-old Olivia (White, girl), said that it was "really weird that they chose [the character to be] a girl. . . . [They] should have done a boy because it's so much more common in boys." Bailey presumably saw the gender skew in autism diagnoses as an immutable biological fact and not a social construction, one that might even shift if Julia's inclusion on *Sesame Street* were to bring attention to gaps in autism diagnoses among girls. Bailey's opinion was likely shaped by the fact that the only autistic girl she personally knew was Olivia. On the basis of gender, Bailey also questioned the extent to which children on the autism spectrum would identify with Julia. She said, "I feel like you're going to find less kids that can relate to it because there's less girls on the spectrum." Bailey's reasoning that autistic boys would ostensibly not relate to Julia belied deeper myths about gender and identification in media, namely that boys will not identify with girl characters, but girls will identify with boy characters.[111]

Bailey's assessment of the majority of autistic children's possible identification with Julia was notably absent any commentary on racial differences. She made no mention of Julia's implicit racial coding as White through her yellow Muppet felt, red hair, and green eyes. This omission may have been because White children are more likely to receive an autism diagnosis, thus following Bailey's logic of "majority rules," or on account of Bailey being White herself. That being said, the fact that Julia is coded White was not a barrier to Amaya's identification with the character. As an Afro-Latina, Amaya found similarities in her and Julia both being girls who liked to stim, even if she did not see her brown skin represented in the Muppet. Ultimately, Amy, mom of 5-year-old Isabella (White, girl), said it best when she noted that "Julia is not gonna represent any one child because they're all so different and a mix of strengths and weaknesses."

MEDIA AND AUTISTIC GIRLHOOD Girls on the spectrum also used media to explore their multifaceted identities. Understanding how Casey's ideas about girlhood were influenced by media like *Free to Be . . . You and Me* requires seeing her identity development as both transgender and autistic as strongly connected and guided by multiple social factors. Casey lived in a household that did not resemble a heteronormative nuclear family. Her mom, Jennifer, was polyamorous, and she and Casey currently resided with Jennifer's boyfriend, his other partner, two other housemates and their two kids, ages 6 and 2. Jennifer said that "most of the folks that live in this house are family, but blood family is just me and her because I've cut the other folks out of my life." Jennifer was not in contact with Casey's biological father, who was abusive, and did not talk to her own parents because they would not refer to Casey by her preferred pronouns and Jennifer wanted to protect her daughter's mental health.

Casey was not just a transgender autistic child living in a household accepting of autism and LGBTQ individuals, but with people who embraced their own autistic and queer identities. Casey "knows she's autistic," Jennifer said. She had explained autism to Casey from an in-group perspective, saying that "we think a little bit differently than some people because we're autistic. It's a pride thing. We talk about it, and we try to remove stigma from it entirely." The fluid composition of Casey's household also brought her into contact with other autistic and queer people. Jennifer said that "a couple years ago, there was another kid who lived here . . . part time, also on the spectrum." Casey and that child "would talk [about the TV show] *Thomas the Tank Engine*, play *Thomas the Tank Engine*. I know, very stereotypical," Jennifer said, alluding to the fact that trains are appealing to many autistic individuals.[112]

Casey's story is unique for a transgender autistic girl in that, from an early age, she received affirmation of her identity and support for her gender- and autism-related needs at home. Adolescents who are both autistic and gender minority (i.e., transgender, nonbinary, gender nonconforming) report social difficulties including "specific challenges with gender discernment and gender affirmation resulting from autism-related self-awareness and/or executive function differences" as well as communicating their needs around gender (e.g., correcting pronouns that other people use to identify them).[113] On a more positive note, some also describe the psychosocial benefits of connecting with other gender-diverse autistic youth and "being able to have a journey and . . . to talk and share that with people."[114] Casey could connect with a number of people in her life who were autistic, gender minority, or both.

Besides *Free to Be*, Jennifer provided Casey with several opportunities through media for her identity exploration to be validated and to see herself and the immediate world around her reflected. "Representation matters," Jennifer said, "We try to do that in all the ways." Casey was very into comic books and graphic novels, which Jennifer indulged by bringing her to PAX, a series of gaming culture festivals. Jennifer said that "at PAX, [I] specifically asked [vendors] for some queer stuff. . . . You know, one princess saving another and falling in love." Jennifer tried to present queer stories as the norm for Casey. "It's not like [Casey] specifically knew that I was looking for queer material," said Jennifer, "just, you know, this is how they come."

Seeing as autistic gender-diverse adolescents report challenges verbalizing and self-advocating for their gender, as well as benefitting from concrete and straightforward explanations about gender,[115] Jennifer was providing Casey with the building blocks of identity exploration through media.

REFLECTIONS ON IDENTITY

The autistic identity of children on the spectrum is but one aspect of their self-concept, which grows more complex over childhood and adolescence. The process by which their identities develop is informed by several layers of social influence. In this chapter, I focused on the role of media—online communities, websites, social media, books, movies, and television programs—as one key factor shaping autistic identity development. This includes the larger media culture and the individuals in a child's immediate environment who directly impact their engagement with media (i.e., family members, peers, teachers). These young people's stories highlight tensions among theories of the self, including the extent to which identity is cohesive. Taken as a whole, a number of discussion topics emerge.

AUTISTIC IDENTITY AND MEDIA
With respect to autistic identity development, I found a great deal of variation in terms of whether or not children knew or could comprehend that they were autistic, disabled, or different in some manner. This is to be expected, considering the relatively wide age range of children and their levels of cognition. As prior work suggests, parents' comfort with disclosing an autism diagnosis to their autistic child also varied. With or without language from their parents to describe autism, children still were attracted to media that made them feel seen, putting a different spin on theories of self and identity. This included depictions and descriptions of similar behaviors (e.g., flapping), communication needs (e.g., using AAC, difficulties communicating sensory needs), and experiences (e.g., bullying). Not every autistic child like Casey and Cody has the same cognitive ability to understand autism as an identity category. But even kids who have not been told about being on the spectrum, like Amaya and Karim, be it because of their age or level of development, might still be using print, screen, and interactive media to figure things out for themselves.

MEDIA REPRESENTATION

Among explicit media representations of autism, with which autistic children might identify or explore what it means to be on the spectrum, very little exists that is accurate and authentic. This may be due to a lack of accessible opportunities for autistic artists, producers, and creators within the creative industries.[116] Books did seem to provide more support than other media among school-age kids on the spectrum to develop a positive autistic identity centered around self-acceptance and the acceptance of others. There is a need for more fictional books to be narrated by child autistic characters and for memoirs written from an autistic adolescent's point of view, like Raul's self-published online book. Autistic kids deserve opportunities to take ownership of their own narratives. Cody's story highlights how, in school settings, books can facilitate conversations about autism that are led by autistic adolescents and scaffolded by trained educators.

These young people's perspectives also highlight how identity development and identification with media characters are not just individual processes, but relational and discursive as well.[117] Interestingly, media did not necessarily have to be about autism explicitly (such as the book *Wonder* and TV show *Speechless*) or even about disability (like *Free to Be*) to make a positive impact on autistic children's identity development. *Sesame Street's* Julia seemed to appeal most to family members of people on the spectrum. Meanwhile, characters like the protagonist of *Rules*, a sibling, were useful for children like Cody in navigating their social worlds. This complicates assumptions about the linearity of autism representation in media and its benefits. Centering *Rules* on a sibling did not detract from the story or its usefulness to Cody because his identity is not completely self-determined. Autistic characters developed in consultation and/or led by autistic individuals are obviously important, but the children in this chapter made it clear that family members, even fictional ones, matter in shaping their identity development, as do experiences other than those labeled as autistic.

SOCIAL FACTORS

This is not to say that media is the only or even the most important social factor influencing children's autistic identity development. Positive representations of autism in the media cannot and should not supplant essential forms of support. Media representation is no replacement for high-quality mental health services provided by schools, health-care providers, and nonprofit community groups, as with the example of Levi. The conversations that autistic children have with their social partners around media also matter. Prior work has illustrated that parents affect their children's autistic identity formation, but this chapter highlights the role that media can play within those exchanges. Parents in general may support their child's positive uses of media by encouraging their child's media creation, scaffolding critical thinking, and using media to cultivate a strong sense of self. Parents of autistic kids can play a significant role by introducing media about autism to their child or giving their child space to play with media and explore their autistic identity. Autistic and otherwise neurodivergent parents like Jennifer have especially important insights to contribute in this respect within online and offline spaces.[118] Jennifer, in fact, also shared how she and some other autistic people had led a discussion with neurotypical parents of autistic children at Casey's school about how to better promote their child's mental well-being based on their own neurodivergent points of view.

There is also much more to explore in how media informs young people's identity development at the intersections of race and autistic identity. White autistic individuals are far more likely to find gainful employment as adults, avoid dangerous encounters with police, and evade other forms of systemic racial bias. Social media platforms are vital spaces where different narratives about race, autism, and childhood are being shared, such as the #BlackAutisticJoy hashtag created by Kayla Smith and multimedia produced by neurodivergent Afro-Latina artist/scholar Jen White-Johnson and her autistic son, Knox.[119] Television, film, and other mass media have not as yet caught up with the intersectionality of multiple marginalized identities and the depth of autistic youth experience outside of one that is primarily White and cisgender male.[120]

IMPLICATIONS FOR SERVICES AND PROGRAMS

Lastly, these findings offer unique insights for educational and therapeutic programs.[121] Clinical formulations of autism may not satisfy how kids on the spectrum understand their own conditions. Identifying with an endearing Beast, for example, might be beneficial in ways that identifying with poor social cognition or a neurological impairment might not be. Media and technology can also help connect autistic youth to one another, provide them with autistic role models, and allow them to develop a sense of pride that is inclusive of being autistic. With regard to families, evaluation research published thus far has focused on the impact of *Sesame Street*'s Julia and Sesame Workshop's corresponding outreach materials on the parents of autistic and nonautistic children, but not on autistic children.[122] Julia has had some success in making a difference, but it is unclear if the primary benefactors of her inclusion on the show are autistic youth themselves.

Though outside factors affect autistic youth awareness of and attitudes toward autism, these young people also actively make meaning of their diagnosis as both a label and a cultural identity through their consumption and creation of media. Identity is an important aspect of the sociotechnical shaping of sociality because what it means to have an identity is influenced by both media and society and because social and technical forces impact the materials available to children to develop a sense of self. As with autistic adults, there are psychological benefits to providing young people on the spectrum with a positive sense of autistic belonging through media. The ethnographic work presented in this chapter can help us to figure out what aspects of mediated identity are helpful to whom and under what circumstances, with complexity and nuance. The next chapter explores the effects of media and technology on another context for autistic children's sense of cultural belonging: that of learning and informal educational settings.

3 LEARNING

Over a cup of coffee at her kitchen table, April—mother of Sofia, a 5-year-old nonspeaking autistic Latina girl—explained that her daughter's sleep, as well as her own, had been completely thrown off lately. "[Sofia is] awake from 2:00 a.m. to 7:00 a.m. every day," April shared, "And then she'll fall asleep until like 11:30, 12:00 [p.m.] because she's exhausted from being up all night." Like many other children across the United States that summer, Sofia was not attending camp and mostly stayed home, spending the day in her Boston apartment. Without a regular schedule, media was increasingly becoming part of Sofia's every waking moment, and she was awake for more of each day. April reported that Sofia will reflexively "grab the iPad, that's the first thing she does [when she wakes up]. Even if she doesn't use it, she needs to touch it." Sofia loved watching the educational preschool cartoon *Clifford the Big Red Dog* on the PBS KIDS video and YouTube apps. She was starting to rely on the iPad not only to structure her day but also to regulate her behavior. April said that "it's the only thing that will keep her calm enough to not start hitting. She doesn't have anything going on . . . she's just not burning that energy at all." Though far from ideal, April felt like there were no alternatives to Sofia's constant media use. "I know why she's not sleeping good and I'm just like . . . can't do anything about it right now," she sighed, "I can only do so much at home."

Frustration over being able to "only do so much at home" was a common refrain among individuals during the summer of 2020 in the wake of the coronavirus pandemic. "Shelter in place," "stay at home," and "safer at home" orders went into effect in mid-March 2020, urging people to leave home only if necessary.[1] In the absence of a coordinated national effort to effectively address the public health crisis, states such as Massachusetts took measures to physically close schools and move learning into virtual classrooms to prevent the spread of COVID-19.[2] Some parents took on another full-time job overseeing their children's schooling in addition to working remotely, while record numbers of Americans became unemployed.[3] Students with disabilities encountered additional educational barriers with the loss of in-person physical, speech, and occupational therapy, and low-income students contended with a lack of high-quality internet access.[4] Being "safer" at home was also relative to the safety within and outside of one's home, including neighborhood and racial health disparities that affected the likelihood of contracting and surviving the coronavirus.

Except all of what April described with Sofia—not going to camp, staying inside, and being tethered to the iPad—happened in July 2019, seven months before the pandemic started. While many people made hard choices and major sacrifices in 2020, interlocking forms of structural inequality meant that Sofia was already intimately familiar with being socially distanced and technologically mediated. Why was she not attending camp? Local programs for autistic kids at $6,000 for just three weeks were far too expensive. April had recently left her job as a daycare provider because she could not function at work after staying up so late with Sofia. April had the option of sending her to summer school but opted out after a terrible summer prior when Sofia was placed, she said, into "an empty room with a blue table and a stack of paper and crayons and that's it." Why was Sofia not leaving home? Her parents had been priced out of their gentrified neighborhood and moved into a more affordable apartment with April's family—but one with no parks, playgrounds, or subway stops in walking distance. Taking the bus somewhere would have overwhelmed Sofia's easily dysregulated sensory system.

And why was Sofia spending so much time with media? On top of the issues that have already been mentioned, she had been on a never-ending waitlist for behavioral and speech therapy for the past nine months. A local hospital's pediatric autism center notified April of openings at therapy practices in the area, but those health-care providers never seemed to have availability when she called. Sofia's experiences match up with research indicating that compared to their White peers, Latino children receive fewer autism services and their parents feel less empowered to advocate on their behalf.[5] Shifting from "waitlist to waitlist to whatever," in April's words, and the resulting gap in therapeutic services led to Sofia having a lot of spare time on her hands. Whatever Sofia was doing, it mostly involved a screen. Sofia's grandmother, Claudia, observed that when her granddaughter is "in school and she has therapy, she doesn't think about technology at all . . . but nothing to do, she's back to *Clifford* all day." Sofia was consuming a significant amount of publicly funded educational media in large part because she had not been receiving the formal enrichment that her public school was legally obligated to provide her.

This chapter focuses on the potential for learning that media and technology offer autistic children like Sofia—with a focus on academic and creative pursuits—and the concurrent barriers they face in accessing a high-quality education. (As for the digital learning obstacles and opportunities borne specifically of the pandemic, I will address those more thoroughly in this book's conclusion.) A common refrain among parents with whom I spoke was that their child learned a great deal through their self-directed and unstructured media use at home, sometimes even more so than in school. Autistic kids also demonstrated and told me enthusiastically about information, skills, and talents that digital tools helped them to cultivate. This may reflect the compelling nature of technology as well as autistic children's attraction to audiovisual media, but it is also an indictment of the lack of engaging, inclusive, and affordable in-person educational and leisure opportunities for kids on the spectrum beyond their homes and in their neighborhoods. The same factors shaping young people's unequal educational opportunities—including structural inequalities rooted in race, class, and geography—also impact the learning possibilities for autistic children in varied ways.

Disabled children's technology use has primarily been understood in society through a curative or rehabilitative lens, placing more emphasis on kids that need fixing than on systems that need overhauling.[6] Neurodivergent students tend to figure into cultural narratives of learning and educational technology on a largely superficial level, thereby reinforcing their outsider or "special" status. Through the analytic lens of the sociotechnical shaping of sociality, in this chapter I unpack popular concepts and key theories in learning and technology and present them from another angle that questions the social norms underpinning them; for example, juxtaposing a recent emphasis in education circles on children's "interest-driven" learning with media and the pathologization of autistic people's so-called special interests. I argue that popular assumptions about the inherent tech-savviness of kids on the spectrum overlook the support, mentorship, and resources that they need to develop a wide range of digital skills and critical literacies to thrive in an uncertain world.

AUTISM, EDUCATION, AND LEARNING WITH TECHNOLOGY

I begin with a broad overview of the formal (i.e., in school) and informal (i.e., out of school) educational landscape for autistic children, with a focus on the US context, and the extent to which technology has been successfully incorporated into their learning outside of the school environment.

FORMAL LEARNING

Students receiving special education services through autism eligibility in the United States comprise approximately 10 percent of all students in special education and around 1 percent of all students enrolled in elementary and secondary schools, or one in eighty-one students.[7] School eligibility for special education services is not a proxy for an autism diagnosis, though; one in eighty-one is far less than the Center for Disease Control and Prevention's medical estimates of autism prevalence as one in forty-four children. There are several reasons for this discrepancy, including the fact that many students on the spectrum are not identified by schools or identified as qualifying for special education services through a different disability category.[8] States also vary in how they determine special education eligibility for autism services due to differences in state-level education spending and the availability of medical providers who can diagnose autism.[9] Individual factors additionally influence autism eligibility in schools; for instance, White families with higher socioeconomic statuses are more likely to advocate that their child be labeled with autism instead of an intellectual disability due in part to the cultural stigma associated with the latter.[10]

The US Individuals with Disabilities Education Act (IDEA) of 1990 (revised in 2004) states that all children have a right to a "free appropriate public education in the least restrictive environment."[11] For students with disabilities, the IDEA mandates the creation of an Individualized Education Program (or Plan) (IEP) to ensure this right. IEPs are personalized to each child and outline educational goals, objectives, and services that a student will receive in school. The IEP is revised annually in a meeting with key stakeholders including parents, teachers, administrators, and students when appropriate. IEPs can leave much to be desired, however. Many parents report finding the process stressful and taxing, especially those who are low-income, immigrant, and/or Black and Latino.[12] Though their attendance at the IEP meeting is mandatory, caregivers are often not provided the opportunity to give meaningful input.[13]

Some disabled students who do not require special instruction or related services but still need some accommodations (e.g., extended time for test taking) have 504 Plans instead of IEPs. These plans derive from Section 504 of the Rehabilitation Act of 1973, a civil rights law prohibiting disability discrimination in programs that receive federal assistance (such as from the Department of Education).[14] Still, whether a child has an IEP or 504— or nothing—is not reflective of the child alone. For example, Meena, an immigrant and mom of 5-year-old Eashan (Asian/Indian, boy), said that he "does not have an IEP at school. It will be a fight to get him. It's just hard for me to push, because I am already going through a lot with my other son [Adhi]," who is also autistic and has complex needs.

"School" itself can take many different shapes for autistic kids. Children on the spectrum may be enrolled in public or private school (the latter of which is not tied to the IDEA or required to follow IEPs), or, alternatively, may be homeschooled. Physical schools can generally be challenging places for students on the spectrum for various reasons, as they "are usually physically large, noisy, and chaotic, transitions between classes occur frequently throughout the school day, and the social milieu becomes ever more complex as children progress."[15] It is important to consider classroom configuration as well. A student might do best in a mainstream school and classroom, a special education classroom in a mainstream school, in a hybrid version of those two arrangements, or in a separate school for kids with neurodevelopmental disabilities. Many autistic children, however, end up in segregated or self-contained classrooms because their schools fail to design individualized instruction and provide staff support in integrated classrooms.[16]

Across these arrangements, there are significant gaps in research on the educational outcomes of autistic students, particularly adolescents and those with intellectual disabilities. Individual education plans for students in specialized settings primarily focus on life skills and developmental areas, whereas mainstream settings emphasize academic progress.[17] Students on the spectrum are often excluded from academic measures like standardized tests and not offered alternative assessments.[18] Studies also show that up to 85 percent of youth in juvenile detention facilities have disabilities like autism that make them eligible for special education services, but only 37 percent received those services while in school, with a disproportionate number being Latino and Black children.[19] Autistic children with intellectual disabilities and from minoritized backgrounds are perpetually being "readied" to learn, in lieu of learning, even in school. The stakes of not having one's educational needs met by schools are simply much higher for some kids on the spectrum than for others.

INFORMAL LEARNING

School may be the primary site of autistic children's education, but it is not the only location. Young people learn in both formal and informal educational settings.[20] Formal learning is primarily classroom-based learning, is provided by trained teachers, and offers a consistent community of fellow learners. It has limited flexibility in terms of incorporating content that does not fit into a specific curriculum or set of educational standards. In contrast, informal learning happens outside the classroom in spaces including afterschool programs, extracurricular clubs, community-based organizations, museums, libraries, and children's own homes. These spaces generally provide more flexibility and experimentation with respect to educational content, though this lack of structure can also make learning outcomes harder to track. Many informal learning opportunities also require major investments of time, money, and other resources (e.g., equipment, supplies) on the part of parents outside of the support they (especially mothers) are already expected to formally provide (e.g., homework help, classroom volunteering).[21]

Questions of formality and informality in education concern not just where one learns but also what counts as learning.[22] Sociocultural learning theory, popularized by developmental psychologist Lev Vygotsky, highlights the pivotal function that social environment and cultural norms serve in a learner's development.[23] High-quality informal learning can have several educational, social, and cultural advantages for children and adolescents. Young people may significantly benefit from developing hobbies and pursuits that follow a less rigid schedule than do the school day and calendar. This includes time for learning that is spontaneous and self-paced and that occurs within longer, uninterrupted stretches. Informal learning also offers opportunities for direct family and intergenerational involvement in a variety of roles such as coaches, collaborators, and onlookers. Out-of-school learning may be self-guided and motivated by personal interests, as well as propelled by social connections, friendships, and relationships.[24]

As with formal learning settings, children on the autism spectrum face unique barriers to accessing informal learning opportunities. Physical spaces can present challenges for autistic youth with sensory sensitivities who find it hard to stay still, quiet, or focused within such environments. Even settings such as museums and libraries that may have "autism friendly" or "sensory sensitive" programming (i.e., special hours with reduced capacity, greater freedom to move about, less harsh lighting, and lowered sound) present their own access barriers. This includes programming that is inconveniently scheduled (i.e., early in the morning), prohibitively expensive, rarely offered, or difficult to access via public transit.[25] Drop-in or casual programs also tend not to provide personalized support for autistic learners unless delivered by a private aide or parent, which inherently privileges families with more resources. For autistic youth like Sofia, all of these issues factor into the outsized function of media as a facilitator of low-cost, convenient, and independent learning at home.

DIGITAL MEDIA AND INFORMAL LEARNING

Media and technology play an increasingly pivotal role in out-of-school learning contexts for children and adolescents. The internet and networked communication technologies blur distinctions between formal and informal learning environments (e.g., school-provided laptops that students take home and use for nonschoolwork-related purposes). Technological and digital media skills may be cultivated through informal learning activities, including those that are mentor-led and learner-initiated.[26] For example, a child can watch YouTube videos to teach themselves digital photo editing, or they can attend a club or camp (in person or virtual) through which they receive personalized instruction. However, significant gaps exist between learners in reaching their goals. There is a difference, for instance, between an adolescent without home internet or computer access watching that same instructional YouTube video on a smartphone shared with younger siblings whom they also must regularly care for while a single parent works, and another viewing the video on their own computer with reliable, high-quality broadband internet at home during ample leisure time. Such disparities tend to result in upper- and middle-class children who come to school "prepared" to learn and poor- and working-class students who have not benefitted from such preparation. The rush to technocentric solutions to educational inequality often leads to greater divides, particularly without an understanding of the social infrastructures, political environments, and cultural expectations into which technologies enter.[27]

With respect to the informal digital learning of disabled and autistic youth, programs focused on science, technology, engineering, and math (STEM) have launched in recent years, though few and far between.[28] Such activities are often borne of partnerships between community organizations, educational institutions, and academic researchers.[29] Many center on job preparation in the tech sector, noting high unemployment among adults on the spectrum.[30] Tech Kids Unlimited, for example, is a nonprofit program in New York City that provides neurodivergent adolescents with computer science and technology training (e.g., app development, video editing) in a social environment with a low student-to-teacher ratio.[31] The IDEAS Maker Program is based on the New York Hall of Science's museum-based maker program and has run as an informal club in New York University's ASD Nest autism-inclusion middle schools.[32] Despite these organized programs, there has been little research into racially and socioeconomically diverse autistic children's mentor-led and self-directed learning with media and technology in out-of-school settings, and there have been few studies on the social, cultural, and political tensions that emerge across their formal and informal learning environments.[33]

NEURODIVERGENT LEARNERS IN A NETWORKED WORLD

I take up this work next by identifying patterns in how digital media and learning play out in the everyday lives of autistic youth. I do so by critically engaging with five key concepts that cut across the learning sciences and the sociology of education: (1) learning ecologies, (2) educational media, (3) media literacy, (4) interest-driven learning, and (5) concerted cultivation. Through my conversations and observations with autistic kids and their parents, I found that many are getting a lot educationally out of media and technology, but what they are learning is often unexpected and hard to measure, and how they are learning it is not always straightforward.

LEARNING ECOLOGIES

Cathleen knew that something was amiss one day when her son, 6-year-old Sebastian (Latino and White, boy), suddenly "had all this *Peppa Pig* language [and was speaking] with a British accent," referring to the animated children's TV show from the United Kingdom starring the eponymous pig. The fact that Sebastian had out of the blue started talking like a Brit was not the surprising part to Cathleen. In addition to autism, Sebastian was diagnosed with Fragile X, a syndrome caused by a genetic mutation on the X chromosome that can also result in difficulties with sensory regulation.[34] Cathleen said that "kids with Fragile X mimic anything," which for Sebastian included things he heard and saw on TV. No, what was curious to Cathleen was that it had been at least a year since her son had even watched an episode of *Peppa Pig*, at least to her knowledge. There was only one place where he could have accessed the show without her direct supervision. "I said, 'Sebastian, are you watching *Peppa Pig* at school?" Cathleen recalled.

After asking him multiple times and eventually talking with one of his teachers, Cathleen deduced that Sebastian had been viewing the program on the iPad every morning at school for the past few months. Upon arrival, Sebastian's school aide brought him straight to the learning resource center, where he could avoid the clamor and chaos of the hallways for 15–20 minutes before joining his kindergarten class. At some point, the center's staff had started to use the iPad as a behavioral management tool to get Sebastian to sit at a table and do work. Cathleen found this pedagogical practice to be frustrating in multiple respects. Her son's time in the "learning resource center" was being spent watching a TV show that to her was more commercial than educational. She did not like that Sebastian was watching TV for fun in the same location where he received academic instruction at other times of the day. She additionally bemoaned the fact that Sebastian's iPad time was an unearned reward at school, which was very different from how she and her husband managed his technology use at home.

Multiple breakdowns in parent-school communication had clearly occurred. "I still don't have all of the information," Cathleen said, "I don't know how long he's watching the iPad for. I don't know if it's a whole show or if it's just a few minutes." She wished that someone in the resource center had sought her consent. "Nobody asked if that was okay, how we feel about iPad use at school," she remarked. No one had solicited her approval of the content either, which she would have objected to. After the fact, Cathleen proposed that her son at least watch an educational show like *Wild Kratts* or play with a letter recognition app on the iPad. She was less than thrilled when the staff came back to her and "suggested that it was going to be *Paw Patrol* and I was like, 'Absolutely no way is he going to school to watch *Paw Patrol*,'" a preschool show that, like *Peppa Pig*, is thin on curriculum. Nor had any representative from school asked about Sebastian's media use or morning routine at home. If they did, they would have learned that he and his younger brother usually watched 30 minutes of TV after breakfast. "Then he goes to school and gets immediately given an iPad," Cathleen said exasperatedly.

Understanding how and why communication had failed between Cathleen and Sebastian's teachers requires taking a closer look at the factors that influence any one child's learning. Psychologist Urie Bronfenbrenner proposed the ecological systems theory to explain the direct and indirect ways that human development shapes and is shaped by society at multiple interconnected levels or "nested systems."[35] The ecological part of the theory highlights how social contexts envelop one another and are in constant interaction. Bronfenbrenner identified five such systems: microsystem, mesosystem, exosystem, macrosystem, and chronosystem. The "microsystem" immediately surrounds a child and includes the activities, spaces, and people they regularly encounter (e.g., Sebastian's parents, aide, and teachers). At the mesosystem level are the interactions between those entities; for example, parent-teacher communication. The "exosystem" surrounds the mesosystem and microsystem, and it encompasses larger institutional factors such as school district policies. These three systems are enclosed by the "macrosystem," or the broader culture and social norms, like White upper-middle-class parents' expectations of a positive relationship with their children's schools. Lastly, the "chronosystem" describes the circumstances impacting how a child grows up at any given era in history and how the individual person and their environments also change over time.

Children are not passive observers in Bronfenbrenner's framework. They both act on and are acted upon by these systems; for instance, kids influence their parents' caregiving practices, which, in turn, impact their own lives. This dynamism holds especially true for the incorporation of digital media and technology into each level of the nested spheres, spanning the online spaces where kids hang out (microsystem), federal and state laws protecting their digital privacy (exosystem), and societal "moral panics" about their potentially excessive media use (macrosystem).[36] The ecology metaphor in Bronfenbrenner's theory extends to the "media ecologies" that young people inhabit, or the structures and conditions of their engagement with digital and nondigital media. It also applies to their "learning ecologies," meaning the social and cultural contexts in which they learn (i.e., formal and informal learning settings, physical and virtual environments).[37]

With respect to the learning ecologies of autistic youth, parents of kids on the spectrum are more likely than those of children with other disabilities to be dissatisfied with their relationship with their child's school and with home-school communication.[38] Dialogue between parents and teachers is of particular importance for autistic children because many like Sebastian have significant communication challenges that limit what they might be able to share at home about school.[39] Ultimately, Cathleen suspected that the cause for the miscommunication about Sebastian's TV time was more institutional than individual, or, in other words, that it concerned the exosystem more so than the microsystem. "I'm not blaming them," Cathleen said of the learning center staff. She explained by bringing up Sebastian's prior educational contexts. "[He] went from this . . . amazing preschool program and you're very connected to what's happening" to elementary school where "you don't get the same information" from teachers, she said. Though he was currently enrolled in one of the most well-funded school districts in Massachusetts, K–12 classrooms were overcrowded, and teachers had increased student caseloads. It was not the biggest deal that Sebastian came home from school talking like Peppa Pig, but the incident represented a larger disconnect within and across the learning spaces that he inhabited daily.

EDUCATIONAL MEDIA

Cathleen's preference for Sebastian watching certain shows at school (if he had to) also speaks to questions of what makes media educational, especially for kids on the spectrum whose cognitive development may not follow a linear path. Children do not only learn from media created with education in mind. They model behavior they regularly see and repeat words they frequently hear from all kinds of media (much to their parents' chagrin). Most explicitly educational media created for US audiences is intended for preschoolers and early elementary-age children. There is a drop-off in educational media consumption around age 8 because children become busier with school and less content is produced for adolescents. Kids can learn both academic skills (e.g., STEM, literacy) and socioemotional skills (e.g., self-awareness, decision-making) from such content; the former, though, is generally easier for younger children to comprehend and the latter, for older kids.[40] Young children can also be confused by media marketed as educational but that has no underlying curriculum or is poorly designed (e.g., too quickly paced).[41] Productions from major industry players (e.g., Nick Jr.,

PBS KIDS) usually go through some form of vetting with education advisors (e.g., script review).

Very little research has been conducted on what autistic kids learn from educational media designed for a mass child audience. Some studies fold such content into interventions for children on the spectrum; for example, determining if certain episodes teach social and emotional skills.[42] Other work centers on the use of media as a reward or reinforcer in behavioral therapy, as well as on the messages that parents receive from clinicians about using media with their autistic child for therapeutic and educational purposes at home.[43] For example, Amy, mom of Isabella (age 5, White, girl), noted, "I think almost all of the games or apps that we have were recommended by her ABA [applied behavior analysis] folks. [Those all] have some educational component." Many kids on the spectrum excel at recognizing patterns and alternative problem solving, talents which lend themselves to educational games and puzzles. The ease of pausing, rewinding, and rewatching content on phones and tablets aids in their retention of letters and words. Difficulties with executive functioning and sensory processing, however, can also limit the efficacy of educational media for this audience, such as apps that have extra "gamified" elements that distract from learning goals.[44]

"IT'S FREE EDUCATION" Many parents, especially of preschool and early elementary-age autistic kids, were excited by the learning potential of You-Tube, mobile devices, and other forms of digital media. YouTube, the world's largest host of video content, would never be characterized as an educational media platform, but it does host material from public broadcasters like PBS and BBC, alongside lower-budget, pseudo-educational material from producers like ChuChuTV.[45] Phil, father of 4-year-old Chris (Asian/Cambodian and White, boy), plainly stated, "YouTube, I'm a big fan. Free. It's free education." Raina thought it was easier for her 4-year-old daughter Zahra (Azerbaijani) to comprehend material on screen than in print: "I believe she can learn more during one hour of media than she would learn from [a] book at this age." Molly, mom of 4-year-old Abbey (White, girl) also noted that traditional media was less effective as an educational tool. "Some [kids] like books. Some like laptops," Molly said, "[Abbey's] thing is going to be either my phone or the tablet. As long as she's learning, I could really care less."

Parents were prepared to make tradeoffs to maximize the educational benefits of media, including what others might characterize as excessive screen time. As Leslie, mom of 3-year-old Oscar (White, boy), put it, "I really wanted to limit his exposure to screens. But I figure . . . it's not like we're watching violent train wrecks on YouTube. We're watching letters." Parents of minimally speaking children regularly said that their child made more attempts at speech and vocalization when they were able to replay sounds and words on a digital device. "Most of [what] he watches on YouTube have things like [the song] 'Farmer in the Dell' in the background while Spider-Man is driving the car off the cliffs," Tara said about the viewing habits of her 3-year-old minimally speaking son Ryan (White)—videos which combined the violent train wrecks and letters mentioned by Leslie. Tara added, "I'll let him watch that video 50,000 times if it's going to make him be able to sing that song." Angelica, mom of 4-year-old minimally speaking Bella (Cape Verdean, girl), likewise claimed that her daughter had learned "a lot of words and speech . . . through these videos on YouTube. And I understand people saying . . . too much of that is bad for them. But for me, I honestly think it's helped her."

Some caregivers considered learning with technology at home to be just as, if not more, beneficial than learning in formal settings. "Basically, the iPad taught him all his colors, all his letters, all his numbers, all his shapes," said Peter, dad of 6-year-old Danny (White, boy). "Do you think more so than school?" I replied, to which Peter said, "Absolutely." Amir, father of 5-year-old Imay (Asian/Nepalese, boy), said of his son's YouTube viewing, "I think he learn from those videos, he learn. In class, in his school, they don't." Educational media could also supplement other kinds of in-person and extracurricular learning. Eight-year-old Karim (Middle Eastern/Algerian, boy), who is Muslim, attended religious and cultural instruction every Saturday. His mom, Nour, who worked in higher education, introduced an app called *Adnan the Teacher of Qu'ran* to him to help him memorize verses and learn Arabic.

Sensory processing played an additional role in how autistic children learned from educational media and managed their attention amid various technological demands. For Abbey, multitasking with media was more a facilitator of learning than a distraction from it. I observed her focused on a game on Molly's iPhone while facing the living room window. Preschool cartoon *Doc McStuffins* played behind her on the television set—a special crossover episode with characters from the classic *Winnie the Pooh* series. "Hi, Eeyore," Abbey said, without looking back at the TV. A few seconds later, an on-screen character said the same line. It was common for Abbey to anticipate and recite speech from shows that she watched repeatedly. "I don't know what it is. Just seeing it on the screen, in the way it's presented, it just absorbs in her mind," Molly remarked. Though "background television" (i.e., when the TV is on, but no one is watching) is generally understood to have various negative impacts on young children's cognition and speech, that research is based on studies of nonautistic kids.[46] Other research has suggested that background television heightens "autism spectrum disorder-like symptoms" for infants and toddlers.[47] The TV on in the background was very much front of mind, however, for Abbey, even as she looked down at the iPhone in her hand. The "education" in educational media can mean different things among autistic children based on social expectations of their learning outcomes and the benefit that they derive relative to other educational contexts.

FOREIGN LANGUAGE   I was surprised by how much one topic—non-English language learning—figured into the media consumed by the autistic kids I spent time with, including those living in English-speaking monolingual and multilingual households. Such media included YouTube videos of letters and words, educational app video screengrabs, and dubbed cartoons. Rob, father of 13-year-old Luke (White, boy) commented, "You'll be sitting here, and you'll hear Elmo [coming from his iPad], and then you'll realize it's in . . . Portuguese." Kids derived pleasure from videos that were identical save for being in a different language, which could be attractive to autistic children preferring patterns and predictability. "There's [a *Sesame Street*] rubber duck song he likes to watch, but he'll watch it in like three different languages," Jessie said of her 4-year-old son Patrick (White). Three-year-old Carter (Black and White, boy) enjoyed "watching [music videos of] 'Wheels on the Bus' in like five different languages," said his mom, Simone. It was hard to say to what extent the kids, the technology, or the global reach of YouTube were driving this phenomenon, or if they were even possible to fully separate.

Another underlying individual factor might have been the condition of hyperlexia, a term derived from the Greek words for "over" (*hyper*) and "word" (*lexis*). Hyperlexia in children is characterized by having advanced reading skills without explicit instruction and a strong orientation toward reading material among those younger than age 5.[48] Hyperlexia is strongly associated with autism: 84 percent of those who have hyperlexia are estimated to be people on the spectrum.[49] Autistic toddlers are more likely than typically

developing children to display interest in literacy-related toys.[50] There is con-
tention over whether hyperlexia is a disability or "superability," a medical
condition or cultural form of "autistic poetics" (i.e., linguistic techniques that
people on the spectrum use to create art and meaning).[51] Hyperlexic children
are drawn to numbers and letters, videos of which there are no shortage of on
YouTube. Oscar's mom, Leslie, noted of his ability to say the Cyrillic letter Я,
"We did not teach him this. He learned this from watching a video."

Some studies have identified a co-concurrence of hyperlexia and difficulties with spoken language.[52] Interestingly, it was primarily nonspeaking or
minimally speaking autistic kids—as with Luke, Carter, and Patrick—who
tended to be the heaviest viewers of this video genre. During her steady consumption of *Clifford* YouTube videos during one of my visits, I noticed Sofia
watching one on her iPad that sounded like it was in Polish and pointed it
out to April. "Oh yeah, you know how many languages I hear?" she replied.
Next thing I knew, Sofia had switched to another *Clifford* video in French.
"She always finds them. They have everything on YouTube," April remarked.
The design of the YouTube app facilitated her daughter's repeated viewing.
"Sofia's watched all these videos on the side," April said, pointing to the app's
sidebar. She also noted the contrast between Sofia's challenges with embodied oral speech and her appetite for dubbed *Clifford* clips. "Sofia, if you end
up speaking many languages when you talk, I will be very impressed," she
joked with her daughter.

April was not alone in seeing a glimpse of her autistic child's future in
her current consumption of foreign language YouTube videos, which to
some parents suggested far greater intelligence than many assumed. During my visit, I must have heard the word "elephant" in about four different
languages in the YouTube videos that Abbey scrolled through on Molly's
iPhone. Molly pointed to Abbey's recitation of foreign language content
as evidence of her cleverness. "For the longest time, we thought she was
speaking a different language because of all of the videos she watched in
Spanish and French," Molly said, "It's honestly amazing. It's the one way
I can guarantee she's processing it." Molly's emphasis on the need to have
proof of Abbey's intelligence speaks to how autistic kids' skills and competencies are often missed or overlooked in formal educational environments.
Her informal learning with media offered a different trajectory than the
path expected of Abbey. Molly spoke with awe about her daughter's talent,
noting that one day she could end up at Harvard or "be a translator."

Nina, mom of 11-year-old Raul (Latino, boy), noted that YouTube was not the only site that kids used to search for and consume such content. Using Google Images, Raul had found a website of bootleg cartoon episodes "that he can't get access to otherwise because YouTube doesn't have all full episodes usually." After finding a video he loved, Raul would search for it in a different language by either reading the title in English or identifying the same visual thumbnail of a screengrab from the video. "I feel like he's learned a lot" from those videos, said Nina, "He's memorized the scripts . . . and the different language could be Spanish, Russian, Mandarin." After watching videos on the website, "sometimes he tries to find these things on iTunes, like the episode in that language and then he changes our iTunes setting to another country to try to purchase." Endless availability and ease of access across different digital media platforms was a significant contributor to autistic children's consumption of educational media and media that they learned from, which were not necessarily the same thing.

MEDIA LITERACY

Though there were obvious educational benefits to the foreign language cartoons, some parents also expressed concerns about inappropriate content that children might encounter through their web browsing. April (who spoke Spanish and English) said of the Polish *Clifford* video, "I don't know what they're saying but hopefully [not] anything bad." Nina mentioned one time when Raul's grandmother, a Cuban immigrant, was watching him, she discovered that he was viewing a YouTube video of the preschool program *Backyardigans* "and they're cussing in Spanish." Nina was also considering restricting Raul's access to the website where he had found the full-length foreign language episodes. "I think I should block it," she mused, "because there's all these advertisements on the side that [have] women posing suggestively. . . . So those are the things I have to be careful of, because usually what he's looking up is pretty innocent."

With advances in touchscreen computing and voice-enabled search (e.g., Apple's Siri), the internet has never been more accessible to children on the spectrum, especially those with difficulties typing and spelling. Parents of autistic kids face a tricky balance in helping their children to maximally benefit from information, media, and communication technologies while protecting them from online risks and vulnerabilities.[53] Concerns include threats to privacy, safety, and mental well-being, and span content risks (i.e., aggressive and hateful material), contact risks (i.e., victimization), conduct risks (i.e., victimizing), and contract risks (i.e., consumer exploitation).[54] Disabled children experience more online harms than their nondisabled peers, and their parents are more worried about them engaging with content that encourages self-harm, promotes political and religious extremist groups, or is sexually explicit.[55] Parents of disabled kids are also more likely to actively manage their child's internet use through rules, discussion, and co-use, in large part because they are likelier to believe that technology can support their child's social and emotional learning. There is a dearth of research, however, on how neurodivergent children learn to analyze, create, and reflect upon the credibility of information and media messages (i.e., media literacy) and how they engage in safe, responsible, and cooperative internet use (i.e., digital citizenship).[56]

On YouTube and in the Apple and Google app stores, there is a great deal of media masquerading as "educational" and "for kids" but that contains explicit (i.e., violent, sexual) content. For example, several parents discussed their child being drawn to fake PBS KIDS videos on YouTube that were not kid friendly. Bella's mom, Angelica, said that she and her husband had stopped letting Bella watch PBS "on YouTube because there [were] videos [with] flashing lights and a bunch of weird sounds. It was kind of creepy because she really wanted to watch it and there was nothing that was productive about it." Karim favored YouTube clips of the animated show *Caillou* (which originally aired on PBS KIDS in the United States). "*Caillou* is my favorite show. I like his bald head," Karim said of the titular character, a boy with no hair. *Caillou* has a cult following on the internet, with his YouTube videos generating significant views, as do ones of Baldi, another hairless boy character from an app called *Baldi's Education in School 3D*. Common Sense Media notes that *Baldi* "is marketed in app stores as an educational game, but it's actually a horror title set in a school."[57]

Nour repeatedly complained about Karim watching fan-produced Caillou and Baldi videos on YouTube that were animated by using the software program GoAnimate. The videos contained gore and violence, and Nour worried about Karim repeating or reenacting what he heard and saw. I sat with Karim as he watched one such video about Caillou bringing a murdered girl back from the dead and another in which a teacher hits Baldi with a ruler. Karim commented that the Baldi video was "funny . . . cause his teacher hits him," but also asked Nour and me questions that indicated his confusion about the inner state of the character ("Does the teacher like him? . . .

Why does he get mad? He made a mistake?"). Nour was concerned that if Karim mimicked the language or behavior in the videos, it "could get him in trouble" with his teachers, who she talked about being "really good or really bad" depending on the school year. Having a disciplinary record at school could also have a disproportionately negative impact on Karim, a Muslim boy of North African descent, if it led to further criminalization. Nour recognized the pleasure that Karim derived from watching the videos, as she did not totally prohibit them, but also felt like she was fighting a losing battle.

Some autistic children recognized the strengths and weaknesses in their media literacy skills. They were also cognizant of gaps in the social support around them to further develop these competences and of the shortcomings of digital tools and platforms. When asked what he does not like about media and technology, 9-year-old Cody (White, boy) said "sharing a lot about yourself with everyone. That's why I don't do YouTube." He did, however, enjoy "making new games for everyone" on Scratch, on which he had an anonymous profile. Thirteen-year-old Adrian (White, boy) regretted that he had used his actual first and last name as his Scratch username when he first signed up at age 7, especially considering that the platform does not allow usernames to be changed.[58] "I was a complete idiot. Or, not I was a complete idiot. I can blame this all on my parents," he remarked half-jokingly. Adrian realized only after the fact that having a personally identifiable username meant that he lacked anonymity. "You can look up a username and then find what they made. Usernames are meant to be a lot less like secure information you shouldn't give away," he said. Having the same username allows for continuity in a virtual space for kids but can also limit the fluidity of youth identity.[59] Adrian worried that his username "would attract attention" to the projects he created as a form of self-exploration and play. He had invested so much time and energy into the online community that leaving the site or creating a new account (from scratch, pun intended) was not an option. There are many gaps in the formal and informal educations that children on spectrum receive, but considering their deep personal investments in online spaces, media literacy and digital citizenship stand out as areas of particular need.

INTEREST-DRIVEN LEARNING

Many of the autistic tweens and adolescents with whom I spoke reported that social media, the internet, and other networked communication technologies

served an educational function in their lives, including for informational purposes and developing creative pursuits. Cody said that his favorite YouTube
channel was SmarterEveryDay. "It's a series of science videos. They do cool
stuff." "Videos that are informal or like entertaining, like this is the stuff I like
to watch," said 12-year-old Saylor (White, girl), who showed me how-to cook-
ing videos and slime making tutorials on her TikTok feed. Eleven-year-old
Rosalita (White, girl) used various forms of media to cultivate a deep interest
in animals and pets, like asking Amazon's Alexa to explain what an Asian
elephant was, comparing the brain sizes of a T-Rex and a pterodactyl on a
dinosaur app, and using her iPad to take videos of her family's new kitten.
Rosalita's mom, Pamela, said that such hands-on technology use has "given
her this sense of self and ability to do for herself. There's a level of independence there." Rosalita confirmed this when she proudly noted, "I like coming
up with videos and talking to the video and if there's a mistake, I just make a
new video."

Over the past decade, educational practitioners, researchers, and designers
have sought to maximize the kinds of technical skills and cultural knowledge
demonstrated by Cody, Saylor, and Rosalita.[60] Such efforts build upon the
democratic ideal that recruiting students' interests leads to more meaningful
and memorable learning.[61] Hobbies and affinities are central to the idea of
"connected learning," which brings together personal interests, supportive
relationships, and academic, civic, and career opportunities against the backdrop of a networked and hypermediated society.[62] Within a connected learning framework, technology promotes learners' choice and access across formal
and informal settings through active engagement with tools, materials, and
other people (i.e., peers, mentors). Digital media can enable kids to cultivate
existing interests and discover new ones, find communities that support these
interests, and apply their interests to new social contexts.[63] Anthropologist
Mizuko Ito and colleagues identify two main motivations for young people's
online participation: interest-driven and friendship-driven.[64] In other words,
young people use technology to primarily stay connected with their friends
and to pursue their passions (which can also lead to the development of new
friendships).[65]

Discussions in educational circles around interest-driven learning have
occurred in parallel—though rarely intersect—with discourses surrounding
the so-called special or circumscribed interests that many (but not all) autistic
people have.[66] This lack of conceptual overlap is surprising considering how

youth on the spectrum are seemingly implicated in the very definition of interest-driven practices: "what youth describe as the domain of the geeks, freaks, musicians, artists, and dorks, who are identified as smart, different, or creative, and who generally exist at the margins of teen social worlds."[67] Why kids on the spectrum have been overlooked as interest-driven learners makes sense, however, when one considers the limited ways in which autistic children are socially configured as learners.[68] In the medical language of behavioral intervention, autistic people's intense passions tend to be framed as "rigid fixations" or "restricted interests" that must be widened and watered down to conform to a more socially acceptable ideal. Studies with autistic children and adults find that there are intrinsic rewards (i.e., pleasure) and mental health benefits (e.g., self-confidence) to being able to explore these passions, and negative effects when that exploration is curtailed.[69]

Putting interest-driven learning and focused interests (a less pathologizing term for special interests) in conversation with one another highlights similarities and differences between the digital experiences of neurotypical and neurodivergent youth. Young people's interests in the internet age are many, are interwoven, and change over time with access to endless information about countless topics.[70] Both autistic and nonautistic kids in school may be discouraged from pursuing passions that are developed at home if those cultural interests do not conform to the White middle-class norms that largely underpin formal education.[71] Adolescence is a critical period for young people to develop interests that become part of their social identities. The relationship between interests and identity development may be forged at a younger age for autistic kids, however, who can express intense interests early on in life.[72] Children on the spectrum may also be adversely impacted by social isolation resulting from difficulties asking others about their interests (i.e., social reciprocity) and talking about topics other than their specific interest (i.e., conversational flexibility).[73]

Whose interests are deemed special, and whose are not? Jennifer, mom of 6-year-old Casey (White, girl) and an autistic person herself, explained that such distinctions were not clear cut. She said that "some of the things in [Casey's] media become her special interests and become the things she wants to talk about. And she doesn't realize that these other people don't know, don't necessarily watch the same shows." Media and technology are common interests among young people on the spectrum,[74] including specific shows and movies (reportedly over 80 percent of autistic kids ages 2–17) and related toys and collectible objects (58–72 percent).[75] Neurotypical and neurodivergent kids overlap in their popular media interests (e.g., superheroes), though older children on the spectrum are more likely than nonautistic children of the same age to enjoy content geared toward a younger audience.[76] Jennifer also noted that, autistic or not, it was common for one child not to want to play what another wanted on the playground if they did not consume the same media. "I mean that even happens between the two kids where one of them might be like, 'That's not a good game.' And [it's] just like, 'Well, nope, you guys are just watching different shows,'" she said.

Perhaps more importantly, what are the implications for such distinctions between marked and unmarked categories of interests on the everyday lives of autistic kids? Research has found that autistic children benefit both academically and behaviorally from educators who draw upon their focused interests.[77] Clinical psychologist Kerri Nowell and colleagues write that "a particular interest may facilitate the development of expertise and rich knowledge, and could promote learning by motivating a child to collect information through books and other avenues," such as YouTube and Google Search.[78] The following stories of Spencer (age 4, Black, boy) and Diego (age 12, White, boy) highlight why it is important to further extend the possibilities of connected learning to young people on the spectrum while recognizing how their experiences can also significantly diverge from one another in terms of the social, cultural, and material support they receive to pursue their unique passions across their learning ecologies.

SPENCER   Spencer took me on an elaborate tour of an elevator right from the living room of his two-story home—which contained no elevators, only stairs—in a middle-class, industrial town outside of Boston. "Do you want timer or elevator?" his mom, Rosie, asked, referring to YouTube videos on different topics, as she cued up the app on their large flatscreen TV. "Elevator," Spencer replied. When she pressed play, he yelled joyously, "It's elevator tour time!" "Elevators are his big passion," Rosie explained. An off-screen narrator discussed tension pullies and counterweights as the camera panned over different elevator parts and button panels. "Let's go to twenty-three. Let's go to four level," said Spencer. He had gotten into the practice of "repeating this and replaying it," Rosie said, "so that he's speaking at the same time as this guy and he's now an elevator tour guide."

Watching virtual elevator tours on YouTube supplemented the in-person trips that Rosie and her husband made with Spencer to different local multi-story buildings. "Since he was 3, we've been going on elevator adventures," she said, sometimes multiple times a week. However, Spencer's difficulty with transitions between activities could make these trips challenging. Rosie recalled the events of the prior weekend, when she and her husband took Spencer to the airport to ride all the elevators in the terminals. "He was absolutely fine until he knew exactly where we were, when we got to the last elevator, and then he started screaming," she said. Rosie relied on media to reduce some of the physical and emotional labor involved in these outings as well as to extend Spencer's experiential learning at home. "I realized if I ever can't [take him] twice a day, I'm kind of screwed," she said, "So I went on Amazon and I found a book about elevators."

There were several educational benefits to Spencer's "big passion." Rosie said that "people have recommended not watching TV and not giving screen time, but he gets a lot of language out of it." Spencer also incorporated elevators into his pretend play. He had taken two small audio speakers and would make believe that they were elevator doors, sliding them together and apart as if they were opening and closing. Elevators were additionally intertwined with his hyperlexia and attraction to numbers and letters. "After he discovered the elevator tour [on YouTube], he then recreated the elevator panel with Play-Doh. That's 'L' and 'P' for lobby and parking," she said, pointing to Spencer's creation on a table. Rosie also purchased a T-shirt with an elevator panel on it, just like the ones Spencer saw on YouTube. He liked to wear it and point on his shirt to the buttons (which he could read upside down) as he watched.

I asked Rosie if Spencer's school drew on his love of elevators in their teaching. "No, he's banned from [riding] the elevators" at school, she replied. This ban was instituted even though Rosie had lobbied to have his focused interest incorporated into his IEP. "I have written a substantial portion of his IEP which is very, very kid specific," she explained, "That they will use items of interest to encourage participation. Whether that happens or not, you know you can't control, but at least it is in there." When Spencer had been at daycare, things were different: "The lady [who ran the daycare] drew him an elevator panel, and it was like, she totally gets it." His preschool classroom, in contrast, was not designed with such flexibility in mind.

Spencer's special education teachers did not draw on any of the elevator-related media like virtual YouTube tours that could have substituted for physical visits to the elevator and that might have made his learning more personally resonant. "What I keep arguing for is, 'You need to know what engages him,'" said Rosie, "But when you're in a classroom that's ABA based and all PECS [Picture Exchange Communication System, an assistive communication program using small, laminated pictures], everything is based off these little squares." Considering that Spencer, a Black boy, lived in a town that was over 80 percent White (based on US Census estimates), his race and disability no doubt also shaped how institutional norms influenced his learning opportunities.[79] His elation over elevators illustrated what artist and activist Jen White-Johnson refers to as "autistic joy" and its importance as an act of resistance in the lives of Black neurodivergent people.[80] Ultimately, it may not have been Spencer's interests that were too rigid, but the mode of instruction employed by his teachers and the educational system itself.

DIEGO   Not all children encountered teachers, therapists, and other autism professionals who were as inflexible as Spencer's. Diego's story shows how the focused media-oriented interests of kids on the spectrum might be incorporated into educational and therapeutic approaches. His experiences also illustrate, though, that there are tradeoffs with respect to autistic children's agency when "play" becomes "work."[81] Diego—a tall, lanky boy with floppy brown hair—received ABA therapy at home from 3:00 p.m. to 6:30 p.m. each weekday from a behavioral therapist named Tiffany. These sessions focused primarily on practicing life skills like personal hygiene and folding laundry. In between these activities, Diego was allowed to use a spare laptop in the family's den, partly as a break, but also as an opportunity for Tiffany to work with him on communication skills. His mom, Francesca, said that if Diego did not follow directions during the sessions, he could "lose the right" to the computer and have to "[earn it] back," a reinforcement structure characteristic of ABA.

Because Diego's free time between therapy and other appointments was limited, I agreed to interview him on a school holiday during which Tiffany was scheduled to work with him all day. Francesca said that she planned for Tiffany to "do the real stuff" with Diego in the morning so that when I came in the afternoon, "it could be all about playing. . . . Because you don't want to do the behavioral stuff; you want to see the communication." Due to these parameters, the time I spent with Diego was technically during an "ABA session" but likely an uncharacteristic one, as it seemed more like he was being watched by a sitter while engaging in the kind of "messing around" with media identified by Ito and colleagues as a core learning activity among adolescents.[82] "This is my computer," Diego said, showing me his laptop,

"When I work, I write notes." While ABA structured his afterschool hours, what Diego did on the computer was largely of his own making. "We work on following his interest," Francesca said, "because otherwise [the therapists] don't really get much out him," indicating that there was both intrinsic and extrinsic value associated with his interest-driven learning at home.

Diego's focused interest was in making "books" on the computer: digital collages of pictures and text about topics from daily life. The idea originally came from Diego's speech therapists, who had worked with him years earlier to make "Social Stories," a technique developed by autism educator Carol Gray in the early 1990s to break novel social situations down into a visual series of sequential steps and written cues for children on the spectrum to more easily comprehend.[83] Continuing the practice at his leisure, Diego liked to craft narratives about the wider world that he saw portrayed in pre-school cartoons (e.g., builders in *Handy Manny*). Diego showed me several books, which had been printed out by his parents and piled in stacks around the den. "This, this, this, this one, this one is all about visiting the dentist," he said, "And this one is all about visiting the fireman." In his memoir *Fall Down 7 Times Get Up 8*, autistic author Naoki Higashida writes about how his own relationship to books as a child changed once he could materially insert himself in them. "Picture books might look very simple, but they require imagination to work," he writes. One day, Higashida's mother put together a photo book using family pictures with short sentences alongside the images. "It was thanks to this that the whole point of picture books 'clicked' for me," writes Higashida.[84] Similarly, Diego's self-made books served as a form of creative expression and way of understanding the social world. As Francesca noted, "I think media for him . . . it's a language."

Diego preferred creating media more so than consuming it, which "was unexpected for [my husband and me] in [his] use of electronics," Francesca said. He used several digital tools to compose the books—including YouTube, Google Image search, a smartphone, and an open-source version of Microsoft Office's PowerPoint called LibreOffice Impress. PowerPoint might not evoke creativity for many, but it was far simpler for Diego to edit visual elements on Impress than on a program like Adobe Photoshop. He had a school-provided Gmail account, through which he received an email address and access to Google Drive for storage. Using Francesca's phone, he took hundreds of photographs while running errands with her, as well as snapshots of images on his computer screen. Diego reported that "I took a lot, a lot of photos on the phone. And then I erase them and then I erase them, erase them to make space for new pictures on the computer," articulating an understanding of the affordances of digital media. Francesca then sent a selected batch to his Gmail. Besides photographs of his computer screen, Diego also made screenshots of the YouTube clips, cutting and pasting them into Impress, three or four to a slide. He explained, "First, first, I stop the movie. And then, and then I . . . and then take it, a picture . . . and then I put it in there."

Diego's books and overall creative process blended fiction and nonfiction. I sat next to him as he viewed an episode of *Caillou* on YouTube. Caillou in the video asked his dad, "Why do you have to work, Daddy?" to which Caillou's dad responded, "Because I enjoy working, and I make money." Diego verbally stimmed on parts of the dialogue, repeating lines while shaping them into something new. "Look, are you working? Are you working?" he said, "I'm making a, a book about . . . about, about, about people working . . . about people working, w-working." It was unclear to what extent Diego understood where his world ended and the one depicted on screen began. "I don't think he has a complete sense that the characters are fictional. In my opinion, he actually feels that these are real people," said Francesca. For example, during a scene in which Caillou's dad went to the bank, Diego remarked, "That's my dad and that's me." "Is that Caillou?" I asked him. "Yes," he replied, "That's my dad, that's me."

Though Diego had some level of digital proficiency, he still needed help from others to execute his projects. "Put the password in," Tiffany reminded Diego when he sat down at the computer. He dictated text for her and Francesca to write on the slides or to spell out for him so that he could independently type the words letter by letter. As he was not a proficient reader, he also required assistance in using the right search terms to find clip art and stock photos on Google Images. For instance, he asked Tiffany how to spell "tape store" so that he could search for pictures of adhesive tape. His search, however, turned up images of video cassette tape stores, so Tiffany told him to try typing just "t-a-p-e" instead. The interaction reminded me of Vygotsky's concepts of scaffolding, in which a more experienced person helps someone less advanced learn through gradual steps, and the Zone of Proximal Development, which is the sweet spot when a step is not too easy or difficult. Francesca hoped that Diego's interest in books could lead to further gains in literacy. "Our goal for these next couple of years is that he can actually type words on his own and Google search," she said, "We are still working on this independent thing."

Diego's digital bookmaking practice does not fit neatly into binaries like dependence and independence; formal and informal learning; child-led and adult-initiated; or structured and unstructured activity. His sessions with Tiffany involved a negotiation of agency across social actors and materials, in ways that were similar to but also very different from the connected learning of neurotypical kids. She was at once a mentor responsive to Diego's interests and a clinician whose expertise was in surveilling and remediating autistic children's behavior. Digital media afforded Diego's self-guided exploration in a way that stood in stark contrast to the adult-driven format of traditional ABA sessions. Francesca reflected on why Diego's computer time was so important for his self-determination. "I think he wants to be in control of the experience," she said, "so if he's handling the pictures and putting them into position, there is a sense of power, of control, that may not be typically there for him." Interest-driven digital learning can be very empowering for young people, and potentially for youth on the spectrum in therapeutic settings,[85] but it is important to keep in mind that disabled and autistic youth are rarely allowed to be in the driver's seat of their own learning.

CONCERTED CULTIVATION

Long before computers entered homes like Diego's, technologies such as pianos and encyclopedias were marketed to middle- and upper-class parents as investments in their children's future careers, happiness, and well-being.[86] The idea that children's free time with media should be focused on meeting educational goals is an example of what sociologist Annette Lareau termed "concerted cultivation," or a parenting style of fostering a child's talents and skills through leisure time and organized activities (e.g., summer camps, lessons, clubs).[87] Children not only learn how to do things through these opportunities but also how to act. They gain social capital (i.e., connections) and cultural capital (i.e., knowledge, mannerisms). Upper- and middle-class kids are generally advantaged in schools because of work done outside of school, though many also report feeling exhausted by being overscheduled with activities.[88]

Recent work has illustrated that concerted cultivation is promoted by families across class, yet resulting advancement is more obtainable for middle-class parents than poor or working-class families.[89] For example,

Crystal, mom of 3-year-old Aaliyah (Black, girl), was currently unemployed and she, Aaliyah, and her husband (who was also not working and on disability leave) lived in subsidized public housing. When Crystal had been working, she was employed by a company that sold educational materials to schools. "I had access to flashcards and manipulating letters and all these free little books," said Crystal, and she brought them home to Aaliyah, who demonstrated a real attraction to educational media like *Sesame Street*. "I definitely just follow her lead and capitalize on what she loved," Crystal said. While they did not have much in terms of money, Crystal had amassed some cultural capital and was able to provide Aaliyah with materials that brought out her natural talents and strengths.

Relatively little has been written about concerted cultivation and children on the autism spectrum, or about the intersection of their technology use and their parents' efforts to channel informal learning opportunities into career potential.[90] Computer coding is one area of digital media and learning that has been well-studied in terms of the challenges that marginalized youth face in leveraging the technical skills they develop in formal and informal learning settings for professional advancement.[91] Several adolescent autistic boys that I spent time with (largely from upper-middle class households) were enrolled in coding classes and/or had highly educated parents who co-used computer coding games and websites with them. Other parents (mostly middle- and working-class) were excited by the idea of their autistic sons gaining greater job security in life through their technical talents but did not have same means to increase the likelihood of such outcomes.[92]

Cody, for example, was offered Scratch programming classes in his after-school program in a wealthy Boston suburb, which his parents supplemented with an additional weekend course. "It ended up just being him, so it basically was like a private Scratch programming class, and I think he got a lot out of that," said his dad, Bobby. Cody showed me one Scratch game he made about falling and exploding watermelons. "I built it. I think gravity is a bit too hard, though," he said of the game mechanics. I also visited 5-year-old Max (Asian/Vietnamese and White, boy) and his mom, Norah, while he played the codeSPARK Academy kids' coding app on an iPad. Norah said that Scratch was a little too open-ended for Max and that he did better with codeSPARK's problem-solving games, which featured a set of characters called The Foos. Norah paid US $8 per month for a subscription because Max tended to speed through the levels. "The Foos is the funnest game I have ever played. The Foos, The Foos, The Foos!" Max exclaimed after Norah let him play an extra level.

In addition to afterschool piano lessons and a math enrichment course, 8-year-old Jeremiah (White, boy) also took live virtual HTML lessons with a private tutor over video chat through a platform called UCode. His mom, Natasha, called it "the ideal learning model for him" because Jeremiah did not have to socialize with other kids, which he found to be stressful. Furthermore, she thought that remote, one-on-one afterschool learning at home was "so great for spectrum kids and kids who have a specialized interest" because "the connection of that topic to a social setting can almost kill the interest." At their own pace, they could pursue their "obsession of the moment in a really safe environment where you're comfortable, all the environment's controlled, [and] there are no unexpecteds or unknowns." Jeremiah's positive experience with UCode enabled him to envision a future in the tech industry. When he was taking the class, Natasha said that "he wanted to work for Minecraft. He wanted to work for Mojang [the video game company that developed Minecraft] and be a game designer, is what he was saying. I think this learning how to program was making him feel like he was working toward that."

Other parents, though, did not have technical fluency like Bobby and Natasha, nor were they able to help their children finish difficult levels on a coding game, as Max sometimes asked of Norah. Pedro, an unemployed immigrant from Brazil, placed a lot of faith in technology. "The future is there," he repeated multiple times during our interview. Pedro dreamed about his autistic sons Bryan (age 7, White) and Matt (age 9, White) having job prospects in the tech industry. Since "everything [they like] is related to technology," Pedro said, "I'm trying to convince them to learn how to code. . . . They can code for Roblox tomorrow and, in 5 years, they can code for Android." The main motive behind Pedro's encouragement was economic in nature; he hoped that Bryan and Matt might be able to parlay recreational coding into eventual employment and financial independence.

In some ways, Pedro's dreams as an immigrant parent were very typical. "I want to see my kids' betterment. They need to survive, make their own money," he said. But his nudging was also related to anxiety about his sons not being able to take care of themselves later in life within a society that offered little support to autistic adults. Pedro was especially worried about Matt being "very very behind in school." He imagined traditional pathways for advancement like college not being available to his son and saw technology as one sector in which he could still have a lucrative job without a degree. Interestingly, while Pedro was more wishful, his wife Beca remained skeptical about Bryan and Matt's future careers in computer coding. "[Pedro] thinks [the internet and technology] could be a breakthrough for the children," she said, "I'm not quite sure, you know, about that." Beca's ambivalence was specific to her sons, but it speaks to the larger social, cultural, and political barriers that autistic children face when it comes to media and technology making a meaningful difference in their learning, to their lives once they age out of the formal education system, and to general critiques of techno-optimism and the belief that technology alone can bridge opportunity gaps for marginalized youth.

REFLECTIONS ON LEARNING

New media and online spaces offer many pathways for informal learning among kids on the spectrum. These areas include language and social communication, STEM education, and creativity. Technical features that enable autistic youth to consume, create, and remix media in a more accessible manner span voice control, predictive text, and automated recommendation systems. Several affordances of new media also make learning easier and simpler for them, such as portability, replicability, repeatability, and predictability.[93] Social and cultural factors play a major role in the effectiveness of these tools for learning, like the physical materials available to a given child at home and the interactions that they have with caregivers and other adult mentors. Factors outside the home—including parents' field of employment and the willingness of schools to adapt to autistic children's needs and interests—additionally shape these dynamics.

Youth on the spectrum have unique challenges navigating media in pursuit of learning and expression. These obstacles are partly related to their disabilities, but they also manifest because of the limiting societal conditions that information and communication technologies make possible. Autistic kids may have difficulty discerning inappropriate content on YouTube that is purposely disguised as educational, videos which have proliferated due to the website's profit model and Google's lack of government regulation. Youth on the autism spectrum who prefer patterns and predictability and have a higher threshold for audiovisual sensory stimuli may be more likely to imitate problematic behavior that they can easily and repeatedly view online. They have much to gain from participating in online learning communities but are also at higher risk for violations of privacy and safety without concurrent support for developing digital literacy skills.[94] Along with these challenges, autistic kids also bring great strengths like persistence, problem solving, and focused interests that can be leveraged for further digital skill- and knowledge-building.

For racially and socioeconomically diverse children on the autism spectrum to thrive into later adolescence and adulthood, and for their engagements with media and technology to contribute to that success, their digital learning must be understood with far more complexity and nuance than it is at present. Considering both the successes and failures of remote school for autistic kids during the COVID-19 pandemic, especially for low-income children of color in the United States, the potential positive impacts of virtual tutoring and video chat for informal learning (as illustrated by Jeremiah) merit further study. Dismissing autistic children's talents as "savant," like being able to read at an early age, oversimplifies the role that context plays in how children acquire knowledge. Their experiences with digital media converge with, but also complicate, current thinking in educational technology circles. For all the hype and hope about technology disrupting education, tools like tablet computers, machine learning, and artificial intelligence often work to make autistic children's behavior easier for others to control and manage more so than to proactively promote their personal growth. For Sebastian, for example, watching Peppa Pig and her classmates in a cartoon on an iPad was no replacement for an in-person inclusive education. The field of education should expect more for autistic kids and presume greater competence in their capacity to learn.

Parents of autistic children have both considerable hopes and fears about the digital world and their child's place in it, including as a space for learning and path toward future job opportunities.[95] These beliefs and attitudes are relative to their dreams and worries about the quality of their child's formal education and informal learning opportunities, as well as the broader individual and societal futures that they imagine.[96] Several parents discussed how their autistic child learned more from unstructured media use at home than from traditional teaching in school. Such statements may say less about the potentials of technology and more about the failures of special education as it currently exists in the United States: woefully underfunded by the federal government and mired by discriminatory practices that disproportionately impact autistic youth of color. The gaps that various parents mentioned between early childhood education settings and elementary school—in incorporating autistic children's interests, in building upon their learning from media at home, and in open dialogue between caregivers and educators—are also worth continued exploration.

Many existing concepts and theories in youth, learning, and technology are helpful for understanding the media and learning ecosystems of autistic kids, but much is missed if their experiences are not incorporated into shifting those discourses too. The affordances of new and mobile media, combined with individual tendencies and preferences, mean that technology can make learning both easier and harder for autistic kids. The educational benefits of digital media for this population are bound up with everything else that they learn through online spaces, for better and for worse. Youth on the spectrum have the potential to significantly benefit from technical and social innovations within and outside of the traditional classroom, but that promise is inconsistently realized for many, if not for most. The next chapter adds to this discussion by providing a more in-depth look at the family context of autistic children's media use for learning, leisure, and connection. In addition, the functional purposes of technology in households with young people on the spectrum will be examined.

Relationships

4 FAMILY

In the winter of 2015, Boston set a record for its snowiest season ever. A January blizzard and an endless series of February snowstorms led to a massive accumulation of just over 110 inches (280 cm). Despite the funny memes shared online about the "Snowpocalypse," that winter was an isolating time for many Bostonians. Three-year-old Alessandra (Latina, girl) was almost 2 then, and her mom, Camilla, said she "was really concerned about her social life at that moment." Alessandra, an only child, was not attending daycare and primarily stayed at home with Camilla, an immigrant from Spain who had only been in the United States for two years and did not yet have a large network of local friends. The media that Camilla most attributed to Alessandra's social development that lonely winter, and in subsequent years, was video chat, specifically with her and her husband's Spanish relatives. "We are the typical family that we are using a lot the technology to communicate with family abroad," Camilla explained.[1] Thanks to mobile apps and smartphones, they could fit video chat in around Alessandra's intense therapy schedule. "It's really difficult to find an open spot for [her]," said Camilla, "Sometimes instead of a Skype [on the computer], we are doing FaceTime [on the phone] in the playground."

Video chatting with Alessandra was a learning process for everyone involved. Her relatives in Spain had to figure out how best to communicate with her. Alessandra—who was minimally speaking and had difficulties with expressive and receptive language—needed help with modeling their greetings and picking up on their conversational cues. At first, Alessandra's relatives spoke too quickly and multitasked while they talked to her, which overwhelmed her sensorially and disoriented her cognitively. With Camilla and her husband's help, their relatives could eventually hold Alessandra's attention for five to ten minutes. "We told them that they have to pace the interaction and . . . ask her questions that she can understand" about simple topics like letters and shapes, Camilla said. They also needed to avoid having "too much noise [in the background and] try to give her time enough to respond," she explained.

I observed Alessandra on such a Skype call at home on the computer with her *tata* (aunt), with whom she sang a Spanish children's rhyming song. In addition to the social benefits, Camilla thought that regular chats in Spanish would be helpful for Alessandra in case the family ended up moving back to Spain. The loose social norms of video chat meant that Alessandra did not have to hold eye contact if she found it uncomfortable. She could move around the living room while the camera was positioned from a distance for her aunt to observe and comment upon her play. Camilla additionally made in-person adjustments to make the chat work, like having Alessandra press the Skype call button to actively engage her in the activity from the start. For Camilla, a strong indication of social growth resulting from the regular calls was that Alessandra had begun requesting to Skype with her extended family members. The format (virtual conferencing), the content (simple conversations), and the context (talking with a familiar loved one) all supported Alessandra's social learning with technology.

This chapter focuses on the role that media and technology play in autistic children's relationships with their family members and in the daily functioning and pace of family life. In some ways, the dynamics of Alessandra's video chats were much like those of any young child or one with relatives abroad. Many little kids have difficulty sitting still and focusing on interacting with the screen on a FaceTime call. Immigrant parents urge their children to stay connected to their culture of origin, with media as one such link. Camilla is also not the only parent to worry about their child's social isolation or to attempt to use media to simulate sociality for them. Parents showed similar concerns and responses during the early months of the COVID-19 pandemic, when families were stuck at home for prolonged periods of time. There were unique considerations for Alessandra and Camilla's experiences in other respects, though. Virtual communication with an autistic child requires certain nuances, such as avoiding sensory overwhelm and scheduling video calls around therapy.

Parents and siblings are young autistic children's most frequent companions for media use. As such, they play an important role in how kids on the spectrum are socialized around and through technology, as well as what it means for them to be "social."[2] On the flip side, autistic children and adolescents also directly and indirectly influence their parents' media management philosophies and their siblings' media use habits. Through my fieldwork, I identified several factors shaping the family context of autistic children's technology use. Parental media management is fluid and shifts in response to changes in their autistic child's preferences and behaviors, which may be significantly more variable than those of a neurotypical child.[3] Household instability caused by issues such as poverty and divorce also impact the overall trajectories of autistic children's care, including their media use.[4] These considerations challenge the utility of broad, overly generalized "screen time" advice that caregivers, including those of children on the spectrum, regularly encounter.

MEDIA, AUTISM, AND FAMILY LIFE

I begin by reviewing current theories of autism and family well-being, what is known about media management strategies implemented by caregivers of autistic children, and how media shapes interpersonal dynamics between kids on the spectrum and their siblings.

THEORETICAL APPROACHES

Understandings of technology, autism, and family life at present are heavily influenced by historical narratives, and often in negative ways. The "refrigerator mother" theory, popularized by psychiatrist Leo Kanner and psychologist Bruno Bettelheim in the mid-twentieth century, falsely claimed that "frigid" unloving mothers caused their child's autism, and promoted the idea that an autistic child was an undesired one.[5] For these same women, their domestic expectations were being reshaped in the postwar era by an influx of electronics and modern appliances (like home refrigerators), in addition to economic, geographic, and social shifts reconfiguring gender politics and the culture of caregiving.[6] Starting in the 1960s, human development researchers began to empirically challenge Bettelheim's psychoanalytic theories about the origins of childhood disability.[7] Many of these studies still presumed that disabled children were a burden to both society and their households, and the research was explicitly motivated by "science as well as sympathy."[8]

Contemporary research on households with children on the spectrum has tended to focus more on individual elements of the family rather than its overall functioning.[9] This has included studies of how having an autistic child impacts dyadic relationships (e.g., marital, parent–child, child–sibling), and affects a family's physical, emotional, social, and financial outcomes.[10] Family system theory argues, though, that the sum of these relationships and outcomes does not equal the whole, and, furthermore, that the family must be understood as its own complex unit of analysis with values, beliefs, and norms.[11] Through a systems approach, family processes shape the developmental trajectory of the autistic child, and, in turn, the child on the spectrum impacts the broader family system.[12]

Proposals for using a family systems approach have similarly been made for the study of media and families. Children and media scholar Amy Jordan suggests that young people's media use reflects and also shapes a family's structural dimensions (like its organization of space in the home and time spent during the day) as well as its social aspects (such as family members' sense of identity).[13] Most research on families, media, and technology has centered on parent–child interactions and relationships, and less so on how siblings factor into a child's media use, broader measures of family well-being (e.g., resilience, quality of life), and changes in familial roles and boundaries.[14] Children and technology use is also a highly gendered issue; on top of other household labor, women in industrialized nations are largely tasked with being the primary managers of their child's media activities as a form of "intensive mothering."[15]

PARENTAL MEDIATION AND AUTISTIC CHILDREN

One helpful concept for understanding how technology fits into family life is "parental mediation," which refers to the formal and informal strategies that caregivers use to oversee, guide, control, and share in their child's use of media.[16] There are four main types of parental mediation: restrictive, social, active, and supervisory.[17] In restrictive mediation, parents establish rules and enforce boundaries like time limits and website restrictions. Social mediation involves family members co-viewing or co-using media for the primary purposes of rapport building and enjoyment. Active mediation has to do with parents' instructive inquiry and critical discussion about media content and functions with their children. Lastly, supervision includes caregivers' attempts to remain in the child's proximity and keep tabs on what they are hearing, seeing, and/or doing with media.[18] Interactive media (e.g., video games) and noninteractive media (e.g., TV) may elicit different mediation forms.[19] Restrictive and active parental mediation reportedly peak around age 8 and decline throughout middle childhood.[20]

Few studies have directly examined how parents influence autistic kids' media and technology use or how kids on the spectrum shape parenting strategies around media. Caregivers of children with emotional struggles and higher levels of hyperactivity are more likely to engage in restrictive mediation.[21] Kuo and colleagues found that parents of adolescents on the spectrum (ages 12–19) most frequently mediate their autistic child's television use with social co-viewing and mediate their videogaming with restrictive strategies.[22] Engelhardt and Mazurek report that 87 percent of parents of autistic boys aged 9 to 19 have rules about video games, including restrictions on mature game content and duration of game play time.[23] In another study by Kuo and colleagues, autistic adolescents who regularly watched television with their parents reported having better relationships with them than those whose parents did not co-view with them.[24] Nally and coauthors additionally found that parents who ceded control of the household's media routines and rituals to their autistic child did so in order to maintain familial balance and harmony.[25]

Since this work was conducted in the 2000s and early 2010s, though, much has changed in the way of technology and society. Over the past decade, young people's engagement with video games has extended far beyond gaming consoles to streaming websites like Twitch and videos of game play uploaded to YouTube by professional and amateur players, as well as youth themselves.[26] Some earlier parental concerns, such as worries about an autistic child preventing other family members' use of the shared television,[27] have lessened over the years with the growing ubiquity of personal mobile devices,[28] while the easy connectivity of these tools has also introduced new parenting challenges.[29] Media management can cause stress among parents of autistic kids, and their strategies may reflect worries about problematic and risky media use.[30] At the same time, media may offer a moment of calm and peace to stressed caregivers, a pleasurable experience to overworked children, and an opportunity for family togetherness amid busy schedules.

AUTISM, MEDIA, AND SIBLING DYNAMICS

Siblings generally spend more time together than with their parents,[31] and their media habits reflect this copresence in several ways. They influence one another's development over their lifespans as well as the care that their caregivers provide to them and their siblings.[32] Parents of multiple children may consciously or unconsciously notice differences in how media affects one of their children and adjust overall media rules and routines as a result.[33] Older siblings can be a positive force by guiding their younger siblings' media use in instructive ways, like helping them type queries into Google Search, while also influencing them negatively by prematurely introducing them to media content intended for an older audience.[34] The effects of media can also differ with media type, genre, and sibling gender; for instance, video games may be associated with both sibling conflict and affection, especially for brothers who play together.[35]

There is more limited research on how siblings shape autistic children's media and technology use. One reason for this may be the higher likelihood that kids on the spectrum do not have a sibling. Retrospective studies of health records indicate that families whose first child was autistic were one-third less likely to have a second child than other families, and families with a later-born child on the spectrum were equally less likely to have more children.[36] The explanation for this difference is not clear; parents may be concerned about the probability of raising another autistic child or lack the support and resources to do so. Among families with an autistic child and later-born children, nearly 19 percent are estimated to have at least one other child who is also on the spectrum, though their children's conditions may be very different.[37]

Most work on autism, siblings, and media use has been comparative studies within families of autistic children and their typically developing siblings (e.g., parent surveys comparing both children's time spent on various kinds of media).[38] Kuo and colleagues, for example, found that parents used similar mediation strategies for their autistic adolescent and their adolescent's nonautistic sibling(s), but more frequently applied restrictive and active strategies for videogaming with kids on the spectrum. Interaction effects were not examined, however, and the authors suggested that managing an autistic child's media use might shape parental management of their sibling's use too. No work has looked closely at families with other autistic and/or disabled children besides the focal child on the spectrum.

AUTISM AND MEDIA IN THE FAMILY SYSTEM

Parents and kids have struggles and positive experiences with digital media and communication technology—individually, interpersonally, and collectively as a family. The discussion that follows focuses on how autistic children's everyday media use impacts and is impacted by parent–child and sibling relationships. Also discussed is the range of individual and contextual factors influencing those dynamics that affect the entire family unit.

PARENT–CHILD RELATIONSHIPS

I found that caregivers of autistic children and early adolescents engage in all four forms of parental mediation (restrictive, social, active, and supervisory) across multiple types of media. Interestingly, many of these parents also incorporate therapeutic and behavioral discourses into their discussions of media use at home. Behavior management is pervasive across childhood (e.g., "No TV until you finish your homework"), but the stakes are higher for autistic children. Rewards and punishments are often viewed as the only means of managing their behavior, while reasoning and negotiation are more prevalent with nonautistic children. Medicalized language is prominent in the parenting of neurodivergent kids and oversight of their media use, shaped in part by their child's development, but also by interactions with clinical providers and related resources.

RESTRICTIVE MEDIATION Parents of children on the spectrum employed several restrictive mediation strategies to both promote positive outcomes and mitigate risks for their child. Strategies changed over the course of early and middle childhood alongside the move from elementary to junior high school. Restrictions included deleting or blocking access to particular apps and websites, imposing time limits or limits during certain times of the day, and monitoring mature or violent content. For some families, restriction was woven into the very social infrastructure of their home. Other parents hesitated to institute restrictions that were too rigid. Autistic children themselves sometimes expressed resistance to these rules, though several thought that it was good to have boundaries.

Parents frequently talked about the need to place hard limits on their autistic child's media use to prevent sensory overload and overstimulation. Julie, for example, used the Guided Access feature on the iPad to lock 4-year-old

Eli (White, boy) into one app at a time because he would otherwise open and close apps every thirty seconds. "If he's doing that for an hour, it's like his brain is fried and the whole rest of the day, he's grumpy and the attention span is shorter," she said. Cathleen, mom of 6-year-old Sebastian (Latino and White, boy), turned off the autoplay feature on Netflix so that it would not advance to another episode right away. Parents also tried to limit media use to certain windows of time or with a curfew. Sara, mom of 8-year-old Isaac (White, boy), recalled that until she and her husband put an 8:30 p.m. limit on Isaac's iPad use: "We would hear it until midnight, 1:00 in the morning because he went so far past that point of tired, he couldn't turn his brain off." Heavy media use outside the home also influenced media rules at home. "My sons Kahlil (age 7) and Orion (age 4) use the tablet at school every day, so no tablets on the weekdays at home," their mother, Monisha, explained.

Caregivers implemented strategies for limiting inappropriate content, but these attempts were not always fruitful, particularly in the case of You-Tube. The introduction of the YouTube Kids app in 2015 offered parents an ostensibly more kid-friendly version of the website, but it was far from universally adopted or trusted. According to parent reports, only 24 percent of children use the YouTube Kids app, approximately the same percentage that do not watch YouTube in any format (app or website).[39] April, mom of 5-year-old Sofia (Latina, girl), had tried to get her daughter to use You-Tube Kids so that she could better filter out inappropriate content. Sofia, however, could tell the difference between the apps and refused the junior version. To feel comfortable with Sofia still using the regular YouTube app, April was resigned to "keep reporting videos every time I hear something weird. And every time I do report, I just clear off as much as I can her history, everything she's liked, and hope that it kind of resets everything."

Other parents had banned all forms of YouTube for their autistic child. "We thought we were safe with YouTube Kids," said Pamela, mom of 11-year-old Rosalita (White, girl), "and we found there was a lot of violence and underlying sexual content that really shouldn't have been there that was masquerading as kids' stuff and so we nixed all of YouTube." When I talked to Rosalita, though, she had interpreted her mom's rule a little differently. "My [younger] brothers aren't allowed to watch YouTube because sometimes they watch unexpected things," she said, "but I can tell. I can tell if this video is okay, then make sure it doesn't have bad language." Unfortunately, not all autistic children were as capable as Rosalita in their ability to tell the difference between appropriate and inappropriate videos for children, nor had YouTube fully addressed the problem; hence, vigilance was required on the part of parents whose autistic kids were mass YouTube consumers.

A few parents had very concrete media rules at home around which children's behavior was organized as a form of social infrastructure. Jamie and Jesse, parents of 10-year-old Levi (Latino and White, boy), had instituted a set of "Family Rules," which were visualized on a poster that hung in their playroom. It listed various policies and consequences for violating them. The first consequence was "Loss of Screen Time," with the description, "Could be for 15 minutes, could be for a week or could be for a different amount of time." Not only could Levi have his screen time taken away by his parents, but he had to earn it in the first place by completing household chores and doing nonscreen activities. Jamie and Jesse had made a very intricate chart (figure 4.1) detailing which tasks earned Levi and Abigail which type of media and for what duration of time, using a unique calculus. For example, "3 Full Bites New Food" equaled a "Half Episode" and "20 Minutes of Work on New Skill" earned "1 Episode." Once a day, Levi and his sister could also trade in a full TV episode for 15 minutes of watching an approved kid-influencer channel on the YouTube Kids app. Levi was not a fan of this reward and reinforcement system. "I get to earn screens, which is terrible. And Abigail thinks that, too, she just doesn't want to do anything about it," he remarked with some bitterness.

Part of the reasoning as to why Jamie and Jesse had created such a firm structure around Levi's media use was because his current elementary school, unlike his former one, did not give homework. Jamie suspected that this led to him requesting screens upon arrival at home without another way to break up his afternoon and evening. His parents were also influenced culturally by their time living in a heavily religious Christian community in the South. The idea for the screen time reward system came from a time when "we went to this one parenting thing that talked about kids that are entitled," Jamie said. She and husband did not like the idea of building their children's moral character by having them earn money for chores, so they used media as a reward instead. Levi's autism factored into the extensive screen time rules in his home, though his disability was far from the only element influencing his parents' caregiving style.

Other kids felt that there were benefits to having some boundaries on their media use or were at least more ambivalent than Levi. Raul (Latino,

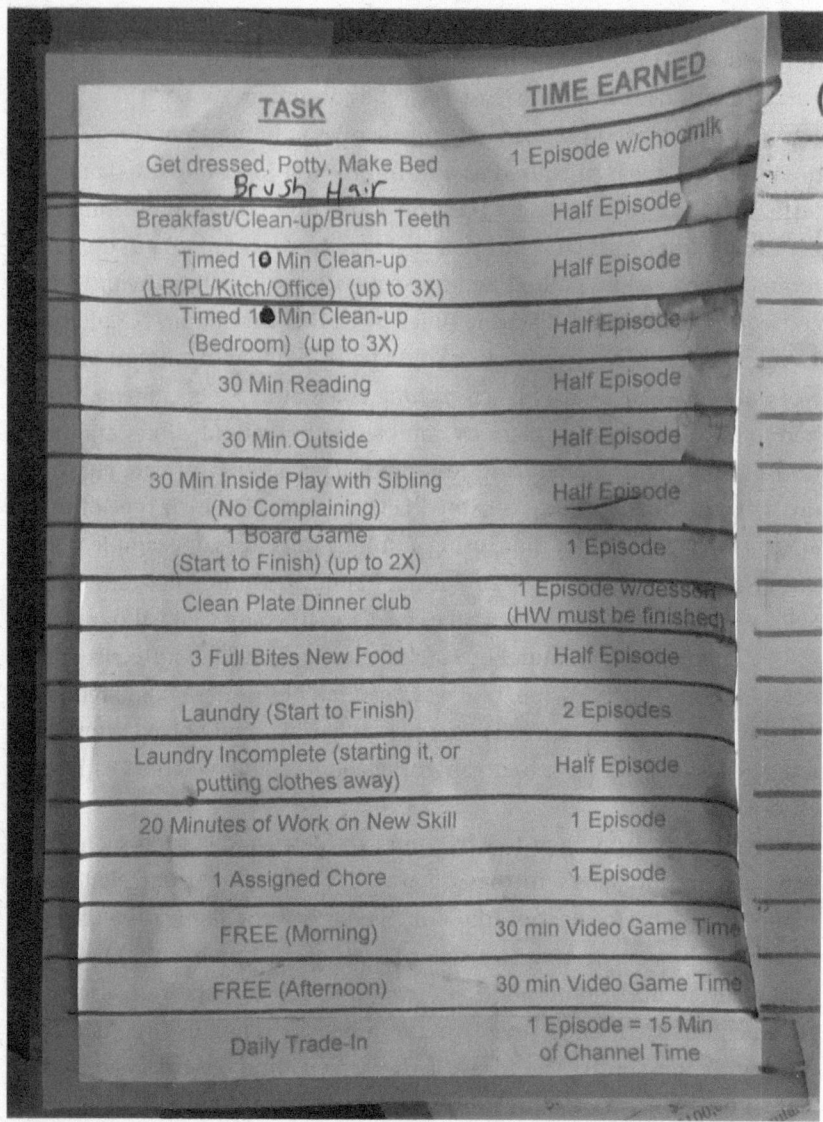

TASK	TIME EARNED
Get dressed, Potty, Make Bed *Brush Hair*	1 Episode w/choc mlk
Breakfast/Clean-up/Brush Teeth	Half Episode
Timed 10 Min Clean-up (LR/PL/Kitch/Office) (up to 3X)	Half Episode
Timed 10 Min Clean-up (Bedroom) (up to 3X)	Half Episode +
30 Min Reading	Half Episode
30 Min Outside	Half Episode
30 Min Inside Play with Sibling (No Complaining)	Half Episode
1 Board Game (Start to Finish) (up to 2X)	1 Episode
Clean Plate Dinner club	1 Episode w/dessert (HW must be finished)
3 Full Bites New Food	Half Episode
Laundry (Start to Finish)	2 Episodes
Laundry Incomplete (starting it, or putting clothes away)	Half Episode
20 Minutes of Work on New Skill	1 Episode
1 Assigned Chore	1 Episode
FREE (Morning)	30 min Video Game Time
FREE (Afternoon)	30 min Video Game Time
Daily Trade-In	1 Episode = 15 Min of Channel Time

FIGURE 4.1
Levi and his sister's chart for earning screen time. *Source*: Meryl Alper.

boy), who was 11 at the time of our interview, wrote that his parents "limit my amount of time with tech depending on my behavior each day." As for what he did or did not like about these rules, Raul said, "I like that they are showing me how to appreciate the technology. I don't like when it's time to get off." Autistic kids thought more positively about their parents' rules when they were aware of how media use could affect their sleep quality, which many autistic people report struggling with.[40] Twelve-year-old Brendan (White, boy) said that his mom had a rule about "no electronics from 8 p.m. to 8 a.m." He had "no opinion whatsoever" about the rule, though he said that when he used to go on his laptop at night, he "slept through half the school day." Now, he said, "I sleep less during the school day. Note, I said 'less,'" suggesting that his difficulties paying attention in school were not entirely related to screen media. Media did not just impact children's sleep; it could also be a tool for nonspeaking kids to communicate their needs at nighttime. April, for example, noted of Sofia, "When it's bedtime, she'll put lullabies on when she's tired."

Some parents were hesitant to restrict their autistic child's media use too heavily due its potential benefits, both for themselves and their kids. Raul's mom, Nina, said that there had been days when her son had met his three-hour iPod quota and found a loophole by watching YouTube on their smart TV. She did not punish him though: "I pick my battles, right?" she said. Kerry, mom of 6-year-old Joey (White, boy), worried that constraining her son's leisurely and creative use of digital media would confuse him, since she envisioned a future in which he would likely need a computer for notetaking and test accommodations. "We have to some way teach him how to use that tool and not fall into the black hole of all the options he has in using that tool, [so] we try not to set limits," she explained. Overall, restrictive mediation was commonly employed by parents of kids on the spectrum, but caregivers had difficulty balancing their child's desires for autonomy and challenges with self-regulation.

SOCIAL MEDIATION   Social mediation was a popular way for parents to connect with their autistic child, but activities did not always go as planned. For instance, Francesca, mom of 12-year-old Diego (White, boy), mentioned a time when she had gotten the new *Postman Pat* movie, a spinoff of the children's TV series beloved by Diego, with the idea that he, Francesca, dad Santos, and younger brother Paolo could all watch it together on the projector in their living room. Diego though could not sit for the film for very long. Francesca found it "frustrating, because when you want to do something as a family, . . . there's no way." Shared viewing sometimes required altered expectations and arrangements. In Eli's home, family movie nights were held a few times a month. At a certain point during the viewing, however, the group often split in two. "Sometimes [it] turns into one parent with Dean and Caila [Eli's older brother and sister] and the other one running after Eli," said Julie, his mom.

In some cases, collaborative media use allowed autistic children to teach their parents and take on a more expert role than usual. Natasha, for example, had taken it upon herself to read up on Minecraft and download the game onto her personal computer when her 8-year-old son Jeremiah (White, boy) expressed interest. Noticing his mom's enthusiasm, Jeremiah encouraged her to learn more. Said Natasha, "I think at some point I finally went and got a YouTube video called 'Minecraft for Kids.' I was watching it and Jeremiah looked over my shoulder and watched along. Then he helped me figure out how to play." Though Jeremiah sometimes had difficulty managing his emotions while playing, Minecraft brought the family together in a special way. Natasha reflected, "[It's] a good example of the family at its best. It's a lot of fun. And also, it's the worst. We have moments [with Jeremiah and his younger sister, Chloe] where it's, 'Chloe, you cannot put that there! This is my world, my rules!'" Caregivers wanted to jointly partake in media as a leisure activity with their child, but there were logistical and personal challenges.

ACTIVE MEDIATION   In terms of active (or instructive) mediation, parents of autistic children found it beneficial to talk through media content with their child, including conversations explaining content and appraising it as positive or negative.[41] For example, the parents of 3-year-old Oscar (White, boy) spent a lot of intensive time with him while he watched YouTube letter videos on the living room TV. "We just don't turn it on and let it play and leave the room," said his dad, Abe, a linguist who suspected that he was likely on the spectrum himself. He shared Oscar's fascination with words and curated related media content for them to discuss together. "I might show the Russian alphabet or the Greek alphabet or I'll find a French song or Spanish song, just to introduce him to these things," he said. Norah, mom of 5-year-old Max (Asian/Vietnamese and White, boy), described how her son initiated active mediation with her while watching one of his favorite TV shows, *Curious George*. "It's very social. He wants to discuss the show and tell me all about it and ask me questions," she remarked. Parents engaged in active mediation with an awareness of their child's cognitive challenges and strengths. Karrie, for example, played the Nintendo game *Scribblenauts* with her 9-year-old son Conor (White, boy). In *Scribblenauts*, players spell objects they wish to make appear. Because Conor struggled with reading, Karrie joined in so that she could help him with the game.

Active mediation sometimes looked different for families with nonspeaking autistic children who communicated using speech generating devices. For instance, Julie engaged in dialogic viewing and questioning with Eli as he watched an episode of *Sesame Street*.[42] "Is that a hexagon?" she said pointing to the screen, then after a few seconds, answered her own question by saying, "No. That's a circle. That's a circle." Afterwards, she went to look up words for shapes in Eli's augmentative and alternative communication device, an iPad with an assistive speech app called Proloquo2Go, with the idea that maybe someday he could comment himself. Julie discovered, however, that Eli's teachers and speech therapists had not made a file folder on his tablet for terms like "hexagon" or "circle"—just a button for the word "shape" itself. "I feel like they're missing vocabulary sometimes," said Julie, as she added the words to Eli's app on her own.

Besides parents' comments on educational material, they also spoke with their autistic children about questionable content (i.e., negative active mediation). Jennifer, mom of 6-year-old Casey (White, girl), enjoyed showing her daughter TV shows and movies that she herself enjoyed as a child. She had to keep an eye out, though, for outdated stereotypical portrayals that Casey might accidentally model. Drawing attention to these depictions could also have the unintended effect of Casey being more likely to mimic them. Jennifer explained one occasion when they were watching a movie in which "they stereotype someone Asian with music." Jennifer paused the film and told Casey, "'You know, . . . they didn't have to do that, and they did it because she was Asian and that's racist and you don't do that.'" Thinking the problem was resolved, Jennifer pressed play again. "But then I heard her sing the song part," she said, "so I just turned off the movie entirely."

Caregivers subjectively make such determinations about content being appropriate or inappropriate for their autistic child. These decisions and conversations are shaped by factors such as race, cultural background, class, and socioeconomic status. Kimberly, for example, thought that it was okay for 8-year-old Amaya (Black, Latina, and White; girl) to watch what she called "teenager cartoons" like *The Simpsons* and *Family Guy* if it made Amaya happy and she did not mimic what she saw and heard. "I don't think I'm a bad parent for letting her watch it as long as she doesn't repeat it or start acting like it," Kimberly said. She also attributed agency to Amaya as a viewer. "These things are not good for her little brain," said Kimberly, "so I told her, 'Hey—what they say, you can't say it,' so she respects that." Amaya's recent consumption of the cartoons was also tied up with Kimberly's current inability to afford a cable television subscription and exclusive reliance on broadcast TV channels, on which *The Simpsons* and *Family Guy* air in the United States. "I think she's just bored and misses her cable channels," Kimberly surmised. The instructiveness of active mediation was relative to the material and institutional conditions surrounding an autistic child's learning from media at home.

SUPERVISORY MEDIATION   Caregivers also oversaw their child's media use by taking on a more peripheral role, like supervising while doing chores. "I'm usually cleaning up, so she can pick up the tablet on her own," said Crystal, mom of 3-year-old Aaliyah (Black, girl), and "if I'm frying something, I don't want her in the kitchen." Sebastian's mom, Cathleen, found that "the only way that I'm able to like make dinner or do some household chores before [Sebastian and his brother] go to bed is to put the TV on because then . . . I know they physically are not going to get on each other." These mothers kept an eye on their children's media use in the same or adjacent room while attending to household tasks. Some parents alternated between supervisory and more active mediation. Oscar's mom, Leslie, noted that she and her husband often oversaw his viewing of alphabet videos in the living room. "This is why pretty much we bring reading material, because we're not too interested in watching these videos," said Leslie. Abe added, "You look up now and again but generally don't pay attention."

The fact that autistic children could easily occupy themselves with media without the need for active or social intervention by adults was also a source of worry for some caregivers. Angelica resented the implication that her daughter, 4-year-old Bella (Cape Verdean, girl), could be babysat with media, because it let others off the hook for engaging with her. It made her angry when people, albeit well-meaning, told her that Bella was "so easy to watch [because] you just give her the phone or the tablet and she's just quiet and she just sits there." Angelica found comments like these dehumanizing because they seemed to prize compliance in autistic children and to justify denying them other social opportunities. "I don't want that to be the reason why you think my daughter is 'easy to watch,' because she just sits on the phone and on the tablet," Angelica said. Media supervision was a valid and necessary form of mediation, but one that could be misused by caregivers of autistic children if it rationalized their social isolation.

THERAPEUTIC DISCOURSES   Beyond the interpersonal communication strategies that parents used to manage their autistic child's media use, and children's own perspectives on these techniques, some of the concerns mentioned by parents did not fit neatly into the categories of restrictive, social, active, or supervisory mediation. One main reason for this was that parental mediation assumes that a child's parents are the sole adults influencing how media is managed at home. For many children on the autism spectrum, however, applied behavioral analysis (ABA) therapists are a constant presence, as such therapy is often intensive and long-term.[43] The primary focus of this clinical field of work is to modify an autistic child's measurable behavior, including increasing "helpful" behavior and decreasing "problematic" ones. Behavioral therapists influence the role that media plays in autistic children's lives by shaping parental conceptions of media as a behavioral reward and reinforcement tool. This influence goes beyond the level of the individual therapist, as behaviorism pervades cultural conceptions of autism more broadly.[44]

For example, many parents absorbed the idea that media was something with which to reward desired behaviors and to withhold until said behaviors were exhibited. "I use [the computer] as leverage against them," said Pedro, dad of 7-year-old Bryan and 9-year-old Matt (White, boys). "It's his reward system at the end of the day," said Gail, mom of 5-year-old Robert (Black and Asian, boy), "I make him work for it." Nelson, father of 10-year-old nonspeaking girl Stephanie (Latina), borrowed clinical language when talking about how he and his wife managed Stephanie's screen media use. "We use it also as a positive and negative reinforcer," he explained, "The positive reinforcer, she can play with it for a certain amount of time and then if she's not compliant or something, she'll be timed out from an iPad." Employing media as a behavioral reward was difficult for some parents to maintain, though. Eli's mom, Julie, explained that "it's a constant balance because we need it to remain motivating, and so there's some measure of withholding it so that when he earns it, it's a big deal and it feels special."

Tara, a stay-at-home mom of 3-year-old Ryan (White, boy), discussed how her son's behavioral therapists used media as a reward with him and how this provided structure to her family's life. "He will get to watch a minute of one of his favorite videos, which keeps him going to the next task," she said, "We use media in a lot of different ways for him to reinforce good behavior." Tara was particularly invested in the assistance provided by her son's therapy team, in part because they personally provided her with stability that was missing in her life. She said that she had "cried" when Ryan aged out of early intervention when he turned 3. "What am I going to do?" she thought, "Because [his early interventionists] were just really, really involved." Tara's husband, Ryan's father, served in the US military reserves and was set to deploy again soon. He was not very active in Ryan's day-to-day life, as he worked a full-time job on top of his military duties and struggled with posttraumatic stress disorder (PTSD). "Unfortunately, my husband's not here a whole lot," she said. Tara instead focused her energies on turning every media moment with Ryan into a therapeutic one. "Where people might just have their kids watching something to keep them busy," she said, "usually whatever he is watching, we're talking about. I'm making him tell me who it is, use his words, what color, what shapes."

Another parent, Nina, pushed back against the guidance of behaviorists and the medicalization of autistic children's screen time because it centered a normative conception of child development. Her son, Raul, enjoyed repetitively watching short portions of videos and cartoons. Nina felt judged by clinicians for allowing her son to do so, particularly behavioral analysts. "People have expressed to me that he really should be watching the whole episode, so it sustains his engagement because it feels, quote unquote, normal to them," she said. Nina did not appreciate their judgement, as media allowed Raul to control his time and for her to have a break. Moreover, she thought that such clinical advice was detached from reality: "Behavioral therapists try to set the same benchmarks for our kids as they do for neurotypical kids. So, if the [American] Academy of Pediatrics says you should only have one to two hours of screen time a day, and a behavioral therapist who doesn't know your family or your habits or your daily practices walks into your home and says the same thing . . . , it's really jarring as a parent in my position." Research suggests that children on the spectrum far exceed the American Academy of Pediatrics' screen time recommendations.[45] The ethos of ABA therapy might lend itself well to enforcing clear media rules, but Nina wished that more health-care providers met her family where they were, which meant much more than two hours of daily screen time for Raul.

Not all clinical interventions for autism are identical. Besides behavioral therapies, there are a growing number of relationship and noncompliance-based options, like the Developmental, Individualized, Relationship-Based model (also known as DIRFloortime or Floortime) and Relationship Development Intervention (RDI). These alternative approaches shaped how other parents approached media management. Norah, for example, thought that Floortime, which involves parents physically getting onto the floor and playing with their young autistic child,[46] influenced her approach to using media with Max. She said that when she did "Floortime stuff [with Max]" when he was 2 years old, "it was really just about getting into that space with him all the time." That interactivity extended to the family's leisure activities. "Max and I do everything together," said Norah, "we play iPad together, we'll watch a movie together, we play stuffed animals together. We're really like playmates." Max, an only child, in turn initiated social uses of media with his parents. I observed him and Norah working on the game *Plants vs. Zombies* together, with Max playing and Norah commenting, Norah and Max jointly playing, and Norah playing while Max watched and sometimes commented or took over for her.

Besides being a parent, some caregivers also took on the role of assistant therapist in how they guided, limited, and shared in media with their autistic child. Such parent-mediated interventions have been intensified by school closures during the COVID-19 pandemic, shifting many of the responsibilities of full-time, one-to-one school aides onto caregivers. For example, Nour, mom of 8-year-old Karim (Middle Eastern/Algerian, boy), described regularly engaging in a media activity that sounded a lot like active mediation but with a more therapeutic purpose. She said that much of her screen time with Karim was "focused around watching things together, just getting the declarative language from him. Because we're doing RDI, which is Relational Developmental Intervention." Nour said further, "We would watch either mute things or cartoons without any words and we just comment on them and share things like that. It's also therapy-based." Besides being a mom watching and commenting on media with her child, Nour became a sort of part-time therapist through this shared media activity. "I'm trying to substitute for his speech therapist or whatever assignments she gives me," Nour said. The many developmental and behavioral intervention approaches to autism have very different therapeutic paradigms, which in turn impacts mediated parent–child relationships in varied ways.

SIBLING RELATIONSHIPS

Besides interactions involving parents and their autistic children, either one-on-one or with other family members, kids on the spectrum also used media with their siblings while their parents were nearby or not copresent. These sibling dynamics were in some ways just like those of nonautistic kids (e.g., fighting over viewing choices on a communal screen). In other respects, they could be more dispassionate or, alternatively, more intense. Relaxed media use rules for an autistic child, for example, might elicit sibling jealousy. Julie noted that "if Eli is watching TV," then his brother or sister will say, "'Well, I want a show then.' And so then suddenly you're like, 'I don't want us all watching TV all day. That's not the plan.'" Parents did not necessarily want to limit their autistic children more than their nonautistic child, either. Brianna said that she sometimes needed to remind Adrian when his video game time was up, but it was not so different with his older brother. "There are certainly days he would play too long," she said, "but both my kids would."

Watching videos and TV together were activities that autistic kids, particularly younger ones, could share in with siblings. Talking about her 3-year-old daughter Emma (White, girl) and her two siblings, mom Nikki said that "socially, that's her way sometimes with them, to draw them to be with her, is to sit with an iPad." Among older children, gaming was a popular sibling activity. Rebecca said that the few times her minimally speaking son Kevin (age 13, Asian/Japanese and White) uses "purposeful speech is when he's watching his brother playing [video games]. 'Oh! Watch out! Watch out, you're going . . . Oh, good job!'" Joey was introduced to Minecraft by his 8-year-old nonautistic older brother, Brian. When I initially visited their home, the brothers were sitting side-by-side in the dining room/office on separate computers but playing on the same Minecraft server with their respective avatars. The server itself was a domestic space, as the brothers had built their own homes and their avatars were currently together in Brian's abode. "These two buildings are our houses," Joey explained, "Our houses are connected together." While their media use was intertwined, there were also major behavioral differences between them. "Brian can better self-regulate his screen time," said Kerry, "whereas Joey, if you did not tell him to turn it off, he never would."

Siblings who were each on the autism spectrum could both instigate and empathize with one another in unique ways, while their overall relationship and how they used media together also reflected general sibling dynamics. Ten-year-old Ronan lightly supervised the media use of his younger brother, Conor, who had greater socioemotional and communication challenges and was more mischievous. Describing the difference between them, and how it shaped their media use, their mom, Karrie, explained, "Ronan will be trying to build this very elaborate thing [in Minecraft] and get it all exactly the way he wants it, and Conor will come around and blow it up." This attraction to chaos fed into Conor's interest in gory video games like *Five Nights at Freddy's* and *Bendy and the Ink Machine*. Though he had never played the games himself, Conor enjoyed watching others' recorded play on YouTube, videos which Conor's parents subsequently told him he was not allowed to watch. "I was banned from horror games," he relayed to me. Despite being aware of the rule, he had a hard time obeying it. Ronan talked about how the videos that his younger brother was drawn to were "actually pretty creepy" and would "make him say scary things. . . . Sometimes I have actually caught him trying to watch them when he was not supposed to." Ronan notified his parents when he discovered Conor attempting to view the videos, motivated to do so out of obeyance and genuine concern for Conor's well-being, but, also, as Karrie joked, because "nothing makes him happier than tattling on his brother."

Some children on the spectrum had a behavioral tendency to act out in ways that could negatively affect their siblings. Even though Adrian was better now at self-regulating, Brianna said that when he was younger, he would become agitated by the competitiveness of video gaming. "I'd always be extremely anxious when he was playing with his brother and I'm glad that's changed because it would be hard on his brother," she shared. Physical conflicts over media could also escalate for some children. Part of 6-year-old Katie's (White, girl) aggression stemmed from her receptive-expressive language disorder. She had difficulty understanding the messages and information that she received from others, as well as expressing her own feelings and thoughts. At one point during my visit, Katie's younger brother, Julian, requested to look at her iPad while she was playing a game, which she did not want him to do. In response, she went into a pop-up tent set up on the living room carpet. When Julian tried to enter, Katie pushed and kicked him hard, leading their mom, Annemarie, to intervene. When I asked her how this event rated in terms of violent encounters on a scale of 1 to 10, Annemarie rated it a "2 or 3 . . . I was kind of pulling them apart but there was a barrier" at least with the tent between them.

Autistic children and their siblings could also have a more distant relationship, through which media did not facilitate social interactivity. During my hour-long observation of Robert and his older brother, 7-year-old Stefan (who had ADHD), the brothers did not interact. Robert watched animal videos on a tablet and Stefan glanced periodically at an episode of a nature reality TV show on in the background, while each talked to themselves and played with their own toys. Their mom, Gail, said this was typical behavior: "They don't really play together. They play side-by-side." Meena, mother of 5-year-old Eashan and his 9-year-old brother Adhi, both of whom were autistic, discussed the boys' video game play together, which I also observed them doing on a Nintendo Wii. "There's no interaction there," Meena said of the game play, "You are running on two parallel tracks. With my kids, the only interaction is when we tell them they have to take turns."

These autistic children and their neurodivergent siblings were copresent but did not consistently co-use media in a manner that required interpersonal interaction. Interactive play is generally more valued than parallel play in social skills interventions for children on the spectrum.[47] Nonetheless, parents like Meena and Gail did not force their neurodivergent children to alter the play patterns with media and technology that came more naturally to them at home. Media provided an important relational touch point for autistic children and their siblings, though watching and playing were not always experienced communally or cooperatively.

INDIVIDUAL AND CONTEXTUAL FACTORS

The different roles that media played in autistic children's relationships with their family members and in their parents' management of their technology use were heavily affected by a variety of individual and contextual factors. These influences included the child's own interest and skills, parents' personal priorities and values, and household-level considerations shaped by neighborhood, employment, and other institutional forces.

CHILD Overseeing autistic children's media use required parents to weigh the benefits and risks of giving their child a device, especially kids with communication, sensory, behavioral, and impulse control challenges. Numerous parents referred to their child as "addicted" to technology and as having difficulty focusing on anything else once in its presence. "If Eli sees an iPad," said his mom, Julie, "there's no sharing. He's not giving it up." As a result, she and her husband had purchased two iPads for their three children to share. Mom Angelica said she had to be careful using her phone when out with her daughter Bella because if "I don't give it to her right away, she sometimes will flip out." Meena hypothesized that autistic kids were not so different from nonautistic kids when it came to an attraction to screen media. "They are all addicted to it," she said. But whereas a typically developing kid might follow a parent's order to put a device away, a child on the spectrum may not as easily obey the request, as Meena described: "I tell them not to touch it and it becomes an anxiety issue. That's the single thing that's running in their mind. When will I get to touch the iPad? When will I get to play the iPad?"

For some parents, restricting access to media was less important than avoiding an upsetting transition away from a screen-based activity. "One of our biggest struggles with him is ending media use and getting off the screen," said Meg, mom of 9-year-old Cody (White, boy). She bemoaned the fact that "media is designed to keep you sucked in and [Cody just wants] to keep going a little bit more." Having to step away was "the biggest source of meltdowns for him," Meg said. One strategy the family had used was setting an alarm with an Amazon Alexa placed in the kitchen. "He needs a countdown, he needs timers, he needs a reminder," said Cody's dad, Bobby. Technology is only helpful, however, if you actually use it, and "a lot of times unfortunately, we're running around and don't remember [to set it]," said Meg.

In terms of physical factors, several children had difficulties with toileting and interoception, or the sense that helps a person feel what is happening inside their body. Interoceptive dysregulation impacted autistic children's media use in different ways. "She'll use it to the point of wetting her pants," Jennifer said of Casey's attachment to the iPad. Bella often felt great discomfort when going to the bathroom, so her parents gave her the phone while on the toilet to help relax her. This strategy sometimes did not work as planned, though. Bella's mom, Angelica, recalled a family visit to Disney World in which Bella requested to go to the bathroom and use Angelica's phone. After 20 minutes of watching videos, Angelica realized that Bella did not need to go, but rather "did it as a kind of way to escape what was going on" sensorially at the busy amusement park. Annemarie similarly discussed the complexities of involving media in toilet training for first grader Katie, which was an ongoing process. Using the tablet as an incentive to sit on the toilet "was starting to backfire," said Annemarie, because her daughter had begun refusing to go unless given a video first.

Lastly, in terms of child factors, multiple parents mentioned concerns about their child engaging in physically risky behavior and saw media as a way to keep them still, safe, and occupied. "We cannot leave these kids off by themselves all the time like other parents can," said Nina, "So it's super unrealistic to think that you can take away electronics or you should limit their screen time and have faith that they'll be safe." Four-year-old Bennett (White, boy), for example, had, on many occasions, run away from his caregivers and into the street in their suburban neighborhood. On one such occasion, he and his twin brother were being watched at home by their grandmother when she realized that Bennett had bolted out the front door. While he had not gotten far, his grandmother had a bad knee and could not run after him. From the porch, Bennett's mother, Shelby, said, "she was like, 'Oh Bennett, we got to see what's on Grandma's phone. Come look what's on Grandma's phone.' And that got him in the house." An autistic child's personal screen time was safer than the physical danger that they could easily get into, which gave their caregivers some peace of mind.

PARENT Parents significantly varied in the degree to which they found managing their autistic children's media use to be stressful. For example, Natasha, mom of 8-year-old Jeremiah (White, boy), claimed to have "never worried about screen time" due to her children being overscheduled. "The amount of free hours anyone could potentially have [is] so small," she explained, "that when we do have free hours, people can decide what they want to do." Other mothers, though, had internalized guilt over letting their autistic child frequently use screen media, and this weighed on their parenting decisions. Nina, for example, felt "like there's this little voice saying I should be doing more with my son [Raul] than giving him the iPod for seven hours on a Saturday." Nina saw no other way for her to stay mentally sane and for Raul to be happy, especially considering that he could not independently occupy himself with sports or other hobbies.

Some parental guilt was rooted in a lack of clear medical guidance and assurance regarding autistic kids and technology. Annemarie was concerned about Katie's reliance on the iPad because "there isn't research that shows how it's going to affect their brains." Crystal worried that she had somehow induced autism in her daughter, 3-year-old Aaliyah (Black, girl), by allowing her to use a phone and tablet at an early age. "There's guilt that I caused her to be . . . who she is, because of the device . . . [that] me giving her the device this whole time was creating her antisocial," said Crystal. At the same time, Crystal mentioned several personal issues that exacerbated Aaliyah's social isolation and her own. Her husband and Aaliyah's father, Mike, had been on disability leave and not working when their daughter was younger. Instead of sending Aaliyah to costly daycare at that time, Mike watched her during the day while Crystal worked, prior to her current unemployment. The situation weighed on Crystal, who blamed herself, though not her husband. "I went to work, and he stayed with her giving her the device all day long, and I thought, 'Nobody is talking to her,'" she said regretfully.

As with caregivers more generally,[48] parents' personal media habits also influenced their mediation strategies, and their autistic children's media preferences shaped their own use as well. For example, April had signed Sofia up for her own YouTube account because she was starting to receive algorithmic recommendations for content geared toward her daughter's preferences instead of her own. "It used to be on mine," April explained, "but then I would just try to watch YouTube to relax and it would be like Clifford, Clifford, Clifford, ABC." Six-year-old Skyler (White, boy) and his mom, Naomi, regularly co-viewed YouTube videos that users had recorded of themselves reading books. Naomi was a former librarian and had felt discouraged when Skyler rejected reading physical books with her. "It's really, really important to me that he loved books, and he wasn't loving books," she recalled, "so this is how we kind of brought books back into his world." Mothers factored their own needs into how they managed their child's media use, despite living in a world that largely requires women to subjugate their feelings and emotional well-being for the sake of others.[49]

HOUSEHOLD   Finally, families of autistic children contended with several home, environmental, and family considerations that impacted how media was integrated into their lives. Extended family could have a meaningful role in autistic children's regular engagement with media, as is highlighted by Alessandra and Camilla's story at the start of this chapter. For instance, the immediate and extended family of 8-year-old Isaac (White, boy) practiced a modern form of Orthodox Judaism that restricted the use of electronics from sundown on Friday to sunset on Saturday (i.e., Shabbat), a time usually spent in prayer and with family. His mom, Sara, said that despite being very religious, her aunt and uncle would "literally will go run to find what their Wi-Fi password is" during Isaac's Shabbat visits to their house "because they know Isaac needs to be on YouTube. . . . [My family is] so supportive."

A lack of consistent high-quality childcare outside of school hours was also a major concern for many parents. When talking to Annemarie, I was struck by how she truly had no one to watch her children besides herself, her husband, or the TV-as-babysitter. All of the other adults who could have potentially cared for Katie and Julian, including a hired regular babysitter and Annemarie's in-laws, had quit. They had done so on account of Katie's physically aggressive outbursts, which included past incidents of kicks to the head and choking her family members, all over relatively minor things. The sitter "doesn't want to come anymore," said Annemarie, and "my husband's parents, they had to take a break because it was too hard, stressful for them."

To get through the day, screens could allow parents to run errands with their autistic child that would otherwise have been difficult to do. Stephanie's parents used a free grocery app when shopping to keep her calm and engaged. She could visualize which items were still needed and check off each item once it was placed in the cart. Other apps that worked offline, like the camera, were also useful in locations without Wi-Fi. Stephanie's father, Nelson, recalled taking selfies with his daughter in the big box store Costco, a location that could be sensorially overwhelming for her. He explained, "We're trying to do as much as we can to get her involved. If she gets bored, she'll start walking around the store, and she'll run away from us." Parents of young kids might use their phones in a similar way in public places,[50] but the caregivers of autistic children with behavioral and communication challenges felt a heightened sense of anticipatory concern.

Beyond the day-to-day, autistic children face the same destabilizing life events that other kids do, including parental divorce, parental separation, or the long-term absence of a parent. Media may be more core to these young people's well-being by offering consistency, routine, and familiarity. Brendan's mother, Marcia, was divorced from his father and shared custody of Brendan and his siblings. "He has to go back and forth between me and his father, which is not easy," she said. What made these transitions smoother was that Brendan could take his laptop with him, a device that held significant affective meaning. "It's his connection, it's his comfort," said Marcia, "He would carry that whole thing with him everywhere." She even recalled times when they would be in the car, about to drive away, and Brendan would ask for five more minutes to finish something on the laptop while connected to their house's Wi-Fi network.

Another single mom, Audrey, was raising Caleb (Black/Haitian, boy), who was 9 years old at our first meeting, and his younger sister, Erika (age 6), having kicked her husband out of the house after nearly 15 years of marriage for being physically and emotionally abusive. Audrey had some relatives in the area, but all were elderly and could not provide consistent childcare. In the small quarters of their apartment, Audrey and her children created both communal and private media spaces. Caleb and Erika had a smart TV in their bedroom so they could view Netflix or YouTube while Audrey watched news in the living room. She kept their remote control outside the door though, on top of the refrigerator in the kitchen, so the children were not able to watch without permission or late at night. Caleb brought up his dad in passing when talking about the TV shared by him and his sister. "Usually, me and my sister fight a lot over the television and usually my sister wins because my father's not here. And I do not want to talk about that," he stated, which I assured him I would not make him do.

Parents of limited financial means additionally balanced their autistic child's access to media with other expenditures. Nour, for instance, said that Karim (who was 11 at the time of our follow-up interview) "had his own phone for a year. Then, you know, expenses were a lot, so I cut on that." Five-year-old Anthony (Black, boy) had his own smartphone from MetroPCS because a family data plan through the cellular provider was cheaper than paying for home internet. Said his mom, Danae, "He don't use the phone. I just get it for the YouTube." Gail downloaded YouTube videos to Robert's tablet for offline viewing because "we don't really have the internet," she said, "Sometimes I'll turn it on from my phone, but it gets pretty expensive, so I don't leave my phone as a hotspot."

When I visited Sofia and her family, it was a particularly hot day during a summer that had already caused frequent power outages in her low-income Boston neighborhood. April had thought of various contingency plans if the electricity and internet were to cease functioning. The family paid for a data plan from a cellular provider on Sofia's iPad in case the Wi-Fi went down. If that were to run out of battery, April made sure that her laptop, which had a DVD player, was charged so that Sofia could watch episodes of her favorite TV show. If worse came to worse, April told the other family members in her intergenerational household, "Next time the power goes out, we're going to a hotel. I don't care if you have to use credit cards; it's just better to not be miserable. She'll be good, she'll have her stuff, and we'll have AC." The economic and infrastructural conditions around autistic children and their families directly shaped their priorities, including their investments in media and technology.

REFLECTIONS ON FAMILY

Among families with children, there is no single factor that determines the role that media and technology play in their lives, including a child's disability. Households with kids on the spectrum are both different from and similar to other families in their joys and struggles. For example, most parents try to balance firmness and looseness in the rules they make and the examples that they set. Medical discourses of behavioral intervention (i.e., rewards, reinforcement), however, are more likely to be woven into media management strategies for the caregivers with whom I spoke. Parents of autistic kids must also handle distinct—and sometimes competing—sensory, behavioral, and socioemotional needs of household members, including siblings.[51] There were significant differences in personal parenting philosophies around media, and there were multiple contextual factors impacting families' everyday technology routines and habits. Media can additionally be a constant, reassuring presence for autistic kids when there is major upheaval in their family life. Below, I discuss theoretical implications of this work for studies of parental mediation, recommendations for clinicians and therapists who work with children on the spectrum, and industry suggestions for better implementing technological guard rails to support parents in keeping their autistic kids safe online.

Concurrent with existing research, I found that parents of children on the spectrum employed active, restrictive, and social mediation with their children; they also engaged in media supervision, which is a more recently identified parental mediation strategy.[52] Yet current theories of parental mediation do not neatly map onto autistic children and their families. For example, in a 2015 study by Kuo and colleagues, parents identified six main strategies for mediating their autistic child's television and video game use.[53] Three were characterized by the researchers as restrictive mediation (removing/limiting access to media, setting rules and being consistent, using monitoring software) and one aligned with active and social mediation (engaging in media activities together). However, within the existing types of parental mediation, the authors observed two strategies that they could not categorize: first, keeping the adolescent busy doing other activities and second, using media as a motivator and removing media as a punishment. These parenting strategies reflect not only individual choices, but also the lack of affordable and accessible leisure activities for children on the spectrum outside of school and the entwinement of behavioral intervention principles in the parenting of autistic kids.

The intersection of autism interventions and parenting strategies around autistic children's media use is complex, as illustrated by the varied experiences of Ryan, Max, and their mothers. Behavioral therapies for kids on the autism spectrum are far more likely to be covered by public insurance providers in the United States than developmental and relationship-based interventions.[54] One of the major critiques of ABA, the most dominant form of behavioral therapy, is that it overfocuses on compliance and that this emphasis leads to deprioritizing the emotional needs of autistic people. In ABA, for example, parents are often encouraged to withhold a reward from their child unless a desired behavior is exhibited, like asking verbally for a toy or snack. Strict ABA programs teach parents to ignore their child's protests and cries. Autistic self-advocates have argued against taking away something extremely pleasurable from an autistic person as a form of punishment due to the disproportionate stress and anxiety it may cause.[55] For many autistic children, media is not ancillary to their lives and something they can manage without; it is a comfort blanket in a highly discomforting world, such as with Brendan's laptop.

Prior work has found that pediatric autism medical providers are advising families on their child's recreational technology use—assistance that could help parents like Annemarie and Crystal—but that the utility of this guidance is mixed.[56] Moving forward, I encourage clinicians to take a family systems perspective on both autism and children's engagement with media. This requires understanding not just individual relationships—like that of kids on the spectrum and their siblings—but the family unit as a whole, along with social and ecological factors beyond the household. For example, a lack of homework from school shaped Levi's parents' family media rules. Many parents, especially mothers, shoulder significant guilt about their child's time with screens.[57] For mothers of autistic children, this shame is intensified by the modern spin on the ableist refrigerator mother theory: that screen media (disproportionately managed by moms) causes autism, which is assumed in such a theorization to be an unquestionably negative outcome.[58] Clinicians should listen to parents to understand the tradeoffs they make when they give a screen to a child on the autism spectrum. This aligns with calls for pediatricians and other health care specialists to, during the COVID-19 pandemic, change their screen time messaging to one that is more positive and avoids stigmatization.[59]

Lastly, industry players like Google should better implement technological guard rails for autistic kids, even if it hurts their bottom line. Outside of self-regulation, government intervention in the United States is needed to push the technology industry toward greater transparency and accountability. Though some parents may curate limited playlists for their children in YouTube Kids, there is no option to do so on regular YouTube, even with a supervised account (which Google promotes for families of children ages 9 and up).[60] This is likely because algorithmic recommendation and targeted advertising generates significant profit for Alphabet, Google's parent company.[61] Considering the number of families with whom I spoke whose autistic children under 9 flatly rejected the YouTube Kids app, their needs are not being served by the website, despite its inescapable presence in their lives. For example, besides playing Whac-A-Mole with the "Report" button, there was no way for April to prevent Sofia from discovering scary videos of her favorite children's cartoon character, Clifford the Big Red dog, especially because videos like these are often preceded by pre-roll advertisements of children's toys.

Better supporting autistic kids in society requires strengthening social support for their families without overemphasizing parents as the only active choice makers in the family system, especially when it comes to technology. Media can be more central to the functioning of families of autistic children, requiring greater reorganization of family life around securing access (i.e., resources, schedules). Siblings may play an outsized role in how children on the autism spectrum learn to navigate the digital world, and more research is needed on this topic. On an even larger scale, it is important to think about not just what is best for individual families of children on the spectrum, but also the greater good of families of autistic kids in society, considering their socioeconomic, ethnic, and racial diversity. It would be a mistake to assume that all families of children on the spectrum are similarly resourced to help their child derive the most benefit from technology and media and to avoid the greatest risks. I turn next to children's social partners outside the familial structure—peers and friends—and the associated opportunities and challenges for connection posed by new media.

5 FRIENDSHIP

Autistic brothers 10-year-old Ronan and 9-year-old Conor (White) dropped their Nintendo Switch controllers and ran over to their mom, Karrie, when the FaceTime call came in from their friend Oliver (technically, from Oliver's mom and on her iPhone). Conor dragged along a fuzzy black blanket, which Karrie said he always wore draped over his shoulders "except when he's at school or in the bath." The six inches that Ronan stood over Conor gave him enough leverage to hold the phone in one hand and gently shove his younger brother offscreen with the other. FaceTime could only track a single face at a time, and Conor was messing up the augmented reality Animoji feature that Ronan was trying to use so that it looked like it was not he who was talking on screen, but an orange cat with his voice. "I don't know if you've noticed anything different about me," Ronan announced to Oliver sarcastically, alluding to his animated appearance. Conor elbowed his way back into the frame and grabbed the phone from Ronan. "Hello, Oliver. Look at my T-Rex creature!" he exclaimed, swapping out the cat filter for a dinosaur one. In reference to his brother's on-screen appearance, Ronan joked, "This is what Conor is in real life."

Oliver had been a new kid in Ronan's class the year before and they instantly clicked. Ronan had a solid group of friends in school "that's a mix of kids who are on the spectrum and kids who are just kind of nerdy. And honestly, I'm not 100% sure which kids are which," said Karrie. When Oliver started to spend lots of time at their house (located in the wealthy, mostly White suburbs of Boston), it was not only Ronan with whom he played, but also Conor, who struggled to make friends of his own in school.

Conor preferred physical play like wrestling and playing chase, which his peers were growing out of. "My brother's actually 9 but he acts a lot younger than he is, so he can be really crazy and annoying," said Ronan. Conor also had trouble "letting other people into the imaginative world" he created with his action figures and ended up giving directions to others more than improvising play, Karrie said. When Ronan had friends over, he was generally good about including his younger brother in the fun—an inclusivity that was heavily facilitated by video games, which the whole group could play together in a structured manner. Gaming allowed Conor to "be involved and part of the group and have that social interaction and not feel like he can't keep up," explained Karrie.

When Oliver moved with his family back to Denmark, it was tough on Ronan, but devastating for Conor. During our interview, when I asked Conor if he ever played video games with his friends, he responded, "I don't have friends. . . . I don't want them anymore. I don't like them because I, because I always lose friends a lot." He spoke specifically of Oliver with the prompting of his dad, Adam, who sat nearby while Conor and I spoke: "Oliver was my, used to be my, I used to have my old friend Oliver. Now he left." Though FaceTime enabled the brothers' friendship with Oliver to persist, it had social and emotional limitations. For one, the boys relied on their parents to facilitate the ongoing relationship, seeing as they and Oliver were too young to own phones. "It's not a thing that's occurred to them yet—talking on the phone with friends," Karrie said, so she would arrange calls with Oliver's mom. Interestingly, Conor was also critical of using video chat to stay connected and discussed the value of tactility and in-person interaction. "Do you know why I don't like friends?" he said, "I can't touch friends. I can't touch my friends. . . . I always like to touch. I always like to touch and talk to people." Conor was frustrated by his inability to literally "reach out and touch someone" (as in AT&T's late twentieth-century advertising slogan for long distance telephone calls), namely Oliver.

This chapter focuses on the social dynamics between autistic kids, their peers, and the popular culture, media, and technology that underpin their relationships and contemporary childhood writ large. The experiences of Conor and Ronan illustrate the heterogeneity of friendships made and lost among kids on the autism spectrum, as well as the myriad ways that media can both ease and hinder companionship between neurotypical and neurodivergent children. Per the theory of the sociotechnical shaping of sociality, technology and society present autistic youth with a range of possibilities for forming relationships, including social media platforms and therapeutic programs for building "social skills." In turn, young people on the spectrum remake and complicate normative assumptions about the nature of friendship in the digital age through their communicative preferences, cognitive and emotional processing, and sensory practices.

By their own account, children and adolescents on the spectrum are not completely unlike neurotypical kids in what they do interpersonally with media. When I asked 12-year-old Saylor (White, girl) if she thought being autistic made her use of social media different from that of her peers, she replied, "I don't think the spectrum is affecting anything, to be honest. I don't know, all my friends are basically doing the same thing, and I'm just doing the same thing." Despite the myth of kids on the autism spectrum self-isolating with technology,[1] I found that many are savvy curators of personal media ecosystems through which they can feel comfortable reaching out and being reached out to by others. Connectivity, however, also exposes kids to social situations that have significant potential for harm and victimization: platforms provide little protection, and autistic children and adolescents can face challenges seeking help from adults. After detailing examples from the everyday lives of kids on the spectrum, I offer reflections on the nature of friendship and implications for theory, design, and practice across the social and digital spaces that autistic youth inhabit.

TECHNOLOGY USE AND MEDIATED FRIENDSHIPS AMONG AUTISTIC KIDS

I begin by providing some background on friendship development in childhood (with an emphasis on kids age 13 and younger) and the role of media and technology in the evolution of those social relationships, the strengths and challenges that youth on the spectrum have in forming such lasting bonds, competing definitions of "friendship" within the context of autism, and what is currently known about how technology poses social risks and rewards for autistic youth by increasing feelings of both belonging and exclusion.

FRIENDSHIP DEVELOPMENT AND MEDIA IN CHILDHOOD
Friendship is a broad term, one that can be either meaningful or meaningless (i.e., a lifelong friend; getting a "friend request" on Facebook). It can be used to

describe any mutually beneficial relationship between peers who engage each other in positive ways that promote future interactions.[2] Research from the field of developmental psychology demonstrates that humans have fundamental social needs and urges from a young age.[3] By around age 8, kids have made close friends outside of their immediate family, though siblings significantly contribute to social learning throughout childhood as close companions.[4] Children vary in their temperaments for friendship, meaning that they have natural preferences for certain social configurations (e.g., one-on-one, trios, large groups of friends.)[5] By age 4 or 5, they have experimented with social power (i.e., excluding or teasing), and test that power in school, which is also the primary site of children's friendship establishment.[6] Popularity becomes a concern for kids starting around second grade, which can distract from the importance of building enduring friendships.[7] With respect to gender, children in grade school generally prefer same gender play groups but have more friends of different genders outside the classroom environment.[8]

Historically, analog and digital communication technologies have played a role in children's ability to exert independence over their social lives apart from their households, be it pen pals forged through written letters sent through the mail or the desire to have a private landline telephone in one's bedroom for conversing with friends.[9] Currently, tweens and teens build relationships in online spaces including social media (e.g., Instagram, TikTok), content-sharing sites (e.g., YouTube), messaging apps (e.g., iMessage, WhatsApp), and virtual worlds and networked games (e.g., Minecraft, *Fortnite*).[10] Social media use is associated with both interpersonal benefits for adolescents (e.g., sense of belonging, social capital) and interpersonal challenges (e.g., relational aggression, perceived isolation).[11] The use of social media is on the rise among tweens; as of 2021, nearly one in five tweens (18% of kids ages 8–12) in the United States used social media on a daily basis, compared to 13% in 2019. Yet watching TV (65%), viewing online videos (64%), and mobile gaming (43%) dominate their free time each day.[12] Boys tend to make more friends online than girls, as regular video game play expands their social circles, and girls are more likely to text frequently and communicate with existing friends.[13]

SOCIAL STRENGTHS AND CHALLENGES OF AUTISTIC CHILDREN

In many ways, neurodivergent children's relationships and their conceptualizations of friendship are like those of their neurotypical peers. Their closest friendships are similarly made mostly at school or through family friends, and they exhibit a preference for same-gender friends.[14] Autistic kids often struggle, though, to establish and maintain stable interpersonal relationships.[15] Children on the spectrum sometimes have difficulty interpreting the nonverbal cues and communicative intent of neurotypical children, regulating their emotions, and understanding often-invisible social rules of conversational and emotional reciprocity.[16] Gail, for instance, described her 5-year-old son Robert (Black and Asian), as "really antisocial. . . . He's in his own little bubble." Some parents were far less concerned, however, about their child's preferences for alone time, understanding it to be a form of self-preservation amid daily emotional and sensory overwhelm. Cathleen noted of her 6-year-old son Sebastian (Latino and White), "I felt sad about, 'Oh he doesn't have any friends,' but I think he's actually quite content in his own world. I think he's happy."

Research on peer relationships among children on the spectrum has primarily focused on White autistic children in mainstream classrooms, not on those with complex communication and intellectual disabilities and who experience compounding forms of exclusion, like 8-year-old immigrant Saaida (Asian/Bangladeshi, girl).[17] Hamza recalled of his daughter, "One day I take her to the playground. She go and try to take a toy. After two or three times, the other kids just go away. They are not playing. They say, 'What she doing?'" Such interactions lead to a cyclical denial of access to social roles. Neurotypical children can be quick to judge autistic kids as awkward and not approachable.[18] They are regularly ignored by peers or nonautistic children who do not reciprocate their social advances.[19] Meena, mom of 5-year-old Eashan (Asian/Indian, boy), felt that his teachers completely misread her son and his social difficulties. "They just think like he's shy and he's quiet. He's not shy! No one is talking to him!" she complained.

What makes an autistic child "social" depends on individual, group, and institutional contexts. For example, Bailey, mom of 6-year-old Olivia (White, girl) was disheartened by a growing awareness that her daughter, who was in an integrated classroom, was being excluded not by her peers, but by their caregivers. "For kids whose parents know that there's a diagnosis, they're less likely to reach out to us for play dates," she said. Autistic children tend to be more accepted by typically developing peers in younger grades but later move toward the periphery of social networks.[20] When I first met Raul (Latino, boy) at age 5, his mom, Nina, talked glowingly about the neurotypical peer buddies that his teachers had arranged for him in his inclusive classroom. Six years later, she remarked that "his friendships at school are not as strong as they were when he was younger. . . . They're ready to be teenagers" and Raul was not. It is not only autistic kids who need help in making friends; nonautistic children also benefit socially and emotionally from learning about how to be supportive friends to their peers on the spectrum.[21] Autistic kids are at increased risk for bullying and cyberbullying, with victimization and its emotional burdens (i.e., depression, anxiety) further compounding difficulties with mental health and in establishing friendships.[22]

Despite their challenges, kids on the spectrum strongly report desiring friends,[23] and say they are generally satisfied by their friendships,[24] though they vary in terms of their preferred frequency and type of social contact.[25] Saylor, for example, said that a good friend is "nice to other people [and] their personality isn't just boring. They can't be . . . like, 'Do you want to watch the same movie over and over again?'" Nine-year-old Caleb (Black/ Haitian, boy) excelled at sports and had frequent playdates with classmates. A good friend, he said, is someone who can "play games and show me stuff and they do cool stuff." His mom, Audrey, also shared that "one of his teachers last year told me, 'Oh he's the mayor, everybody knows him. He's friends with everybody.'" Autistic kids' peer relationships can sometimes look different, however, from nonautistic children's friendships (i.e., less emotional intimacy and affective reciprocity). For instance, Audrey said of Caleb, "It's not like he's friends with you and he'll come home, be talking about you. You know, he's friends with you, he comes home, he forgets about you."

Parents and siblings of autistic kids regularly facilitate social access and provide practical support in maintaining friendships, like Conor's family, as well as help children cope with victimization.[26] This can offer some, but not complete, psychological protection from negative outcomes like loneliness.[27] Autistic children's friendships are additionally shaped globally by cultural differences in interpersonal relationship norms (e.g., expectations for social harmony in East Asian countries) as well as intersections of race, socioeconomic status, and neighborhood (e.g., public school classroom composition in the United States).[28] For example, Kimberly, mom of 8-year-old Amaya (Black, Latina, and White; girl), said that her daughter "doesn't have any friends," but that the free gatherings offered by a local autism resource center mostly serving low-income autistic children of color were important "especially if you don't have friends. The only way, if they have parties, [Amaya] looks forward to that."

MEDICAL AND SOCIAL MODELS OF AUTISTIC FRIENDSHIP

Given that difficulties in making friends is named as part of the autism diagnostic criteria in the DSM, it is worth noting how few studies there are on autistic children's friendships relative to other expressions of autism (e.g., language difficulties).[29] Childhood friendship itself has a clinical definition within the Autism Diagnostic Interview-Revised assessment, a standardized tool used to diagnose autism. The relationship has to be between kids approximately the same age, the activities that they do together have to be varied and take place outside of prearranged groups, and there has to be reciprocity and mutual responsiveness in the relationship.[30] To scaffold this model of friendship, autistic children are regularly enrolled in social skills groups and programs that support "social thinking."[31]

Some parents spoke enthusiastically of such programs. For instance, Jessie said that in the group of her then 6-year-old son Patrick (White), which included two other autistic kids, "they play board games or do things with the iPad where they each select. I think that's been a huge, a huge factor in his socialization." Though these programs can increase knowledge of social rules, several ethical and empirical critiques have also been raised by disability and education scholars.[32] Social skills interventions that largely focus on teaching normative social behaviors to autistic kids (e.g., making eye contact, initiating greetings) may work to inhibit authentic expression, normalize adult surveillance, and increase stigma.[33] Acquired skills also may not transfer outside of the pseudo-naturalistic therapeutic environment, as the "bottom up," organic nuances of conversation are generally overlooked within curricula in favor of more "top down," predetermined communicative repertoires.[34]

The contemporary framing of autistic children's social development as deviant coincides with a late modern societal shift that emphasizes personal choice in selecting with whom we socialize and rewards individual likeability and self-disclosure.[35] Some clinicians and educators have looked to build curated social spaces in which autistic kids' belonging is not solely tied to personal characteristics. Adolescents on the spectrum report preferring taking part in social skills groups with self-selecting peers who have similar interests (also known as "affinity spaces"),[36] as opposed to programs that focus centrally on teaching social norms.[37] Countering deficit-oriented views of autistic sociality, many adults on the spectrum contend that there is value in social spaces that are predominantly for neurodivergent people or that center "autistic friendship," relationships built on modes of interaction and communication that come more naturally to them.[38] For example, Casey's mom, Jennifer, also an autistic person, said that she feels "a lot more comfortable talking with other autistic people generally speaking." The fact that she is "very direct [is] not necessarily a deficit. . . . It's just, you know, neurotypical people talk in a certain way and autistic people talk another way."

NAVIGATING AUTISM, MEDIA, AND YOUTH FRIENDSHIP

Mass media and communication technology can allow such alternative forms of friendship to flourish, though online environments are far from a social utopia for kids on the spectrum.[39] There is a direct and indirect relationship between the participation of autistic youth in physical social spaces and their use of media and technology. For instance, autistic children ages 3–11 who are excluded from in-person play by other kids are more likely to occupy their time with media (especially on weekends), an exclusion which is additionally compounded by structural barriers such as a lack of affordable and accessible leisure and recreational activities.[40] Online gaming spaces like Autcraft, an autism-focused Minecraft server, can offer a safe, social community for autistic children. Supporting their relationship building, though, also requires intense parental investments of time, money, and technical knowledge.[41] Online spaces are additionally important because they may be one of the few arenas where autistic youth do not have a constant adult presence, particularly those with one-on-one aides for their entire school day, which may be detrimental to their forming friendships.[42]

A very important part of childhood is having common experiences to talk about with friends. Among youth, knowledge of mass media, technology, and popular culture serves as a form of social currency as well as a means of social distinction (i.e., cool, uncool).[43] Due to their often-deep investment in media culture (e.g., bands, anime),[44] kids on the spectrum may look online and offline (i.e., at recess, on TikTok) to clear symbols of shared affinities with other youth as a means of more confidently initiating spontaneous social interactions.[45] For instance, Jamie recalled of her 10-year-old son Levi (Latino and White, boy), "I'll see him on the playground and he'll see a kid with a Spiderman shirt and . . . he'll be like, 'Oh you like Spiderman? Let's play Spiderman.'"

Among autistic adolescents, social media use is associated with high self-reported friendship quality.[46] It is unclear what aspect of social media might be associated with strong friendships for this population (e.g., messaging, likes). Also uncertain is the directionality and causality of this association (i.e., if social media improves autistic kids' friendships or if those with strong friendships use more social media).[47] Adolescents on the spectrum report finding texting etiquette challenging, such as initiating and responding to messages.[48] Guidebooks to navigating social interaction for adolescent autistic audiences (some written by autistic adults) address anxieties that kids might have about social conduct online and how to identify different types of online friends. For example, *The Asperkid's (Secret) Book of Social Rules* distinguishes between "possible friendship" ("someone who 'liked' you on Facebook or decided to follow your blog") and "evolving friendship" ("this is someone you could text or email/Facebook to see what they're up to or tell them about something funny that happened.")[49] As social media platforms rapidly change and new ones develop, though, this advice can quickly become obsolete and outdated.

How adolescents on the spectrum engage with technology for social purposes parallels and deviates from media use and peer engagement among typically developing kids in multiple ways. Like boys who are nonautistic, autistic boys report that video gaming is the media activity they engage in most frequently with friends and that this play largely strengthens their friendships.[50] Girls on the autism spectrum and nonautistic girls both acknowledge that while online friends are easier to make, such friendships have risks and limitations, and in-person socializing can lead to more authentic, affective connections.[51] However, autistic adolescents reportedly use social media more for entertainment than for friendship building.[52] No studies to date have focused on autistic children age 13 and under with diverse backgrounds and abilities, their understandings of friendship, and the role that different media forms (i.e., mass, digital, social, interactive) play in their experience of peer relationships and social interactions.

NAVIGATING AUTISM, FRIENDSHIP, AND DIGITAL CHILDHOODS

The following analysis does not reveal a universal theory of autism, media, and youth friendship but rather four key themes: (1) media as social *scaffolding*, (2) autistic children's *agency* in using media for social purposes, (3) navigating online *safety* in social interactions, and (4) *contextual factors* impacting the centrality of peer relationships in their social uses of media.

SCAFFOLDING

Media and technology serve in various ways as an on-ramp to online and offline social participation for kids on the spectrum. Watching YouTube videos and engaging in different forms of digital writing allow for a kind of scaffolded, or supported, sociality, removed from the immediacy of live interaction, that enables practice with modes of social address.

SOCIAL SCRIPTING FROM MEDIA   Several children adopted the speech and phrasing of media characters, celebrities, and other online personalities to help them engage with their peers, play pretend, and take on imagined personas. For example, Olivia's mom, Bailey, credited the Disney Junior animated show *Jake and the Neverland Pirates* (a spinoff of the film *Peter Pan*) for providing Olivia with concrete social language that she could memorize (a cognitive strength of hers) and deploy in novel peer interactions. Bailey offered one such example, a time when Olivia came across a boy with a skateboard, to whom she said, "Look, a skateboard. Cool, sweet, awesome. Let's take a ride," a line that she had heard on the show. "How really she learned a lot of her social norms in the beginning was from watching these videos, from picking up on the conversation skills of these kids interacting together, and then flushing them into her conversations," Bailey said.

Kids on the spectrum also used online video to converse with on-screen personas, known in media psychology as "parasocial interactions."[53] Rosie, mom of 4-year-old Spencer (Black, boy) described how YouTube facilitated his "pretend play—which he supposedly doesn't have," she said, alluding to clinical judgements of her son's sociability. Spencer mimicked and remixed play that he observed from a toy unboxing video on YouTube for a Melissa & Doug–brand dollhouse with tiny doorbells, a toy which he himself owned. Spencer had turned the dollhouse upside down, found the toy name on the label, and then typed it into YouTube. The video included an adult man (whose face never appears on-screen) using his hands to puppeteer four figurines who ring the doorbells on the playhouse. Spencer came up with his own language to self-narrate the video. Said Rosie, "He's like, 'Come on friends.' Then he goes, 'Well, let's see who's behind door number one.'" YouTube also enabled autistic kids to watch social action up close yet from a distance, leading some to develop feelings of intimacy, friendship, and identification with media personae, or "parasocial relationships."[54] Natasha, mom of 8-year-old Jeremiah (White, boy), hypothesized that watching videos of YouTubers playing games together allowed her son to observe social interaction and learn about conflict resolution. "The social piece is appealing to him for some reason," she said, "I think it's a safe way to watch people interact and learn how to interact with friends, and not be doing it yourself."

Twelve-year-old Brendan (White, boy) showed me videos from one of his favorite gamers on YouTube, Markiplier, who currently has over 30 million channel subscribers. We watched one video that Brendan had viewed many times before, in which Markiplier played a horror-adventure game called *Little Nightmares*. Brendan enabled the video's captions so that he could read aloud what Markiplier was saying, as well as simulate conversation with the YouTuber. "I don't know where I am now," Markiplier said in reference to his in-game location, to which Brendan replied with friendly familiarity, "You never know where you are, Mark." Brendan interestingly remarked that he appreciated the attention Markiplier paid to his captions ("This guy edits them, so it looks nice," he said). YouTube was not the only digital media that enabled Brendan to play along without playing. He also enjoyed spending time on the gaming website Roblox, and I observed him adopting the game narration style of Markiplier while he played on a server called "Reason 2 Die." After his own avatar met his demise, Brendan watched the game in "spectate survivors" mode and made humorous comments on the game much like Markiplier would. Parasocial interactions and relationships, along with media scripts, enabled autistic kids to play with sociality using existing cultural material.

BUILDING ONLINE SOCIAL SKILLS WHILE OFFLINE Digital but nonnetworked media could also offer a sandbox for autistic kids to practice online communication with peers before they were fully ready to have their own connected devices. First-grader Olivia, who lived in a wealthy Boston suburb in which a number of her peers already had personal mobile devices, became curious about texting through her exposure to popular culture as well as her personal observations, such as text messages popping up on her mom's cell phone. An emoji pattern covered her school backpack, and she was anticipating the imminent release of *The Emoji Movie*. For her upcoming seventh birthday then, it was not entirely unexpected that Olivia requested "a real phone with a real plan" as a present, as Bailey said. Giving Olivia a fully functional smartphone was out of the question—not only because of her age, but also due to concerns about her social vulnerabilities. Bailey shared one such example: "There's a boy in school who offered her tickets to [the amusement park] LEGOLAND. He's like, 'I'll give you three tickets if you don't talk for the rest of the day.' She came home and she was over the moon because she thought she was going to get three tickets to LEGOLAND" for having remained silent.

Instead of a smartphone, Bailey offered to get Olivia a "diary computer," or an iPad with a keyboard case. "She likes to just type and write stories, so we discussed that we would do a diary computer," said Bailey. When I spoke to Olivia though, she seemed less interested in the nonsocial functions of the tablet and more intrigued by the idea of messaging friends, perhaps through Apple's preinstalled iMessage app. "One of my friends has a diary computer so I can text them on the computer," said Olivia. "Do you know that you can't text on a computer, honey?" Bailey responded. I asked Olivia what she would like to type on her diary computer, and she replied, "'Would you like to come out for pizza?' Yeah. That's what I would like to do with my friends. It's called texting back. Texting means you can like text your person and then they text you back." When I visited a few weeks later after her birthday, Olivia had indeed received a diary computer—along with her mom's old, disconnected iPhone 4. And while Bailey had encouraged Olivia to write "diary" stories on the Notes app on the iPad, Olivia was more eager to use the tablet to watch *Monster High* videos on YouTube Kids. Children on the autism spectrum may be excited to chat with friends outside of school by using technology, but parental concerns about the ease with which they might be connected loom large, with parents like Bailey trying to find a middle ground.

AGENCY

Far from being passive actors, many young people on the spectrum make active choices about the media they use, how and when they use it socially, and in what circumstances. Autistic kids deploy technology to build interpersonal and group relationships that center on a shared passion, hobby, or interest related to media, as well as to create physical and psychological distance from an upsetting social situation.

TECHNOLOGY AS SOCIAL RESPITE   Autistic children inhabit social spaces in which they have relatively little control and environments that can overwhelm their sensory systems. Personal devices like tablet computers allow kids on the spectrum to be copresent with others while minimizing the effects of distressing stimuli around them.[55] For example, Raina, mom of 4-year-old Zahra (Azerbajani, girl), said that her daughter "always wanted to play with kids, but she was scared or uncomfortable. So, she would just permit herself with watching videos, iPad, or playing a game." Zahra had grown more relaxed around other children over the past year and had less sensory sensitivity to their cries and screams, to the point that "she's very friendly. I would say too friendly," said Raina, "If there are other kids, she doesn't even need [media] anymore." However, April, mom of 5-year-old Sofia (Latina, girl), did not see media and sociality as necessarily mutually exclusive. She reflected on the idea that "they always say like the kids with autism don't really want to be around people, but [Sofia] always wants to be where everyone's at." Her tablet allowed her some power over of her immediate social space. "Like if she's able to, she'll sit here and browse her iPad and just be near you, which is her way of being involved," April said. To the outside observer, Sofia's way might not look social, but to her family, it was easily interpretable.

FRIENDSHIP THROUGH MEDIA PLAY AND PRODUCTION   Adolescents on the spectrum talked about bonding with other kids through their shared interests in talking about, playing with, and producing media. When friends came over to hang out with 11-year-old Rosalita (White, girl), "We do like a video together and take pictures," she said, using her iPad or Instax instant camera. Similarly, for Cody and Jeremiah, video games helped structure peer relationships and interactions. "Sanjay plays Minecraft," 9-year-old Cody (White, boy) told me, "He's a friend in my class. The day I told him about that if you are trying to activate a rail and you go over it in a minecart, the minecart rattles and you fall out—he apparently discovered that, too." As for Jeremiah, "Those games help [him and his friends] find something to do" afterschool together, said his mom, Natasha, "They allow him to have a common language and be social." Jeremiah had grown especially close with another boy on the spectrum in his class who shared his love of Minecraft. Whereas neurotypical kids in the class preferred having three- or four-hour playdates, Jeremiah and the boy were well-matched in that neither could handle socializing in person for more than one and a half or two hours at a time. Natasha explained that Jeremiah and the boy initially spent their time together watching Minecraft videos on YouTube, "picking which ones to watch [and] talking about them after. They've evolved as we've done more play dates. Now they've started to play games themselves together."

Virtual and in-person clubs and groups, organized around specific media genres and franchises, also allowed autistic tweens to regularly connect with peers who had similar interests, and under social conditions that they did not find overly taxing.[56] When 13-year-old Adrian (White, boy) was bouncing between schools during a turbulent period in his life, his mom, Brianna, said that "Minecraft helped him get together with people . . . he wasn't seeing at school on a daily basis." He was also involved in a Scratch computer programming club at the local Boys and Girls Club. "As long as your kid doesn't get beaten up in the other areas [of the club], the tech room is pretty cool," Brianna said sardonically, alluding to Adrian's struggles with bullying. Beyond digital media, organized tabletop and card games also kept Adrian regularly connected with other kids. "I have this thing called Pokémon League every Saturday," he said, which was a small group of teens that gathered weekly at a local gaming store to compete in a turn-based combat game with Pokémon trading cards. In general, Adrian reported that "honestly, I don't actually usually have many friends. I'm much more of an introvert." For his recent *Dungeons & Dragons* (*D&D*)–themed birthday party, he had six friends over to play the video game *Super Smash Bros*. "But other than that, I rarely have enough friends over for there to actually be like, uh, fun having 'screen time' and stuff," Adrian said, slightly mocking adult-driven terminology for young people's media use.

Ronan also played *D&D*, getting together with friends to play in an organized group every other Sunday, in addition to attending a live-action role playing class (LARP) each Saturday. When I asked Ronan what he liked about playing *D&D* with his friends, he joked, "You can't really single-handedly take down like a million monsters when they all have to make attacks against you. [You're] the only thing out there for them to attack if there's no friends." In his LARP class, Ronan enjoyed being part of a group while developing his own character, Dark Ronan, who is "descended from Gandalf the Grey" from *The Lord of the Rings* and "wears a random cloak with fur that my mom made me," he said. Though his LARPing group was not specifically for kids on the spectrum, his mom, Karrie, thought that the company that ran it had created a really accommodating space for autistic kids. "They have certain sections of the gym [you can] go if you just need a time out and you don't want anyone to mess with you for a little bit and you can take a little sensory break," she said. Kids on the spectrum made decisions and expressed their desires to be social on their own terms, with media enabling varying degrees of togetherness with individuals physically near and far from them.

SECURITY

Preadolescent kids on the spectrum are coming of age in a networked environment with, unfortunately, endless potential for their social vulnerabilities to be taken advantage of by cruel actors and for their data to be exploited by companies for profit.[57] Several autistic kids learned these lessons the hard way, some were challenged by the nuances of online visibility management, and a few were developing their own strategies for coping with cyberbullying.

CYBERBULLYING AND ONLINE ANTAGONISM Video games are a major site of networked aggression where autistic kids are frequently targeted.[58] Brendan, for example, talked about feeling harassed and misunderstood by anonymous players while on the online gaming platform Roblox. When I asked him if there was anything that he did not like about electronics, he reported, "People who think I'm a hacker just because my Roblox username is all numbers." Because of his suspicious username, Brendan was regularly kicked off Roblox servers by players typing "Kick due to name" into the chat, a directive to the game's moderators. This expulsion made Brendan "sad, because I'm not a hacker!" although he was usually able to rejoin the game. He spoke about developing a kind of resiliency in response to his frustrations ("I'll just [rejoin] over and over until they realize I can keep doing this all day") and finding comfort in the consequences for harassment on Roblox ("They'll lose five things for every time they kick me, so they're just wasting things. Trust me, it's kind of nice to see that they're actually punishing themselves for hurting someone, for what they're not.")

Unlike the aggression against Brendan, which was carried out by strangers in a video game, the antagonism toward Saylor was enacted by girls she knew from school and whose torment spanned online and offline spaces. Girls on the spectrum regularly report anxiety over social disapproval.[59] Back in sixth grade, Saylor had difficulty distinguishing between "somebody who would accept her or somebody who would pretend to be her friend but [was] not really looking out for her," said her mom, Maggie. Saylor talked about how her relationship with these girls "was kind of confusing" in terms of how they treated her in person and on social media: "On my old Instagram, these girls who bullied me, they called me fat and stuff. . . . The day before they said that we were like friends because they said that I could try on some of their clothes at their house because [they said] my clothes were awful [and] because we're about the same size." These same girls later told Saylor that she should post on Snapchat about wanting to take her own life, which Saylor then posted out of peer pressure. Another mother saw the message on her child's Snapchat and contacted Maggie, who "went into crisis mode." The incident led to Saylor attending "counseling steadily to just sort of have that place to talk about all these different issues," Maggie reported.

By age 12, Saylor could reflect on her experiences with bullying and talk about them as part of her past as well as within the current context of pervasive toxicity online. Like other preteens, she was aware of the overt dangers of having an online presence and had used the affordances of social media to engage in impression management, curate her self-presentation, and recognize the influence of social norms on her posts.[60] "The year I got bullied," she said, "I always got picked on for having really bad Instagram photos. . . . I was like 9 and I didn't know. I just wanted to be cool and stuff." She subsequently changed some of her privacy settings, creating more intimate audiences through private Snapchat stories as well as separate 'finsta' (private) and 'rinsta' (public) Instagram accounts. Saylor explained that she did not post "awkward" photos on her nonprivate Snapchat story anymore "because if everyone just sees a weird picture of me then everyone's gonna screenshot it—which actually did happen when I was little, but I think they forget about that now." With the help of her family, her local community, and licensed therapists, Saylor was able to create some psychological distance from her challenges with cyberbullying, but the process was ongoing, as was the evolution of social media platforms with which she and her peers engaged.

MAKING ONLINE "FRIENDS" Besides targeted attacks from known and unknown actors, children on the spectrum also navigate relationship building online with people from school and from parts unknown, particularly through video games. Roblox was central to these discussions, considering both its popularity and its role as a social networking platform for kids under 13.[61] For example, Brendan's mom, Marcia, recalled a time in which her son wrote "can we be friends?" into the chat on Roblox, which surprised her. "Even though he wants friends," she said, "he doesn't know how to probably maintain those relationships." She worried about Brendan not being able to pick up on another person's bad intentions, "not only from the outside world . . . but also children from school" with whom Brendan sometimes played. She was also nervous about others online interpreting Brendan's sometimes "goofy or annoying" behavior as aggressive and reacting as such, which she knew happened to him at school.

"Friendship" took on multiple meanings across the digital platforms used by autistic brothers Matt and Bryan (ages 9 and 7, White, boys). I sat with them as they showed me their favorite Roblox games and noticed that Matt had a long list of 200 Roblox-designated "friends" along with 165 messages from said individuals. "It's kind of like texting," he said, as he picked one person from his friends list and typed, "sup." I asked the brothers how you become friends with someone on Roblox. "You just friend them! And wait for them to accept it. If they accept it then, then it's a new friend," said Bryan. Unlike in-person situations, the clearly marked indicator of a friend request took the guesswork out of approaching and determining if someone was receptive to interaction. "You can play what they're playing, but if it says they're offline then you can't," said Bryan. When I asked him if he always accepted friend requests on Roblox, his response reflected a broader interest in internet celebrity. "Yeah, because we're YouTubers," he said, in reference to the videos that he and Matt sometimes posted to the site, "and the YouTuber rule [is] if you get famous, lots of people are going to friend you." Bryan, like many children today, wanted to be "YouTube famous"; however, he also said, "but most people don't watch" our videos.

Bryan and Matt's parents, Pedro and Beca, recent immigrants to the United States from Brazil, had different reactions to their sons' forays into networked social interaction. Pedro thought that maintaining an online presence was important for the boys' future social advancement, and that practice navigating these spaces was valuable, even if it involved upsetting experiences. "I've been raising them in a world that friends are online friends," Pedro said, "You have to teach to prepare for a different world." After an incident in which Matt was very upset by being verbally harassed over a headset by a teenage player on PlayStation 4, and another in which Bryan told a stranger on Roblox that he was 6 years old, Pedro tried to impart an ethos of personal responsibility for privacy and safety to his sons. He recalled telling them that online, "nobody is your friend. . . . You don't share your name, your age, your school." With respect to online antagonism, Pedro told them that "you have to learn how to ignore these people."

Beca was more fearful that the boys did not have the capacity to exhibit such control or display critical awareness due to the intersection of their autism and their age. Of Matt, she noted that he "doesn't know when people want him to stop, or people are not comfortable with something." It was especially difficult for Beca to set clear rules regarding online exchanges and relationships, considering that her sons interacted with both friends from school and total strangers on Roblox. "There's a few kids from the school, actually, that they add each other," said Beca, "So I try to . . . make it very clear that if [Matt] says 'Oh, I have 200 friends,' that's not friendship; that's just random people that you add."

Saylor had herself made online friends and thought about the risks of interacting with unknown people on the internet. "I have internet friends," Saylor said, "I have one that's nice and so we met on Roblox, even though it's kind of weird to meet friends on Roblox, but she just needed some friends." She discussed the importance of verifying the girl's identity, noting, "we've FaceTimed like on Snapchat and I know what she looks like and she's very funny. I don't really trust her 100 percent because like, I don't know her, but we still talk and stuff and play Roblox." Other friends, Saylor reported, had engaged in far riskier social interactions on Roblox, such as playing a game that simulated going on dates and having a romantic relationship with players of unknown ages ("I'm just like, how do you not know about stranger danger?! You can date someone that's like 83 and you'll be like, 'Oh, you're so cute,'" Saylor remarked). In all, some autistic kids had difficulty determining the appropriateness of contacting and being contacted by anonymous video game players, while others were savvier in their understanding of the potential consequences for safety, security, and privacy beyond the game.

CONTEXTUAL FACTORS

Lastly, the social relationships that kids on the spectrum do or do not develop around media or through technology have to do with far more than the choices they actively make or even the specific devices and platforms they have access to. The extent to which a given child may been seen by others as "friendly" or approachable in the United States is heavily shaped by societal factors like racism, and this is especially true for autistic youth in online and offline spaces. Family members (i.e., siblings, parents) additionally play another important contextual role in how they model and introduce the social uses of media and technology to autistic kids.

RACE Caleb went to an elementary school in Boston attended mostly by White children. There were different public safety considerations in his friends' neighborhoods and in his own, which had a high crime rate. When Caleb went over to play at the home of one White school friend on the spectrum, Audrey said that "[the] mom lets them outside on the street. . . . I'm worried about that. Their street is very quiet. I don't care; I'm not letting Caleb outside by himself." In addition to gaps in safety, Audrey was also keenly aware of how her Black autistic son with ADHD was vulnerable to being read by others as aggressive and violent, which could directly impact interactions with powerful institutions like the police. For example, Audrey did not want Caleb listening to rap songs with lyrics about guns and murder that he might be overheard repeating. She explained that "being Black, you have to know your boundaries," describing the material and symbolic impacts of racism. "If you want to become President Obama, you have to be clean because if he wasn't clean, he wouldn't have been president. So, this," she said, referring to her rules about rap music, "is where you start making sure you're clean."

At the same time that Audrey was concerned about how Caleb would navigate a racial hierarchy that privileged White individuals in society, she had been avoiding talking to Caleb explicitly about race. She worried that he might have a hard time interpreting and relaying the social nuances of racism. Audrey was especially concerned that Caleb might talk to his White friends about race relations in a way that would prove alienating. "Things about being Black, about violence, I don't want to explain to him in details because I don't want him to go to school and try to explain it and for other kids to see him in a whole different way," said Audrey. Structural racism pervaded many aspects of Caleb's life, shaping his friendships, media consumption, and their complex entwinement with his autism.

FAMILY CO-USE The immediate social environment around a child at home also influenced their use of technology with friends. In addition to one sibling expanding another's social network, as with Conor and Ronan, parents and other adult family members could support an autistic child's engagement with media as a means of connecting with peers. Norah, for example, thought that the frequent media co-use that she and her family engaged in with her 5-year-old son Max (Asian and White, boy), an only child, directly contributed to his extraversion with peers and his social uses of media with them.

"For him and autism," Norah said of Max, media has "been a way for him to connect with other people." She, her husband, and their extended family all enjoyed watching TV and playing iPad games with him as a way of understanding his interests. Max, in turn, modeled his family members' enthusiasm with his peers. For instance, Norah said, "We'll get [to swim class] early or something and somebody is playing [a mobile game]. He's like, 'What are you doing? Can I watch?'" Norah hypothesized that her and her family "just made him that way by being very social at home and just always always socializing like 24/7."

For less well-resourced families, however, such joint media engagement was not possible, nor was highly social peer interaction an end goal. Nour regretted the fact that she herself was not a gamer and felt some guilt that she was not able to support 8-year-old Karim's (Middle Eastern/Algerian, boy) media use in a way that might have led to friendships. "Unfortunately, I am not a person who is technology oriented," she said, "so I did not push for any video games. . . . But I realize that if I had, that would create a connection because I've seen his friends, all of them playing Roblox, Minecraft." Using media socially with family members may not have necessarily led to peer relationships but was still a valid form of social interaction. Twelve-year-old Diego (White, boy) was a frequent user of social technologies. Said his mom, Francesca, "He's interested in messaging. He takes selfies. . . . I mean he's doing all of the social things. He gets the social." But Diego's online conversations were exclusively with family members, like sending his mom emoji and Skyping with his grandparents in Europe—people who were patient, consistent, and always available to Diego. As for using media with classmates, "He doesn't really have peer friends," Francesca said, but family fulfilled Diego's desires for mediated social interaction.

REFLECTIONS ON FRIENDSHIP

Autistic kids are kids, and like all kids, they have fundamental needs for feeling known to others and in the world. The interpersonal relationships that they forge can look like those of neurotypical children and yet may be quite different in other respects. Media and technology provide them with what nonautistic youth also seek, like community among those with similar interests and practical coordination of offline plans. Autistic children's desires for mediated friendship may also conflict, though, with what is expected of contemporary online sociality, such as carefully calibrated self-disclosure.[62] Understanding autistic kids' mediated peer relationships—through the lenses of scaffolding, agency, safety, and contextual factors—allows us to reframe dominant considerations of technology, society, and what it means to be social. After all, social media use is not analogous to online social interaction. Empirically speaking, platforms like Facebook, Instagram, and Twitter are primarily used for browsing and broadcasting, and most "social interactions" happen outside of social media (defined as mutual acknowledgment by both partners of a shared relationship, conversational exchange, and focused attention).[63] Social media is not really all that social, and "nonsocial" media like video game play and online video consumption may cultivate richer relationships, especially for people on the spectrum.[64]

In their 2019 meta-analysis of qualitative studies of autistic adolescents' self-described experiences of peer relationships (ages 10–19), clinical psychologist Lily Cresswell and colleagues identified four key themes generated by youth on the spectrum: *understanding friendship* (i.e., describing friendship and its important qualities), *having and wanting friends* (i.e., desiring friendship and reputation concerns), *challenges of peer relationships* (i.e., making friends, peer rejection and victimization), and *overcoming challenges* (i.e., responding to bullies, support from others). I found that media and technology cut across these areas, including Jeremiah's observations of YouTubers' relationships, Olivia's wanting to ask classmates out to pizza with her "diary computer," Bryan and Matt's difficulties with evaluating trustworthy friendships on Roblox, and Saylor's carving out of a space for positivity on her Snapchat and Instagram accounts after negative peer experiences online. With regard to autistic kids, it is especially important to understand social differences in their usage across types of media content and technology; demographic differences by age, gender, race, and class; and variations in communication skills and intellectual disability with respect to how media meets their social needs.

This analysis lends itself to several implications for parents, clinicians, policy makers, and other stakeholders in autistic children's social engagement with media and technology. First, there is significant value in kids on the spectrum being able to play and learn about interpersonal interactions and relationships online without all of the risks that come with being fully or publicly networked. For example, Autcraft has allowed autistic adolescents to practice and define sociality in a way that allows them to have more control over what and how they share their feelings, views, and ideas with others.[65] The term "walled garden" has been used by digital learning and education scholars, generally in a negative way, to refer to online spaces for kids that significantly bound their ability to connect with outside contacts as well as limit their potential interactions within.[66] There are good reasons for kids to be protected before they can responsibly explore the world outside the garden, times when the boundaries are too limiting and paternalistic, and instances when the artifice of the walls forces kids into finding ingenious ways to leap over them. Despite not being fully realized, Olivia's "diary computer" is a good example of a walled garden that might scaffold autistic children's entry into the broader online world as a form of social rehearsal while still being very much "real" to them.

Such places might even give autistic adolescents opportunities to reflect on what education scholar Katie Davis terms "spheres of obligation" for presenting oneself online (i.e., you, your interpersonal connections, online social norms, broader cultural norms).[67] Older adolescents on the spectrum may be able to critically reflect on online risks and employ strategies to keep themselves safe, such as accepting friend requests only from people they know.[68] Nonautistic parents and professionals potentially underestimate autistic adolescent users' social media competence, as youth on the spectrum may be more vulnerable online but also more risk averse than nonautistic adolescents.[69] Different social media platforms have different social rules that are constantly changing, and it is not always clear to autistic kids when those norms have been transgressed. Parents need help with creative ideas for easing their preadolescent children into the complexity of networked interpersonal communication through small steps, especially with tools that are free or low-cost, protect young people's data privacy, and do not require significant technical knowledge for caregivers to guide their child.[70]

Next, the reductive binary of children's technology usage as either social (and active and productive) or antisocial (and passive and consumptive) centers neurotypical children's friendships and relational norms.[71] Kids on the spectrum may be repeatedly watching YouTube videos, for example, that provide them instructive examples of social situations, like Olivia memorizing scripted lines from *Jake and the Neverland Pirates*. Solitary media time can be important to their personal and social growth, including the copresent use of technology with others in close proximity sans interaction,[72] as with Sofia. Neurotypical parents' ideas about appropriate online and offline friendships (e.g., texting friends to maintain a close relationship) might not sync up with the degree of social gratification that some youth on the spectrum desire.[73] Parents limiting video game play among autistic kids for valid reasons (e.g., to shield from them harassment) may also inadvertently be cutting them off from important social connections.

Lastly, certain customizable features of interactive technology could better facilitate social relationships for kids on the spectrum if integrated more fully into the platforms that kids use the most.[74] Digital ethnographer Kathryn Ringland, for example, has highlighted various affordances of Minecraft that take unnecessary social pressure off autistic kids in the virtual space, options that a child would not have on an in-person play date (e.g., using the "teleport" function to leave an uncomfortable interaction in-game).[75] She and her colleagues also developed an iPad game focused on supporting collaboration among autistic children and identified three levels of social relationship (without adult intervention) that new media could scaffold. First, design features that allow for joining in can support membership or participation in a group. Second, coordination features in an app's design can facilitate the partnership of people working toward a shared goal. And lastly, features that enable commentary on a shared experience can bolster the development of friendships around mutual interests and affinities.[76] These may be good design practices for all children's digital play, but especially useful for those on the spectrum.

Reflecting on childhood friendship, autistic author Naoki Higashida writes that children on the spectrum do not have to be social in expressly neurotypical ways. "Whether or not we have lots of friends, every single one of us is the main protagonist of our own existence," he writes. "Having no friends is nothing to be ashamed of. Let's all follow and be true to our singular path through life."[77] Media and communication technologies provide more ways than ever for kids on the spectrum to start, maintain, and dissolve friendships. As with neurotypical children, some autistic kids have concerns about fitting in with peers and belonging online, while others prefer the social companionship of media personae who cultivate intimate relationships with their audiences. Friendships enabled by digital media can both offer relief for and add stress to the lives of autistic kids, especially for those already predisposed to anxiety, depression, and other mental health issues. The solutions to their challenges cannot solely be technological in nature, as the mediated friendships of autistic kids are forged against the backdrop of offline spaces in which their specific interpersonal needs are not always fully accepted and met. The next chapter focuses on some of those needs, specifically their unique modes of sensory processing and the role of media in making their immediate physical environments more or less accommodating.

Embodiment

6 SENSES

Patrick and his mom, Jessie, sat on the living room couch, engaged in their near-daily viewing of the animated film *Despicable Me 2*. Jessie is a single parent by choice, having conceived Patrick, a 4-year-old minimally speaking White autistic boy, through donor sperm and in vitro fertilization. Her deep love and singular dedication to him was evident in her attentiveness to his sensory sensitivities. Patrick giggled gleefully as Jessie ran her fingers along the soles of his feet. "He loves being tickled," she said, loudly kissing him behind the ears. "I could eat you! I could eat you!" she exclaimed, to which Patrick responded with bursts of laughter. Jessie was not only the parent of a disabled child, but a special education preschool teacher as well. Owing to this, she employed language reflecting someone who knew quite a bit about autistic children and their unique responses to sensory stimuli. Jessie remarked how Patrick got "his sensory needs met" over the course of the film. "He had a lot. A lot. You have the oral. Between his feet, his hands. His vestibular," she said.

For those less familiar with terminology like "sensory needs," while growing up you may have learned that there are five senses: visual (sight), auditory (sound), tactility (touch), olfactory (smell), and gustatory (taste). We can think of these traditional five senses as external, meaning they have to do with stimuli that come from outside of the body. However, insights from the clinical and scientific fields of occupational therapy, educational psychology, and neurobiology suggest that sensory processing also includes at least two internal senses that tell us where the body is in space.[1] These senses—vestibular and proprioceptive—have to do with body movement and body awareness. Imagine the vestibular sense as knowing when a car speeds up or slows down, and proprioception as feeling the weight of yourself in the seat and your feet on the floor.

Humans vary in their ability to process sensory stimuli, manage its intensity, and organize bodily sensations. Sensory experiences can be not only unpleasant for some, but overwhelming and distressing enough to trigger "meltdowns" (i.e., a temporary loss of behavioral control) and "shutdowns" (i.e., a temporary retreat).[2] Not everyone with difficulty responding to and receiving sensory information is autistic, but sensory processing challenges are a common feature of autism. Ninety to 95 percent of school-age autistic children reportedly have some sensory issues.[3] Overreactivity or underreactivity to sensory input and "unusual interest in sensory aspects of the environment" are diagnostic criteria for autism in the fifth edition of the American Psychiatric Association's *Diagnostic and Statistical Manual of Mental Disorders*.[4] Autistic individuals report processing sensory input in ways that can significantly diverge from those of the nonautistic population.[5] This includes being extremely bothered by clothing tags, possessing a low or high pain threshold, and having difficulty measuring spatial proximity.[6] Their sensory experiences can also be intensely pleasurable. For example, Ido Kedar notes in his memoir *Ido in Autismland* that blinking lights or the sun's glare on the water are "visually harmonious sights" to him. "I see woven patterns of shapes and colors. No one who sees this isn't amazed at the lovely details of the lights," writes Kedar.[7]

As with the rest of the population, autistic individuals are also users of information and communication technologies. The senses play a complex role in how all of us perceive media content and interact physically with technology.[8] However, the ways that autistic people process sensory information and how they use media and technology to create more pleasurable and less painful sensory environments tend to be understood as pathological in nature.[9] For example, some parents and behavioral therapists consider a child's repeated viewing and rewinding of selected parts of an animated film to be a problematic fixation in need of correction instead of a self-soothing stimulatory practice (or "stim") that creates a pleasurable visual and/or auditory sensation.[10] Some children on the spectrum reportedly have strong visual-spatial abilities and prefer processing information in a visual rather than a written form, which may heighten the appeal and ease of using screen and digital media.[11] At the same time, the intense sensory stimulation of interactive media might be challenging for autistic children to filter out, particularly if that content is violent and highly arousing, and impede their ability to engage in meaningful learning or attend to others in their social environment.[12]

In this chapter, I explore how children on the spectrum like Patrick process sensory information through their media use, and, in doing so, ground the sociotechnical shaping of sociality in the sensuous study of media.[13] The internal and external human sensory systems are interrelated in complex ways, and this sensemaking influences the design and arrangement of autistic children's domestic spaces, intimate relationships with family members, and media use when it is solitary, proximal (i.e., with others nearby), and joint (i.e., with social partners).

THEORIES OF MEDIA, AUTISM, AND THE SENSES

I start here by providing a brief background on the intersection of technology, society, and sensory differences. This includes understanding sensory processing from a neurodiversity perspective, how normative approaches to the senses are embedded in the study of media technologies, and theoretical explanations for how people regulate their senses through media.

NEURODIVERSE APPROACHES TO SENSORY PROCESSING
Sensation affects human development, functioning, and behavior across the lifespan in complex ways. Sensory integration theory explains how individuals may experience difficulties integrating and processing sensory information in two respects: having high or low *thresholds* for sensory stimuli and *responding* actively or passively to sensory input.[14] Based on these thresholds and responses, there are four types of sensory processing challenges that a person could have: (1) a high threshold and passive response (i.e., low sensory registration), (2) a high threshold and active response (i.e., being sensory seeking), (3) a low threshold and passive response (i.e., being sensory sensitive), and (4) a low threshold and active response (i.e., being sensory avoiding). Even between two autistic kids in the same family, sensory thresholds and responses can look very different. One mom, Karrie, noted that her 9-year-old son Conor (White, boy) "is very hyposensory, so he's really sensory seeking. He likes a lot of physical touch and physical input. He sometimes gets overwhelmed with loud noises," while 10-year-old Ronan (White, boy) "doesn't really have any sensory issues."

All senses are implicated in sensory regulation, but the proprioceptive and vestibular senses are lesser known.[15] Proprioception refers to sensory information regarding the body's location in space created by the contraction, stretching, and compression of muscles, joints, and tendons. Signs of proprioceptive processing difficulties include frequent crashing and bumping into objects and experiencing relief from deep pressure on the body, such as being under heavy blankets or hugged tightly. The body's vestibular receptors in the inner ear are responsible for maintaining a sense of gravity and balance, which tells the body if it is moving, how fast, and in what direction. Signs of vestibular sensory integration dysfunction include appearing to never become dizzy while spinning and craving activities in which the feet leave the ground (i.e., swinging, jumping). Activities can stimulate both senses; bouncing on a trampoline, for instance, provides deep pressure through the feet and a feeling of flight.

Sensory regulation and dysregulation are not solely individual or biological in nature but are culturally and socially situated as well.[16] Language reflects and generates distinctions between marked and unmarked categories, with one example being the difference between having sensory "needs" and sensory "preferences." Within the US cultural context, the prioritization of values such as independence and self-reliance effectively turns having needs and needing others into a weakness (i.e., neediness, dependency).[17] This is particularly true if the needs in question are those of people with disabilities.[18] With respect to autism, the mannerisms that many autistic individuals develop in order to cope with environmental sensory overload—such as hand flapping and avoiding eye contact—are often socially stigmatized.[19] Autistic children may be actively discouraged or punished for exhibiting these self-soothing behaviors.[20] Humans have a wide range of sensory needs and make valid attempts to fulfill those needs in relation to their environments, in which media and technology are increasingly pervasive.

SENSORY NORMS IN DIGITAL MEDIA

Without directly considering the lived experiences of autistic and neurodivergent people with significant sensory processing challenges, researchers have long attended to the phenomenological, social, and cultural construction of sensation. Those in the social sciences and humanities have broadened ways of thinking about the senses beyond the medical fields of physiology and neurology.[21] Psychologists, designers, and historians have illustrated how cultural norms, social roles, and aesthetic preferences around the senses form a basis for human interaction and differentiation.[22] The anthropological and sociological study of the senses has interrogated how people have used sensory knowledge to structure culture and society[23] and how we live in and move through the world is shaped by our perception and embodiment.[24]

In media and communication studies, the senses have provoked ongoing scholarly conversation about acuity and the body in relation to technology.[25] Digital and nondigital media objects have "affordances" and "constraints," concepts that have come to encompass not only the possibilities and limitations of design features,[26] but how people get a feel for a given technology and perceive its potential uses.[27] The individual senses that media use recruit may less likely be singular modes of bodily perception and more like sensory "ensembles" of different affective, kinesthetic, and somatic ways of knowing.[28] Others have theorized that the sensing of media is synesthetic in nature (as in, processing information from several senses at once); for example, communication theorist Marshall McLuhan described televisual images as "tactile promptings."[29] Symbolic representations of the senses have also shaped understandings of the cognitive affordances of media technologies and content. McLuhan proposed, for instance, that specific media have standardized effects on the senses (i.e., "sensory ratios").[30]

Disability disrupts such universalizing claims to sensory experiences and expands the broader social and political potentialities of media and technology.[31] Normative bodies are popularly understood as ideal media users,[32] or what media studies scholar Elizabeth Ellcessor terms the "preferred user position."[33] Technological affordances are relative to diverse forms of sensory embodiment.[34] Research in feminist science and technology studies explores the cultural politics of sensory impairment.[35] Such work reveals, for example, how cognition researchers in the mid-twentieth century drew on computing metaphors like "processing," "input," and "feedback"— language now used to describe the senses—to position their field as more science than art (i.e., cognitive science). Cyberneticists, engineers, and psychologists at the time also designed experiments testing how tactility (i.e., touch) and haptics (i.e., force and touch) might simulate or replace the "lost" senses of sight (blindness) and sound (deafness).[36] These deficit-oriented sensory norms are incorporated into today's technological developments and shape participation in and exclusion from everyday media use,[37] such as the uneven quality and availability of closed (i.e., can turn off) and open (cannot turn off) captioning in user-generated online video.[38]

MEDIA SENSORY CURATION THEORY

The various channels through which media transmits sensations—sight, sound, touch, movement, and activity—influences a user's overall sensory experience. In the academic subfield of media psychology, media sensory curation theory proposes that media devices are tools that people purposefully use to regulate their sensory systems by amplifying input (i.e., sensory capturing) and limiting input (i.e., sensory curbing) from their surrounding environments.[39] Media psychologist Kristen Harrison (who is autistic) and colleagues identify three sensory environments nested within each other that people regularly manage—the natural environment (e.g., sunlight), the built environment (e.g., indoor lighting), and the media environment (e.g., the brightness of an iPad's screen). In another example, through what media studies scholar Mack Hagood calls "sonic self-control," a person can use headphones to increase auditory input in an environment that they find too quiet to concentrate in or, alternatively, cancel out noise in a space that is too loud.[40] In fact, Apple announced in 2021 that it would be adding a background noise reduction option for its phones and headphones explicitly "in support of neurodiversity."[41]

Media sensory curation is reportedly higher among children with disabilities that may cause sensory dysregulation (e.g., autism, ADHD) than those without.[42] Within a household, different thresholds and regulatory responses to media sensory stimuli can generate conflict between family members (i.e., turning the volume up too high), particularly between neurotypical parents and neurodivergent children.[43] Conflict may be preemptively avoided through physical, social, and symbolic modifications that autistic children and their caregivers make to the home environment that can reduce sensory challenges and contribute to well-being.[44] Cathleen, for example, placed media in the same category as objects she had purchased for 6-year-old Sebastian (Latino and White, boy) that were designed for sensory regulation purposes. "I think [media is] a tool that we use just like we use a swing or a rocking chair or a body sock," she said. "[It's a] way for him to decompress and reorganize himself."

Home environments and their sensory features can look very different among autistic children. Few parents have the social, cultural, or economic means to install sound insulation for reducing noise if their autistic child screams or pounds on the floor during high-stress times.[45] Families who live in neighborhoods with spaced apart homes are privileged in this respect. For instance, Hamza, father of 8-year-old nonspeaking Saaida (Asian/Bengali, girl), was worried about what would happen over Saaida's winter break from school when it was too cold to take her outside to play. The lack of vestibular input would likely lead to her having a meltdown inside their apartment. "In snow time, when school close," Hamza said, "sometimes this situation will make us so much trouble to control her. The other people in this building . . . I know if police come . . . somebody told me they'd call police." This fear of law enforcement being summoned was compounded by Hamza's status as a Bangladeshi citizen living in the United States with his family on a temporary visa. Saaida and her parents were not only managing the natural, built, and media sensory environments within their home, but also an ableist, racist, and xenophobic world outside it.

SENSING SOCIALITY AND MEDIA

Media plays some role in autistic children's sensory seeking and avoiding at home and their encounters with pleasurable and painful sensory stimuli. But what does this look like up close? I found that the external senses (auditory, tactility, visual, and gustatory),[46] the internal senses (proprioceptive and vestibular), and their complex interrelation are central to autistic children's media and technology activities. These mediated behaviors are integrated into how they interpret their physical environment, the people around them, and their own sensoria.

AUDITORY
Autistic children can have challenges with auditory processing in at least two ways that shape their media use: sound volume and types of sounds. With respect to volume, loud media causes extreme discomfort for some. Nelson, father of 10-year-old Stephanie (Latina, girl), said that she would accidentally "put the volume all the way up to a hundred" using the TV remote, "and she would be freaking out because she was trying to adjust herself." Because Stephanie also did not have an effective way to communicate, this sudden auditory overload caused her increased stress. A number of children, though, preferred the volume to be very loud, which could be a source of minor or

major conflict between the child and their family members. During my interview with Kerry in the family's living room, her 6-year-old son Joey (White,
boy) sat down on the sofa and turned on the television set. The TV show
began to play very loudly, to which Kerry remarked, "Where are the remote
controls? Here they are. Let's turn them down, let's turn this down a little
bit, okay?" She explained that Joey's grandmother, who babysat him and his
brother afterschool, "lets them put it on like, 40, and I keep it on 12."

While Joey was not visibly bothered by Kerry lowering the volume,
4-year-old Bennett (White, boy) was resistant to a similar intervention from
his mom, Shelby. Bennett (who is autistic) and his twin brother, Kyle (who
has a sensory processing disorder) were playing games on their tablets in the
living room. When Bennett turned the volume up on his device, Kyle left for
the adjacent sunroom on the first floor of the house. Shelby walked over to
Kyle to ask if he had left "because Bennett's [tablet] is loud?" to which Kyle
replied, "Yeah." A few minutes later, Bennett went to join his brother but
with his tablet still set at the higher volume. Kyle protested Bennett's intru-
sion, causing Shelby to intervene. "Bennett," she asked, "can I turn you guys
down just a little bit?" "No," said Bennett, his voice slightly rising in anger
and his body tensing. Kyle, sensing conflict, moved further away from his
brother toward the other end of the sofa. "[Bennett] likes everything loud,"
Shelby shrugged, the tension defused, "Last night, he turned the TV up to 90.
I'm like, 'Really?'"

Mobile technologies with simple volume controls allowed kids like Bennett to put auditory pleasure into their own hands, both for better and for
worse. While I interviewed Stephanie's parents on a weeknight, she held the
speaker of the iPad close to her ears as she sat nearby bouncing on an exercise
ball, creating a sensory experience more to her liking than the incident with
the TV remote. Nina said that her son Raul (Latino), who was 11 years old at
the time of our second interview, liked to "keep the volume on low, but he
will press the phone or the iPod against his ear during certain parts. . . . No
visual, just listening." April, mom of 5-year-old Sofia (Latina, girl) put tape
over the speaker of her daughter's iPad to muffle the sound because Sofia
preferred it loud but also refused to wear headphones.

Other children had no issue using headphones with mobile devices, which
enabled them and other family members to each maintain their preferred
sound levels while remaining in the same room or enclosed space. "When
we are all together and it's getting too loud," said Esosa of her 7-year-old

son Chike's (Black, boy) preference for loud music on his iPod, "we are like, 'Here. Put this on.'" Kameelah mentioned that she and her husband had purposefully turned the volume setting on 6-year-old Talen's (Black, Latino, and White; boy) headphones down low so that he could raise the volume on his iPad as high as he wanted. "He ideally likes both loud," said Kameelah. Limiting the headphone's audio output bounded Talen's volume control to just one device.

Headphones were also actively chosen by children, sometimes in tandem with other objects, to curate a more comforting auditory environment. Six-year-old Olivia (White, girl) hung out on the couch while I jointly interviewed her and her mom, Bailey. Olivia had turned the volume up high on the Spotify app on Bailey's phone, and since the music was interfering slightly with our conversation, Bailey initiated a negotiation process with Olivia. She offered Olivia the option of taking a break in her bedroom upstairs, to which Olivia responded, "I think I'm going to stay here and put the blanket on me." As that did not address the issue of volume, Bailey replied, "If you want, you can go up and get headphones and put them into the phone and you can listen to it that way, okay?" Olivia agreed and the interview kept going, with the blanket and headphones allowing Olivia to meet both her social and sensory needs.

In addition to volume, certain sound qualities could also set off meltdowns. Three-year-old Aaliyah (Black, girl) was unable to bear one particular video in a series of short, educational videos about careers that aired between TV shows on PBS KIDS. Her mom, Crystal, explained, "There's a pilot, there's a scientist, and there's a teacher. But the teacher [video] bothers her." Crystal did not know what about the male teacher's voice disturbed Aaliyah, but she knew how to identify warning signs. "[Aaliyah will] get a sense when it's coming on," said Crystal, "Like the show will end and she'll think it's coming. She'll block her ears or curl her body into [her] mind." Those behaviors alerted Crystal to immediately change the channel or mute the TV in response to what Crystal described as Aaliyah's physically painful response to the auditory stimuli. "It's like a fear in her eyes," Crystal said, "when that commercial comes on. It's like, ugh. I want to save you from that pain."

TACTILITY
Autistic children incorporated tactile feedback into their media routines in a number of respects, including by playing with "fidget toys" during television viewing, using game controllers to keep their fingers busy, and

watching YouTube videos of other people's hands manipulating objects. One pervasive fidget object in children's homes were "mermaid pillows," named for sequins affixed to pillows that shimmer like scales on the mythical creature's tail. The sequins are sewn as to be flipped in two directions, with each side of the sequin reflecting a contrasting color. With the sequins, one can write messages, play with the reflecting colors, or enjoy the smooth feeling. While the low-cost trend is enjoyed by both disabled and nondisabled children,[47] the pleasure of a mermaid pillow might be felt more intensely or differently by those on the autism spectrum. In fact, on craft websites like Etsy, they are often listed for sale as a "sensory fidget."[48]

Amanda worked part-time at a home decor store where she came across the mermaid pillow and purchased it because she thought her son 3-year-old son Noah (White, boy) might enjoy the feel. "He has a lot of textural aversions," she said, "so this is just kind of like a funky texture for him to play with." The mermaid pillow stayed in the living room, but instead of being placed on the couch, it was kept atop a small table in front of the large flatscreen television. Amanda said, "He's usually not sitting. He doesn't sit very often. He's usually standing over here going—" at which point she rubbed her fingers along the sequins. Jessie had also purchased an inexpensive mermaid pillow on Amazon for Patrick to play with "when he needs to fidget" while sitting in front of the TV. She had learned about the pillowcase on a sensory processing disorder Facebook group. "It's like a disco ball," said Jessie, "That's like a sensory thing that he'll use while he is watching things."

Not all moms, though, spend significant time on Facebook groups, make Amazon purchases, or even have internet, like Danae, mother of 5-year-old Anthony (Black, boy). As an episode of the animated Disney Junior show *Doc McStuffins* played on the TV, Anthony and one of my research assistants sat next to each other on a small sofa. When Anthony began to play with her coat, Danae reprimanded him, saying, "Anthony, leave her buttons alone." Danae explained of her son's behavior, "He like the feeling. You know, if I have a shirt on and it have the thing, he be like scratching it." A few minutes later, Anthony affectionately sat in Danae's lap facing the TV set, his arm laid behind his head and his fingers lingering on the raised printed design on her T-shirt.

For some children, their media viewing habits involved seeking or avoiding certain textures. As 4-year-old Eli (White, boy) watched *Sesame Street*, he rubbed his hands over the green bristles of a toy wooden broom and pressed his palm into the cold prickliness of a pin screen, a toy in which hundreds of flat metal pins are arranged to create a three-dimensional relief when an object is pressed against the pins. Eli also placed the pin screen on his head and under his T-shirt while he watched. Sometimes the physical texture of technologies themselves shaped children's sensory experiences. When I commented on the fact that Patrick's tablet did not have a case on it, considering the high cost of the device and good chance of it breaking in a child's hands,[49] Jessie explained that the tablet was caseless because Patrick "does not like the feeling. He has wrecked tons of them. The ones that have more of the rubber feel, he has bit off."

Computer and console video gaming offered added tactility for autistic children. During my interview with then-12-year-old Saylor (White, girl), she was constantly doing something with her hands, be it rolling a tube of lip gloss around or fiddling with a Band-Aid on her toe. Saylor explicitly identified haptic feedback as part of what made gaming pleasurable to her. Besides the fun of building and playing with friends, Saylor said that she liked Minecraft and Roblox because "it was just a good way to get your hands working." In fact, the minute after she put down the Xbox controller after showing me the video game *Fortnite*, she picked up her iPhone—adorned with a *Fortnite*-branded PopSocket grip accessory—without looking at the screen and held it in her lap. These behaviors and reflections from Saylor suggested that her need to hold the phone was partly about the materiality of the object and not just the media content or social connection it provided.

Children's fascination with YouTube videos of hands manipulating objects was also an extension of their cravings for tactility. It is well documented that children and adults alike are fascinated by product unboxing videos and Kinder Surprise Egg toy videos that show close-up shots of hands twisting and turning pieces. Media studies scholar Sharif Mowlabocus writes that "the hands . . . offer a sense of vicarious touch."[50] For children who process sensory stimuli differently, these videos are appealing not just for their commercial or noncommercial content, but also for their tactile simulation and stimulation. Three-year-old Oscar (White, boy) watched hours of videos on repeat of hands making letters out of Play-Doh. Rosie pulled out her phone to show me a photo of 4-year-old Spencer (Black, boy) "making the time with Play-Doh" as he watched YouTube videos of timers counting down. "This is an example of sensory," she said, explicitly referencing the visual and tactile stimulation that the activity produced.

VISUAL

Irrespective of content or messaging, the formal features of visual media can provide sensory stimulation favored by some autistic children. This includes adjusting proximity to the screen, amplifying color contrast, and shifting visual perspectives. Various parents reported that their children preferred to keep screens very close to their faces as they watched. Nina said that Raul will "press his face up to a specific spot in the TV screen" and the screen will fill his entire field of vision. Molly reported that 4-year-old Abbey (White, girl) "has to get so close to the TV. I'm like, 'Back up,' but she gets so excited that she gets way too close to it . . . especially when they sing." With a smaller screen, I watched Abbey hover over her mom's iPhone, her face two inches from the device. Nikki, mom of 3-year-old Emma (White, girl), noted how unlike Emma's neurotypical siblings' tablet use, "Everything is close. Her eyes are fine. They were tested. But I know that there's a word for it, and I can't think of it right now, where she tends to put a lot of things up close."

A few children were visually drawn to digital media content that had been altered through device settings or effects to amplify the contrast between colors. During my interview with Esosa at her dining room table, Chike walked over to us with her iPhone. He had switched the Accessibility setting on iOS in order to play the mobile gaming app *Temple Run* in an inverted color mode. "He likes to put it in negative mode," said Esosa, "He likes the visual." Among the array of YouTube videos that I observed Abbey watching on her mom's iPhone, three of them consisted of screen recordings of apps and animated shows (e.g., *Talking Tom Cat, Pocoyo*), arranged in a grid on screen of anywhere from three to ten small video screenshots, with a different color filter added to each video so that the recordings moved identically but in assorted colors.

Mobile devices also afforded children easy manual control over the visual pace of video platforms and playback modes, including pausing, rewinding, and fast-forwarding video clips in a repetitive manner. Eight-year-old Amaya (Black, Latina, and White; girl) enjoyed the blurred visuals of scrolling up and down through YouTube's list of recommended videos on her iPad without necessarily clicking on one to watch. While watching *Sesame Street* on Jessie's iPhone, Patrick would repeatedly flip the phone 180 degrees back and forth in his right hand while viewing, a one-handed move that would have been hard to pull off with a tablet. When he turned it around, the picture on the phone shifted between vertical portrait mode and horizontal landscape mode. There were many levels of sensory pleasure for Patrick: the moving of his hands, the jostling of the screen, and the activity taking place within the *Sesame Street* content itself. Some parents, though, actively worked to limit their child stimming with mobile video. Stephanie's dad, Nelson, reported that "we started working with this new therapy where [Stephanie is] not repeating the video over and over again. She can see the whole video, but she needs to start getting out of that, going over and over it."

GUSTATORY

The gustatory system, associated with eating and taste, can also be a part of children's sensorial media experiences. For example, 13-year-old Pargev (Armenian, boy) routinely liked watching *High School Musical* on Netflix while moving potato chips back and forth between four blue plastic bowls as he ate. Media could also distract autistic children from aversions they had to particular foods.[51] Rosie recalled that Spencer will "multitask no matter what he's doing . . . [so] one of the strategies to actually get him to eat when he was younger was to put something on, because he had so many sensory things." Norah said that she will sometimes put her son Max (Asian/ Vietnamese and White, age 5) "in front of the TV to get him to eat something healthy" because he will "just blindly eat whatever is in front of him," whereas he will not eat vegetables at the dinner table. "One way I rationalize this is like, 'Well he's going to eat carrots, so it's okay for him to watch *Curious George* again,'" said Norah.

When placed into one's mouth, media objects themselves could become a problematic gustatory stim. Like Saaida in chapter 1, Patrick had an issue with trying to consume paper, leading Jessie to avoid buying print books or borrowing them from the library. "Sometimes if you're not looking, or you turn your back for a second, . . . he'll eat paper. We've had some paper issues with books," said Jessie. April mentioned that Sofia "loves puzzles, but she's been eating them lately so we've kind of put them away for now until this phase is over." They also had difficulty locating a tablet case that Sofia would not chew on. "It's kind of hard to find a case that's not edible," said April, "because anything soft is edible for her. But if we kind of just go, 'No you can't eat that, you can't eat that,' eventually she'll stop because she's like, 'They're just going to keep getting on my nerves.'"

Children found other ways to have their gustatory needs met while (metaphorically) consuming media. I found it ironic that one of the books that Sebastian repeatedly wanted renewed from the library was *The Magic School Bus Explores the Senses,* considering his own sensory issues. His mom, Cathleen, noted that he will wear a sweatband on his wrist at all times, including while watching TV, because he will otherwise chew on himself. For Patrick, the mermaid pillow provided a solution to some of his self-harm behaviors by redirecting his need for gustatory sensory stimulation. He "will bite his hand," Jessie said, "It's not anxiety related. It's just sensory seeking and behavioral. . . . [The mermaid pillow is] great because when he's watching or playing, he'll have one hand here [instead]."

PROPRIOCEPTIVE

Media additionally provided opportunities for proprioceptive input and close physical intimacy for autistic children at home. The sofa was one site of sensory ritual and pleasurable pressure on muscles and joints. Molly said that while watching TV with Abbey's dad, "they'll cuddle and he'll squeeze her and she loves that." Besides an immobile television set, mobile devices also enabled sitting side-by-side over the shared small screen. Molly noted that Abbey will "need to be thigh-to-thigh with me. . . . She'll definitely be on the phone and sit right next to me." I observed Abbey engaging in this behavior, curling up next to Molly, who rubbed Abbey's leg, arm, and back. Chike also preferred this sensation, as Esosa explained, "If everybody is down here [watching television]," pointing to the living room, "[Chike] will come and squeeze himself between people."

Children employed verbal and nonverbal communication to directly solicit proprioceptive input from their caregivers. Noticing that Olivia was having difficulty paying attention to an episode of *Kids Baking Championship* and staying in the living room during my observation, her mom, Bailey, asked her to sit down and watch the rest of the episode together. Olivia acquiesced, but conditionally, as she asked, "Will you pat my back [while we watch]? This time you got to pat fast!" Olivia lay across the lap of Bailey, who made a hand chopping motion across Olivia's back. As Jessie and Patrick watched *Despicable Me 2* together, Patrick took Jessie's hands and clapped them gently in front of his face. "Where do you want me to put the hand? You want me to rub behind your ears?" Jessie asked in response to Patrick's gestures. As she rubbed, Patrick vocalized an "ahhhhh!" of pleasure. "Oh, that's so good," she replied.

Besides stimuli from other people, children also used furniture, mattresses, and mattress-like objects to generate proprioceptive input during media use.

Saaida's bed consisted of a mattress on the floor in the living room of her family's one-bedroom apartment. Hamza reported that she preferred to watch videos on his tablet in "some gap between the bed and [the wall]. . . . She tried to fit there in a very tiny space." For families with additional room and resources, a crash pad—a large air- and foam-filled mat—provided proprioceptive input. Noah encouraged his mom, Amanda, to chase him onto the blue crash pad set up in their living room while music played on the TV. "Oh, you want to crash on the crash pad?" asked Amanda. "Crash!" Noah replied, as he set off running across the room onto the pad. Eli used the couch as a kind of crash pad while watching *Sesame Street* with Julie. As she sat on the couch, he climbed behind her and perched himself atop her shoulders. Julie then stood straight up in a pretty remarkable feat of strength and balance, lifting Eli into the air at eye level with the flatscreen TV. After pacing a bit, she dumped him onto the couch, and he laughed with delight.

As with gustatory sensations, children's unmet needs for proprioceptive input could also lead to behaviors that resulted in bodily discomfort for themselves or others. Anthony's near constant physical activity while he lay on or near Danae while they watched TV appeared to pain and maybe annoy her. "He was trying to scratch me earlier. He was like digging his nails," said Danae, "He always want me to put my arm over his face. I'm like, 'Boy . . .'" Parents who were more permissive of their children's sensory seeking behaviors used materials to redirect these actions and incorporated such objects into the home environment. As Patrick sat in Jessie's lap in front of the TV, he dug his fingernails hard into her hands and his thighs. In response, Jessie pulled out a squishy purple ball partly filled with sand from her side of the couch. "It's an Everlast [fitness brand] one," she explained, "If he's trying to dig . . . , we give him this." With a gentle firmness, she placed the ball in Patrick's hands and said, "You get my hands, you get the ball. You know the drill." Patrick dug in, literally, making happy vocal grunts as he squeezed.

VESTIBULAR

Some children sought intense vestibular input during media use, including jumping, swinging, and spinning. Six-year-old Skyler (White, boy), for example, enjoyed *Just Dance* for the Nintendo Wii gaming system, but rather than playing the game using the controller, he moved along to the songs with the help of his mom, Naomi. She explained, "He just runs in circles or jumps and does headstands because he's a big sensory seeker, and

FIGURE 6.1
Small trampoline set up in front of the television set in Noah's living room. *Source*:
Meryl Alper.

I play the music." While watching TV, children used bouncy surfaces like
small trampolines or sofas to generate vestibular input. Amanda noted that
"even when the TV's on, [Noah] won't just sit and watch a show usually.
He's jumping up and down on the trampoline while he's playing" (figure 6.1).
Jessie usually kept a trampoline for Patrick "in front of the TV and he'll jump
on it," though it was temporarily put away when I visited because Patrick
was in a full leg cast as the result of a recent corrective surgery.

Similar to proprioception, vestibular input must also be understood in
relation to the room that sensory objects take up and the square footage
of homes within which children roam. Conor and Ronan had a dedicated
playroom in their large suburban home. Karrie noted how "when watching TV or playing video games, [Conor is] very mobile. . . . He climbs up
onto the arm of the couch and then jumps off and runs around." The small
trampoline was a permanent fixture in Eli's large TV room, situated within
the spacious ground floor of his suburban house. "He kind of goes in a loop

sometimes," Julie noted, as Eli leaped across the love seat, sofa, and trampoline, frequently departing and reentering the room. "We have a whole obstacle course going now," she remarked. Anthony also made use of his couches for jumping, but within a small apartment in one of Boston's poorest neighborhoods. His exuberance while watching television in the limited floor space was marked on the wall by a hole kicked through the plaster, now covered with masking tape.

And as with YouTube videos of hands manipulating objects and simulating tactile pleasure, audiovisual media content depicting energetic movement also influenced the behaviors that children emulated and the kinds of sensory input they sought. Crystal said that if "someone is upside down in a video, [Aaliyah] wants to be upside down. Running, bumping into things intentionally because of something that she watched." While viewing an episode of the TV show *American Ninja Warrior* with Kerry, Joey jumped off the couch and waved socks on his hands while the participants on-screen swung from obstacle to obstacle. Said Kerry, "You're going to enact your Ninja Warrior–ness. You keep on, what?" "Keep on falling," responded Joey, "I was trying to fall." Julie suspected that the media content Eli liked best was also related to depictions of characters receiving vestibular input. "I do think it's the sensory. It's the episodes where characters are bouncing," she said, "There's another [*Sesame Street*] episode that has a pogo stick in it. He likes to jump, and I think he likes these episodes about the pogo sticks."

Ritualistic vestibular movement can itself be interpreted as expressing one's pleasure or displeasure with media content. This is true for nearly everyone (i.e., clapping after a staged performance), but especially among nonspeaking and minimally speaking autistic children. As Eli jumped on his trampoline, Julie pointed out, "And this is classic trampoline." Eli began to jump even more enthusiastically while watching a *Sesame Street* segment of *Abby's Flying Fairy School*, to which Julie responded, "Whoa, this is a good Abby!" Similarly, "when [Patrick] really likes a scene, he'll go on the floor and he'll do his dance thing," Jessie said. At one point, Patrick got up to dance along with *Despicable Me 2*, despite his full-leg cast. "He's able to get through even with the cast on. He's figured out how to get his sensory needs met even without [his trampoline]," she said.

Children's body movements are additionally shaped by the mobile affordances of communication technology and the extent to which media can be enjoyed hands-free or sitting still.[52] Three-year-old Ryan (White, boy), for instance, used Google Chromecast to project the YouTube Kids app onto the large flatscreen TV in the living room. The app algorithmically automated a playlist of videos while he moved about, jumping on the sofa and running back and forth between the living room and the kitchen. Julie remarked that "one of Eli's biggest challenges is he will not sit still—actually unless he is watching television. . . . And I should even clarify that. It's really only if he has an iPad, because even when he's watching television, he is jumping." Books did not hold staying power, either. Julie remarked, "As he started to move more, and it seemed his body really needed that [sensory] input, I feel like it's been much more difficult, and he is no longer interested in reading books with us."

INTERCONNECTED INTERNAL AND EXTERNAL SENSES

The internal and external sensory experiences that I have described allude to the interplay between various senses. At times, the multisensory nature of these media rituals was particularly pronounced and manifested in complex cultural, spatial, and social relations within a given child's environment. With respect to culture, 4-year-old Zahra (Azerbaijani, girl) derived great pleasure from continuous spinning while listening to music in a manner that conveyed cultural meaning for her mom, Raina. As Raina and her girlfriend Becky (who also identifies as autistic) played the song "Cheap Thrills" by musical artist Sia on Raina's phone, Zahra skipped quickly in an oval path around the living room. Raina compared Zahra's ability to seemingly turn around endlessly without getting dizzy to the Whirling Dervishes of the Mevlevi sect in her former home of Turkey. "In Turkish culture, they have these people who just go around and around," explained Raina, "They find balance and spiritual something. [Zahra] can do that for hours." "More Sia!" Zahra demanded in an authoritative manner befitting a preschooler. "She loves that feeling," Raina responded, to which Becky agreed, "She's one of those people."

Spatially, vestibular movement could be entwined with a child's preferred viewing position for audiovisual media. On ten different occasions while watching *Sesame Street*, Eli exited the TV room and reentered from the adjoining dining room. Julie hypothesized that this was not only related to his vestibular needs, but visual as well, remarking, "He often circles [the dining room table], which you can still see the TV from. . . . He likes the peripheral. He just paces." Skyler also took pleasure from the combination of body movement and peripheral vision during viewing. An indoor home gym product called the Gorilla Gym—a sort of deluxe pull-up bar with a swing and trapeze—was mounted to the top of the door frame intersecting Skyler's kitchen, dining room, and hallway. While sitting facing the kitchen, Skyler could see the dining room on his left side. The family used the room less for dining and more for computing, for on the dining room table stood a large iMac computer surrounded by stacks of DVDs in and out of their cases. The iMac was pivoted not only toward a seat at the table, but Skyler's kitchen-facing swinging position, from which he could peer sideways at the screen. While singing along to a kids' music DVD, Skyler swung to and fro on the thick ropes.

REFLECTIONS ON THE SENSES

Autistic children's engagement with new media, at home and among family members, reveal normative assumptions about the senses and sensory processing that underpin prevailing ideas about media, sociality, and neat distinctions between minds and bodies.[53] Their solitary and shared rituals and routines demonstrate how the external and internal sensory systems are connected to one another as well as complexly entwined with ordinary media use. Their stories also illustrate how intimate associations with others are co-configured not only by joint technology use, but also by the senses. Two concepts from the field of critical disability studies—"misfitting" and "access intimacy"—further highlight the centrality of sensation in the sociotechnical shaping of sociality.

According to philosopher Maurice Merleau-Ponty,[54] embodiment is intercorporeal, which means that surrounding bodies shape our sensations and that we shape the sensory experiences of other people. Feminist disability scholar Rosemarie Garland-Thomson extends this social view of embodiment to nonnormative bodies through the critical concept of the "misfit."[55] The term misfit usually has a pejorative connotation, meaning a person who is set apart from others and is not accepted based on their behavior or attitude (e.g., "social misfit"). Garland-Thomson reframes the word as neither inherently negative nor based on individual deficiency. Fitting and misfitting, Garland-Thomson explains, reflect congruent and incongruent relationships, similar to placing a square peg in either a square hole or a round one, as the metaphor goes.

Garland-Thomson's idea of the misfit locates conformity not in the peg or the hole, or in the sensing person and the sensory environment, but in their co-constitution. The concepts of misfit and misfitting are useful for understanding the extent to which one's immediate surroundings accommodate variations in the human senses. Autistic children and their families developed active strategies and designed accommodations for countering sensory misfitting at home, what some have called "therapeutic landscapes"[56] or "prosthetic environments."[57] Some of these materials, like crash pads, were specially designed to provide sensory input; in other cases, children made use of preexisting furniture and objects such as mattresses in their living spaces. Children and parents developed creative ways to work with sensoria that "misfit" their environments and enabled the child to interact with media and with their family members in a more comfortable manner.

Beyond children's immediate environments, these alterations are also relative to the wider sensory culture.[58] Some of the very therapeutic objects and toys used by autistic children—such as gyroscopes, Therapuddy, and weighted blankets—are increasingly repackaged for a mass audience as fidget spinners, slime, and gravity blankets.[59] Autonomous sensory meridian response (ASMR) videos on YouTube, which generate a pleasurable tingling sensation for some through recorded sound and movement, have gone from fringe internet content to a profitable global phenomenon.[60] There are obvious benefits for neurodivergent people to these tools becoming cheaper, more widely available, and less socially stigmatizing, especially for those without official diagnoses. Yet these fads do not automatically translate into greater disability acceptance. Stigma has long been associated with technologies considered "assistive" when used by people with disabilities but merely "helpful" for the general population.[61] The boundaries maintained between materials designated "for sensory needs" and "for play" are inherently political because acceptable use is contingent on compulsory able-bodiedness and the idealization of nondisabled bodies.[62]

Sensory cultures also exist within wider social structures. Though each body will experience some sensory misfitting, certain bodies are more likely than others to consistently misfit and face significant consequences for doing so in public and private spaces. Less socioeconomically privileged families like Saaida's must work harder to support their child's sensory self-regulation in smaller living areas with closer proximity to neighbors. Autistic people of color may be at a higher risk of physical victimization and deadly encounters with law enforcement if their behaviors, stims, or sensory meltdowns are interpreted as threatening, which may explain Danae's urge to discipline an energetic Anthony.[63] Rosie, who is White, expressed grave concern for her son Spencer, who is Black. "What if he has a melt-down in society?" she wondered aloud, "This society is very frightening right now with a Black son. It is. He has a meltdown and ends up in jail and they don't know that he has autism." The potential for autistic children to self-regulate their senses through media is relative to other degrees of free-dom, autonomy, and mobility within and outside their homes.

In addition to misfitting, the concept of "access intimacy," developed by disability justice activist Mia Mingus,[64] also helps to understand the politi-cal and social dimensions of sensory engagement with media and tech-nology. Access intimacy is "produced when interdependence informs the making of access."[65] In other words, access depends not only on accessible infrastructures and built environments, but on disabled people who are cared for and who care for others.[66] People with disabilities have long devel-oped practices of mutual aid within systems that actively work to isolate them from one another and deny them care.[67] In addition to technologies, people become affordances for each other when there are no readily avail-able tools, devices, systems, architecture, or infrastructure to address their needs.[68]

Autistic children and their families illustrate how media and technology are in many ways central to access intimacy in the context of sensory sen-sitivities. They use media content, devices, and settings as "care structures" to actively cope with a world that is often sensorially chaotic and pain-ful.[69] Mediated relationships, practices, and intimacies are forged around and through family members with different sensory processing capacities.[70] These processes are akin to what clinician and social anthropologist Brendan Hart refers to as "joint embodiment," or "an improvised social choreogra-phy whereby parents and child prompt each another verbally, gesturally, and physically as they together move through the social world,"[71] epitomized by Patrick and Jessie at the start of this chapter.

Caregivers balance the competing sensory needs of different family members, though not without conflict. Tension emerges when there is a mismatch between individuals inhabiting the same mediated space. One person's sensory comfort may cause discomfort to someone else. The unique adaptive functions that children develop through media sensory curation may not be fully understood by parents and caregivers.[72] Disabled people are intimately aware that access needs can conflict and need to undergo a negotiation process to reach a resolution, which is not always possible.[73] Sensory needs can be temporarily met through media and technology, but maintaining a sense of comfort also means regular negotiation and trade-offs. Media may be an effective method for reducing sensory overload, but it can also become problematic if it becomes a primary coping strategy.[74]

In closing, media does not just inform, entertain, and connect us to others; it also soothes and comforts sensorially. All of us have preferences for media content, settings, devices, accessories, and spaces that allow us to adjust sensory input and maintain a sense of physical and emotional well-being. By observing autistic children and their caregivers at home, as well as by talking to them about their favorite media routines and layered stimming practices, I found that responses to sensory stimuli are shaped not only by immediate social partners (e.g., parents, siblings) and social environments (e.g., living rooms, bedrooms), but also by broader social structures (e.g., immigration, housing, policing). Richer consideration of the senses allows for deeper, more critical understandings of the social norms at play and power dynamics around everyday media and technology use. Next, I conclude with this book's final body chapter, connecting autistic children's sensory experiences to their embodied emotions and how they use media to navigate complex feelings.

7 EMOTIONS

It was a humid afternoon in late June 2019 when I met Amaya, an 8-year-old Afro-Latina girl, wearing a cotton-candy-pink satin wrap on her head to protect her hair in the summer heat. I sat side-by-side with her on a white leather couch in her Boston apartment as she played games on an iPad. Kimberly, a single mom, described her daughter Amaya as an "extremely sensitive" child, one who fiercely protected other kids in class that she saw crying or thought might be hurt. Amaya's emotional intensity was bound up with her dual diagnoses of autism and obsessive-compulsive disorder (OCD). She sometimes felt intense anxiety, which was compounded by the environmental stress of living in a neighborhood with a high incidence of gun violence. Her anxiety had additionally been exacerbated the year prior by a teacher who assaulted her, leading Kimberly to transfer Amaya to another public school. "She refuses to even drive by the old school. I think she was traumatized," Kimberly said of Amaya. On top of all this, Kimberly had been fighting for the past three months with the state health insurance provider to cover additional OCD therapy for her daughter. "I will not accept it," said Kimberly, "She needs professionals that can help her."

Since the incident at school, Kimberly had seen Amaya's ongoing mental health issues manifest in a drastic change in her daily habits, including her media use. "I don't know what she's going through," Kimberly said, "but as far as any fun, I don't see that anymore." Amaya had lost interest in recreational activities like playing in the park and going swimming. Her motivation to occupy herself with LOL Surprise dolls and activities outside the home had also waned. Kimberly explained that "she doesn't want to play with toys.

Doesn't want to read books. . . . She used to be so excited to watch a new movie [and now] she doesn't want to go to the theater." Instead, Amaya was self-isolating and soothing herself within the security of her living room and through the predictability of screen media. "I know she's comfortable here," Kimberly said, "She loves laying in that sofa watching TV."

In the absence of professional help, Amaya and Kimberly had turned to an unlikely source for clinical support: YouTube. Kimberly said that Amaya will see "a [YouTube] video of people being violent or hurting each other [and] she'll stay stuck on that for a while," viewing it on repeat. The videos served some purpose for Amaya in processing her emotions, though the success of this coping mechanism was unclear. Kimberly tried to shape whatever lessons her daughter was possibly learning by talking to Amaya about the content. "I have to sit there and explain to her, 'There's a lot of bad people in this world and a lot of good people,'" Kimberly said. She also attempted to use Amaya's fascination with on-screen violence to educate her about reporting physical abuse. Kimberly had seen "a video of a teacher hitting a kid and [Amaya] saw it. So, I kind of teach her like, 'No teacher hit you, okay? Anybody hit you, you tell Mommy.'" Kimberly hoped that watching the video with Amaya and talking to her about it would offer some protection. Yet she recognized the futility of using such an individual strategy to solve institutional problems at the intersection of ableism and racism. "I'm telling my daughter to trust these people and they're hurting her," she noted, "That's messed up."

This chapter focuses on the complex ways that media and technology affect and reflect the emotions and emotional development of autistic children, including those like Amaya who have experienced significant emotional trauma and live with additional mental health conditions that are often insufficiently addressed. I begin with Amaya's story because her deep sensitivity provides a radical counterpoint to the pervasive and persistent cultural stereotype that people on the autism spectrum lack empathy, act robotically, and are unable to understand and display emotion. To the contrary, many adults on the spectrum report feeling emotions in an intense manner that can sometimes negatively impact the ease of their social communication and rapport, leading to a state of exhaustion and fatigue known as "autistic burnout."[1] In social interactions, people on the spectrum often find it uncomfortable or stressful to maintain eye contact with neurotypical people, who may instead prefer looking at or being looked at by someone straight ahead as they talk.[2] For their part, however, nonautistic people also have a hard time interpreting, recognizing, and validating the mental states and emotional expressions of autistic individuals,[3] suggesting that such miscommunication is bidirectional in nature (i.e., the "double empathy" problem).[4]

Amaya's story also highlights how emotions intersect with the sociotechnical shaping of sociality, and why it is important to understand this co-construction better, particularly its effects for autistic kids who are marginalized in multiple ways. An individual's social and emotional development is influenced directly and indirectly by technology. For Amaya, this includes how easy it was for her to replay violent YouTube videos on her iPad and a recommendation algorithm that served her such content. Sociological factors also matter, like her health insurer's denial of therapy services coverage and the systemic violence that Black girls and autistic people of color are all too often subjected to in the United States.[5] Technology and society also fundamentally affect how emotions are felt, shared, and coped with. This involves, as in Amaya's case, neurotypical expectations of emotional expression, how these norms are raced and gendered, and their impact on online and offline activities.[6]

Media and technology can both positively and negatively impact the emotional health of nonautistic children, and I found in my fieldwork for this to be true for autistic youth as well. Print, screen, and interactive media factor into how kids on the autism spectrum understand, experience, express, and manage their emotions. This relationship, however, is not always straightforward; for example, playing video games can aid autistic children in dealing with their emotional extremes as well as make emotion regulation very difficult for them. While kids on the spectrum sometimes express emotion differently than their neurotypical peers, this difference is not inherently a deficit. Gaining a richer understanding of the emotional complexity of autistic children, as well as how media impacts their emotional development, can result in educational, therapeutic, and social services that better addresses their diverse needs.[7] Their perspectives also offer a unique view of broader societal and ethical discussions about computers and computer algorithms that sense and respond to emotions, the neurotypical models of emotionality that such tools largely employ, and the unexpected role of autistic children in the development of these widespread technologies.

THEORIES OF EMOTION, AUTISM, AND TECHNOLOGY

The role of emotions in human development, culture, and social organization is well studied and touches upon a wider range of academic disciplines than can possibly be explored here in depth.[8] Three topics, though, are of particular relevance for understanding autistic children's emotional engagement with media: theoretical frameworks for emotion and human development; the relationship between autism and emotionality; and how computers impact the ways that feelings are experienced, conveyed, measured, and sometimes manipulated. Taken together, this body of literature illustrates that normative conceptions of emotion shape how autistic children are configured through and by the sociotechnical systems that they engage with on a daily basis.

EMOTIONS AND EMOTIONAL DEVELOPMENT

In broad terms, emotional development involves learning what emotions are, understanding how and why we feel them, recognizing one's feelings and those of others, and developing strategies for managing emotions.[9] Debates and discussions about the basic foundations of human emotions are ongoing.[10] Sociologist Arlie Hochschild theorized that there are two main models of emotion: organismic and interactional.[11] In an organismic approach, emotions are driven primarily by our biological processes and urges. From an interactional perspective, our emotions strongly depend on social and cultural factors. Arguments for the former are rooted in the intellectual traditions of psychology, neurobiology, and evolutionary biology, and for the latter in sociology and anthropology. Within the organismic tradition, there are also the discrete and functional views of emotion, in that emotions are biologically set in motion (discrete) or emerge with age (functional).[12]

One of the primary theorists behind the discrete view is psychologist Paul Ekman, who proposed a core set of universal human emotions: happiness, anger, sadness, disgust, surprise, fear, and (later in his work) contempt.[13] Ekman's influence on popular understandings of emotion is wide reaching; for example, Pixar consulted with him in developing their hit animated film *Inside Out*, in which emotions are personified through fictional characters.[14] Even if one accepts the premise of Ekman's view, that some emotions are universal, the functional approach argues that just certain primary ones are present at birth, like contentment, interest, and distress. Other emotions are learned or require greater cognitive development.[15] Only at around 6 months do children begin to experience joy, surprise, sadness, disgust, anger, and fear. Secondary feelings like embarrassment and empathy emerge between 18 and 24 months of age, with pride, guilt, and shame appearing closer to 24 to 36 months.[16] Key developmental phases (i.e., puberty) are also associated with widespread changes in young people's emotional regulation.[17]

This standardized, linear understanding of emotions leaves little room for contextual, cultural, and social influences, which the interactionist approach expands upon. For example, frequent periods of instability in the family environment (e.g., divorce) and societally (e.g., war) may cause children to suffer from short-term stress and long-term challenges with socioemotional adjustment. The beliefs and values of a child's culture also shape their emotional development. Certain societies emphasize individual responsibility for one's emotions more so than collective concern for mental well-being.[18] Children additionally learn over time to internalize the displayed emotional rules of their given cultures, including hiding the outward appearance of their inner feelings. A variety of environmental, family, and child factors and stressors affect how any one child develops. The emotional competencies that children are expected to acquire are reflective of the broader society, cultural context, and historical moment in which they live.[19]

AUTISM AND EMOTIONS

It is through this dynamic lens that the emotional development of autistic children must be understood, as well as the role that autism plays in how cultures think about emotion.[20] Society discursively positions people on the spectrum as "emotional suspects," in that they are "defined by their atypical emotions and then subject to modification and regulation" through a range of often intensive and sometimes coercive behavioral, therapeutic, and educational interventions.[21] Within biomedical discourse, autism is frequently called upon to frame typical emotional development.[22] In the field of psychology, for example, "theory of mind" gained prominence in the late twentieth century as a concept that describes an individual's ability to empathize with and understand the desires, intentions, and beliefs of other people.[23] The claim that autistic people by definition lack a theory of mind pervades clinical psychology, though autistic researchers and collaborators have recently challenged its empirical rigor.[24]

The emotional challenges that many autistic adults and children experience are very real, but they are reflective of far more than just the individual autistic person. Beginning in early childhood and lasting into adulthood, kids on the autism spectrum are more likely to have difficulty regulating their emotions than their nonautistic peers. This includes trouble calming down after getting upset, rapid mood changes, temper outbursts, and becoming easily frustrated.[25] Social factors also shape autistic children's emotional regulation, including parent stress levels in the home environment and negative peer relationships.[26] Research suggests that autistic kids may additionally have more difficulty identifying, labeling, and communicating their feelings and emotions, also known as alexithymia (translated from Greek as "without words for emotions").[27]

Yet focusing primarily on difficulties may distract us from how kids on the spectrum experience a full range of emotions (i.e., affect), including happiness and satisfaction. People on the spectrum commonly say that they feel emotions intensely, both their own and those of others, and that these feelings are linked to their sensory processing.[28] Autistic memoirist Ido Kedar writes that he sees "qualities in people like color. . . . It's like a hint of their soul. . . . My mom is blue but she can be red if she is angry."[29] Expressions like Kedar's also complicate the already highly critiqued idea that our observable behaviors are necessarily indicative of our internal emotional states and perceptions.[30] Those on the spectrum may display emotion differently than neurotypical people in terms of the frequency, duration, and intensity of their emotional presentation.[31] Current research suggests that these differences extend to facial expressions, body movement, and vocalization.[32] Autistic people's differing styles of emotion expression, recognition, and interpretation, however, are all too often falsely assumed to be a lack thereof.

AFFECTIVE TECHNOLOGIES AND AUTISM

Considering their unique affective experiences, individuals on the spectrum have much to add to ongoing discussions about how accurately computers can interpret emotions and the ethics of whether technologies should be used to do so at all.[33] Powered by artificial intelligence (AI) and machine learning algorithms, affective computing technologies process and attempt to predict human emotion.[34] They have been deployed in contexts as varied as remote test taking, job interviews, and mental health assessments.[35]

Critics contend that individual and social harms may result from inferences that are made by using these automated tools, many of which are predicated on reductive models of emotion like Ekman's.[36] Inferring affect from biological markers like tone of voice and eye contact can lead to psychological profiling that would disproportionately impact the most marginalized in society.[37] Others argue that affective technologies may lead to a resurgence in physiognomy, a pseudoscience claiming to use measures of the body to make determinations about a person's moral, mental, and emotional fitness.[38] If used without consent, these tools threaten civil liberties, especially when linked to other personal data. Emotion recognition technologies can also be highly unreliable, raising questions about whether their intrusiveness and lack of transparency are worthwhile trade-offs.[39]

Among these many criticisms, an often-overlooked critique of affective technologies is their complicated entwinement with autism.[40] Founded in 2009, software company Affectiva markets itself as "the largest emotion data repository in the world."[41] The start-up packages its facial emotion recognition system Affdex for mass market uses including audience analytics and automotive sensing, and partners with other companies to combine its algorithm with biometric sensors that capture physiological data like heart rate. Crucially, Affectiva's emotion AI was originally based on autism intervention technologies designed by cognitive scientists and computer engineers at Cambridge University and the Massachusetts Institute of Technology (MIT) Media Lab. The technology was initially intended to help autistic children read and respond to the social and emotional cues of neurotypical people through a wearable device worn prosthetically, like glasses.[42]

When Affectiva spun out of MIT, it was on the premise that future developments in emotion AI would inevitably feed back into improved assistive technologies (or that "a device that could work for [television pilot audience testing at] FOX could also better assist the autistic.")[43] Aiding autistic people is Affectiva's "assistive pretext," a term introduced by media historian Mara Mills to describe "the resourcing of disability within technoscience." It applies to a number of technologies, such as the telephone, whose inventors first gained access to resources and capital investment under the pretense of their innovation assisting disabled populations. However, over time, these technologies have become increasingly distanced from the needs, hopes, and desires of people with disabilities.[44] Autism is drawn upon materially and discursively in the field of emotion AI and affective computing, without much critical reflection on the harms done to disabled individuals in this field's technological developments.

Beyond emotion recognition algorithms, ordinary media and communication technologies may additionally play an important role in autistic people's emotional lives. Cultural studies scholar Raymond Williams described how cultural artifacts can symbolize and concretize the fluid experience of emotion as a "structure of feeling."[45] This includes social media platforms that analyze the sentiment in our messages and allow us to "heart" one another's posts, actions which then feed back into platforms' recommendation algorithms.[46] One of the more ubiquitous media forms that exemplify a structure of feeling are emoji. These small graphical icons—which began in Japan as emoticons (punctuation marks arranged to look like facial expressions)—are standardized across our phones and computers. Emoji punctuate communication by relaying mood and affect in a quick and efficient manner.[47] They may simplify emotion, but that is not necessarily a bad thing. Autistic people report that having a shared and widely available emotional language through emoji helps make their written communicative intent clearer and aids them in understanding the social cues of others.[48]

In short, how we understand emotions and how we understand technology are not only connected but are also socially shaped by how we understand autism and autistic people.[49] In writing about early twentieth century thinkers and how they imagined electronic mass communication, media scholar Brent Malin uses the term "media physicalism" to describe the "[location of] emotion in media technologies themselves as well as in a decidedly technologized version of the human body."[50] Contemporary discourses of media physicalism reduce the experiences of autistic people to a narrow set of mental and physical traits that are isolated from the complexity of their everyday emotional lives. Autistic children are more likely to have their affective responses studied in the controlled setting of a lab and operationalized through algorithms than to be understood as fully fledged individuals whose daily uses of mass, digital, and interactive media influence their emotional development, and in sometimes unexpected ways.

MEDIA, TECHNOLOGY, AND THE EMOTIONS OF AUTISTIC CHILDREN

Media offers all young people endless ways to observe, feel, and learn about emotions, which can have both positive and negative effects on their emotional development in the short and long terms.[51] These span young children developing fears and phobias as a result of early exposure to scary movies, school-age kids playing video games that boost their mood, and teenagers using social media to cope with stressful feelings during the COVID-19 pandemic.[52] Media can also be a tool that helps kids put into words the feelings that they have difficulty expressing otherwise. For example, children in preschool or early elementary school grades may engage in pretend play using violent or dark themes from media texts because these stories allow them to examine human emotions up close and without serious repercussions.[53]

For autistic children and adolescents, there is limited research on how popular media and mainstream technology impact their emotional development, as well as the many factors that may mediate this influence. In terms of benefits, the video game platform Minecraft and associated web-based forums for autistic players can enable youth on the spectrum to express their emotions in ways they likely would not have in face-to-face settings and to receive emotional support and reassurance.[54] On the other hand, pediatricians have raised concerns about parents of young autistic children overusing media as a way of keeping their child calm and occupied, warning that this may lead to maladaptive behaviors (e.g., difficulty transitioning to nonmedia activities).[55] Autistic children who have a high threshold for sensory input may also seek out very arousing content with vivid imagery, like violent video games, which can then negatively impact their emotion processing and regulation if they do not have the maturity to fully understand that content.[56]

In my fieldwork with autistic kids and their families, I identified four main themes in terms of how technologies play into their emotional lives: (1) *understanding*, (2) *experiencing*, (3) *expressing*, and (4) *managing* emotions. These themes could apply to any one child, such as Kahlil, a minimally speaking 7-year-old Black boy. His mom, Monisha, thought that media was emotionally beneficial for him in a number of ways. She said, "I think him watching certain stuff shows him certain emotions that he might have difficulty learning otherwise" (understanding). Kahlil could also "be watching something that's like sad to him [and] he starts crying" (experiencing). Monisha tried to use media to help Kahlil convey his emotions, but it was not always successful. "I want to know what he's feeling" (expressing), she said, "[I try] to show him different things [but] when he gets overwhelmed, he starts crying sometimes" (managing). Kahlil's experiences also exist against a societal backdrop of institutional racism, in which Black boys and girls are more likely to be misperceived as angry by institutional authority figures than are their White peers.[57] An array of media could help and hinder the emotional development of autistic kids like Kahlil, which was in turn shaped by a range of individual and social factors.

UNDERSTANDING EMOTIONS

First, media can help scaffold autistic children's emotion recognition in various beneficial ways. Donna, mom of Sam—an 8-year-old White boy who is nonspeaking and has an intellectual disability—described her son as an avid viewer of the Nick Jr. preschool show *Blue's Clues*, which is about a mystery-solving dog named Blue. Sam would use his Dynavox voice output communication device while watching the program to label and name the character's emotional states, like "Blue happy" or "Blue sad." Sam would also express empathy in embodied ways besides speech. Rubbing his shoulder "means he's sorry for people," Donna said. When she cried, Sam would use his Dynavox to say "'Mom is sad' and then [try] to wipe the tears off my face." Though *Blue's Clues* has a curriculum emphasizing reasoning skills, media that was not expressly educational could also be a learning tool. Raina, mother of Zahra, a 4-year-old girl of Azerbaijani descent, said that "even emotions, she learns from videos. . . . She knows the difference of scary and not scary. Let's say, 'Halloween videos [on YouTube] are scary.'"

The emotional awareness of 11-year-old Karim, an Algerian American boy, was shaped by educational content that he found on YouTube. He liked to repeat lines from short videos that aired between 30-minute episodes on the linear PBS KIDS television channel and that YouTube users had recorded and uploaded to the site. When I spoke with Karim about his favorite TV shows, he kept repeating the line, "Visit PBSKIDS.org. There's a lot of great information for grown-ups, too." The first time that he said it, our conversation went as follows:

Karim: Visit PBSKIDS.org. There's a lot of great information for grown-ups, too.

Meryl: There *is* a lot of great information for grown-ups, I would say.

Karim: What's the information of?

Meryl: So sometimes they'll give information for how parents can have conversations and talk with their kids after they see episodes.

Karim: If kids are sad, they ask them to use their words?

Meryl: Yeah, yeah. If you have feelings, if you ever feel sad, that you can always talk to your parents about how you feel, yeah.

Karim: *Daniel Tiger's Neighborhood?*

Meryl: Oh, yeah, that's good. *Daniel Tiger's Neighborhood* is a lot about talking about how you feel.

Karim: Visit the neighborhood at PBSKIDS.org.

Based on my professional background working in the children's media industry, I recognized Karim's scripting (or repetition) of content from a short PBS KIDS video that drove television viewers of the educational preschool program *Daniel Tiger's Neighborhood* (an animated spinoff of *Mister Rogers' Neighborhood*) to the network's website ("Visit the neighborhood at PBSKIDS .org"). I also saw his choice of phrasing as a valid form of communication. Some linguists have argued that scripting and echolalia (i.e., precisely repeating aloud words and sounds that one has heard) are tools accessible to autistic people to draw upon in conversation.[58] They are an interactional resource that we might consider akin to a type of technology. In his own way, Karim had conveyed a lesson about emotions ("If kids are sad, they ask them to use their words?") that he had learned from *Daniel Tiger.*[59]

Research has shown that animated content—including material from *Daniel Tiger*—can provide straightforward visual representations of emotions that are easier for autistic children to comprehend and learn from.[60] The children and parents that I spent time with confirmed this in a number of ways. Becky, girlfriend of Zahra's mom, Raina, and an autistic woman herself, offered insights as to why Zahra was attracted to animated content more so than live action shows, especially when it came to interpreting emotional cues. "Social interactions, or looking people in the eye, or their facial expressions can be complicated for [Zahra] to interpret," Becky said, "Usually cartoons or computer animation, the facial expressions are pretty simple." Because of the exaggerated emotional expressions of animated characters, Zahra "knows if they're happy because they're really excited, versus a human [who] can really be confusing," Becky explained.

Molly, mom of Abbey, a 4-year-old White girl, also credited cartoons, specifically YouTube videos and mobile games that labeled emotions and feelings, with positively influencing her daughter's emotional development. Molly said that as a toddler, Abbey "never could process emotions. You could sit there and hurt yourself and bawl your eyes out and she would just not know what to do." Abbey had instead learned to mimic empathetic responses from a game she played on Molly's smartphone that involved taking care of a baby panda. When Abbey saw little kids crying on the playground, she would say,

"'Oh, the baby's sad. Oh, do you need a kiss?' She'll repeat it as if the child is a panda," Molly said. She concluded that "media has definitely played a huge role" in Abbey "[knowing] kind of the social cues that a child should understand." The fact that Abbey may have been mimicking these responses, more so than spontaneously generating them, did not take away from their meaningfulness for Molly. In all, media and technology in both digital and nondigital forms could help autistic children identify and label emotions that were also interpretable by their closest social partners.

EXPERIENCING EMOTIONS

Print, screen, and interactive media could directly influence the emotional experiences of kids on the spectrum and elicit disproportionately strong emotions. Leslie, mom of 3-year-old Oscar (White, boy), thought that her son's deep interest in alphabet videos on YouTube was tied to his emotions. "I guess he feels things for letters that the rest of us don't," she surmised, "And I don't know if that's just because [in] kids' shows, often the letters are anthropomorphized, they have faces, and they do things." Sometimes strong emotions generated by media had the potential to overwhelm autistic children. "Could be the content, and the movie could be anything," said Marcia, mom of Brendan, a 12-year-old White boy, but "if it's sad, he'll just outright cry." Jamie, mom of 10-year-old Levi (Latino and White, boy), said that "for movies, we'll be watching and he'll get emotional and then he'll get mad at himself for being emotional if there's a sad part." Pamela, mom of Rosalita, an 11-year-old White girl, reported that "if a sad song comes on, [Rosalita will] cry. So . . . just very much a feeling kid. . . . But in the same respect, we can put on a happy song, she's a happy kid." This strong reactivity was not universal, though. Jennifer, a genderqueer autistic person and mom of Casey (a 6-year-old White transgender girl), said that her daughter "has plenty of emotions. And I have plenty of emotions." But when it came to media, Jennifer said of Casey, "I don't think she's one to get really tied into the emotions of the things so much."

Some parents compared their children's emotional reactions to media to other situations and stimuli. Julie, for example, found it interesting that her 4-year-old nonspeaking White son Eli was "very sensitive" to sad moments in TV content but displayed almost no reaction to the emotional distress of others in person. "If one of his siblings gets hurt in real life," Julie said, "it's not even on his radar screen. He shows very little sensitivity to others except for when it's been on television." Because of Eli's heightened sensitivity to on-screen emotionality, Julie suspected that he preferred watching *Sesame Street* over *Daniel Tiger* because he found the latter to be too emotionally intense. She described an episode of *Daniel Tiger* that Eli had seen in which a bird's nest falls out of a tree. "Nothing bad happens to Daniel Tiger," Julie said, "but Eli is crying and very upset during that scene. He'll really whine and react negatively. . . . That's an interesting window into Eli." It should be noted that Eli struggled to consistently use his iPad and augmentative and alternative communication app to communicate, so the "window" that media provided into Eli's emotional state was of particular value to Julie.

Karrie saw a connection between her 9-year-old son Conor's (White) reactions to strongly emotive media and his impulsive reactions more broadly. She described his challenges as very "all or nothing. He'll be all the way sad or all the way happy and it'll flip." She mentioned a time when Conor refused to get ready for school and reacted by wanting to throw out his toys. When she asked why, he responded, according to Karrie, "'Because, should I always be in school and never have fun and never get to play with my toys and always have to be at school?'" Karrie recognized that same high degree of arousal and impulsivity in his response to movies that elicited strong feelings. She said that "Conor, in movies, he doesn't like um . . . emotional distress? He really doesn't like it when characters are mean to each other." She gave an example of when their family went to see the Pixar film *Coco* and Conor stormed out at the beginning of the film during a scene in which the grandmother destroys her grandson's guitar. Karrie said, "He's like, 'I don't like that mean grandma. I don't know why she's so mean. I'm not going to watch this with the mean grandma.'" As a result, Karrie stayed with Conor in the theater lobby while the rest of the family finished watching.

Besides media with themes of sadness and grief, autistic children could be profoundly affected emotionally by physiologically arousing violent or sexually explicit content that they encountered online, sometimes unintentionally. For instance, 11-year-old Rosalita said that she did not like seeing violent media content. "I don't like seeing rude stuff on YouTube. Like, I don't like seeing somebody shooting guns or learning how to shoot guns in public," she said. Rosalita was visibly upset—frowning and tearing up—just by talking about such material with me, and I did not dwell on it further. It seemed likely that this content was not something that Rosalita sought out but had found its way to her through YouTube's recommendation algorithms.

Brianna described an incident in which her 13-year-old White son Adrian had accidently discovered online pornography featuring Pokémon characters, much to his horror and dismay. "Unfortunately, it was with characters that he likes, so it was very disturbing to him," she said. Brianna had discovered Adrian's viewing history when conducting a regular review of his smartphone. When she approached her son about it, "He cried and he cried and [said,] 'And it's just really weird, Mom,'" she reported. Because Adrian had already been seeing a therapist for his anxiety, Brianna and her husband turned to her for assistance. "We talked to his therapist. 'How do we talk to him? How do we get through this?'" she recalled asking.

When I later interviewed Adrian, he did not bring up this incident, nor did I ask him about it. He did, however, mention a very different instance of media eliciting strong emotions. "I had probably the most conflicting feelings ever when I got a *Warrior Cats* graphic novel for Christmas," he said, "It was probably the most emotionally diverse time in my life so far." (*Warrior Cats* is a young adult fantasy fiction series about clans of feral cats living in the forest.) It was not the media itself that elicited a strong and varied emotional reaction for Adrian, but the social context around its consumption. Adrian's "most conflicting feelings ever" stemmed from perceived social pressure to express public appreciation of the series. He explained, "I felt like no matter how good the series is, I was like, 'Oh my gosh, this is what everyone else does. It's trendy.'" Since Christmas, Adrian had somewhat learned to manage his feelings. "I'm not a hundred percent over it," he said, "but if somebody says the [name of the] series, I'll be like, 'Oh, cool' and talk to them about it rather than me like cringing away or like getting awkwardly silent about it." Such attunement to the perspectives of others clearly evidences theory of mind and Adrian's understanding of social expectations, running counter to dominant autism theories. It was not only media content that could elicit strong emotions, but its social reception as well.

EXPRESSING EMOTIONS

Besides arousing emotions, popular media and technology could also act as a conduit for autistic children's affective expression, including talking about their feelings and communicating their emotional states to others. For nonspeaking and minimally speaking autistic children, media can be an especially powerful tool of self-expression.[61] Four-year-old Bella, who was of Cape Verdean descent, loved the Pixar film *The Incredibles* and its sequel, which I observed her at home watching on the Netflix app on her father's iPhone. Bella's mom, Angelica, said that the intense emotions displayed by characters in the film gave her daughter a vocabulary to use to express her own feelings. When Bella is angry, Angelica said, "She's been saying 'Mr. Incredible' because when [the character] Mr. Incredible gets mad he'll say, 'I'm Mr. Incredible!'" For 10-year-old Stephanie, a Mexican American girl, her parents interpreted the music that she played loudly on her iPad as an expression of her mood, in large part because she could not talk, and she was not receiving enough therapeutic services from either the state or her school to support her use of an alternative communication system at home.

Some autistic adolescents reflected upon their own trajectories of emotional expression and the role of media in that aspect of their development. When I asked Saylor, a 12-year-old White girl, what fictional character she most identified with, she said that when she was little, "I used to be like Judy Moody," referring to a book series about a third-grade girl with a temperamental personality. "I was never happy. I used to cry all the time. And I had like no friends because I would cry every time I made friends." She added, however, "Now, I'm the total opposite and I talk to people all the time." Her experiences expressing emotions were in some respects typical of a tween girl and in other ways more connected to her autism. Saylor primarily used social media, she said, "to spread positivity. . . . People just like joke around and I try to join in some of the people stuff." This included sending silly Snapchat photos, sharing funny TikTok videos, and making posts about body positivity. ("This one says, 'Real girls are never perfect but perfect girls are never real,'" Saylor said, showing me one such Instagram post.)

Kids on the spectrum may also use media to cope with uncertainty in their lives. Levi enacted a desire to feel powerful through his engagement with fictional narratives involving battles between good and evil. "He likes the bad guys," his mom, Jamie, said, "I almost feel like to him, that's how he makes sense of his emotions." Levi himself talked of deriving pleasure from his identification with villainous media characters. When I asked him about his favorite characters, he said, "I like supervillains," especially Loki from the Marvel Comics universe. As to why he liked this character so much, he explained that "Loki is the evil one and I love evil. Because I am evil." It was hard to tell if Levi had an active imagination, underlying emotional issues, was processing traumatic experiences, or some combination of all of the above. Certain dark emotions did seem to stem from his parents' frequent relocation of the family. His father, Jesse, had difficulty securing full-time work, and the family regularly moved as a result.

Levi incorporated his emotions into his fantasies, often with violent or aggressive themes from media. One of his favorite television programs was *Liberty's Kids*, a relatively tame animated series for grade schoolers about historical events leading up to the US Revolutionary War. Levi imagined himself and his sister on the side of the colonists and his parents were the British seeking to maintain control of the colony through a pretend edict called "the Watching Act." Levi spoke to his parents as if the Watching Act were real. With some sadness, Jamie recalled, "He'll talk about, 'My mom . . . I used to trust her, but she made the Watching Act.'" Levi brought up the Watching Act during our interview in specific reference to his frequent relocating. He said, "If the Watching Act survives, it will not survive any moving, any more moving." Using narrative material from *Liberty's Kids*, Levi was casting himself as a patriot rebelling against his parents as the creators and enforcers of rules that he thought were unfair.

Liberty's Kids was not the only media property that Levi drew upon when working through his anger and resentment. As I observed him on the computer viewing LEGO *Star Wars* stop-motion animation videos on YouTube, Levi said out loud, "I'm building an army right now." "An army? Of *Star Wars*?" I asked. "Yeah," Levi responded, "Obviously, to take over my parents." Jamie and Jesse figured prominently in his *Star Wars* fantasy play. "I want, really, to start my own empire and destroy the Republic," Levi said. I asked him what he would get if he did so, to which he replied, "Revenge." "[And] who would you seek revenge upon?" I asked in response. At this moment in the interview, we could both hear his parents' laughter coming from the living room. "That," Levi replied, which I interpreted as revenge upon his parents, represented in his fantasy as "the Republic."

For their part, Jamie and Jesse struggled in knowing where to draw the line in letting Levi have his fantasies. Levi spoke of imaginary friends who "want me to be evil." He also said that his favorite *Star Wars* character was Kylo Ren, who in the most recent films kills his father and makes multiple attempts to kill his mother. Jesse and Jamie's efforts to curb Levi's media fantasy play involved limiting his access to screen media as a form of punishment. In the playroom where I observed Levi, a handwritten poster listing "Family Rules" was taped to the wall. I asked Levi if he could read them aloud to me. "Be safe. Be kind. Stop pretending when it's not pretending time—do not like that one," he added. Media with themes of war and violence connected with Levi and likely made him feel empowered. He figured his parents into these fantasies, either as victims or villains. Though Levi openly expressed these imaginings to them, it was unclear if they were able to help him process and resolve his underlying distress.

MANAGING EMOTIONS

Autistic children's ability to self-manage their emotions could be both supported and challenged by their use of print, screen, and interactive media, as well as bound up with parenting strategies for instilling emotional self-regulation in their children.

SUPPORT Media and technology can aid autistic children in regulating the extremes of their emotions. Sometimes these behavior management techniques are parent-initiated. Hamza, a Bengali immigrant, said that his 8-year-old daughter Saaida loves "traditional songs, in my country," so much so that when "she becomes more hyperactive or she shouts loud, then we give this type of song. She stops." Nina noted that her nonspeaking Latino son Raul, who was 11 at the time, was starting to have "a harder time with anger and emotion and tantrums" at the start of puberty. He could earn up to three hours of iPod time at night for managing his behavior well but could lose time if not. Nina and her husband explained to Raul that his feelings were valid but learning to keep them in check was important. "We always tell him, 'We honor your feelings,'" Nina said, "'But at the same time, we still have to be not destructive in class and not throw a tantrum and scream at the top of our lungs.'"

Autistic children themselves also turned to media to work through their emotions. Thirteen-year-old Moira, a nonspeaking White girl, employed media to situationally calm herself; in her case, to reduce anxiety before regularly getting her blood drawn. Moira's mom, Vanessa, explained that her daughter frequently stimmed on YouTube, repeatedly watching "videos of kids getting shots and vaccinations." Vanessa was baffled that "many families post [videos] like 'Watch my child freak out,'" garnering hundreds of thousands of views, but she saw the effect they had on Moira specifically as a viewer. "Now, when she gets blood work," reported Vanessa, "she's just a champ." Moira habitually viewed YouTube videos of minors in distress at the doctor's office, doing so ostensibly to manage her own discomfort in a similar situation. Far from being an exceptional habit, Vanessa compared Moira's behavior to how the general population uses different strategies for emotion management. She said, "All of us need self-soothing time, and I'm sure there are behaviors that we engage in when we're alone that maybe we wouldn't do in front of other people." Autistic kids, especially those with limited speech, may be getting something extra out of the emotional language and sensory gratification that media provides.[62]

Like Moira, Rosalita had developed tactics for self-managing stressful feelings through her media use. When I asked her if she could show me some of her favorite toys, Rosalita pulled out a box of Pokémon cards from her closet. "My favorite Pokémon card is Meditite," she said of the character (figure 7.1). I asked Rosalita what she liked about Meditite, to which she responded, "When I see it, I feel like meditating." The name of the Pokémon not only sounded like the word "meditate" to Rosalita, but the character also resembled a person meditating, sitting in a yoga position with their arms extended and thumb and forefinger curled together. The Pokémon card prompted Rosalita to check in with her emotions. "When I get angry," she said, "I just meditate myself out to get calm."

Besides helping during periodic moments of emotional dysregulation, media could also provide autistic children with a means of processing complex emotions during turbulent time periods in their life. For example, Amaya, discussed at the beginning of this chapter, had been abused and used YouTube to process her trauma. Jackson, an 11-year-old White boy, used media to cope with a highly distressing experience, but in a different way. Jackson's dad had been in and out of the hospital for colon cancer, and while it was affecting him emotionally, he had difficulty expressing those feelings with words. His mom, Linda, reported, "Sometimes with me, he still can't express when he gets mad. He'll want to hit or scream." At one point during his extended hospital stay, Jackson's dad had called home from the hospital and Jackson did not even want to speak to him "because he was just so mad with him," Linda said.

Upon Jackson's dad returning home from the hospital, though, a nightly ritual of father–son TV viewing (of the game and variety shows *Jeopardy*, *America's Funniest Home Videos*, and *Ellen's Game of Games*) helped to mend and strengthen the relationship between Jackson and his dad. "They watch this special TV program together certain nights," said Linda, "It wasn't like that before [my husband] got cancer. So, it's like a little closeness and a

FIGURE 7.1
Rosalita holds up her Pokémon card for the character Meditite. *Source*: Meryl Alper.

thing that he has." These shows clearly held some resonance for Jackson, as he asked me out of the blue during our interview, "Did you see the *America's Funniest [Home] Videos* videos on Sunday?" I said that I had not, but I asked (having already spoken to Linda), "Do you watch them with your dad sometimes?" "Yep, we watched them yesterday," he happily replied.

CHALLENGES   While media and technology could help with autistic children's self-management of emotions, it could also contribute to and dovetail with their existing emotional regulation difficulties. Some parents were conflicted about using media as a coping mechanism. Rosalita's mom, Pamela, thought that telling her daughter, "'If you calm down, you can have the tablet,' is just very counterproductive. . . . It's like, 'Okay, we need to calm ourselves. Understand we're not using the tablet to do that.'" Rosalita herself recognized that unlimited access to media could have negative cognitive effects. When I asked her if her parents had any rules about screens, she replied, "The rule of screen time is, if you play like too much screen, it will make your brain melt," a feeling of overstimulation that she said she had experienced before.

Some autistic children had trouble keeping their feelings in check while engaging in very physiologically arousing media, most notably video games. Nine-year-old Matt (White, boy) was described as cold and emotionless by his dad, Pedro, and mom, Beca. "He doesn't have feelings, to be honest," said Pedro. "He has no empathy," Beca said. Pedro added that even if Matt saw "somebody crying [in front of him], he's going to keep playing his game." While it was impossible to confirm Pedro and Beca's claims and determine whether Matt was capable of empathizing with others, he did seem to experience a vast range of feelings, including excitement, anger, and sadness, particularly as it related to video games.

With respect to excitement, Matt displayed a high threshold for video games that were very stimulating. When I observed him and his younger brother, 7-year-old Bryan—who was also autistic—playing side-by-side on the computers in their bedroom, Matt had selected a game with rather graphic violent content: a prison-themed role-playing game on Roblox. An online game platform and game generation system, Roblox allows users to program and play games created by other users, some of which are far more violent and sexually explicit than Roblox's blocky, child-friendly aesthetic suggests.[63] In the first-person shooter game that Matt chose, inmates, criminals, and guards fight each other using guns and crude knives. "Oh my god! O-M-G," Matt yelled aloud as he played, "They got the most insane guns. Look here, criminals. I got him! I got them! We got the totally insane criminals!"

In terms of anger, Matt had difficulty controlling his impulses. He "hurts his brother, a lot. Since he was a baby," Pedro said. Playing video games together often escalated this baseline level of conflict. Beca reported, "They excite each other and sometimes Bryan does something and Matt doesn't like it. He physically will hurt Bryan, will punch him." Matt had a hard time stopping himself from being physically aggressively outside of the digital game space. "Like, 'He push me in the game, he push me in reality' . . . Matt, he doesn't know the limits," Beca said. She and Pedro were not only worried about Matt's lack of impulse control, but also his younger brother's submission to it. Bryan would make excuses for Matt to keep him out of trouble. Bryan understood that "his brother loves him and he doesn't have control of this," Beca said, but at the same time, she and Pedro did not want Bryan to associate love with suffering. It's "very concerning for us," Beca explained, "I don't want him to understand that [it's okay for] anybody else . . . to hurt him."

Yet Matt was quite emotionally sensitive. He cried and was "devastated," Pedro said, when a teenage player online that Matt did not know verbally called him a "dumb jerk" over the headset connected to the PlayStation 4 game they were playing together. Pedro drew a distinction between Matt's own feelings and his recognition of others' emotions. He said that Matt was "egocentric" because he was "ultra, mega, hypersensitive about himself" when others were mean to him online and offline, but that he lacked "self-awareness" because "he never sees that the same thing that he does all the time hurts other people." Though Matt and Bryan both had a diagnosis of autism, they had diverging emotional experiences, which were themselves shaped by the technology they used, by the people they interacted with on those platforms, and by one another within the digital game space and inside their shared bedroom.

Like Matt, Jeremiah, an 8-year-old White boy, had difficulty controlling his emotions during video game play. His mom, Natasha, reported that the staff at his afterschool program "were mentioning to us that Jeremiah never plays games [there] because he gets too mad when he loses. He has meltdowns." I observed these outbursts firsthand while he played Minecraft on the Xbox at home with Natasha, dad Neil, and younger sister Chloe. Jeremiah got very upset when Chloe did not notice that the sun was going down in the game environment, leaving the rest of the family vulnerable when night fell because of monster attacks. "Chloe!" Jeremiah exclaimed, "Stop looking at the ceiling or else you're going to die! . . . We're all going to die because of you!" His parents tried to calm him down. "Jeremiah. Jeremiah, honey," said Natasha, "Shh. It's okay." Interestingly, in my interview a few weeks prior, Natasha had said that Minecraft was "the perfect game" for Jeremiah because "it's this world where there are no unknowns and you're in complete control. You can decide everything, up to a point." That point was reached multiple times during my observation, for although video games have clear mechanics, humans (especially little sisters) are far more unpredictable.

REFLECTIONS ON EMOTION

This chapter has examined how parents and family members interpret their autistic children's emotions, how youth on the spectrum describe their own emotional experiences, and the role that media and technology play in that interchange. Some autistic kids can be very empathetic, while others might express emotions in a more reserved way, and this influences the media content they choose. Those who have additional challenges with language may also be drawn to certain technological tools and media texts for their affective qualities. Cyberbullying from both anonymous strangers and known peers online can have an emotional impact on autistic youth. Pixar films may oversimply their feelings (*Inside Out*), provide them with emotive language (*The Incredibles*), or be too intensely emotionally arousing (*Coco*). I identified four key ways in which the mediated practices of kids on the spectrum are bound up with their emotional development: through understanding (i.e., learning how to recognize and name emotions through media), experiencing (i.e., media influencing their emotions, such making them very happy or very sad), expressing (i.e., media as a tool for processing and sharing emotions), and managing (i.e., media as playing a role in the regulation and management of emotions).

This work speaks to practical issues of supporting autistic children's emotional well-being in the digital age as well as to conceptual and theoretical debates about the relationship between computers, autism, and emotion. First, a great deal is still unknown about autistic children's emotional lives. Some underexplored factors may be affecting these kids' uses of media and technology as a coping mechanism. For example, there is a lack of clinical measures to evaluate trauma among kids on the autism spectrum like Amaya, whose mother noted a marked change in her media use habits following an abusive incident at school.[64] Autistic children additionally marginalized on account of their race, ethnicity, and socioeconomic background are more likely to encounter environmental risk factors for mental health issues, such as lack of community resources and poor neighborhood safety.[65] The compounding social crises of the past few years in the United States, including the COVID-19 pandemic, school shootings, and racial violence, have only intensified the mental and physical trauma experienced by children and heightened the necessity of measures that better assess the socioemotional needs of autistic kids from these populations.

Second, the affordances of media and communication technology play a clear but varied role in shaping autistic kids' emotional development. Handheld, personal, and mobile media connected to the internet put highly salient tools for emotion regulation directly into children's hands. Smartphones and tablets allow those with disabilities to have greater independence and agency in how they spend their leisure time.[66] There is potential, though, for overuse or misuse. Parents should be attentive to how media can both stress and soothe their child, as well as how their child's processing of emotions may be related to their sensory processing.[67] It is important to help autistic children learn to regulate their emotions in ways that do not always rely on the comfort of a screen, because the technology may impede social interactions that are helpful for development.[68] Many caregivers were actively invested in finding out what their children were feeling and what they knew about emotions, providing them with materials for sharing their feelings, and helping them manage their mood. Parents drew on the resources available to them to make those decisions—resources, however, that were not equally accessible by all parents across socioeconomic and educational backgrounds.

YouTube can be a particularly tricky online platform for autistic kids and their parents to handle in terms of emotional well-being. Animated content on the site may make emotions more concrete and easier for children on the spectrum to comprehend. This can backfire, though, for kids like Eli who are vulnerable to heightened emotional arousal caused by screen media. The algorithmic, informational, and economic infrastructure of YouTube serves children "related" videos, but those recommendations can be more harmful than calming, as in the case of Amaya earlier in the chapter. Some cartoons on YouTube might also appear to have an educational element but can actually contain graphic material likely to upset young children and alarm caregivers.[69] Additionally, autistic children themselves may be the subject of distressing content on the site. Several parents have posted videos on YouTube of their autistic child having an involuntary behavioral meltdown (on the premise that they are of educational value to other parents). Many in the disability community have condemned these clips, arguing that no one deserves to have their worst moments shared online.[70] Videos of kids in pain might be appealing or gratifying in some way to autistic kids like Moira, but young people also need to be protected from unanticipated algorithmically driven exposure to upsetting material.

Lastly, studying the emotional contours of autistic children's media and technology use up close highlights flaws in universal frameworks for emotional development, the widespread deployment of emotion AI, and enthusiasm for "emotionally aware" robots that interact with autistic children—and have been repackaged as a "distance learning" tool for isolated children during the COVID-19 pandemic.[71] Few people who interact with these technologies are aware of their origins in autism research. Neurotypical people are the standard against which affect is measured through artificial models of emotional intelligence. Affective computing largely fails to capture the emotional nuances of autistic people and neurodivergent experiences, and, moreover, encodes neurotypical biases into algorithms.[72] The field of "empathic media" has been underwritten by experimental research with autistic children and driven by the false idea that they fundamentally lack empathy.[73] Models of emotion recognition based on the individual overlook how affective meaning is shaped by the media environment and by social partners like parents, siblings, and peers (who may also be autistic themselves). Autistic children can react intensely to the affective states of others, including those emotions depicted in mass media, suggesting that empathy is far more intersubjective than commonly assumed.

The emotions of children on the spectrum are rarely, if ever, considered beyond a deficit-oriented perspective. This inhibits researchers from identifying the creative and constructive ways that media offers autistic children powerful tools for making sense of their emotions and learning how to handle them. The diversity of emotional experiences evidenced in the ethnographic material in this chapter complicates the narrow conceptions of autism, empathy, and theory of mind that have been drawn upon in the development of affective computing and associated philosophies. The medicalized models of emotionality that are embedded in socioemotional prosthetics for autistic children center nonautistic minds and bodies as the ideal.[74] These frameworks neatly define emotion and bound technology within the realm of the curative, but they ignore the messy, porous world of autistic children's feelings while growing up in the digital age. In the next chapter, I offer a holistic reflection on young people on the spectrum as they navigate a social world that actively denies the validity of autistic sociality, and I propose ways that media—along with other social institutions—could better recognize and react to the significant inequalities that exist among children on the spectrum, particularly in the wake of the COVID-19 pandemic.

8 CONCLUSION

The research for this book wound down right as the COVID-19 pandemic began. It may, in fact, be one of the last books to be published for a while that is based on the ethnographic study of young children conducted from physically inside their homes. In April 2020, I pivoted to Skype to speak with two autistic kids whom I had interviewed a few years prior—now 13-year-old Saylor (White, girl) and 10-year-old Caleb (Black, boy)—and their respective mothers, Maggie and Audrey.[1] By then, in-person public school in Massachusetts had been suspended and moved online, and an assortment of social distancing measures had commenced across the state. For Caleb and Saylor, the pandemic had already begun to alter how they sought connection with their peers and how technology facilitated those interactions and relationships.

Right before the lockdown, Saylor had started to exercise more physical and social independence from her parents. "She did get to a point where she's walking home from school with a friend, [and telling me,] 'Oh, we're going to go to Dunkin' Donuts and hang out,'" shared Maggie, whose family lived in a predominantly White and mostly residential Boston suburb. Maggie did not take these typical teenage freedoms for granted, considering her daughter's prior struggles with bullying. When Saylor spoke about what had changed in her life due to the pandemic, the loss of her newfound mobility stuck out. "I've gotten a little stressed out because I think people in my town might have it and everything shut down so fast," she said, "I thought this whole week, I'm just going to go to Dunkin' and get a coffee and come home and quarantine, but Dunkin' is pretty much closed." The internet is always open, however, and much of Saylor's socializing, as well as that of her peers, had migrated online. She was feeling somewhat neglected by her friends, who were enticed by endless entertainment options at home. "Corona has been pretty lonely," Saylor shared, "None of my friends really communicate with me anymore because . . . they're all just playing video games. . . . I'll be like, 'Hey, do you want to FaceTime?' They'll be like, 'I can't right now, I'm on *Fortnite.*'"

While Saylor spoke of gaming displacing richer online and offline social opportunities, video games opened up new ways for Caleb to play with classmates during quarantine. His in-person playdates had already been limited prior to the pandemic. There was not a lot of spare room in his seven-hundred-square-foot apartment, and Audrey—a single mom and immigrant from Haiti—did not think it was safe for friends to come over and play with her son outside because they lived on a busy main road in a part of Boston with a high crime rate. In our earlier interview, Caleb had reported with respect to his media habits, "I don't chat with people on games. I've never done that before." This had changed a month into the pandemic. He and a few classmates would log on to their school-supplied Google Chromebooks to video chat while working on homework together. Those sessions led to scheduled online meet ups on weekends to play Roblox while each boy kept their camera on. Though Caleb might have eventually started social gaming when he got older, Audrey believed that the pandemic was a catalyst. "[It's] changed the way he's interacting with his friends. He's using technology. He wasn't doing that at all before," she said.

Saylor and Caleb's experiences are particular to the COVID-19 era, but also gesture toward key themes that I have discussed throughout this book. First, their usage of media was not entirely different from that of their non-autistic peers. For example, both kids reported increased screen time. In the United States, 72 percent of parents with children in grades K–12 indicated in April 2021 that their child had spent more time in front of screens since the start of the pandemic a year earlier.[2] Mobile devices and video games allowed Caleb and Saylor to self-organize social spaces outside of school. Second, despite the same autism diagnosis and similar profiles (e.g., sharp conversational skills, challenges with focusing), their social uses of media differed in important ways. Technology seemed to exacerbate Saylor's loneliness while minimizing Caleb's. These distinctions may have resulted from how they were being socialized as a teen girl and a tween boy. Beyond age and gender, their social possibilities were also influenced by issues of race and power outside their homes, like housing segregation and neighborhood safety. Being autistic no doubt impacted how Saylor and Caleb were handling disrupted routines and constrained geographies due to COVID-19,[3] including using media to cope,[4] but it was not the only factor in how they each demonstrated resiliency.

Third, their stories exemplify my theorization of the sociotechnical shaping of sociality, or how the relationship between society and technology shapes and is shaped by neurotypical interpersonal expectations and norms. Though some people on the spectrum have difficulty reading facial expressions,[5] both children valued seeing their friends' faces online (Saylor through FaceTime and Caleb using Google Hangouts). This echoes research indicating that autistic children missed embodied social contact during the pandemic and that technology was not a panacea for this longing.[6] Parents widely reported that autistic children who required substantial support struggled with the medium of remote learning and regressed academically, socially, and behaviorally as a result of the pandemic,[7] while some thrived taking classes virtually from the comfort of home.[8] Autistic young people may have been better equipped than their nonautistic peers in some ways to make the sudden switch to distanced socializing. Many already had intimate experience with barriers to physical participation and had been using media and technology to navigate uncertain futures.

It will take years to understand the pandemic's long-term impact on the mental health of young people, including kids on the spectrum like Caleb and Saylor. It is my hope, though, that the vivid perspectives of children and their families in this book—the first to chronicle autistic young people's media and technology practices in depth—are both timeless and timely, universal yet specific. In the remainder of this concluding chapter, I review how the three overarching themes that I identified in my fieldwork—cultural belonging, social relationships, and physical embodiment—define autistic children's media use. Next, I summarize the contribution that this book makes to theoretical understandings of sociality and technology. I then propose practical advice for how these empirical findings can be applied in several contexts. Lastly, I suggest how future research on autism, media, and social technologies can be more inclusive. Such topics are immediately relevant to autism researchers, but they also concern scholars of technology and society, children and media, education, human-computer interaction, sociology, cultural anthropology, psychology, human development, and family communication.

BOOK SUMMARY

In this book, I approach the question of what young people on the spectrum are doing with media by taking care to avoid simplistic and damaging tropes about autism and "mechanical boys" that have circulated within mainstream culture for well over fifty years.[9] I identify three main technological caricatures of autistic children that these narratives produce: (1) computer-savvy and intensely focused geeks who are valuable societal and economic assets to the technological and scientific sectors; (2) heavy internet users at social risk for online and offline peer isolation and aggressive behavior; and (3) those whose autism has been caused by too much screen time and not enough people time.

In their own way, the first and second narratives each encourage the regulation and management of autistic bodies, either for the extraction of capital or as a pretext for increased surveillance. Some young people on the spectrum are indeed using their technological talents to important ends, including developing apps that help themselves and others manage their own conditions.[10] But prevailing techno-centric autism stereotypes are largely based on notions of the prototypical autistic child as White, male, and upper-middle class,[11] which also does a disservice to these boys by flattening out the nuances of their social and emotional lives.[12] The third myth concerns the idea that technology and specific media texts (like the preschool TV show *Peppa Pig*) make children more "autistic," cause "autistic symptoms," or put children "at risk" for autism.[13] Research asserting causal claims between autism and screen media are empirically flawed in several ways. Autism is a developmental condition, meaning it develops prior to birth. Fetuses cannot view screens, so the idea that media causes autism is beyond belief. Such studies describe "connections" and "links" that are correlational or cyclical, but not directly causal.[14] These studies also presume that the complex characteristics of autism are easily definable and reducible.

I found this to be far from the case when tracing the role of media and technology in autistic children's social lives. I examined how they make sense of where they belong culturally in terms of their identities (chapter 2) and learning environments (chapter 3). I studied the kinds of personal relationships that they forge with family (chapter 4) and friends (chapter 5). And I tried to understand their embodied experiences of neurodivergence, namely their sensory (chapter 6) and emotional (chapter 7) processing.

Each child had different strengths and challenges, as well as varied backgrounds. While autism is inseparable from autistic children, children on the spectrum are more than their autism alone, and this extends to their digital, mass, and social media use. This book demonstrates how prevailing views of the relationship between autism and technology reflect a bias that does not account for gender, race, ethnicity, class, and other aspects of human difference. For example, though the idea of autistic youth as "naturally" geeky is persistent and pervasive, there is nothing natural about having access to hardware and software, to necessary infrastructure like high-quality internet, and to enriching opportunities outside of school.[15] To deny these realities in the lives of autistic people is to oversimplify and reduce their existences.

THEORETICAL IMPLICATIONS

Viewing autistic youth and their technology use as homogenous not only shortchanges children and families, but it is a missed opportunity to understand communication and social technologies themselves in a more nuanced way. My last book centered around the idea of "voice" (and a population of nonspeaking disabled individuals), and this one has focused on what it means to be "social." Autism is clinically characterized by an individual's lack or deficit of sociality, but I was driven to ask, how do autistic children enact "the social"? How do they do so through an array of media and technology? And what can this tell us about the relationship between society and technology more broadly? I found that autism does not only concern being social (or not), but it is profoundly sociological and sociotechnical.[16] The modern media and technology practices of autistic children reveal tensions and contradictions in how social norms are made, remade, and unmade through highly complex interactions and relationships on interpersonal and institutional levels. This book has adopted an asset model of disability, inverting a deficit view that can overshadow strengths. It looks toward those who are clinically defined as having "social deficits" to learn how technology shapes social experiences as well as how to critically contextualize social communication.[17]

It is a paradox that autism is insufficiently theorized in media and technology, yet these same tools and materials are pervasive in the lives of autistic children and adults. Borrowing a typology of youth media practices developed by anthropologist Mizuko Ito and colleagues, some autistic kids are "geeking out" (exploring media interests), but they are also "messing around" (producing media) and "hanging out" (using media to socialize).[18] Some autistic kids engage in these activities more so than others do. Their social preferences, however, may not look like those of neurotypical children and thus get invalidated or ignored, even when engaging with the same digital platforms.

Consider the parasocial relationships formed by multiple children on the spectrum with YouTube media personae, discussed in chapter 5. These online experiences were socially meaningful in and of themselves to kids like Brendan, though they could also scaffold mutually beneficial relationship building with peers offline, as with Jeremiah. The binary between "social" and "nonsocial" media does not hold in the case of autistic youth, who may form affective bonds with media in its material and symbolic forms. As Brendan's mom, Marcia, noted of these seeming contradictions, "I can't explain it. The electronics mean more to him than the social connection. So, it's not that he doesn't want friends. It's not that he doesn't love his family. It's just that it means a lot to him, and he really enjoys it, so he would prefer that."

This book captures only a subset of mediated autistic socialites, or possibilities for being social and on the spectrum through information, media, and communication technologies. Some of these socialites are seen as more valid now than before the COVID-19 pandemic, though this approval is conditional. For example, children's video game play reportedly soared during the pandemic due to physical distancing measures.[19] In that time, news articles began to appear in major publications not only assuaging parents of guilt over their more relaxed screen time rules, but also extolling the social benefits of intensive game play.[20] Many neurodivergent youth, however, were already comfortable with and even preferred cultivating and maintaining relationships via online means, such as chatting and socially sharing in game play through digital platforms like Twitch and Discord.[21] Ways of being that are favored by minoritized populations are often not considered socially acceptable until they are adopted and assimilated by nonminoritized groups. Cultural approval of socially adaptive technology is contextual and contingent, and it does not automatically extend to all aspects of autistic people's lives that could be made more accessible during the pandemic or beyond.[22]

RECOMMENDATIONS

This book arrives at an encouraging cultural moment in which more and more individuals, industries, and institutions are talking about neurodiversity as an important dimension of inclusion. In addition to theoretical contributions, this book makes several recommendations for different kinds of audiences, with members who may or may not be autistic themselves.[23] I distill my reflections into actionable media advice for parents of kids of the spectrum. I make suggestions for those who work directly with autistic children (e.g., teachers, therapists), many of whom may not necessarily understand the overall context of technology in these children's lives or who see it only as a problem. I also critically intercede in discussions about high-tech behavioral, social, and emotional interventions whose stated intention is to help kids on the spectrum, but that I argue do not account for the many ethical issues that these technologies raise. I have additionally included advice for media producers, technology developers, and policy makers who have significant influence over structural forces shaping how kids on the spectrum, as well as their siblings and peers, grow up in the digital age.

PARENTS
During the COVID-19 pandemic, psychologists likened parents' more relaxed media rules for their children in the absence of childcare to a "babysitter of last resort."[24] Screen media may have lightened an impossibly heavy load for parents, but it has long served that role for caregivers of autistic youth—in addition to de facto teacher, therapist, and social worker. Parents of kids on the spectrum report receiving inconsistent messaging from medical providers about how to manage their child's media use, especially if that management style differs for their neurotypical siblings and if the autistic child also has any other co-occurring conditions such as ADHD.[25] Following other strengths-based work on technology use in marginalized families,[26] I highlight in this book what children and families are doing well so that these assets can be built upon. In terms of how parents might navigate challenging issues in practice, I have identified six developmental areas, while each of the other chapters in this book also present additional takeaways.

SOCIAL Parents of autistic kids can support their child's use of media to communicate and connect in ways that respect their preferred modes of sociality. Autistic children like Caleb may find it easier to socialize with classmates through video games with chat functions. This format could be particularly beneficial for those who might not be regularly included in after-school play. There is a difficult balance, however, in giving kids autonomy and opening them up to disempowering situations (i.e., cyberbullying, online harassment), like Matt and Bryan's risky, unmonitored Roblox use (chapter 5). For parents, using media together, like family movie nights, can help build a child's social communication skills. That being said, there are often challenges beyond a caregivers' immediate control, like being a single parent and not having a second caregiver to rely upon for attending to the needs of other children in the household.

EMOTION   Emotionally, parents should pay attention to how media can soothe or stress their child, even if the child is nonspeaking and may not articulate their mood in traditional ways. Children on the spectrum can be very empathetic, like Sam, who used both gestures and his augmentative and alternative communication device to express how he understood the feelings of his mom and the character Blue from *Blue's Clues* (chapter 7). Other autistic kids might convey emotions in a more reserved way, which then shapes the media content that they choose. It is important, though, to help children on the autism spectrum learn to regulate their emotions in ways that do not always involve the relief provided by a screen, especially as technology can also sometimes make emotion regulation more difficult for some. Parents can additionally scaffold children's emotion management, like talking together about the emotionally intense situations in which media characters find themselves.

COGNITION   In terms of cognitive development, parents can help autistic children become critical thinkers about media and technology to the fullest extent of their abilities. Some kids on the spectrum can fully grasp the complexity of what they see and read online, while others might not know what is inappropriate to post on social media or understand that what they are watching on YouTube is an advertisement. Parents should meet their children where they are and watch videos together to explain what could be confusing for their child. Caregivers, however, face challenges of staying informed themselves. For example, neither Adrian nor his well-educated parents were aware that he could not change his original, non-anonymized username in Scratch when he first joined the site, leading to privacy concerns later on (chapter 3).

BEHAVIOR Behaviorally, parents should set reasonable boundaries around media but also give kids on the spectrum an active role in defining parameters. Media can provide a sense of routine for autistic children who thrive with clear schedules and plans, as well as for those like Amaya living with unresolved trauma (chapter 7). But for some, constant media use might negatively impact their ability to self-regulate and transition to nonmedia activities. Sensory dysregulation can also trigger a loss of behavioral control, which certain media might ameliorate or intensify. For example, Aaliyah loved to watch PBS KIDS and sing along to songs, but specific content that played between episodes elicited a physically painful response (chapter 6). To help, parents can involve kids in making predictable and safe choices about their media and technology use while being attentive to when they have become overstimulated.

SLEEP With respect to sleep, media can work both with and against an autistic child's sleeping habits. Many kids on the spectrum, like Sofia, tend to have nonnormative sleeping habits to begin with (chapter 3). When others in the home are sleeping, media could be what is keeping these children company at night and thus keeping them from disrupting their parents' sleep or waking up their siblings. But, if media before bed is making things worse, then parents should consider enacting small changes for developing new routines, like not using screens in the hour leading up to bedtime. Adolescents on the spectrum, like Brendan, may also be self-aware of how technology impacts their sleep and understand the benefits of rules and moderation (chapter 4).

CREATIVITY Lastly, parents should give autistic kids large canvases, metaphorically speaking, to explore their interests and create things, both physical and digital. Some children on the spectrum have amazing artistic skills and an eye for detail, but there are many with minimal resources who lack basic internet access, such as Robert and Anthony, limiting the possibilities of their creativity as well as their vocational potential. Making and reading paper comic books and graphic novels can be a great way for autistic kids to build worlds in a nondigital way too, especially in the case of kids like Casey who use the medium to explore their multifaceted identities (chapter 2).

PRACTITIONERS

Parents, of course, should not and cannot bear the entire responsibility for helping their kids on the spectrum grow up happy and healthy. Clinicians, therapists, and other medical professionals with whom they interact regularly can be partners in enabling autistic children to thrive in a highly mediated world, provided that caregivers can access this health care to begin with, which is not a given in the United States. Recreational media may be a helpful clinical tool; for example, popular games like Minecraft have been used in therapy to enable autistic children to process trauma.[27] From my conversations with parents and observations of kids, it became clear, however, that not all therapists are equally well-trained to carry out this work, nor are all therapeutic interventions equally concerned with autistic children's overall well-being. I was encouraged, though, by the work between Diego and his behavioral therapist, Tiffany (chapter 3), which required her to relinquish control to Diego and allow him to create his countless PowerPoint "books" during their sessions with her technical and social support.

Teachers and therapists who work in schools (i.e., speech-language, occupational, and physical therapists) have had more glimpses as of late into the domestic spaces of their students through the screens of Zoom, Skype, and Google Meet. The stories in this book, told from the perspectives of autistic kids and their parents, as well from families with a diverse array of backgrounds, hopefully generate creative pedagogical ideas and offer alternative explanations for student behavior and performance. For example, unexamined racial biases may be at work when diagnoses are made and Individualized Educational Programs (or Plans) are developed. These prejudices can contribute to understandings of some children as more "stereotypically" autistic in their technological engagement and, subsequently, to those kids being offered additional resources. Other autistic children may not be seen that way and hence may not receive that help,[28] as in the case of Clayton (chapter 1).

MEDIA PRODUCERS

While there have been more fictional on-screen representations of autism over the past five or so years, it is almost as if autistic girls of color do not exist in the eyes of the media. Though kids on the spectrum can identify with media characters with other disabilities or autistic characters with different racial or gender backgrounds (chapter 2), they deserve more options. TV shows could play an important role in continuing to push back against the status quo in this respect, having already made major inroads for autism representation on programs like *Sesame Street*, *Hero Elementary*, and *Daniel Tiger's Neighborhood* in the United States, *Pablo* in the United Kingdom, and *Heartbreak High* in Australia.[29]

Such work necessitates a more diverse set of autistic producers, creators, and creative consultants. Mass media can add new layers to our general understandings of autism in an authentic and diverse way, including websites, books, movies, podcasts, and social media accounts. The online publication *Spectrum* covers scientific research on autism and autism's more social and cultural dimensions (though it would benefit from having more autistic writers). There are documentary movies about the experiences of nonspeaking autistic people who express themselves through alternative communication systems. An increasing number of autistic people of color and their parents are using digital media to share their points of view and develop community, such as the *Autism in Black* (autisminblack.org) podcast.

TECHNOLOGY DEVELOPERS

There are rising calls within and outside the tech industry to grapple with the morality and ethics of deploying technologies without considering the possible disproportionate negative impacts on marginalized groups. By and large, this critical reckoning has yet to extend to the field of autism technologies and popular media technologies regularly used by autistic children.[30] Most "autism apps" (i.e., applications that tout their therapeutic potential for autism) not only are low quality, but are poorly maintained and updated in app stores, leading to their abandonment by users.[31] Autistic children themselves are rarely involved in the process of designing assistive autism technologies in a meaningful way.[32] The fetishization of high-tech interventions like humanoid robots and Google Glass has led many in the technology sector to overlook the developmental areas in which kids on the spectrum already show interest and a desire to learn. For example, I dedicated a significant amount of space in chapter 3 to detailing autistic children's fascination with literacy and numeracy, which, for some of these children, is likely a result of being hyperlexic. Research on embodied artificially intelligent agents as assistive technologies focuses mainly on controlled experiments in laboratory environments and does not account for the habits, routines, and rituals cultivated inside the home media environment of children on the spectrum.

As discussed in earlier chapters, many autistic kids turned to YouTube and other websites to easily access material, like foreign language videos, but also shown were the ways in which those platforms may not be entirely positive for children's mental and emotional health (e.g., exposing them to adult or overly commercial content). Therefore, there is an opportunity for more playful, weird, and delightful digital tools and content to be put safely and securely in their hands by actors that, at a minimum, follow the current guidelines outlined in the US Children's Online Privacy and Protection Act (COPPA). COPPA's regulatory strength, though, is much weaker than newer online child consumer privacy legislation such as the United Kingdom's Age Appropriate Design Code. YouTube is many things to autistic children out of necessity, including a makeshift clinical tool for coping with mental health distress (e.g., Amaya in chapter 7), so it is hard for parents, especially those who are underresourced, to opt out altogether. As I discuss in chapter 4, Google has a responsibility to offer parents better, more customizable choices for how to manage their child's consumption without limiting the agency of children, while the US government, federally and on the state level, should take legal measures to shore up online child safety, data protection, and algorithmic transparency.

POLICY MAKERS

Lastly, besides these technology policy changes, this book highlights the unsustainability of pushing the collective needs and agency of children, people with disabilities, and their families even further away from the center of societal priorities.[33] A culture of "intensive parenting" that demands the prioritization of individual choice over collective responsibility for child rearing disproportionately affects disabled children and their caregivers.[34] I have drawn attention to the understudied role of health-care systems, clinical providers, and health disparities in shaping children's digital media use, such as April and Kimberly's challenges in scheduling therapeutic services for their daughters (chapters 3 and 7). Community-based organizations with multilingual and racially diverse staff play an essential role in brokering access and lessening labor for parents of autistic children who may be already significantly limited in resources like money, time, and flexible schedules. Such groups merit greater funding on local, state, and federal levels. Enabling autistic children to derive the greatest benefit from media in their daily lives demands addressing structural forms of racism, bigotry, ableism, and various overlapping forms of inequality and discrimination head on.[35]

FUTURE RESEARCH

There are a number of topics related to autism, childhood, and technology that are beyond the scope of this book but warrant additional attention. One underexplored issue is the deployment of mobile and wearable GPS tracking devices for children on the spectrum as risk-prevention tools. Critical scholars of technology and society have analyzed the political economy of child location tracking technologies as well as their social benefits and drawbacks (e.g., decreased child autonomy and increased surveillance; the intensification of parenting).[36] These discussions, though, have barely extended to the safety and security of disabled and autistic youth, who already have more limited control over their time and space. The concerns and anxieties of these children's caregivers have not been sufficiently considered, either.[37] For example, Saylor's afterschool in-person socializing before the pandemic was in part facilitated by such technology. Her parents kept track of her whereabouts through the Life360 family tracking app and location services enabled on her iPhone. Maggie did not want to be "the parent that watches every step someone is taking," but felt it necessary, as Saylor had trouble keeping track of time and remembering to text her parents if she was running late.

GPS technologies worn on or near the body (i.e., wristwatches, anklets) by autistic children are primarily intended for those with a tendency to run suddenly or "bolt" into dangerous situations, like Bennett in chapter 4. Such technologies gained a higher profile after the death of 14-year-old Avonte Oquendo, a Black boy who managed to run away from his Queens, New York school in 2013 and whose body was tragically found months later in the East River. A law in his name funding parental procurement of wearable location tracking technology for autistic children was passed on the US federal level in 2018.[38] To date, though, very little empirical research has been conducted on the pros and cons of these surveillance technologies, how they are understood by autistic people of different racial and ethnic backgrounds and their families, or their implementation alongside or in place of other educational and behavioral supports.[39]

There are also methodological improvements to be made in the study of autistic children's socioemotional development and engagement with media. For instance, I discussed research in chapter 7 suggesting that autistic children are more likely to have a condition known as alexithymia, which concerns an inability to communicate, label, and identify emotions and feelings. Interestingly, children's engagement with media and the emotional responses that it may or may not elicit are part of the very assessment tool used to study alexithymia in school-age kids. The Toronto Alexithymia Scale for Children (TAS-C) was designed to measure children's alexithymia.[40] Two items on the modified TAS-C are "I like watching funny TV shows, more than TV shows about people's problems" and "I don't like movies where I have to concentrate to understand the story."[41] A child responding to these items with "sometimes" or "a lot like me" would increase their TAS-C score. From the perspective of children and media scholarship, however, these statements are not good proxies for a child's ability to talk about feelings. School-age children are drawn to humorous stories, may be accustomed in the YouTube era to content that is much shorter than film length, and prefer movies with simple plots.[42] Children and media researchers should be drawn upon as resources by psychologists and psychiatrists who lack this domain expertise.

Future research also needs to be more representative, longitudinal, qualitative, and global in nature.[43] Autism research must more frequently report the race, ethnicity, and gender of participants.[44] Greater efforts should be made to generate knowledge from the media experiences of autistic girls and non-White children on the spectrum. More studies are warranted of children on the spectrum living in the Global South, as well as of media use among autistic teens ages 14–18 and their transitions to adulthood.[45] For example, how do autistic TikTok personalities influence the self-concept of youth on the spectrum who use the platform? How do teens on the spectrum handle social pressures to manage their self-presentation online? Might social media have a unique impact on autistic girls at risk of developing an eating disorder? Considering that a great deal of research is drawn from parent report and surveys, more inroads should be made to conduct ethnographic work that is embedded in the daily lives of autistic children and adolescents. This includes directly engaging with them in a manner that best accommodates their diverse cognitive, behavioral, and communication profiles. Beyond a given medium or platform, content is also understudied as a central aspect of autistic kids' media usage.[46]

Finally, more space needs to be made for research on autism and technology across academic disciplines that study media and society. One thread running through this book is the push and pull between the medical establishment and autistic people, who historically have been excluded from designing and developing research that could best improve their lives and livelihoods. This is currently undergoing a major shift, with more autistic people getting involved as clinicians and researchers themselves and lay autistic individuals on social media advocating for new research directions.[47] Parents can be important partners in this process, but there is a long history of their voices sometimes drowning out those of others in the autism community. One way forward may be through taking a systems approach that recognizes the macro- and micro-level influences on autistic people's life trajectories. As I discuss in chapter 4, this angle helped to identify a significant gap in the study of families with two or more children on the autism spectrum and the role of media in their family functioning.

There is a pressing need to move beyond rhetoric that characterizes technology as either a social cure or social harm while also identifying the areas in which marginalized young people need psychological, physiological, social, and emotional support. Intersectional approaches to childhood and autism can help us understand how race, ethnicity, gender, and religion differentially impact the lives of kids on the spectrum at home, at school, and in their communities. In this book, I have suggested new strategies and advocated for better resources in supporting autistic children and adolescents in the digital age, while, along the way, rethinking assumptions about the relationship between autism, technology, and society. Autistic youth deserve more inclusive online and offline spaces that better leverage the potential of media and technology to promote their fullest possible expression, independence, and communication.

APPENDIX: METHODS

In this appendix, I provide additional methodological background on the empirical research on which this book is based. I highlight several opportunities and challenges of conducting qualitative research with diverse youth on the autism spectrum and capturing the significance of media and technology in their lives. I further detail my positionality as a researcher and explain the participation criteria, recruitment methods, study design, and limitations of the study.

QUALITATIVE RESEARCH WITH AUTISTIC CHILDREN

There is no single approach for maximizing the involvement of young people on the autism spectrum in research, as the methods need to be adapted to cater to their individual needs. Inclusive education scholar Carmel Conn details six general best practices for conducting qualitative research with this population, which I drew upon for this book.[1] First, researchers should aim for naturalistic inquiry. I did so by observing children engaging in routine activities with familiar people and by asking them concrete questions about their immediate surroundings. Second, research should be strengths-based. Parents took on a key role during our initial interviews by suggesting support strategies that would enable their child to participate, including how to pace interview questions.[2] Additionally, children were free to meet their sensory needs during interviews. I did not stop them from playing with stim toys and other objects or from scooting under tables if they preferred to answer my questions from there (as Caleb did for part of our interview). I also offered nonspeaking children who used AAC (augmentative and alternative communication) the option to type question responses or use other preferred methods.

Third, Conn contends that the research ought to involve mixed methods. For this book, I employed a combination of interviews and observations with parents and autistic kids. I was also flexible with the child interview format in the moment,[3] such as making certain open-ended questions more structured if children were having difficulty responding.[4] Fourth, research with autistic young people should enable their participation. One strategy that I used toward the end of my interview with kids was telling them that they could ask me questions too. Rosalita, for instance, inquired whether I had any pets, which reflected her own interest in animals. Fifth, Conn writes that researchers should be reflexive and offer children on the spectrum opportunities to share their own interpretations. As I detail later in this chapter, several offered commentaries on the research process with me, which then informed my ongoing work. Lastly, research should be practice-oriented, as in geared toward producing actionable change. Throughout this book, I have made recommendations for parents and professionals.

POSITIONALITY

As the primary ethnographer on this project, I was my own research instrument.[5] As such, it is important to reflect upon my positionality and the ways that I drew upon multiple visible and invisible aspects of my identity during the course of research,[6] including the ease with which I was socially accepted into homes and physically navigated fieldwork. It was both beneficial and detrimental in some cases that as a upper-middle class monolingual English-speaking White-appearing young woman, I looked and sounded like many of the health professionals that regularly provide in-home services to autistic children.[7] Upon my arrival at their house, for example, Emma's brother, Mikey, asked if I was there to teach his sister "how to talk," confusing me for a speech-language pathologist making a home visit.

But not all therapy providers are as warmly welcomed. Maya's father, Ismail, mentioned that his daughter had a traumatic experience with the applied behavior analysis (ABA) therapists who had worked with her at home. In discussing the timing of my return visit to observe Maya, Ismail said, "If you come to our house at 3 p.m., she'll start crying because that's when the ABA therapists came." We planned for me to arrive later in the afternoon next time, to avoid unnecessarily upsetting Maya.

During the period when I conducted field research, I did not yet have child-care responsibilities, so I could flexibly schedule my interviews and observations based on families' needs, including weeknight evenings and weekends. Additionally, an orientation to what I have elsewhere termed "inclusive sensory ethnography" shaped my fieldwork in homes.[8] I have no physical mobility constraints or chronic conditions such as chemical sensitivities or severe allergies. Studying how autistic children related sensorially to their built environment made me notice that I never had to think logistically about how I would enter homes or bother to ask parents if they had any pets before I came by. The "unsettled times" of the COVID-19 pandemic has limited in-person ethnography within personally intimate spaces, but such work was not so easily undertaken by many in the "settled times" prior to the pandemic either.[9] Reflexivity is not limited to a postscript discussion here or elsewhere in this book; rather, continuous reflection was central to the research process and the interpretation of data.[10]

PARTICIPANTS

Table A.1 summarizes demographic information collected about all of the autistic children and caregivers who took part in my study from 2013 to 2020, while table A.2 offers more descriptive data on each child and family. All child participants were required to have an autism diagnosis as confirmed by their parents, which prior research has indicated to be a valid and reliable source.[11] Children had to be between the ages of 3 and 13 when I first met them and their parents. I selected this age range for several reasons. The global average age of an autism diagnosis is 3 years old.[12] Three is also the age at which children in the United States qualify under the US Individuals with Disabilities Education Act for an Individualized Education Program (or Plan) (IEP). Fourteen is the age by which students on the spectrum with an IEP must begin to receive services from public school districts to ease their transition to adulthood.[13] I also conceived of this population in terms of two age groups: 3–8 and 9–13. In the former age range, family members tend to be a child's primary social partners, and during the latter, nonfamilial relationships become more central to a child's life.[14]

Families participating in the research included those with employed, unemployed, or underemployed parents; mothers with graduate degrees and those with a high school education or less; caregivers who were software engineers and those who were Uber drivers (and Uber drivers with

Table A.1
Demographics of Autistic Child Participants and Their Parents

Age (Median, years)	7
Gender[a]	
Boy	44
Girl	18
Parent-reported co-occurring conditions (in addition to autism)[b]	
Communication impairment[c]	26
Attention-deficit/hyperactivity disorder (ADHD)	6
Anxiety	3
Epilepsy	3
Other[d]	9
Race	
White	32
Nonwhite	30
Black[e]	11
Asian[e,f]	10
Latino/Latina[e]	9
Middle Eastern[e]	1
Other[e,g]	3
Yearly household income	
≥ $100,000	29
$99,999–$50,000	12
$49,999–$25,000	11
< $25,000	10
Parent/s born outside the United States	
Yes	17
Language other than English used at home	
Yes	16
Parent relationship status	
Married or unmarried/cohabitating	50
Other[h]	12
Mother's education	
College or advanced degree	47
Some college, high school, or less	15

Table A.1
(continued)

State of residence	
Massachusetts	50
California	12

[a] Cisgender and transgender children.
[b] "Autism" includes parent-reported diagnoses of autism, autism spectrum disorder, Asperger's syndrome, and Pervasive Developmental Disorder-Not Otherwise Specified (PDD-NOS).
[c] Parent reported that child used augmentative and alternative communication (AAC), had a communication disorder, had a speech delay, was "non-verbal," had childhood apraxia of speech, and/or had mixed expressive-receptive language disorder.
[d] Asthma, obsessive-compulsive disorder (OCD), dyslexia, intellectual disability, visual impairment, Fragile X syndrome, Pediatric Autoimmune Neuropsychiatric Disorders Associated with Streptococcal Infections syndrome (PANDAS), other genetic disorder.
[e] Children with at least one biological parent with that racial background.
[f] Bengali, Cambodian, Filipino, Indian, Japanese, Nepali, Pakistani, and Vietnamese.
[g] Cape Verdean, Armenian, and Azerbaijani.
[h] Divorced, separated, or single parent.

graduate degrees); and those who were married, divorced, remarried, separated, single, or polyamorous. Some parents and caregivers identified as neurodivergent or autistic, though most without a formal diagnosis. Parents had immigrated from countries such as Algeria, Bangladesh, Haiti, and Pakistan. The study required that at least one parent speak English. In the majority of households, only English was spoken, but in other homes, languages including Hebrew, Dutch, and Swahili were spoken as well. In addition to autism, several parents indicated that their children had additional diagnoses including attention-deficit/hyperactivity disorder (ADHD), anxiety, and epilepsy.

RECRUITMENT

Research was conducted in two waves: first from 2013 to 2014, when I was a graduate student at the University of Southern California in Los Angeles, and then from 2016 to 2020, when I was an assistant professor at Northeastern University in Boston. Twelve children and their families were recruited in Wave 1, and fifty families were recruited in Wave 2. Wave 1 families included nonspeaking and minimally speaking children on the autism spectrum recruited for the study on which my prior book, *Giving Voice*, is based. Ethnographic material included in this book but collected during Wave 1 did not appear in

Table A.2
Descriptive Data of Autistic Child Participants

First Name	Age[a]	Gender	Race (Ethnicity)	Parent-reported diagnosis/disability[b]	Yearly household income	Parents/caregivers name/s	Year(s) interviewed or observed
Aaliyah	3	Girl	Black	Autism	Less than $25,000	Crystal & Mike	2019
Abbey	4	Girl	White	Autism	$25,000–$49,999	Molly & Steve	2017
Adhi[c]	9	Boy	Asian (Indian)	Autism	$50,000–$99,999	Meena & Arjun	2017
Adrian	13	Boy	White	Autism, Asperger's syndrome, dyslexia, anxiety	$100,000 or more	Brianna & Stewart	2018
Alessandra	3	Girl	Latina	Autism, AAC user	$25,000–$49,999	Camila & Felipe	2017
Amaya	8	Girl	Black, Latina, and White	Autism, PDD-NOS, OCD, anxiety	Less than $25,000	Kimberly	2019
Anthony	5	Boy	Black	Autism, asthma	Less than $25,000	Danae & Darnell	2017
Bella	4	Girl	Other (Cape Verdean)	Autism	$100,000 or more	Angelica & Dave	2019
Bennett	4	Boy	White	Autism, PDD-NOS, communication disorder	$50,000–$99,999	Shelby & Keith	2017
Brendan	12	Boy	White	Autism, PDD-NOS	$50,000–$99,999	Marcia	2018
Bryan[c]	7	Boy	White	Autism	$25,000–$49,999	Beca & Pedro	2019
Caleb	9	Boy	Black	Autism, ADHD	Less than $25,000	Audrey	2019, 2020
Carter	3	Boy	Black and White	Autism, AAC user	$25,000–$49,999	Simone & Prince	2018
Casey	6	Girl	White	Autism, ADHD	Less than $25,000	Jennifer	2019
Chike	7	Boy	Black	Autism, AAC user	$100,000 or more	Esosa & Adamu	2014
Chris	4	Boy	Asian (Cambodian) and White	Autism, AAC user	$100,000 or more	Chanda & Phil	2017

Name	Age	Gender	Race/Ethnicity	Diagnosis	Income	Parents	Year
Cody	9	Boy	White	Autism, PDD-NOS	$100,000 or more	Meg & Bobby	2018
Conor[c]	9	Boy	White	Autism	$100,000 or more	Karrie & Adam	2019
Danny	6	Boy	White	Autism, epilepsy, AAC user	$100,000 or more	Alice & Peter	2013
Diego	12	Boy	White	Autism, intellectual disability, epilepsy	$100,000 or more	Francesca & Santos	2018
Eashan[c]	5	Boy	Asian (Indian)	Autism	$50,000–$99,999	Meena & Arjun	2017
Eli	4	Boy	White	Autism, AAC user	$100,000 or more	Julie & Jason	2017
Emma	3	Girl	White	Autism	$100,000 or more	Nikki & Seth	2017
Imay	5	Boy	Asian (Nepali)	Autism, AAC user	$25,000–$49,999	Geetu & Amir	2019
Isabella	5	Girl	White	Autism	$100,000 or more	Amy & Brandon	2018
Isaac	8	Boy	White	Autism, AAC user	$100,000 or more	Sara & Daniel	2013
Jackson	11	Boy	White	Autism, PDD-NOS, epilepsy, ADHD	$25,000–$49,999	Linda & Roger	2019
Jeremiah	8	Boy	White	Autism, Asperger's syndrome	$100,000 or more	Natasha & Neil	2017
Joey	6	Boy	White	Autism, PDD-NOS	$100,000 or more	Kerry & Doug	2016
Kahlil[c]	7	Boy	Black	Autism, speech delay, "nonverbal," AAC user	Less than $25,000	Monisha	2019
Karim	8	Boy	Middle Eastern (Algerian)	Autism, PDD-NOS	$25,000–$49,999	Nour & Hakim	2016, 2019
Katie	6	Girl	White	Autism, ADHD, anxiety	$50,000–$99,999	Annemarie & Frank	2019
Kevin	13	Boy	Asian (Japanese) and White	Autism, speech delays, AAC user	$25,000–$49,999	Rebecca & Eric	2014
Levi	10	Boy	Latino and White	Autism, PDD-NOS	$100,000 or more	Jamie & Jesse	2018
Lucas	5	Boy	Latino and White	Asperger's syndrome	$100,000 or more	Melissa & Brady	2016–2017

(continued)

Table A.2
(continued)

First Name	Age[a]	Gender	Race (Ethnicity)	Parent-reported diagnosis/ disability[b]	Yearly household income	Parents/caregivers name/s	Year(s) interviewed or observed
Luke	13	Boy	White	Autism, AAC user	$100,000 or more	Debra & Rob	2013
Matt[c]	9	Boy	White	Autism	$25,000–$49,999	Beca & Pedro	2019
Max	5	Boy	Asian (Vietnamese) and White	Autism	$100,000 or more	Norah & Mark	2017
Maya	8	Girl	Asian (Pakistani)	Autism, vision impairment, AAC user	$100,000 or more	Nazanin & Ismail	2019
Moira	10	Girl	White	Autism, childhood apraxia of speech, AAC user	$50,000–$99,999	Vanessa	2014
Noah	3	Boy	White	Autism	$25,000–$49,999	Amanda	2017
Olivia	6	Girl	White	Autism	$100,000 or more	Bailey	2017
Orion[c]	4	Boy	Black	Autism, speech delay	Less than $25,000	Monisha	2019
Oscar	3	Boy	White	Autism	$100,000 or more	Leslie & Abe	2017
Pargev	13	Boy	Other (Armenian)	Autism, AAC user	Less than $25,000	Karun & Mihran	2013
Patrick	4	Boy	White	Autism, AAC user	$50,000–$99,999	Jessie	2017, 2019
Raul	5	Boy	Latino	Autism, AAC user	$100,000 or more	Nina & Javier	2013, 2019
Robert	5	Boy	Black and Asian	Autism, ADHD	$50,000–$99,999	Gail	2017
Ronan[c]	10	Boy	White	Autism	$100,000 or more	Karrie & Adam	2019
Rosalita	11	Girl	White	Autism, Asperger's syndrome	$100,000 or more	Pamela & William	2019

Ryan	3	Boy	White	Autism, mixed developmental disorder, mixed receptive-expressive language disorder, AAC user	$50,000–$99,999	Tara & Craig	2017
Saaida	8	Girl	Asian (Bengali)	Autism, AAC user	Less than $25,000	Tanvi & Hamsa	2017
Sam	8	Boy	White	Autism, intellectual disability, genetic disorder, AAC user	$100,000 or more	Donna & Marc	2014
Saylor	12	Girl	White	Autism, PDD-NOS	$100,000 or more	Maggie & Jon	2018, 2020
Sebastian	6	Boy	Latino and White	Autism, Fragile X syndrome	$100,000 or more	Cathleen & Michael	2019
Skyler	6	Boy	White	Autism, ADHD	$100,000 or more	Naomi & Jacob	2017
Sofia	5	Girl	Latina	Autism, AAC user	$50,000–$99,999	April & Seb	2019
Spencer	4	Boy	Black and White	Autism, PANDAS, AAC user	$50,000–$99,999	Rosie & John	2017
Stephanie	10	Girl	Latina	Autism, AAC user	$25,000–$49,999	Marisa & Nelson	2013
Talen	6	Boy	Black, Latino, and White	Autism, AAC user	$50,000–$99,999	Kameelah & Marcus	2013
Thomas	11	Boy	Asian (Filipino) and White	Autism, intellectual disability, AAC user	$100,000 or more	Daisy & Joe	2013
Zahra	4	Girl	Other (Azerbaijani)	Autism	Less than $25,000	Raina & Becky[d]	2017

[a] Child's age at the beginning of research.
[b] Parent selections of "autism" and "autism spectrum disorder" reported together.
[c] Autistic sibling.
[d] Domestic partnership.

Abbreviations: AAC = augmentative and alternative communication; ADHD = attention-deficit/hyperactivity disorder; OCD = obsessive-compulsive disorder; PANDAS = Pediatric Autoimmune Neuropsychiatric Disorders Associated with Streptococcal Infections syndrome; PDD-NOS = Pervasive Developmental Disorder-Not Otherwise Specified.

that earlier publication. In each wave, recruitment began after approval from the university's institutional review board (IRB). The recruitment strategy and study design for Wave 1 has been detailed elsewhere, so the discussion here will focus on Wave 2.[15] Families in Wave 2 were recruited via professional referrals, electronic communication, print flyers, and community meetings. Parents were screened via phone, email, or text message to confirm their eligibility, and they signed a consent form prior to participating.

Families received a USD $30–$50 gift card after completion of the study. Parents' primary motivations to participate, however, were not financial in nature. Most wanted to help researchers such as myself learn more about autism and ultimately better support their child and children like them. Some parents provided specific insights, like Nour, who thought of my interview with her son, Karim, as a kind of therapeutic intervention. She explained that not many people visited her home because no relatives lived nearby, let alone in the country. Due to the novelty of visitors, Karim was "very interested [in] people who come to [their] house." My visit was an opportunity to capitalize on that interest and have Karim work on social communication skills like introducing himself and "presenting one's relatives to another person."

STUDY DESIGN

This study employed three primary qualitative methods: semi-structured interviews (with parents and autistic children), semi-naturalistic observation (with autistic children and their families), and participant observation. During Wave 2, I was aided in conducting observations and interviews by three undergraduate and graduate student research assistants on eleven different occasions. Collectively, they had professional experience at an autistic self-advocacy nonprofit organization, personal experience as the sibling of an autistic person, and graduate training in public health and qualitative research on youth mental health.

PARENT INTERVIEWS

Parent interviews were primarily, though not exclusively, conducted with mothers. Fathers sometimes joined in or were the primary interviewee, especially if mothers were not proficient in English. As noted in chapter 1, I conducted follow up interviews (as well as child observations) with several families (one from Wave 1 and four from Wave 2). Interviews with parents in Wave 2 lasted from one to two and a half hours and were conducted by using a semi-structured interview guide. Interviews began with warm up questions about the family and child's background (i.e., autism diagnosis process, child's average weekday and weekend schedule). The interview then covered eight main topics regarding their child's media and technology use: overall media preferences and experiences, specific types of media use and media environments, cognitive and behavioral development, sleep and physiological development, social and emotional development, communication and self-expression, fun and learning, and social norms and values. The interviews concluded with an opportunity for parents to talk about any topic not discussed or point that they wanted to clarify.

Nearly all parent interviews took place at their homes to gain richer insights into the family milieu. One parent requested that we meet at a coffee shop near her child's preschool, and two wanted to be interviewed in their office spaces at work. For interviews conducted at homes, other family members (e.g., grandparents) and the autistic child were sometimes present and took part peripherally as a subject of discussion (i.e., the parent commenting on the child using media in the background) or as an active member of the conversation. For instance, when Meg mentioned that Cody went through phases of being interested in certain video games, like *War Robots*, he interjected from the other room, "I don't play that anymore!" to which Meg responded with a laugh, "Yeah, I know you don't play that anymore, but you did for a while."

Following the interview, parents filled out a family background form to provide demographic information about their household (e.g., average yearly household income). Before leaving, parents and I discussed plans for my follow-up visit with their child, which would entail either a media use observation or a combined interview and observation. I asked parents whether or not their autistic child was capable of being interviewed, and if so, what communication support they might require (e.g., having the parent also be present). Return visits were scheduled around optimal times for the child to be engaged. For instance, Melissa said that any time would be fine for her son, Lucas, "as long as it's not right after school because that's when he needs his alone time." Fieldwork with each family was spread out over one to three weeks, depending on availability.

FAMILY OBSERVATIONS

Some children were not able to be interviewed, so I instead observed them at home engaging in a routine media activity that was typically undertaken with another family member (i.e., parent, sibling). Field notes focused on social interactions between autistic children and their social partners, the child's media consumption practices, and any parent commentary on the activity. Parents sometimes helped to interpret their child's nonspoken behavior. For example, at one point during my initial observation with Karim, Nour turned to me and said of her son, "He's getting more comfortable with you because he's singing." Family observations lasted thirty to ninety minutes. The specific media activity and social configuration was left purposefully open for families to choose. Observations primarily occurred in communal areas of the home (e.g., living room), but sometimes in a child's bedroom if it was the regular site for a particular media ritual (e.g., Skyler and Naomi's afterschool parent–child "book reading" on YouTube).

CHILD INTERVIEWS AND OBSERVATIONS

Prior to each child interview, assent was obtained by reading a printed document aloud to the child that explained the purpose of the study. Based on best practices,[16] autistic children were told that they did not have to answer all of my questions, could skip any, and were able to stop or take a break. Interviews were mostly conducted on the living room sofa, sitting side-by-side without forcing the child on the spectrum to make eye contact. Children could instead look at the page of interview questions that I had printed out on paper and see the interview's progression.[17] I used a semi-structured interview guide designed to aid in children's comprehension. Each question was typed in large print and was accompanied with a small graphic that symbolized the question (e.g., the YouTube logo next to a question about YouTube). Either I or the child checked a box in a column next to the question after it was answered or skipped. Sample questions included, "Who is your favorite character from a TV show, movie, book, or video game? What do you like about them?" and "What do you not like about media or technology?" Interviews lasted approximately thirty minutes, after which I asked children to show me their favorite media or technology activity, which I then observed and discussed with them for an additional thirty minutes.

During the child interviews, parents of older children with more cognitive and verbal capacity mostly left the child and me alone to talk in a nearby room. Other caregivers provided more direct and indirect support by scaffolding their child's conversation and helping me gain an understanding of their child's "sociocommunicative lifeworld."[18] For example, at one point during my interview with Conor, he turned to his dad, Adam, who sat a few feet away at the kitchen table, and asked, "Daddy, daddy! You help her answer questions. Which YouTube, which videos I was banned from?" In reporting children's responses in this book, I also tried to keep their language patterns intact; for example, Diego's word repetition when discussing his digital bookmaking in chapter 3.

CHILD FEEDBACK

As noted earlier, young people on the spectrum could be reflective about their research participation. For example, Adrian noted, regarding his loquaciousness, "I always talk as if I'm doing a TED Talk." Some expressed annoyance at my presence. I ended up conducting Levi's interview in between him watching videos on YouTube, which was less than ideal due to the distraction of the screen. I periodically asked him to pause so that I could pose another question. "You know this is like school," he said during our interview. "What's like school? Me asking you questions?" I replied. "Yep. And I get to earn screens," he said, perhaps reflecting on the reward structure within his household that was noted in chapter 4. With an awkward laugh, I responded, "Hopefully it's a little more fun," to which Levi declared, "Yeah, it isn't."

My passable knowledge of popular culture helped in rapport building, something which could go a long way for other adults working with autistic kids. I know next to nothing about the Pokémon franchise, except for the fact that there is one character with essentially the same name as me—Marill, a cute blue mouse-like creature. I shared my single Pokémon fact with Adrian after he expressed his love for the series, to which he responded, "So you're not just *studying* studying. You're not just here to study autism. You're here because you're a geek." Adrian then added how it put him at ease when the clinicians with whom he regularly interacted took the time to engage him in discussions about such things: "I'll just happen to wear a Pokémon sweatshirt or like some geeky shirt [to the doctor's office]—because I seriously don't run out of those at all—and I'm so excited anytime a doctor says, 'Oh hey, that's Sandslash [another Pokémon character]. Are you into that?' I can start the conversation and they'll be like, 'Oh, we're going to put this needle in your arm,' and I'm like, 'What? Oh, sure.'"

Other kids offered metacommentary on interviewing as a methodology. During my interview with Casey, she started scribbling with pencil on a piece of scrap paper. I noticed that she had drawn a question mark and I asked her what it was. "You," she responded. Seeing as I do not look particularly question mark–shaped, I asked her if she drew me that way because I was asking a lot of questions. Without directly answering me, she added, "I'm the exclamation mark," drawing one on the page as well. Maybe, I thought, Casey considered herself the exclamation mark because of the focused attention that I was giving her. Playing along, I asked what her mom, Jennifer, was. Casey declared that she was a period, which she drew in between the question mark and the exclamation mark. Jennifer was in a way playing the role of a "period" during our conversation: an emotionally neutral authority figure with final say, mediating the space between myself and Casey. She had directly conveyed her interpretation of our social roles through punctuation—? . !—and the symbolic meanings she assigned to them. With more than words alone, Casey not only playfully and creatively communicated to me who she was, but also who I might be to the children I was observing.

PARTICIPANT OBSERVATIONS

In addition to these interviews and observations, I attended a dozen public gatherings for children on the autism spectrum and their families, as well as some targeted toward parents exclusively. These observations added context to my knowledge about the availability of local autism resources. Sites included sensory-friendly film screenings at suburban movie theaters and in-person parent support group meetings in underresourced neighborhoods. Observations lasted one to two and a half hours each.

ANALYSIS

All interviews and semi-naturalistic observations were audio recorded and later transcribed by research assistants and the transcription service Rev .com. In addition, field notes or "jottings" were taken by members of the research team during each encounter.[19] Transcripts and notes were supplemented with reflective memos written by researchers immediately following site visits, supported by written field notes. Digital photographs of relevant activities, environments, and materials were also taken, both to aid in interpreting written material and to supplement the eventual interpretations shared publicly. All typed memos, notes, and transcripts were entered into the qualitative data analysis software program MAXQDA to create a customized searchable database of documents.

In developing grounded theory, open and selective coding and recoding of the data were employed to identify key concepts and categories.[20] I also applied a constant comparative method approach to analyzing the data by coding throughout the course of fieldwork and being attentive to patterns that I noticed emerging, such as parent language regarding the use of media rewards and restrictions as a behavior modification tool for autistic children.[21] Although I served as the sole coder, I discussed data exclusions and interpretations with participants and research assistants during fieldwork and data analysis to validate findings, a practice known as "member checking."[22] I used a combination of inductive and deductive approaches to coding the data;[23] for example, theoretical work on autistic sociality informed coding for parents' discussions of how their child might be described as "social," particularly in the context of their media use. I also benefited immensely from feedback on early drafts of the manuscript by autistic scholars who encouraged me to avoid centering the neurotypical experience as necessarily preferable to or entirely separate from that of neurodivergent people, and they also urged me to reconsider sections of writing that drew on the rather unstable epistemic authority of biological autism science.

RESEARCH LIMITATIONS

Though this book adds to understanding of autistic children's everyday media and technology practices and of theories of social technologies, there are a number of limitations to address. The first is that I was not able to recruit a significant number of nonspeaking and minimally speaking autistic children who were also able to be interviewed. Access to communication is not a right that all young people on the autism spectrum have realized, especially those additionally marginalized on the basis of their race, ethnicity, or class. Though the recruitment material for parents of autistic children ages 9–13 explicitly stated their child did not need to "be verbal" or speak, that the interview format could be adapted, and that parents could provide communication support for their child, few parents of adolescent autistic AAC users responded. Inclusion of more of these young people may have added complexity to the themes discussed in this book. To fill in some gaps, I have woven relevant quotes into the text from nonspeaking autistic memoirists who were adolescents at the time of their writing, such as Ido Kedar and Naoki Higashida.

Second, due to time constraints and the coronavirus pandemic, I was unable to interview non-English-speaking parents and observe their autistic children. Right before the pandemic struck, I had been planning to conduct research with primarily Spanish-speaking parents. All of the recruitment materials had been translated into Spanish with additional IRB approval, I had a Spanish-speaking research assistant join my team, and we had already recruited one parent. Unfortunately, those plans had to be canceled once much of Boston went into lockdown. Future work on autistic children's media use should incorporate the perspectives of non-English-speaking parents from the outset.

Next, one critique that some may make is that I did not separate out my findings by autism severity or use any formal quantitative autism assessments (e.g., the Autism Diagnostic Observation Schedule). This is partly related to the fact that I did not recruit families through established research databases and programs. Not being a clinician myself, I followed the lead of autistic self-advocates who have pointed out there is often much in common between autistic people with high support needs and those with low support needs.[24]

Lastly, though this book delves into issues surrounding friendship, including both parents' and autistic children's discussions of the topic, I had few chances to directly observe kids on the spectrum playing with their peers around and through media. This is largely due to my focus on the home environment. For example, in another version of this book, I could have recruited whole classrooms of children on the spectrum, mapped out their social networks, and studied the role of media and communication technology in mediating their online and offline relationships and interactions. This is yet another opportunity for future researchers to extend the work described in this book.

NOTES

CHAPTER 1

1. Bettelheim offered an expanded discussion of Joey in his 1967 book *The Empty Fortress*: Bruno Bettelheim, *The Empty Fortress: Infantile Autism and the Birth of the Self* (New York: Free Press, 1967). For a more extensive discussion of the "boy-machine" in psychoanalytic literature, see Sungook Hong, "Joey the Mechanical Boy, Revisited," e-flux, March 18, 2018, https://www.e-flux.com/architecture/superhumanity /179228/joey-the-mechanical-boy-revisited/; Jeffrey Sconce, *The Technical Delusion: Electronics, Power, Insanity* (Durham, NC: Duke University Press, 2019); Hannah Zeavin, "Hot and Cool Mothers," *differences* 23, no. 3 (2021): 53–84.

2. Bruno Bettelheim, "Joey: A 'Mechanical Boy,'" *Scientific American* 200 (1959): 117.

3. Bettelheim, *The Empty Fortress*, 127.

4. Bruno Bettelheim, *The Uses of Enchantment: The Meaning and Importance of Fairy Tales* (New York: Knopf, 1976).

5. Richard Pollak, *The Creation of Dr. B: A Biography of Bruno Bettelheim* (New York: Simon & Schuster, 1997).

6. Bettelheim, "Joey," 117.

7. Neil Brewer, Jordana Zoanetti, and Robyn L. Young, "The Influence of Media Suggestions about Links between Criminality and Autism Spectrum Disorder," *Autism* 21, no. 1 (2017): 117–21; Christopher R. Engelhardt et al., "Effects of Violent-Video-Game Exposure on Aggressive Behavior, Aggressive-Thought Accessibility, and Aggressive Affect among Adults with and without Autism Spectrum Disorder," *Psychological Science* 26, no. 8 (2015): 1187–1200; Konnor Davis et al., "Video Game Use, Aggression, and Social Impairment in Adolescents with Autism Spectrum Disorder," *Journal of Autism and Developmental Disorders* (2022), https://link.springer.com/article/10.1007 /s10803-022-05649-1.

8. Jordynn Jack, *Autism and Gender: From Refrigerator Mothers to Computer Geeks* (Urbana: University of Illinois Press, 2014). Notions of children on the spectrum as innately technologically savvy is also grounded in the idea that many are a product of marriages between autistic engineers, computer scientists, and programmers in high-tech regions like Silicon Valley; Steve Silberman, "The Geek Syndrome," *Wired*, December 2001, http://archive.wired.com/wired/archive/9.12/aspergers_pr.html.

9. Dominque Browning, "Talking Face to Face Is So . . . Yesterday," *New York Times*, December 4, 2011, http://www.nytimes.com/2011/12/04/opinion/sunday/actual-con versation-so-yesterday.html.

10. Anne Balsamo, *Technologies of the Gendered Body: Reading Cyborg Women* (Durham, NC: Duke University Press, 1996): 132. See also Karen F. Heffler and Leonard M. Oestreicher, "Causation Model of Autism: Audiovisual Brain Specialization in Infancy Competes with Social Brain Networks," *Medical Hypotheses* 91 (2016): 114–22.

11. Scientific research strongly refutes the claim that childhood vaccinations are an environmental risk factor for autism, despite the pseudoscience circulated by so-called anti-vaxxers; Susan Hyman et al., "Identification, Evaluation, and Management of Children with Autism Spectrum Disorder," *Pediatrics* 145, no. 1 (2020): 1–64.

12. Sue Fletcher-Watson and Francesca Happé, *Autism: A New Introduction to Psychological Theory and Current Debate*, 2nd ed. (New York: Routledge, 2019).

13. In this book, I employ primarily identity-first language as well as the "spectrum" metaphor, though imperfect, while avoiding reference to any one individual as "low" or "high" as a reflection of their value or needs, preferring to instead paint a fuller narrative picture of their successes and challenges.

14. Gil Eyal et al., *The Autism Matrix: The Social Origins of the Autism Epidemic* (Cambridge: Polity Press, 2010); Jennifer C. Sarrett, "Trapped Children: Popular Images of Children with Autism in the 1960s and 2000s," *Medical Humanities* 32, no. 2 (2011): 141–53.

15. Ortal Slobodin, Karen F. Heffler, and Michael Davidovitch, "Screen Media and Autism Spectrum Disorder: A Systematic Literature Review," *Journal of Developmental & Behavioral Pediatrics* 40, no. 4 (2019): 303–11.

16. Rebecca Lane and Jenny Radesky, "Digital Media and Autism Spectrum Disorders: Review of Evidence, Theoretical Concerns, and Opportunities for Intervention," *Journal of Developmental & Behavioral Pediatrics* 40, no. 5 (2019): 364–68.

17. Jaimie Ellis, "Researching the Social Worlds of Autistic Children: An Exploration of How an Understanding of Autistic Children's Social Worlds Is Best Achieved," *Children & Society* 31, no. 1 (2016): 23–36; Juliet Scott-Barrett, Katie Cebula, and Lani Florian, "Listening to Young People with Autism: Learning from Researcher Experiences," *International Journal of Research & Method in Education* 42, no. 2 (2019): 163–84; Karen G. Sirota, "Narratives of Distinction: Personal Life Narrative as a

Technology of the Self in the Everyday Lives and Relational Worlds of Children with Autism," *Ethos* 38, no. 1 (2010): 93–115.

18. For example, the user-generated short-form music video app Musical.ly became TikTok.

19. Guillermo Montes, "Children with Autism Spectrum Disorder and Screen Time: Results from a Large, Nationally Representative US Study," *Academic Pediatrics* 16, no. 2 (2016): 122–28; Melissa H. Kuo, Joyce Magill-Evans, and Lonnie Zwaigenbaum, "Parental Mediation of Television Viewing and Videogaming of Adolescents with Autism Spectrum Disorder and Their Siblings," *Autism* 19, no. 6 (2015): 724–35.

20. Barney G. Glaser and Anselm L. Strauss, *The Discovery of Grounded Theory: Strategies for Qualitative Research* (New Brunswick, NJ: Aldine, 1967); Anselm L. Strauss and Juliet Corbin, *Basics of Qualitative Research: Techniques and Procedures for Developing Grounded Theory* (Thousand Oaks, CA: Sage, 1998).

21. C. Wright Mills, *The Sociological Imagination* (Oxford: Oxford University Press, 1959).

22. Elizabeth Ellcessor, *Restricted Access: Media, Disability, and the Politics of Participation* (New York: New York University Press, 2016); Faye Ginsburg, "Disability in the Digital Age," in *Digital Anthropology*, ed. Heather A. Horst and Daniel Miller (London: Berg, 2012), 101–26; Gerard Goggin and Christopher Newell, *Digital Disability: The Social Construction of Disability in New Media* (Lanham, MD: Rowman & Littlefield, 2003); Mara Mills and Jonathan Sterne, "Dismediation: Three Propositions and Six Tactics (Afterword)," in *Disability Media Studies*, ed. Elizabeth Ellcessor and Bill Kirkpatrick (New York: New York University Press, 2017), 365–78.

23. Katherine Ott, "Disability Things: Material Culture and American Disability History, 1700–2010," in *Disability Histories*, ed. Susan Birch and Michael Rembis (Urbana: University of Illinois Press, 2014), 120.

24. Meryl Alper, *Giving Voice: Mobile Communication, Disability, and Inequality* (Cambridge, MA: MIT Press, 2017).

25. Mizuko Ito et al., *Hanging Out, Messing Around, and Geeking Out: Kids Living and Learning with New Media* (Cambridge, MA: MIT Press, 2010); Sonia Livingstone and Julian Sefton-Green, *The Class: Living and Learning in the Digital Age* (New York: New York University Press, 2016).

26. Meryl Alper, *Digital Youth with Disabilities* (Cambridge, MA: MIT Press, 2014).

27. Kristen Harrison, "Rude or Shrewd? Reframing Media Devices as Care Structures and Child Use as Accommodation," *Journal of Children and Media* 13, no. 3 (2019): 367–75; Nicole Martins, Andy King, and Rebecca Beights, "Audiovisual Media Content Preferences of Children with Autism Spectrum Disorders: Insights from Parental Interviews," *Journal of Autism and Developmental Disorders* 50, no. 9 (2020): 3092–100.

28. Jeanette M. Garcia et al., "Brief Report: The Impact of the COVID-19 Pandemic on Health Behaviors in Adolescents with Autism Spectrum Disorder," *Disability and Health Journal* 14, no. 2 (2021): 101021; Micah O. Mazurek et al., "Prevalence and Correlates of Screen-Based Media Use among Youths with Autism Spectrum Disorders," *Journal of Autism and Developmental Disorders* 42, no. 8 (2012): 1757–67.

29. Brenda Nally, Bob Houlton, and Sue Ralph, "Researches in Brief: The Management of Television and Video by Parents of Children with Autism," *Autism* 4, no. 3 (2000): 331–37; Howard C. Shane and Patti D. Albert, "Electronic Screen Media for Persons with Autism Spectrum Disorders: Results of a Survey," *Journal of Autism and Developmental Disorders* 38, no. 8 (2008): 1499–1508; Anja Stiller and Thomas Mößle, "Media Use among Children and Adolescents with Autism Spectrum Disorder: A Systematic Review," *Review Journal of Autism and Developmental Disorders* 5, no. 3 (2018): 227–46. Some parent memoirs provide glimpses into the mediated lives of autistic children, but these books reflect individual families who are unrepresentative of the majority of households; Judith Newman, *To Siri with Love: A Mother, Her Autistic Son, and the Kindness of Machines* (New York: Harper, 2017); Ron Suskind, *Life, Animated: A Story of Sidekicks, Heroes, and Autism* (Los Angeles: Kingswell, 2014).

30. Lydia Plowman, "Rethinking Context: Digital Technologies and Children's Everyday Lives," *Children's Geographies* 14, no. 2 (2016): 190–202.

31. Vasilis Galis, "Enacting Disability: How Can Science and Technology Studies Inform Disability Studies?," *Disability and Society* 26, no. 7 (2011): 825–38; John Law, "Introduction: Monsters, Machines, and Sociotechnical Relations," in *A Sociology of Monsters: Essays on Power, Technology, and Domination*, ed. John Law (New York: Routledge, 1991), 1–23; Susan Leigh Star, "Power, Technology, and the Phenomenology of Conventions: On Being Allergic to Onions," in *A Sociology of Monsters: Essays on Power, Technology, and Domination*, ed. John Law (New York: Routledge, 1991), 26–56; Ingunn Moser, "Disability and Promises of Technology: Technology, Subjectivity and Embodiment within an Order of the Normal," *Information, Communication & Society* 9, no. 3 (2006): 373–95.

32. Anne McGuire, *War on Autism: On the Cultural Logic of Normative Violence* (Ann Arbor: University of Michigan Press, 2016); Majia H. Nadesan, *Constructing Autism: Unraveling the "Truth" and Understanding the Social* (New York: Routledge, 2005); Chloe Silverman, *Understanding Autism: Parents, Doctors, and the History of a Disorder* (Princeton, NJ: Princeton University Press, 2012); Jennifer S. Singh, *Multiple Autisms: Spectrums of Advocacy and Genomic Science* (Minneapolis: University of Minnesota Press, 2015).

33. Alicia A. Broderick and Ari Ne'eman, "Autism as Metaphor: Narrative and Counter-Narrative," *International Journal of Inclusive Education* 12, no. 5–6 (2008): 459–76.

34. David T. Mitchell and Sharon L. Snyder, "Introduction: Disability Studies and the Double-Bind of Representation," in *The Body and Physical Difference: Discourses of Disability*, ed. David T. Mitchell and Sharon L. Snyder (Ann Arbor: University of Michigan Press, 1997), 8.

35. Law, "Monsters, Machines, and Sociotechnical Relations," 7.

36. "About iOS 14 Updates," https://support.apple.com/en-us/HT211808.

37. Nouchine Hadjikhani et al., "Look Me in the Eyes: Constraining Gaze in the Eye-Region Provokes Abnormally High Subcortical Activation in Autism," *Scientific Reports* 7, June 9, 2017, https://www.nature.com/articles/s41598-017-03378-5.

38. Elinor Ochs and Olga Solomon, "Autistic Sociality," *Ethos* 38, no. 1 (2010): 69–92.

39. Nelya Koteyko, Martine van Driel, and John Vines, "Autistic Sociality on Twitter: Enacted Affordances and Affiliation Strategies," *Discourse & Communication* (in press); Amit Pinchevski, "Displacing Incommunicability: Autism as an Epistemological Boundary," *Communication and Critical/Cultural Studies* 2, no. 2 (2005): 163–84; Amit Pinchevski and John Durham Peters, "Autism and New Media: Disability between Technology and Society," *New Media & Society* 18, no. 11 (2016): 2507–23; Jessica S. Rauchberg, "Imagining a Neuroqueer Technoscience," *Studies in Social Justice* 16, no. 2 (2022): 370–88.

40. Bettelheim, "Joey," 117.

41. Joyce Davidson and Michael Orsini, eds., *Worlds of Autism: Across the Spectrum of Neurological Difference* (Minneapolis: University of Minnesota Press, 2013).

42. M. Remi Yergeau, *Authoring Autism: On Rhetoric and Neurological Queerness* (Durham, NC: Duke University Press; 2017). See also Julia Bascom, ed., *Loud Hands: Autistic People, Speaking* (Washington, DC: The Autistic Press, 2012); Lydia X. Z. Brown, E. Ashkenazy, and Morénike Giwa Onaiwu, eds., *All the Weight of Our Dreams: On Living Racialized Autism* (n.p.: DragonBee Press, 2017).

43. Being a Jewish person and a member of an ethnoreligious minority group strongly shapes my commitment to social justice. Though I am conditionally read as White in the social spaces that I largely inhabit in the United States, I and members of my community are no strangers to the ills of white supremacy, antisemitism, and anti-Jewish hatred.

44. Carmel Conn, "'Sensory Highs', 'Vivid Rememberings' and 'Interactive Stimming': Children's Play Cultures and Experiences of Friendship in Autistic Autobiographies," *Disability & Society* 30, no. 8 (2015): 1192–206.

45. Anne Pasek, "Errant Bodies: Relational Aesthetics, Digital Communication, and the Autistic Analogy," *Disability Studies Quarterly* 35, no. 4 (2015).

46. Marisa H. Fisher et al., "A Population-Based Examination of Maltreatment Referrals and Substantiation for Children with Autism Spectrum Disorder," *Autism* 23, no. 5 (2019): 1335–40.

47. All personal names that appear in the book are pseudonyms and all personally identifiable information has been anonymized, removed, or obscured.

48. Ron Eglash, "Appropriating Technology: An Introduction," in *Appropriating Technology: Vernacular Science and Social Power*, ed. Ron Eglash et al. (Minneapolis:

University of Minnesota Press, 2004), vii–xxi; Lisa Rhee et al., "Social by Definition: How Users Define Social Platforms and Why It Matters," *Telematics and Informatics* 59 (2021): 1–16.

49. Stefanie Duguay, "You Can't Use This App for That: Exploring Off-Label Use through an Investigation of Tinder," *The Information Society* 36, no. 1 (2020): 30–42.

50. Claude S. Fischer, *America Calling: A Social History of the Telephone to 1940* (Berkeley: University of California Press, 1994).

51. Ron Westrum, *Technologies and Society: The Shaping of People and Things* (Belmont, CA: Wadsworth, 1991).

52. M.G.L. c. 766, or Chapter 766, was passed in 1972 under Massachusetts General Law and served as a model for the first federal special education legislation. It later moved to a new statutory home under M.G.L. c. 71(b), but it is still referred to as Chapter 766; Massachusetts General Law, Chapter 71B, Children with Special Needs, https://malegislature.gov/Laws/GeneralLaws/PartI/TitleXII/Chapter71B.

53. Lorella Terzi, "The Social Model of Disability: A Philosophical Critique," *Journal of Applied Philosophy* 21, no. 2 (2004): 141–57.

54. Nicole E. Rosen, Catherine Lord, and Fred R. Volkmar, "The Diagnosis of Autism: From Kanner to DSM-III to DSM-5 and Beyond," *Journal of Autism and Developmental Disorders* 51, no. 12 (2021): 4253–70.

55. American Psychiatric Association, *Diagnostic and Statistical Manual of Mental Disorders: DSM-5* (Washington, DC: American Psychiatric Association, 2013).

56. Silverman, *Understanding Autism*.

57. Herb Kutchins and Stuart A. Kirk, *Making Us Crazy: DSM: The Psychiatric Bible and the Creation of Mental Disorders* (New York: Free Press, 1997).

58. Eyal et al., *The Autism Matrix*.

59. Silverman, *Understanding Autism*; Irving K. Zola, "Medicine as an Institution of Social Control," *Sociological Review* 20, no. 4 (1972): 487–504.

60. Eli Clare, *Brilliant Imperfection: Grappling with Cure* (Durham, NC: Duke University Press, 2017); Hannah Ebben, "The Desire to Recognize the Undesirable: De/constructing the Autism Epidemic Metaphor and Contagion in Autism as a Discourse," *Feminist Formations* 30, no. 1 (2018): 141–63.

61. Eyal et al., *The Autism Matrix*; McGuire, *War on Autism*; Sarah M. Parsloe, and Avery E. Holton, "#Boycottautismspeaks: Communicating a Counternarrative through Cyberactivism and Connective Action," *Information, Communication & Society* 21, no. 8 (2018): 1116–33; Jim Sinclair, "Don't Mourn for Us," *Our Voice* 1, no. 3 (1993): 3–6.

62. Alison Kafer, *Feminist, Queer, Crip* (Bloomington, IN: Indiana University Press, 2013).

63. Mia Mingus, "Access Intimacy, Interdependence and Disability Justice," *Leaving Evidence*, April 12, 2017, https://leavingevidence.wordpress.com/2017/04/12/access -intimacy-interdependence-and-disability-justice/; Rayna Rapp and Faye Ginsburg, "Enabling Disability: Rewriting Kinship, Reimagining Citizenship," *Public Culture* 13, no. 3 (2001): 533–56.

64. Nicole Krueger, "The Story of Autism as Told By a 10-Year-Old with Autism," *International Society for Technology in Education (ISTE)*, December 18, 2018, https:// www.iste.org/explore/Student-voices/The-story-of-autism--as-told-by-a-10-year-old -with-autism.

65. Catherine J. Crompton et al., "Autistic Peer-to-Peer Information Transfer is Highly Effective," *Autism* 24, no. 7 (2020): 1704–12; Morton Ann Gernsbacher and M. Remi Yergeau, "Empirical Failures of the Claim That Autistic People Lack a Theory of Mind," *Archives of Scientific Psychology* 7, no. 1 (2019): 102–18.

66. Fletcher-Watson and Happé, *Autism*.

67. Fletcher-Watson and Happé.

68. Linda Beckman, Lisa Hellström, and Laura von Kobyletzki, "Cyber Bullying among Children with Neurodevelopmental Disorders: A Systematic Review," *Scandinavian Journal of Psychology* 61, no. 1 (2020): 54–67; Robin M. Kowalski and Allison Toth, "Cyberbullying among Youth with and without Disabilities," *Journal of Child & Adolescent Trauma* 11, no. 1 (2018): 7–15.

69. Alexia Ostrolenk et al., "Hyperlexia: Systematic Review, Neurocognitive Modelling, and Outcome," *Neuroscience & Biobehavioral Reviews* 79 (2017): 134–49.

70. Viktoria Lyons and Michael Fitzgerald, "Humor in Autism and Asperger Syndrome," *Journal of Autism and Developmental Disorders* 34, no. 5 (2004): 521–31.

71. Lorcan Kenny et al., "Which Terms Should Be Used to Describe Autism? Perspectives From the UK Autism Community," *Autism* 20, no. 4 (2016): 442–62; Riley Buijsman, Sander Begeer, and Anke M. Scheeren, "'Autistic Person' or 'Person with Autism'? Person-First Language Preference in Dutch Adults with Autism and Parents," *Autism*, August 11, 2022, https://journals.sagepub.com/doi/full/10.1177 /13623613221117914.

72. Martijn Dekker, "On Our Own Terms: Emerging Autistic Culture," Autscape, October 7, 1999, http://www.autscape.org/2015/programme/handouts/Autistic-Culture-07 -Oct-1999.pdf; Joseph N. Straus, "Autism as Culture," in *The Disability Studies Reader*, 4th ed., ed. Lennard J. Davis (New York: Routledge, 2013), 460–84.

73. Lorna Wing, "The Definition and Prevalence of Autism: A Review," *European Child & Adolescent Psychiatry* 2 (1993): 61–74.

74. Heather Thomas and Tom Boellstorff, "Beyond the Spectrum: Rethinking Autism," *Disability Studies Quarterly* 37, no. 1 (2017), https://dsq-sds.org/article/view /5375/4551.

75. Steve Silberman, *NeuroTribes: The Legacy of Autism and the Future of Neurodiversity* (New York: Penguin Random House, 2015), 479.

76. Elizabeth Fein, "Making Meaningful Worlds: Role-Playing Subcultures and the Autism Spectrum," *Culture, Medicine, and Psychiatry* 39, no. 2 (2015): 299–321; Elizabeth Fein, *Living on the Spectrum: Autism and Youth in Community* (New York: New York University Press, 2020); Elinor Ochs et al., "Autism and the Social World: An Anthropological Perspective," *Discourse Studies* 6, no. 2 (2004): 147–83; Sirota, "Narratives of Distinction."

77. Eugen Bleuler, *Dementia Praecox or the Group of Schizophrenias* (Madison, CT: International Universities Press, 1950 [1911]).

78. Leo Kanner, "Autistic Disturbances of Affective Contact," *Nervous Child* 2 (1943): 217–50.

79. Lorna Wing and Judith Gould, "Severe Impairments of Social Interaction and Associated Abnormalities in Children: Epidemiology and Classification," *Journal of Autism and Developmental Disorders* 9, no. 1 (1979): 11–29.

80. Autism self-advocates are those who claim autism as central to who they are and agency over their self-determination.

81. Douglas Biklen, *Autism and the Myth of the Person Alone* (New York: New York University Press, 2005); Edmund Coleman-Fountain, "Uneasy Encounters: Youth, Social (Dis) Comfort and the Autistic Self," *Social Science & Medicine* 185 (2017): 9–16; Roy Richard Grinker, "Commentary: On Being Autistic, and Social," *Ethos* 38, no. 1 (2010): 172–78; Steven K. Kapp, "Social Support, Well-Being, and Quality of Life among Individuals on the Autism Spectrum," *Pediatrics* 141, no. Supplement 4 (2018): S362–68.

82. Vikram K. Jaswal and Nameera Akhtar, "Being versus Appearing Socially Uninterested: Challenging Assumptions about Social Motivation in Autism," *Behavioral and Brain Sciences* 42 (2019): 1–73. For response to commentaries, see Vikram K. Jaswal and Nameera Akhtar, "Supporting Autistic Flourishing," *Behavioral and Brain Sciences* 42 (2019): e115.

83. Nameera Akhtar and Vikram K. Jaswal, "Stretching the Social: Broadening the Behavioral Indicators of Sociality," *Child Development Perspectives* 14, no. 1 (2020): 28–33.

84. Dara Shifrer and Angela Frederick, "Disability at the Intersections," *Sociology Compass* 13, no. 10 (2019): 1–16; Lauren R. Strand, "Charting Relations between Intersectionality Theory and the Neurodiversity Paradigm," *Disability Studies Quarterly* 37, no. 2 (2017), https://dsq-sds.org/article/view/5374/4647.

85. Harvey Blume, "Neurodiversity," *The Atlantic*, September 1998, https://www.theatlantic.com/magazine/archive/1998/09/neurodiversity/305909/.

86. Steven K. Kapp et al., "Deficit, Difference, or Both? Autism and Neurodiversity," *Developmental Psychology* 49, no. 1 (2013): 59–71.

87. Damian E. M. Milton, "On the Ontological Status of Autism: The 'Double Empathy Problem,'" *Disability & Society* 27, no. 6 (2012): 883–87.

88. Georg Simmel, "The Sociology of Sociability," *American Journal of Sociology* 55, no. 3 (1949): 254–61.

89. Ochs and Solomon, "Autistic Sociality."

90. Joyce Davidson and Mick Smith, "Autistic Autobiographies and More-than-Human Emotional Geographies," *Environment and Planning D: Society and Space* 27, no. 5 (2009): 898–916; Olga Solomon, "Doing, Being and Becoming: The Sociality of Children with Autism in Activities with Therapy Dogs and Other People," *Cambridge Journal of Anthropology* 30, no. 1 (2012): 109–26.

91. Ido Kedar, *Ido in Autismland: Climbing Out of Autism's Silent Prison* (n.p.: Sharon Kedar, 2012), 42.

92. Ben Belek, "Autism and the Proficiency of Social Ineptitude: Probing the Rules of 'Appropriate' Behavior," *Ethos* 46, no. 2 (2018): 162.

93. Belek, "Autism and the Proficiency of Social Ineptitude," 175–76.

94. Silberman, *NeuroTribes*.

95. Jonathan Sterne, "Bourdieu, Technique, and Technology," *Cultural Studies* 17, no. 3/4 (2003): 367–89.

96. Donna Z. Davis and Tom Boellstorff, "Compulsive Creativity: Virtual Worlds, Disability, and Digital Capital," *International Journal of Communication* 10 (2016): 2096–118.

97. Roy Richard Grinker, "Autism, 'Stigma,' Disability: A Shifting Historical Terrain," *Current Anthropology* 61, no. S21 (2020): S55–67.

98. Justine Egner, "#ActuallyAutistic: Using Twitter to Construct Individual and Collective Identity Narratives," *Studies in Social Justice* 16, no. 2 (2022): 349–69; Annuska Zolyomi, Ridley Jones, and Tomer Kaftan, "#ActuallyAutistic Sense-Making on Twitter," in *Proceedings of the 22nd ACM SIGACCESS Conference on Computers and Accessibility (ASSETS '20)* (New York: ACM, 2020), 1–4.

99. Kristen Gillespie-Lynch et al., "Intersections Between the Autism Spectrum and the Internet: Perceived Benefits and Preferred Functions of Computer-Mediated Communication," *Intellectual & Developmental Disabilities* 52, no. 6 (2014): 456–69; Brett Heasman and Alex Gillespie, "Neurodivergent Intersubjectivity: Distinctive Features of How Autistic People Create Shared Understanding," *Autism* 23, no. 4 (2019): 910–21.

100. Star, "Power, Technology, and the Phenomenology of Conventions."

101. Harry M. Collins, "Socialness and the Undersocialized Conception of Society," *Science, Technology, & Human Values* 23, no. 4 (1998): 502.

102. Aimi Hamraie and Kelly Fritsch, "Crip Technoscience Manifesto," *Catalyst: Feminism, Theory, Technoscience* 5, no. 1 (2019): 1–33; Rauchberg, "Imagining a Neuroqueer Technoscience."

103. Donald MacKenzie and Judy Wajcman, eds., *The Social Shaping of Technology*, 2nd ed. (Buckingham, UK: Open University Press, 1999).

104. Paul du Gay et al., *Doing Cultural Studies: The Story of the Sony Walkman*, 2nd ed. (Thousand Oaks, CA: Sage, 2013); Leah Lievrouw and Sonia Livingstone, "Introduction," in *Handbook of New Media: Social Shaping and Social Consequences*, ed. Leah Lievrouw and Sonia Livingstone (Thousand Oaks, CA: Sage, 2006), 1–14; Raymond Williams, *Television: Technology and Cultural Form* (London: Fontana, 1974).

105. Mills and Sterne, "Dismediation," 366.

106. Nancy Baym, "Social Media and the Struggle for Society," *Social Media + Society* 1, no. 1 (2015), https://journals.sagepub.com/doi/10.1177/2056305115580477; Nick Couldry, *Media, Society, World: Social Theory and Digital Media Practice* (Cambridge: Polity Press, 2012); Zizi Papacharissi, "We Have Always Been Social," *Social Media + Society* 1, no. 1 (2015), https://journals.sagepub.com/doi/full/10.1177/2056305115581185.

107. Nick Couldry and Jose Van Dijck, "Researching Social Media as if the Social Mattered," *Social Media + Society* 1, no. 2 (2015), https://journals.sagepub.com/doi/10.1177/2056305115604174; Nicholas A. John, *The Age of Sharing* (Cambridge: Polity Press, 2016); Stine Lomborg, *Social Media, Social Genres: Making Sense of the Ordinary* (New York: Routledge, 2014); Caleb T. Carr and Rebecca A. Hayes, "Social Media: Defining, Developing, and Divining," *Atlantic Journal of Communication* 23, no. 1 (2015), https://www.tandfonline.com/doi/abs/10.1080/15456870.2015.972282.

108. Mazurek et al., "Prevalence and Correlates of Screen-Based Media Use," 1757.

109. David Morley, *Family Television: Cultural Power and Domestic Leisure* (New York: Routledge, 1988); Lynn Spigel, *Make Room for TV: Television and the Family Ideal in Postwar America* (Chicago: University of Chicago Press, 1992).

110. James Lull, "Family Communication Patterns and the Social Uses of Television," *Communication Research* 7, no. 3 (1980): 319–34.

111. Kathryn E. Ringland, "Playful Places in Online Playgrounds: An Ethnography of a Minecraft Virtual World for Children with Autism" (PhD diss., University of California, Irvine, 2018).

112. Lily Cresswell, Rebecca Hinch, and Eilidh Cage, "The Experiences of Peer Relationships amongst Autistic Adolescents: A Systematic Review of the Qualitative Evidence," *Research in Autism Spectrum Disorders* 61 (2019): 45–60; Andrew J. O. Whitehouse et al., "Friendship, Loneliness and Depression in Adolescents with Asperger's Syndrome," *Journal of Adolescence* 32 (2009): 309–22.

113. Mary Wagner et al., "Social Activities of Youth with Disabilities," *NLTS2 Data Brief: A Report from the National Longitudinal Transition Study-2* 3, no. 1 (2004): 1–4.

114. Jessica C. O'Toole, *The Asperkid's (Secret) Book of Social Rules* (London: Jessica Kingsley, 2013).

115. Erik W. Carter et al., "Promoting Social Competence and Peer Relationships for Adolescents with Autism Spectrum Disorders," *Remedial and Special Education* 35, no. 2 (2014): 91–101.

116. Wendy B. Martin et al., "Promoting Science, Technology, and Engineering Self-Efficacy and Knowledge for All with an Autism Inclusion Maker Program," *Frontiers in Education* 5 (2020): 1–18.

117. Rebecca Cokley, "Reflections from an ADA Generation," *TEDxUniversityofRochester*, April 2018, https://www.ted.com/talks/rebecca_cokley_reflections_from_an_ada _generation.

118. Lori M. Takeuchi and Michael H. Levine, "Learning in a Digital Age: Toward a New Ecology of Human Development," in *Media and the Well-Being of Children and Adolescents*, ed. Amy B. Jordan and Daniel Romer (Oxford: Oxford University Press, 2014), 20–43.

119. Lane and Radesky, "Digital Media and Autism Spectrum Disorders."

120. Urie Bronfenbrenner, *The Ecology of Human Development* (Cambridge, MA: Harvard University Press, 1979); Urie Bronfenbrenner, *Making Human Beings Human: Bioecological Perspectives on Human Development* (Thousand Oaks, CA: Sage, 2005); Arnold Sameroff, "A Unified Theory of Development: A Dialectic Integration of Nature and Nurture," *Child Development* 81, no. 1 (2010): 6–22.

121. Jeffrey Danforth, "Ecological Model of Autism," in *Encyclopedia of Autism Spectrum Disorders*, ed. Fred R. Volkmar (New York: Springer, 2013).

122. Micah O. Mazurek and Colleen Wenstrup, "Television, Video Game and Social Media Use among Children with ASD and Typically Developing Siblings," *Journal of Autism and Developmental Disorders* 43, no. 6 (2013): 1258–71.

123. Christopher R. Engelhardt and Micah O. Mazurek, "Video Game Access, Parental Rules, and Problem Behavior: A Study of Boys with Autism Spectrum Disorder," *Autism* 18, no. 5 (2014): 529–37; Micah O. Mazurek and Christopher R. Engelhardt, "Video Game Use and Problem Behaviors in Boys with Autism Spectrum Disorders," *Research in Autism Spectrum Disorders* 7 (2013): 316–24.

124. Parts of this section are adapted from Meryl Alper and Madison Irons, "Digital Socializing in Children on the Autism Spectrum," in *The Routledge Companion to Digital Media and Children*, ed. Leila Green et al. (New York: Routledge, 2020), 348–57.

125. Mazurek et al., "Prevalence and Correlates of Screen-Based Media Use."

126. Julie J. Blais et al., "Adolescents Online: The Importance of Internet Activity Choices to Salient Relationships," *Journal of Youth and Adolescence* 37, no. 5 (2007): 522–36.

127. Lane and Radesky, "Digital Media and Autism Spectrum Disorders."

128. Bethany Good and Lin Fang, "Promoting Smart and Safe Internet Use among Children with Neurodevelopmental Disorders and Their Parents," *Clinical Social*

Work Journal 43, no. 2 (2015): 179–88; Kathryn E. Ringland, "A Place to Play: The (Dis)abled Embodied Experience for Autistic Children in Online Spaces," in *Proceedings of the 2019 ACM CHI Conference on Human Factors in Computing Systems* (New York: ACM, 2019), paper 288.

129. Melissa H. Kuo et al., "Media Use among Adolescents with Autism Spectrum Disorder," *Autism* 18, no. 8 (2014): 914–23.

130. Mazurek et al., "Prevalence and Correlates of Screen-Based Media Use."

131. Mazurek and Wenstrup, "Television, Video Game and Social Media Use."

132. Kathryn E. Ringland et al., "Making 'Safe': Community-Centered Practices in a Virtual World Dedicated to Children with Autism," in *Proceedings of the 2015 ACM International Conference on Computer Supported Collaborative Work (CSCW)* (New York: ACM, 2015), 1788–1800.

133. Victoria Rideout et al., *Common Sense Census: Media Use by Tweens and Teens, 2021* (San Francisco: Common Sense Media, 2021).

134. Julie A. Kientz et al., *Interactive Technologies and Autism*, 2nd ed. (San Rafael, CA: Morgan & Claypool, 2020).

135. Katta Spiel et al., "Agency of Autistic Children in Technology Research—A Critical Literature Review," *ACM Transactions on Computer-Human Interaction* 26, no. 6 (2019): 1–40.

136. Cynthia L. Bennett, Erin Brady, and Stacy M. Branham, "Interdependence as a Frame for Assistive Technology Research and Design," in *Proceedings of the ACM SIGACCESS Conference on Computers and Accessibility (ASSETS '18)* (New York: ACM, 2018), 161–73; Kiley Sobel et al., "Incloodle: Evaluating an Interactive Application for Young Children with Mixed Abilities," in *Proceedings of the 2016 ACM CHI Conference on Human Factors in Computing Systems* (New York: ACM, 2016), 165–76.

137. Gerardo Herrera et al., "Development of Symbolic Play through the Use of Virtual Reality Tools in Children with Autistic Spectrum Disorders," *Autism* 12, no. 2 (2008): 143–57.

138. Thoroughly analyzing the ethics of cognitive behavioral therapy and applied behavior analysis are beyond the scope here, but such techniques are greatly debated within and outside the autism community; Patrick Kirkham, "'The Line between Intervention and Abuse'—Autism and Applied Behaviour Analysis," *History of the Human Sciences* 30, no. 2 (2017): 107–26.

139. Nuria Aresti-Bartolome and Begonya Garcia-Zapirain, "Technologies as Support Tools for Persons with Autistic Spectrum Disorder: A Systematic Review," *International Journal of Environmental Research and Public Health* 11, no. 8 (2014): 7767–802.

140. Catalin Voss et al., "Effect of Wearable Digital Intervention for Improving Socialization in Children with Autism Spectrum Disorder: A Randomized Clinical Trial," *JAMA Pediatrics* 173, no. 5 (2019): 446–54.

141. Kristen Bottema-Beutel, Haerin Park, and So Yoon Kim, "Commentary on Social Skills Training Curricula for Individuals with ASD: Social Interaction, Authenticity, and Stigma," *Journal of Autism and Developmental Disorders* 48, no. 3 (2018): 953–64.

142. Scot Danforth and Srikala Naraian, "Use of the Machine Metaphor within Autism Research," *Journal of Developmental and Physical Disabilities* 19, no. 3 (2007): 273–90.

143. Temple Grandin, *Thinking in Pictures: And Other Reports from My Life with Autism* (New York: Doubleday, 1995).

144. Olga Solomon, "What a Dog Can Do: Children with Autism and Therapy Dogs in Social Interaction," *Ethos* 38, no. 1 (2010): 143–66.

145. Kathleen Richardson et al., "Robot Enhanced Therapy for Children with Autism (DREAM): A Social Model of Autism," *IEEE Technology and Society Magazine* 37, no. 1 (2018): 30–39.

146. Eve Müller, Adriana Schuler, and Gregory B. Yates, "Social Challenges and Supports from the Perspective of Individuals with Asperger Syndrome and Other Autism Spectrum Disabilities," *Autism* 12 no. 2 (2008): 173–90.

147. Carmel Conn, *Autism and the Social World of Childhood: A Sociocultural Perspective on Theory and Practice* (New York: Routledge, 2014).

148. Gerrit I. van Schalkwyk et al., "Social Media Use, Friendship Quality, and the Moderating Role of Anxiety in Adolescents with Autism Spectrum Disorder," *Journal of Autism and Developmental Disorders* 47, no. 9 (2017): 2805–13.

149. Olivia Tucker, "TikTok Creators Like Paige Layle Are Redefining Narratives about Autism," *Teen Vogue*, January 20, 2021, https://www.teenvogue.com/story/tiktok-creators-paige-layle-autism.

150. Ringland et al., "Making 'Safe'"; Kathryn E. Ringland et al., "'Will I Always Be Not Social?' Re-conceptualizing Sociality in the Context of a Minecraft Community for Autism," in *Proceedings of the 2016 ACM CHI Conference on Human Factors in Computing Systems* (New York: ACM, 2016), 1256–69.

151. Dan Goodley and Katherine Runswick-Cole, "Emancipating Play: Dis/abled Children, Development, and Deconstruction," *Disability and Society* 25, no. 4 (2010): 499–512.

152. Puzzle pieces are a contested symbol of autism for many autistic people. For further explanation, see Roy Richard Grinker and David Mandell, "Notes on a Puzzle Piece," *Autism* 19, no. 6 (2015): 643–45; Liz Pellicano et al., "A New Era for Autism Research, and for Our Journal," *Autism* 22, no. 2 (2018): 82–83.

153. Angela Frederick and Dara Shifter, "Race and Disability: From Analogy to Intersectionality," *Sociology of Race and Ethnicity* 5, no. 2 (2019): 200–214. The "spectrum" is a useful metaphor for social stratification, though it might not be the best one; Marianne Cooper and Allison J. Pugh, "Families across the Income Spectrum: A Decade in Review," *Journal of Marriage and Family* 82, no. 1 (2020): 272–99. Social class cannot

exist as a spectrum if one sees class as inherently about power relations and shifting distinctions between ruling and subjugated classes; Pierre Bourdieu, *Outline of a Theory of Practice*, trans. Richard Nice (Cambridge: Cambridge University Press, 1972); Pierre Bourdieu, *Distinction: A Social Critique of the Judgment of Taste*, trans. Richard Nice (Cambridge, MA: Harvard University Press, 1984). With respect to media, I am also alluding to "radio spectrum," or the electromagnetic waves widely used in modern technology and telecommunication.

154. Kristy Anderson et al., *National Autism Indicators Report: Children on the Autism Spectrum and Family Financial Hardship* (Philadelphia: Life Course Outcomes Program, Drexel Autism Institute, Drexel University, 2020).

155. Eyal et al., *The Autism Matrix*.

156. Matthew J. Maenner et al., "Prevalence and Characteristics of Autism Spectrum Disorder among Children Aged 8 Years—Autism and Developmental Disabilities Monitoring Network, 11 Sites, United States, 2018," *Morbidity and Mortality Weekly Report (MMWR) Surveillance Summaries* 70, no. 11 (2021): 1–16.

157. National Center for Education Statistics, "Children 3 to 21 Years Old Served under Individuals with Disabilities Education Act (IDEA), Part B, by Type of Disability: Selected Years, 1976–77 through 2019–20," *Digest of Education Statistics* (n.d.), https://nces.ed.gov/programs/digest/d20/tables/dt20_204.30.asp.

158. Hyman et al., "Identification, Evaluation, and Management."

159. Anne de Leeuw, Francesca Happé, and Rosa A. Hoekstra, "A Conceptual Framework for Understanding the Cultural and Contextual Factors on Autism across the Globe," *Autism Research* 13, no. 7 (2020): 1029–50.

160. Sandra Magaña et al., "Racial and Ethnic Disparities in Quality of Health Care among Children with Autism and Other Developmental Disabilities," *Intellectual and Developmental Disabilities* 50, no. 4 (2012): 287–99.

161. Sarah Garcia, Jennifer Hall-Lande, and Kelly Nye-Lengerman, "Factors Influencing Low Prevalence of Neurodevelopmental Disabilities among US Hispanic/Latino Children," *Journal of Racial and Ethnic Health Disparities* 6, no. 6 (2019): 1107–21.

162. Bryn Harris, Erin E. Barton, and Maryellen Brunson McClain, "Inclusion of Racially and Ethnically Diverse Populations in ASD Intervention Research," *Research in Autism Spectrum Disorders* 73 (2020): 101551; Elizabeth A. West et al., "Racial and Ethnic Diversity of Participants in Research Supporting Evidence-Based Practices for Learners with Autism Spectrum Disorder," *Journal of Special Education* 50, no. 3 (2016): 151–63.

163. Katharina Dworzynski et al., "How Different Are Girls and Boys above and below the Diagnostic Threshold for Autism Spectrum Disorders?," *Journal of the American Academy of Child & Adolescent Psychiatry* 51, no. 8 (2012): 788–97.

164. Maenner et al., "Prevalence and Characteristics of Autism Spectrum Disorder."

165. David Mandell et al., "Disparities in Diagnoses Received Prior to a Diagnosis of Autism Spectrum Disorder," *Journal of Autism and Developmental Disorders* 37, no. 9 (2007): 1795–802. These categorical determinations have a significant impact on disabled children's life trajectories. For example, students of color labeled with emotional disabilities have higher rates of school suspensions and expulsions. These forms of punishment send children on a path toward the juvenile and criminal justice system, also known as the "school-to-prison pipeline"; Charles Bell, "Special Needs Under Siege: From Classrooms to Incarceration," *Sociology Compass* 10, no. 8 (2016): 698–705.

166. Maenner et al., "Prevalence and Characteristics of Autism Spectrum Disorder."

167. Maenner et al.

168. Linda Blum, *Raising Generation Rx: Mothering Kids with Invisible Disabilities in an Age of Inequality* (New York: New York University Press, 2015).

169. Silberman, *NeuroTribes*.

170. Blum, *Raising Generation Rx*.

171. Various additional disabilities may accompany autism: classic medical problems (such as epilepsy and gastrointestinal issues), developmental diagnoses (like intellectual disability and language delay), mental health conditions (such as anxiety and eating disorders, especially among autistic girls), and genetic conditions (such as Fragile X syndrome); Hannah Furfaro, "Conditions That Accompany Autism, Explained," *Spectrum*, July 25, 2018, https://www.spectrumnews.org/news /conditions-accompany-autism-explained.

172. Lawrence D. Shriberg et al., "Speech and Prosody Characteristics of Adolescents and Adults with High-Functioning Autism and Asperger Syndrome," *Journal of Speech, Language, and Hearing Research* 44, no. 5 (2001): 1097–115.

173. Spiel et al., "Agency of Autistic Children in Technology Research."

174. Michael Burawoy, "Revisits: An Outline of a Theory of Reflexive Ethnography," *American Sociological Review* 68, no. 5 (2003): 645–79.

175. Thomas R. Lindlof and Bryan C. Taylor, *Qualitative Communication Research Methods*, 2nd ed. (Thousand Oaks, CA: Sage, 2002).

176. Nadesan, *Constructing Autism*; Mitzi Waltz, "The Production of the 'Normal' Child: Neurodiversity and the Commodification of Parenting," in *Neurodiversity Studies*, ed. Hanna Bertilsdotter Rosqvist, Nick Chown, and Anna Stenning (London: Routledge, 2020), 15–26.

177. Margaret H. Laurie et al., "An International Survey of Parental Attitudes to Technology Use by Their Autistic Children at Home," *Journal of Autism and Developmental Disorders* 49, no. 4 (2019): 1517–30.

178. Sandra B. Vanegas and Randa Abdelrahim, "Characterizing the Systems of Support for Families of Children with Disabilities: A Review of the Literature," *Journal of Family Social Work* 19, no. 4 (2016): 286–327.

179. Cynthia L. Bennett and Os Keyes, "What Is the Point of Fairness?," *Interactions* 27, no. 3 (2020): 35–39.

CHAPTER 2

1. Though *Free to Be* is not currently available on any video streaming services, Jennifer had years ago downloaded it onto the iPad through a peer-to-peer file sharing network.

2. Gerrit I. van Schalkwyk, Katherine Klingensmith, and Fred R. Volkmar, "Gender Identity and Autism Spectrum Disorders," *Yale Journal of Biology and Medicine* 88, no. 1 (2015): 81–83; Daniel E. Shumer et al., "Brief Report: Autistic Traits in Mothers and Children Associated with Child's Gender Nonconformity," *Journal of Autism and Developmental Disorders* 45, no. 5 (2015): 1489–94.

3. Geoffrey C. Bowker and Susan Leigh Star, *Sorting Things Out: Classification and Its Consequences* (Cambridge, MA: MIT Press, 1999); Lisa Nakamura, "Race in/for Cyberspace: Identity Tourism and Racial Passing on the Internet," in *The Cybercultures Reader*, ed. David Bell and Barbara M. Kennedy (New York: Routledge, 2000), 712–20.

4. William R. Penuel and James V. Wertsch, "Vygotsky and Identity Formation: A Sociocultural Approach," *Educational Psychologist* 30, no. 2 (1995): 83–92; Susan Harter, *Construction of the Self: A Developmental Perspective* (New York: Guilford Press, 1999).

5. Lingling Zhang and Beth Haller, "Consuming Image: How Mass Media Impact the Identity of People with Disabilities," *Communication Quarterly* 61, no. 3 (2013): 319–34.

6. Jean Piaget, *The Construction of Reality in the Child*, trans. Margaret Cook (New York: Basic Books, 1954).

7. Erik H. Erikson, *Childhood and Society* (New York: W. W. Norton, 1950).

8. Dan P. McAdams and Claudia Zapata-Gietl, "Three Strands of Identity Development across the Human Life Course: Reading Erik Erikson in Full," in *The Oxford Handbook of Identity Development*, ed. Kate C. McLean and Moin Syed (Oxford: Oxford University Press, 2015), 81–94.

9. Carl R. Rogers, "Theory of Therapy, Personality and Interpersonal Relationships as Developed in the Client-Centered Framework," in *Psychology: A Study of Science*, vol. 3, *Formulations of the Person and the Social Context*, ed. Sigmund Kock (New York: McGraw-Hill, 1959).

10. James E. Marcia, "Identity in Adolescence," *Handbook of Adolescent Psychology* 9, no. 11 (1980): 159–87.

11. Peggy A. Thoits and Lauren K. Virshup, "Me's and We's: Forms and Functions of Social Identities," in *Self and Identity: Fundamental Issues*, ed. Richard D. Ashmore and Lee Jussim (Oxford: Oxford University Press, 1997), 106–33.

12. Henri Tajfel and John Turner, "An Integrative Theory of Intergroup Conflict," in *The Social Psychology of Intergroup Relations*, ed. William G. Austin and Stephen

Worchel (Monterey, CA: Brooks/Cole, 1979), 33–47; S. Alexander Haslam et al., "Social Identity, Health and Well-Being: An Emerging Agenda for Applied Psychology," *Applied Psychology* 58, no. 1 (2009): 1–23.

13. Mary Bucholtz and Kira Hall, "Identity and Interaction: A Sociocultural Linguistic Approach," *Discourse Studies* 7, no. 4–5 (2005): 585–614.

14. Erving Goffman, *The Presentation of Self in Everyday Life* (New York: Doubleday, 1956).

15. Anthony Giddens, *Modernity and Self-Identity* (Cambridge: Polity Press, 1991).

16. Anjali Forber-Pratt et al., "Disability Identity Development: A Systematic Review of the Literature," *Rehabilitation Psychology* 62, no. 2 (2017): 198–207; Joyce Davidson and Victoria L. Henderson, "'Coming Out' on the Spectrum: Autism, Identity and Disclosure," *Social & Cultural Geography* 11, no. 2 (2010): 155–70.

17. Sarah M. Parsloe, "Discourses of Disability, Narratives of Community: Reclaiming an Autistic Identity Online," *Journal of Applied Communication Research* 43, no. 3 (2015): 336–56.

18. Ian Hacking, *The Social Construction of What?* (Cambridge, MA: Harvard University Press, 1999). Such fluidity has led some autistic people to adopt the infinity loop as a shared symbol of autism meant to convey the nonlinearity of the condition, the lack of a clear beginning or end to the "spectrum," and a diversity of lived experiences; Sara Luterman, "The Biggest Autism Advocacy Group Is Still Failing Too Many Autistic People," *Washington Post*, February 14, 2020, https://www.washingtonpost.com/outlook/2020/02/14/biggest-autism-advocacy-group-is-still-failing-too-many-autistic-people/.

19. Laura F. Lewis, "Realizing a Diagnosis of Autism Spectrum Disorder as an Adult," *International Journal of Mental Health Nursing* 25, no. 4 (2016): 346–54.

20. Ellen Samuels, *Fantasies of Identification: Disability, Gender, Race* (New York: New York University Press, 2014).

21. Some within the autism community debate the validity of self-diagnoses and thus the legitimacy of self-diagnosed autistics to represent autism to the outside world. The internet offers an ever-expanding space for individuals with and without diagnoses to discuss autism as an identity outside of professional authority; Jennifer C. Sarrett, "Biocertification and Neurodiversity: The Role and Implications of Self-Diagnosis in Autistic Communities," *Neuroethics* 9, no. 1 (2016): 23–36.

22. Catherine D. Tan, "'I'm a Normal Autistic Person, Not an Abnormal Neurotypical': Autism Spectrum Disorder Diagnosis as Biographical Illumination," *Social Science & Medicine* 197 (2018): 161–67.

23. Kate Cooper, Laura G. E. Smith, and Ailsa Russell, "Social Identity, Self-Esteem, and Mental Health in Autism," *European Journal of Social Psychology* 47, no. 7 (2017): 844–54.

24. Rosalind Cooper et al., "'I'm Proud to Be a Little Bit Different': The Effects of Autistic Individuals' Perceptions of Autism and Autism Social Identity on Their

Collective Self-Esteem," *Journal of Autism and Developmental Disorders* 51, no. 2 (2021): 704–14.

25. Henry Angulo, Michelle Chan, and Laura DeThorne, "Life Is a Stage: Autistic Perspectives on Neurotypicality," *Autism in Adulthood* 1, no. 4 (2019): 276–85; Anna-Kaisa Newheiser and Manuela Barreto, "Hidden Costs of Hiding Stigma: Ironic Interpersonal Consequences of Concealing a Stigmatized Identity in Social Interactions," *Journal of Experimental Social Psychology* 52 (2014): 58–70.

26. Barry Carpenter, Francesca Happé, and Jo Egerton, eds., *Girls and Autism: Educational, Family and Personal Perspectives* (New York: Routledge, 2019).

27. Qtd. in Angulo, Chan, and DeThorne, "Life Is a Stage," 281.

28. Rosemarie Garland-Thomson, *Extraordinary Bodies: Figuring Physical Disability in American Culture and Literature* (New York: Columbia University Press, 1997); Simi Linton, *Claiming Disability: Knowledge and Identity* (New York: New York University Press, 1998); Tom Shakespeare, "Disability, Identity and Difference," in *Exploring the Divide: Illness and Disability*, ed. Colin Barnes and Geof Mercer (Leeds, UK: Disability Press, 1996), 94–113; Tobin Siebers, *Disability Theory* (Ann Arbor: University of Michigan Press, 2008).

29. Charlotte Brownlow, "Presenting the Self: Negotiating a Label of Autism," *Journal of Intellectual and Developmental Disability* 35, no. 1 (2010): 14–21; Steven K. Kapp et al., "Deficit, Difference, or Both? Autism and Neurodiversity," *Developmental Psychology* 49, no. 1 (2013): 59–71.

30. Nancy Bagatell, "Orchestrating Voices: Autism, Identity and the Power of Discourse," *Disability & Society* 22, no. 4 (2007): 413–26; Lennard Davis, *The End of Normal: Identity in a Biocultural Era* (Ann Arbor: University of Michigan Press, 2013); Sarrett, "Biocertification and Neurodiversity."

31. Lydia X. Z. Brown, E. Ashkenazy, and Morénike Giwa Onaiwu, eds., *All the Weight of Our Dreams: On Living Racialized Autism* (n.p.: DragonBee Press, 2017).

32. Patricia Hill Collins, *Fighting Words: Black Women and the Search for Justice* (Minneapolis: University of Minneapolis Press, 1998); Kimberlé Crenshaw, "Mapping the Margins: Intersectionality, Identity Politics, and Violence against Women of Color," *Stanford Law Review* 43, no. 6 (1991): 1241–99.

33. Ange-Marie Hancock, "When Multiplication Doesn't Equal Quick Addition: Examining Intersectionality as a Research Paradigm," *Perspectives on Politics* 5, no. 1 (2007): 63–79. For incorporation in feminist disability studies, see Rosemarie Garland-Thomson, "Feminist Disability Studies," *Signs: Journal of Women in Culture and Society* 30, no. 2 (2005): 1557–87; Sami Schalk, "Coming to Claim Crip: Disidentification with/in Disability Studies," *Disability Studies Quarterly* 33, no. 2 (2013).

34. Justine Egner, "'The Disability Rights Community Was Never Mine': Neuroqueer Disidentification," *Gender & Society* 33, no. 1 (2019): 123–47.

35. Jennifer S. Singh, *Multiple Autisms: Spectrums of Advocacy and Genomic Science* (Minneapolis: University of Minnesota Press, 2015).

36. Andrea MacLeod, Ann Lewis, and Christopher Robertson, "'Why Should I Be Like Bloody Rain Man?!' Navigating the Autistic Identity," *British Journal of Special Education* 40, no. 1 (2013): 41–49; Anders Nordahl-Hansen, Magnus Tøndevold, and Sue Fletcher-Watson, "Mental Health on Screen: A DSM-5 Dissection of Portrayals of Autism Spectrum Disorders in Film and TV," *Psychiatry Research* 262 (2018): 351–53.

37. John Fiske, *Understanding Popular Culture* (New York: Routledge, 1989); Henry Jenkins, *Textual Poachers: Television Fans and Participatory Culture* (New York: Routledge, 1992).

38. Stuart Hall, "Encoding/Decoding," in *Culture, Media, Language*, ed. Stuart Hall et al. (London: Hutchinson, 1980), 128–38.

39. Sarah Kurchak, "Imagining a Fuller Spectrum of Autism on TV," *Pacific Standard*, February 22, 2018, https://psmag.com/social-justice/autistic-license.

40. Samuels, *Fantasies of Identification*.

41. Jade Budowski, "Autistic Voices, Community Members, and Experts Look Back (and Forward) at Autism Representation on TV," Decider, August 18, 2017, https://decider.com/2017/08/18/autistic-voices-community-members-and-experts-look-back-and-forward-at-autism-representation-on-tv/.

42. Variety, "Sia Talks Directing Her First Feature Film 'Music,'" YouTube, October 29, 2020, https://www.youtube.com/watch?v=SIVppt0YPio.

43. Douwe Draaisma, "Stereotypes of Autism," *Philosophical Transactions of the Royal Society B: Biological Sciences* 364, no. 1522 (2009): 1475–80.

44. Sonya F. Loftis, *Imagining Autism: Fiction and Stereotypes on the Spectrum* (Bloomington: Indiana University Press, 2015).

45. Julia Bascom, "Someone Who Moves Like You," *Thinking Person's Guide to Autism*, August 13, 2012, http://www.thinkingautismguide.com/2012/08/someone-who-moves-like-you.html.

46. Kurchak, "Imagining a Fuller Spectrum," para. 7.

47. Baden Gaeke-Franz, "Rejection or Celebration? Autistic Representation in Sitcom Television," *Studies in Social Justice* 16, no. 2 (2022): 308–22; Christa Mullis, "Reflection: Autistic-Coded Characters and Fans in Fandom," *Canadian Journal of Disability Studies* 8, no. 2 (2019): 147–56.

48. Erving Goffman, *Stigma: Notes on the Management of Spoiled Identity* (New York: Touchstone, 1963).

49. So Yoon Kim and Kristen Bottema-Beutel, "Negotiation of Individual and Collective Identities in the Online Discourse of Autistic Adults," *Autism in Adulthood* 1, no. 1

(2019): 69–78; Vered Seidmann, "On Blogs, Autistic Bloggers, and Autistic Space," *Information, Communication & Society* 24, no. 15 (2021): 2277–92.

50. Rosalind W. Picard and Jonathan Klein, "Computers that Recognise and Respond to User Emotion: Theoretical and Practical Implications," *Interacting with Computers* 14, no. 2 (2002): 157.

51. Nomy Bitman, "'Authentic' Digital Inclusion? Dis/ability Performances on Social Media by Users with Concealable Communicative Disabilities," *New Media & Society* 24, no. 2 (2022): 401–19.

52. Henry Angulo-Jiménez and Laura DeThorne, "Narratives about Autism: An Analysis of YouTube Videos by Individuals Who Self-Identify as Autistic," *American Journal of Speech-Language Pathology* 28, no. 2 (2019): 569–90; Joyce Davidson, "Autistic Culture Online: Virtual Communication and Cultural Expression on the Spectrum," *Social & Cultural Geography* 9, no. 7 (2008): 791–806; Joyce Davidson and Michael Orsini, "The Shifting Horizons of Autism Online," in *Worlds of Autism: Across the Spectrum of Neurological Difference*, ed. Joyce Davidson and Michael Orsini (Minneapolis: University of Minnesota Press, 2013), 285–304.

53. Anne-Marie DePape and Sally Lindsay, "Lived Experiences from the Perspective of Individuals with Autism Spectrum Disorder: A Qualitative Meta-Synthesis," *Focus on Autism and Other Developmental Disabilities* 31, no. 1 (2016): 60–71.

54. Lise Mogensen and Jan Mason, "The Meaning of a Label for Teenagers Negotiating Identity: Experiences with Autism Spectrum Disorder," *Sociology of Health & Illness* 37, no. 2 (2015): 255–69.

55. M. Ariel Cascio, "'Asperger's Syndrome Does Not Exist': The Limits of Brain-Based Identity Discourses around Asperger's Syndrome and Autism in Italy," *BioSocieties* 16, no. 2 (2021): 196–224; Mary C. King, Emma I. Williams, and Kate Gleeson, "Using Photographs to Explore Self-Understanding in Adolescent Boys with an Autism Spectrum Condition," *Journal of Intellectual & Developmental Disability* 44, no. 2 (2019): 232–43. For a notable exception, see John F. Strang et al., "'They Thought It Was an Obsession': Trajectories and Perspectives of Autistic Transgender and Gender-Diverse Adolescents," *Journal of Autism and Developmental Disorders* 48, no. 12 (2018): 4039–55.

56. Megan Clark and Dawn Adams, "The Self-Identified Positive Attributes and Favourite Activities of Children on the Autism Spectrum," *Research in Autism Spectrum Disorders* 72 (2020): 1–10.

57. Bagatell, "Orchestrating Voices"; Anthony Lee and R. Peter Hobson, "On Developing Self-Concepts: A Controlled Study of Children and Adolescents with Autism," *Journal of Child Psychology and Psychiatry and Allied Disciplines* 39, no. 8 (1998): 1131–44.

58. Jennifer L. Jones et al., "'Are You by Chance on the Spectrum?' Adolescents with Autism Spectrum Disorder Making Sense of Their Diagnoses," *Disability & Society* 30, no. 10 (2015): 1490–504.

59. Lily Cresswell and Eilidh Cage, "'Who Am I?' An Exploratory Study of the Relationships between Identity, Acculturation and Mental Health in Autistic Adolescents," *Journal of Autism and Developmental Disorders* 49, no. 7 (2019): 2901–12.

60. Lauren D. Berkovits, Christine T. Moody, and Jan Blacher, "'I Don't Feel Different. But Then Again, I Wouldn't Know What It Feels Like to Be Normal:' Perspectives of Adolescents with Autism Spectrum Disorder," *Journal of Autism and Developmental Disorders* 50, no. 3 (2020): 831–43; Jones et al., "'Are You by Chance on the Spectrum?'"

61. Cascio, "'Asperger's Syndrome Does Not Exist.'"

62. AnnMarie D. Baines, "Positioning, Strategizing, and Charming: How Students with Autism Construct Identities in Relation to Disability," *Disability & Society* 27, no. 4 (2012): 547–61; Cascio, "'Asperger's Syndrome Does Not Exist.'"

63. Tomisin Oredipe et al., "Does Learning You Are Autistic at a Younger Age Lead to Better Adult Outcomes? A Participatory Exploration of the Perspectives of Autistic University Students," *Autism*, April 11, 2022, https://journals.sagepub.com/doi/10.1177/13623613221086700.

64. Bridget Kiely et al., "Patterns and Outcomes of Diagnosis Disclosure to Youth with Autism Spectrum Disorder," *Journal of Developmental & Behavioral Pediatrics* 41, no. 6 (2020): 443–51.

65. Laura Crane et al., "Parents' Views and Experiences of Talking about Autism with Their Children," *Autism* 23, no. 8 (2019): 1969–81.

66. Barbara J. Myers, Virginia H. Mackintosh, and Robin P. Goin-Kochel, "'My Greatest Joy and My Greatest Heart Ache:' Parents' Own Words on How Having a Child in the Autism Spectrum Has Affected Their Lives and Their Families' Lives," *Research in Autism Spectrum Disorders* 3, no. 3 (2009): 670–84.

67. M. Ariel Cascio, "Neurodiversity: Autism Pride among Mothers of Children with Autism Spectrum Disorders," *Intellectual and Developmental Disabilities* 50, no. 3 (2012): 273–83; Brendan Hart, "Autism Parents & Neurodiversity: Radical Translation, Joint Embodiment and the Prosthetic Environment," *BioSocieties* 9, no. 3 (2014): 284–303; Ariana Riccio et al., "How Is Autistic Identity in Adolescence Influenced by Parental Disclosure Decisions and Perceptions of Autism?," *Autism* 25, no. 2 (2021): 374–88.

68. Isaac C. Smith et al., "Parental Disclosure of ASD Diagnosis to the Child: A Systematic Review," *Evidence-Based Practice in Child and Adolescent Mental Health* 3, no. 2 (2018): 98–105.

69. Cooper, Smith, and Russell, "Social Identity, Self-Esteem, and Mental Health."

70. Laura Crane et al., "Autistic Parents' Views and Experiences of Talking about Autism with Their Autistic Children," *Autism* 25, no. 4 (2021): 1161–67.

71. Nick Hodge, Emma J. Rice, and Lisa Reidy, "'They're Told All the Time They're Different': How Educators Understand Development of Sense of Self for Autistic

Pupils," *Disability & Society* 34, no. 9–10 (2019): 1353–78; Emma I. Williams, Kate Gleeson, and Bridget E. Jones, "How Pupils on the Autism Spectrum Make Sense of Themselves in the Context of Their Experiences in a Mainstream School Setting: A Qualitative Metasynthesis," *Autism* 23, no. 1 (2019): 8–28.

72. Wendy B. Martin et al., "Promoting Science, Technology, and Engineering Self-Efficacy and Knowledge for All with an Autism Inclusion Maker Program," *Frontiers in Education* 5 (2020): 1–18.

73. Yellow Ladybugs, "About Us," Yellow Ladybugs, https://www.yellowladybugs .com.au/AboutUs.

74. Alana Whitlock et al., "Recognition of Girls on the Autism Spectrum by Primary School Educators: An Experimental Study," *Autism Research* 13, no. 8 (2020): 1358–72.

75. Yenn Purkis and Emma Goodall. *The Parents' Practical Guide to Resilience for Children Aged 2–10 on the Autism Spectrum* (London: Jessica Kingsley, 2017).

76. Martin et al., "Promoting Science, Technology, and Engineering."

77. Katie Davis, "Tensions of Identity in a Networked Era: Young People's Perspectives on the Risks and Rewards of Online Self-Expression," *New Media & Society* 14, no. 4 (2012): 634–51; Jackie Marsh, "Ritual, Performance and Identity Construction," in *Popular Culture, New Media, and Digital Literacy in Early Childhood*, ed. Jackie Marsh (London: RoutledgeFalmer, 2005), 28–50.

78. danah boyd, "Why Youth (Heart) Social Network Sites: The Role of Networked Publics in Teenage Social Life," in *Youth, Identity, and Digital Media*, ed. David Buckingham (Cambridge, MA: MIT Press, 2008), 119–42; Patti M. Valkenburg, Alexander P. Schouten, and Jochen Peter, "Adolescents' Identity Experiments on the Internet," *New Media & Society* 7, no. 3 (2005): 383–402.

79. Detra Price-Dennis, Kathlene A. Holmes, and Emily Smith, "Exploring Digital Literacy Practices in an Inclusive Classroom," *The Reading Teacher* 69, no. 2 (2015): 195–205.

80. Berkovits, Moody, and Blacher, "'I Don't Feel Different'"; Cascio, "'Asperger's Syndrome Does Not Exist.'"

81. Soraya Giaccardi et al., *See Jane 2019 Report* (Los Angeles: The Geena Davis Institute for Gender in Media, 2019).

82. Elizabeth A. Wheeler, *HandiLand: The Crippest Place on Earth* (Ann Arbor: University of Michigan Press, 2019). Some autistic scholars have argued that some narratives for youth audiences that concern issues of neurodiversity inconsistently value neurological variation; Alyssa H. Zisk, "Pulling the Rug out from under (Neuro) Divergence in the *Divergent* Universe," *Critical Disability Discourses* 9 (2019), https:// cdd.journals.yorku.ca/index.php/cdd/article/view/39757.

83. Sarah Kapit, *Get a Grip, Vivy Cohen!* (New York: Dial Books for Young Readers, 2020); Ido Kedar, *In Two Worlds* (n.p.: Double Buck Publishing, 2018); Jen Malina, *Too Sticky! Sensory Issues with Autism* (Chicago: Albert Whitman & Company, 2020).

84. Siena Castellon, *The Spectrum Girl's Survival Guide: How to Grow Up Awesome and Autistic* (London: Jessica Kingsley, 2020).

85. Haley Moss, "How Video Games Gave Me a Foundation of Acceptance Growing Up Autistic," Mic, December 12, 2019, https://www.mic.com/p/how-video-games -gave-me-a-foundation-of-acceptance-growing-up-autistic-19446436.

86. Kathryn Ringland et al., "Making in Minecraft: A Means of Self-Expression for Youth with Autism," in *Proceedings of the 2017 Conference on Interaction Design and Children* (New York: ACM, 2017), 340–45; Kathryn E. Ringland, "'Autsome': Foster-ing an Autistic Identity in an Online Minecraft Community for Youth with Autism," in *Proceedings of iConference 2019* (New York: Springer, 2019), 132–43.

87. Wheeler, *HandiLand*.

88. Asaka Park, "I'm a Disabled Teenager, and Social Media Is My Lifeline," *New York Times*, June 5, 2019, https://www.nytimes.com/2019/06/05/learning/im-a-disabled -teenager-and-social-media-is-my-lifeline.html.

89. Olivia Tucker, "TikTok Creators Like Paige Layle Are Redefining Narratives about Autism," *Teen Vogue*, January 20, 2021, https://www.teenvogue.com/story/tiktok -creators-paige-layle-autism.

90. Patrick Barkham, "Natural Talent: The 16-Year-Old Writer Taking the World by Storm," *Guardian*, May 16, 2020, https://www.theguardian.com/books/2020/may/16 /dara-mcanulty-nature-writing-diary-of-a-young-naturalist; Thomas Olesen, "Greta Thunberg's Iconicity: Performance and Co-performance in the Social Media Ecology," *New Media & Society*, November 25, 2020, https://journals.sagepub.com/doi/full/10 .1177/1461444820975416.

91. Chang Sup Park, Qian Liu, and Barbara K. Kaye, "Analysis of Ageism, Sexism, and Ableism in User Comments on YouTube Videos about Climate Activist Greta Thunberg," *Social Media + Society* 7, no. 3 (2021): 1–14.

92. Cascio, "'Asperger's Syndrome Does Not Exist'"; Elizabeth Fein, "Making Mean-ingful Worlds: Role-Playing Subcultures and the Autism Spectrum," *Culture, Medi-cine, and Psychiatry* 39, no. 2 (2015): 299–321.

93. Elizabeth Fein, *Living on the Spectrum: Autism and Youth in Community* (New York: New York University Press, 2020); King, Williams, and Gleeson, "Using Photographs."

94. Clark and Adams, "The Self-Identified Positive Attributes."

95. Laura Sterponi, Kenton de Kirby, and Jennifer Shankey, "Rethinking Language in Autism," *Autism* 19, no. 5 (2015): 517–26; Roy D. Pea, "The Social and Techno-logical Dimensions of Scaffolding and Related Theoretical Concepts for Learning, Education, and Human Activity," *Journal of the Learning Sciences* 13, no. 3 (2004): 423–51.

96. Riki Entz, "Review: *Rules* by Cynthia Lord," Disability in Kidlit, April 12, 2015, https://disabilityinkidlit.com/2015/04/12/review-rules-by-cynthia-lord/.

97. *Speechless* was also notable because it featured a disabled person playing a disabled character. However, though the actor who played the role, Micah Fowler, does have cerebral palsy, he does not also have a speech disability.

98. Rebecca Black, *Adolescents and Online Fan Fiction* (New York: Peter Lang, 2008).

99. Rebecca Black et al., "Representations of Autism in Online *Harry Potter* Fanfiction," *Journal of Literacy Research* 51, no. 1 (2019): 30–51.

100. Ricarose Roque, Yasmin Kafai, and Deborah Fields, "From Tools to Communities: Designs to Support Online Creative Collaboration in Scratch," in *Proceedings of the 2012 Conference on Interaction Design and Children* (New York: ACM, 2012), 220–23.

101. Gabriela T. Richard and Yasmin Kafai, "Blind Spots in Youth DIY Programming: Examining Diversity in Creators, Content, and Comments within the Scratch Online Community," in *Proceedings of the 2016 CHI Conference on Human Factors in Computing Systems (CHI '16)* (New York: ACM, 2016), 1473–85.

102. Haley Moss, "For Autistic People, *Star Trek* Can Be a Lens into the World," StarTrek.com, April 2, 2020, https://www.startrek.com/news/for-autistic-people-star-trek -can-be-a-lens-into-the-world.

103. The name of the Scratch studio has been anonymized.

104. Yasmin Kafai, *Minds in Play: Computer Game Design as a Context for Children's Learning* (New York: Routledge, 1995).

105. This text has been edited for the purposes of anonymity.

106. Chandra Lebenhagen, "Including Speaking and Nonspeaking Autistic Voice in Research," *Autism in Adulthood* 2, no. 2 (2020): 128–31.

107. Jordynn Jack, *Autism and Gender: From Refrigerator Mothers to Computer Geeks* (Urbana: University of Illinois Press, 2014).

108. Joy Resmovits, "Why *Sesame Street*'s New Character Isn't Representative of Most Kids with Autism," *Los Angeles Times*, October 22, 2015, https://www.latimes .com/local/education/community/la-me-edu-sesame-street-autistic-muppet-girl -julia-20151022-htmlstory.html. One of those organizations, the Autistic Self Advocacy Network, ended its partnership with Sesame Workshop in 2019 due to the Workshop's collaboration with autism charity Autism Speaks in the production of outreach materials for parents of autistic children; Lindsey Bever, "How a 'Sesame Street' Muppet Became Embroiled in a Controversy over Autism," *Washington Post*, September 19, 2019, https://www.washingtonpost.com/health/2019/09/19/how-sesa me-street-muppet-became-embroiled-controversy-over-autism.

109. Besides being a girl, Julia also challenges autism stereotypes because she is nonspeaking and uses an AAC device.

110. Julia's introduction also built upon a longer tradition of disability and autism representation in television for young children. For example, Sivan, a wheelchair-using girl Muppet, was introduced in 2009 on *Rechov Sumsum*, Israel's version of

Sesame Street; Charlotte F. Cole and June H. Lee, *The Sesame Effect: The Global Impact of the Longest Street in the World* (New York: Routledge, 2016).

111. Jennifer S. Aubrey and Kristen Harrison, "The Gender-Role Content of Children's Favorite Television Programs and Its Links to Their Gender-Related Receptions," *Media Psychology* 6, no. 2 (2004): 111–46.

112. So strong is the connection between autistic viewers and *Thomas the Tank Engine* that the latest *Thomas & Friends* TV series introduced an autistic train character in 2022, voiced by an autistic child actor; Mark Sweney, *"Thomas the Tank Engine* to Introduce First Autistic Character," *Guardian*, September 7, 2022, https://www.theguardian.com/global/2022/sep/07/thomas-the-tank-engine-to-introduce-first-autistic-character.

113. Strang et al., "'They Thought It Was an Obsession,'" 4048.

114. Strang et al.

115. Strang et al.

116. Eleanor Buckley, Elizabeth Pellicano, and Anna Remington, "'The Real Thing I Struggle with Is Other People's Perceptions': The Experiences of Autistic Performing Arts Professionals and Attitudes of Performing Arts Employers in the UK," *Journal of Autism and Developmental Disorders* 51, no. 1 (2021): 45–59.

117. Bucholtz and Hall, "Identity and Interaction."

118. Jessy E. Fletcher-Randle, "Where Are All the Autistic Parents? A Thematic Analysis of Autistic Parenting Discourse within the Narrative of Parenting and Autism in Online Media," *Studies in Social Justice* 16, no. 2 (2022): 389–406; Bridget Liang, "Divided Communities and Absent Voices: The Search for Autistic BIPOC Parent Blogs," *Studies in Social Justice* 16, no. 2 (2022): 447–69.

119. Timotheus "T. J." Gordon Jr., "#BlackAutisticJoy in ADA 30," *Disability Visibility Project*, July 19, 2020, https://disabilityvisibilityproject.com/2020/07/19/blackautisticjoy-in-ada-30/; Alice Wong, "#BlackDisabledLivesMatter: Q&A with Artist Jen White-Johnson," Pop Culture Collaborative, September 9, 2020, https://popcollab.org/blackdisabledlivesmatter-qa-with-artist-jen-white-johnson/.

120. John Aspler, Kelly D. Harding, and M. Ariel Cascio, "Representation Matters: Race, Gender, Class, and Intersectional Representations of Autistic and Disabled Characters on Television," *Studies in Social Justice* 16, no. 2 (2022): 323–48.

121. Dana L. Baker, "Neurodiversity, Neurological Disability and the Public Sector: Notes on the Autism Spectrum," *Disability & Society* 21, no. 1 (2006): 15–29.

122. Bruno J. Anthony et al., "Increasing Autism Acceptance: The Impact of the *Sesame Street* 'See Amazing in All Children' Initiative," *Autism* 24, no. 1 (2020): 95–108; Cheryl L. Dickter et al., "Assessment of *Sesame Street* Online Autism Resources: Impacts on Parental Implicit and Explicit Attitudes toward Children with Autism," *Autism* 25, no. 1 (2021): 114–24.

CHAPTER 3

1. National League of Cities, "What's The Difference between Shelter in Place, Safer at Home, and Stay Home Orders?," CitiesSpeak, March 30, 2020, https://citiesspeak .org/2020/03/30/whats-the-difference-between-shelter-in-place-safer-at-home-and -stay-home-orders/.

2. James Vaznis and Bianca Vázquez Toness, "Baker Orders Schools Stay Closed through the End of the School Year," *Boston Globe*, April 21, 2020, https://www .bostonglobe.com/2020/04/21/nation/coronavirus-boston-massachusetts-april-21/.

3. Congressional Research Service, *Unemployment Rates during the COVID-19 Pandemic*, August 20, 2021, https://fas.org/sgp/crs/misc/R46554.pdf.

4. Hallie Levine, "Parents and Schools Are Struggling to Care for Kids with Special Needs," *New York Times*, March 31, 2020, https://www.nytimes.com/2020/03/31 /parenting/kids-special-needs-coronavirus.html.

5. Meghan M. Burke et al., "Examining Differences in Empowerment, Special Education Knowledge, and Family–School Partnerships among Latino and White Families of Children with Autism Spectrum Disorder," *International Journal of Developmental Disabilities* 66, no. 1 (2020): 75–81; Sandra Magaña et al., "Access to Diagnosis and Treatment Services among Latino Children with Autism Spectrum Disorders," *Intellectual and Developmental Disabilities* 51, no. 3 (2013): 141–53.

6. Meryl Alper, *Digital Youth with Disabilities* (Cambridge, MA: MIT Press, 2014).

7. The states where this book's study took place have some of the highest percentages, with California at approximately 13 percent and Massachusetts at 11 percent; Jonathan Safer-Lichtenstein and Laura Lee McIntyre, "Comparing Autism Symptom Severity between Children with a Medical Autism Diagnosis and an Autism Special Education Eligibility," *Focus on Autism and Other Developmental Disabilities* 35, no. 3 (2020): 186–92.

8. Rachel Aiello, Lisa Ruble, and Amy Esler, "National Study of School Psychologists' Use of Evidence-Based Assessment in Autism Spectrum Disorder," *Journal of Applied School Psychology* 33, no. 1 (2017): 67–88.

9. David S. Mandell and Raymond Palmer, "Differences among States in the Identification of Autistic Spectrum Disorders," *Archives of Pediatrics & Adolescent Medicine* 159, no. 3 (2005): 266–69; Malinda L Pennington, Douglas Cullinan, and Louise B. Southern, "Defining Autism: Variability in State Education Agency Definitions of and Evaluations for Autism Spectrum Disorders," *Autism Research and Treatment* 2014 (2014): 1–8.

10. Rachel E. Fish, "Standing Out and Sorting In: Exploring the Role of Racial Composition in Racial Disparities in Special Education," *American Educational Research Journal* 56, no. 6 (2019): 2573–608; Colin Ong-Dean, *Distinguishing Disability: Parents, Privilege, and Special Education* (Chicago: University of Chicago Press, 2009).

11. *Individuals with Disabilities Education Improvement Act*, 20 U.S.C. § 1400 et seq. (2004).

12. Linda Blum, *Raising Generation Rx: Mothering Kids with Invisible Disabilities in an Age of Inequality* (New York: New York University Press, 2015); Audrey A. Trainor, "Reexamining the Promise of Parent Participation in Special Education: An Analysis of Cultural and Social Capital," *Anthropology & Education Quarterly* 41, no. 3 (2010): 245–63.

13. William H. Blackwell and Zachary S. Rossetti, "The Development of Individualized Education Programs: Where Have We Been and Where Should We Go Now?," *SAGE Open* 4, no. 2 (2014): 1–15.

14. *Section 504, Rehabilitation Act*, 29 U.S.C. § 701 (1973).

15. Liz Pellicano, Sven Bölte, and Aubyn Stahmer, "The Current Illusion of Educational Inclusion," *Autism* 22, no. 4 (2018): 386–87.

16. Martin Agran et al., "Why Aren't Students with Severe Disabilities Being Placed in General Education Classrooms: Examining the Relations among Classroom Placement, Learner Outcomes, and Other Factors," *Research and Practice for Persons with Severe Disabilities* 45, no. 1 (2020): 4–13; Mary E. Morningstar, Jennifer A. Kurth, and Paul E. Johnson, "Examining National Trends in Educational Placements for Students with Significant Disabilities," *Remedial and Special Education* 38, no. 1 (2017): 3–12.

17. Jennifer Kurth and Ann M. Mastergeorge, "Impact of Setting and Instructional Context for Adolescents with Autism," *Journal of Special Education* 46, no. 1 (2012): 36–48.

18. Rebecca Wood and Francesca Happé, "Barriers to Tests and Exams for Autistic Pupils: Improving Access and Longer-Term Outcomes," *International Journal of Inclusive Education*, December 30, 2020, https://doi.org/10.1080/13603116.2020.1866685.

19. National Council on Disability, "Breaking the School-to-Prison Pipeline for Students with Disabilities," 2015, https://www.ncd.gov/publications/2015/06182015.

20. Julian Sefton-Green, *Learning at Not-School: A Review of Study, Theory, and Advocacy for Education in Non-Formal Settings* (Cambridge, MA: MIT Press, 2013).

21. Brigid Barron et al., "Parents as Learning Partners in the Development of Technological Fluency," *International Journal of Learning and Media* 1, no. 2 (2009): 55–77; Annette Lareau, *Unequal Childhoods: Class, Race, and Family Life* (Berkeley: University of California Press, 2003).

22. David W. Livingstone, "Informal Learning: Conceptual Distinctions and Preliminary Findings," in *Learning in Places: The Informal Education Reader*, ed. Zvi Bekerman, Nicholas C. Burbules, and Diana Silberman-Keller (New York: Peter Lang, 2006), 203–27; Sefton-Green, *Learning at Not-School*.

23. Michael Cole, *Cultural Psychology: A Once and Future Discipline* (Cambridge, MA: Harvard University Press, 1996); Jerome Bruner, *Actual Minds, Possible Worlds* (Cambridge, MA: Harvard University Press, 1986); Barbara Rogoff, *The Cultural Nature of Human Development* (Oxford: Oxford University Press, 2003); Lev S. Vygotsky, *Mind*

in Society: The Development of Higher Psychological Processes, ed. Michael Cole et al. (Cambridge, MA: Harvard University Press, 1978).

24. Flávio S. Azevedo, "The Tailored Practice of Hobbies and Its Implication for the Design of Interest-Driven Learning Environments," *Journal of the Learning Sciences* 22, no. 3 (2013): 462–510.

25. Meryl Alper, "Critical Media Access Studies: Deconstructing Power, Visibility, and Marginality in Mediated Space," *International Journal of Communication* 15 (2021): 840–61; Amelia N. Gibson and Dana Hanson-Baldauf, "Beyond Sensory Story Time: An Intersectional Analysis of Information Seeking among Parents of Autistic Individuals," *Library Trends* 67, no. 3 (2019): 550–75.

26. Jackie Marsh et al., "Play and Creativity in Young Children's Use of Apps," *British Journal of Educational Technology* 49, no. 5 (2018): 870–82; Kylie Peppler and Yasmin Kafai, "From SuperGoo to Scratch: Exploring Creative Digital Media Production in Informal Learning," *Learning, Media and Technology* 32, no. 2 (2007): 149–66.

27. Matthew Rafalow, *Digital Divisions: How Schools Create Inequality in the Tech Era* (Chicago: University of Chicago Press, 2020); Ellen Seiter, "Practicing at Home: Computers, Pianos, and Cultural Capital," in *Digital Youth, Innovation, and the Unexpected*, ed. Tara McPherson (Cambridge, MA: MIT Press, 2008), 27–52; Christo Sims, *Disruptive Fixation: School Reform and the Pitfalls of Techno-Idealism* (Princeton, NJ: Princeton University Press, 2017).

28. Kaisa Pihlainen, Calkin S. Montero, and Eija Kärnä, "Fostering Parental Co-development of Technology for Children with Special Needs Informal Learning Activities," *International Journal of Child-Computer Interaction* 11 (2017): 19–27.

29. Matthew Jones et al., "Identifying the Essential Components of Strength-Based Technology Clubs for Adolescents with Autism Spectrum Disorder," *Developmental Neurorehabilitation* 24, no. 5 (2021): 323–36.

30. Marissa L. Diener et al., "Tapping into Technical Talent: Using Technology to Facilitate Personal, Social, and Vocational Skills in Youth with Autism Spectrum Disorder (ASD)," in *Technology and the Treatment of Children with Autism Spectrum Disorder*, ed. Teresa A. Cardon (New York: Springer, 2016), 97–112.

31. Arianna Skibell, "More People with Autism Are Getting Training for Technology Jobs," *The Hechinger Report*, November 15, 2015, https://hechingerreport.org/more-people-with-autism-are-getting-training-for-technology-jobs/.

32. Wendy B. Martin et al., "Promoting Science, Technology, and Engineering Self-Efficacy and Knowledge for All with an Autism Inclusion Maker Program," *Frontiers in Education* 5 (2020): 1–18.

33. Sonia Livingstone and Alicia Blum-Ross, *Parenting for a Digital Future: How Hopes and Fears about Technology Shape Children's Lives* (Oxford: Oxford University Press, 2020); Jessica Z. Pandya, Nat Hansuvadha, and Kathleah C. Pagdilao, "Multimodal,

Digital Composition for Children with Autism: Lessons on Process, Product, and Assessment," *Language Arts* 93, no. 6 (2016): 415–29.

34. Fifty percent of boys with Fragile X are reportedly also on the autism spectrum; Donald B. Bailey Jr. et al., "Co-occurring Conditions Associated with FMR1 Gene Variations: Findings from a National Parent Survey," *American Journal of Medical Genetics Part A* 146, no. 16 (2008): 2060–69.

35. Urie Bronfenbrenner, *The Ecology of Human Development* (Cambridge, MA: Harvard University Press, 1979); Urie Bronfenbrenner, *Making Human Beings Human: Bioecological Perspectives on Human Development* (Thousand Oaks, CA: Sage, 2005). Bronfenbrenner later revised ecological systems theory as bioecological systems theory. The biological component recognizes that personal and genetic factors shape developmental trajectories over the lifespan. Bronfenbrenner's work is of particular relevance to disability politics. His 1979 book *The Ecology of Human Development* furthered the case for the deinstitutionalization of disabled people. His analysis was heavily shaped by his upbringing on the grounds of Letchworth Village, an institution in Rockland County, New York, where his father worked as a neuropathologist. Shut down in 1996, Letchworth was infamous for its inhumane treatment of residents, which included testing the polio vaccine on child patients in 1950; Margalit Fox, "Urie Bronfenbrenner, 88, An Authority on Child Development, Dies," *New York Times*, September 27, 2005, https://www.nytimes.com/2005/09/27/nyregion/urie-bronfenbrenner-88-an-authority-on-child-development-dies.html.

36. Amy B. Jordan, "The Role of Media in Children's Development: An Ecological Perspective," *Developmental and Behavioral Pediatrics* 25, no. 3 (2004): 196–206; Lori M. Takeuchi and Michael H. Levine, "Learning in a Digital Age: Toward a New Ecology of Human Development," in *Media and the Well-Being of Children and Adolescents*, ed. Amy B. Jordan and Daniel Romer (Oxford: Oxford University Press, 2014), 20–43.

37. Brigid Barron, "Learning Ecologies for Technological Fluency: Gender and Experience Differences," *Journal of Educational Computing Research* 31, no. 1 (2004): 1–36; Brigid Barron, "Interest and Self-Sustained Learning as Catalysts of Development: A Learning Ecology Perspective," *Human Development* 49 (2006): 193–224; Heather A. Horst, Becky Herr-Stephenson, and Lisa Robinson, "Media Ecologies," in *Hanging Out, Messing Around, and Geeking Out: Kids Living and Learning with New Media*, ed. Mizuko Ito et al. (Cambridge, MA: MIT Press, 2010), 29–78.

38. Samantha E. Goldman and Meghan M. Burke, "The Perceptions of School Involvement of Parents of Students with Autism Spectrum Disorders: A Systematic Literature Review," *Review Journal of Autism and Developmental Disorders* 6, no. 2 (2019): 109–27.

39. Gazi F. Azad et al., "Parent–Teacher Communication about Children with Autism Spectrum Disorder: An Examination of Collaborative Problem-Solving," *Psychology in the Schools* 53, no. 10 (2016): 1071–84.

40. Patti M. Valkenburg and Jessica T. Piotrowski, *Plugged In: How Media Attract and Affect Youth* (New Haven, CT: Yale University Press, 2017).

41. Marisa Meyer et al., "How Educational Are 'Educational' Apps for Young Children? App Store Content Analysis Using the Four Pillars of Learning Framework," *Journal of Children and Media* 15, no. 4 (2021): 526–48.

42. Wesley H. Dotson et al., "Evaluating the Ability of the PBS Children's Show *Daniel Tiger's Neighborhood* to Teach Skills to Two Young Children with Autism Spectrum Disorder," *Behavior Analysis in Practice* 10, no. 1 (2017): 67–71.

43. Meryl Alper, "U.S. Parent Perspectives of Media Guidance from Pediatric Autism Professionals," *Journal of Children and Media* 15, no. 2 (2021): 165–82.

44. Rebecca Lane and Jenny Radesky, "Digital Media and Autism Spectrum Disorders: Review of Evidence, Theoretical Concerns, and Opportunities for Intervention," *Journal of Developmental & Behavioral Pediatrics* 40, no. 5 (2019): 364–68.

45. Alexis C. Madrigal, "Raised by YouTube," *The Atlantic*, November 2018, https://www.theatlantic.com/magazine/archive/2018/11/raised-by-youtube/570838/.

46. Heather L. Kirkorian et al., "The Impact of Background Television on Parent–Child Interaction," *Child Development* 80, no. 5 (2009): 1350–59.

47. Karen F. Heffler et al., "Association of Early-Life Social and Digital Media Experiences with Development of Autism Spectrum Disorder–Like Symptoms," *JAMA Pediatrics* 174, no. 7 (2020): 690–96.

48. Norman E. Silberg and Margaret C. Silberberg, "Hyperlexia—Specific Word Recognition Skills in Young Children," *Exceptional Children* 34, no. 1 (1967): 41–42.

49. Alexia Ostrolenk et al., "Hyperlexia: Systematic Review, Neurocognitive Modelling, and Outcome," *Neuroscience & Biobehavioral Reviews* 79 (2017): 134–49.

50. Claudine Jacques et al., "What Interests Young Autistic Children? An Exploratory Study of Object Exploration and Repetitive Behavior," *PLOS One* 13, no. 12 (2018): 1–17.

51. Julie M. Rodas, *Autistic Disturbances: Theorizing Autism Poetics from the DSM to Robinson Crusoe* (Ann Arbor: University of Michigan Press, 2018).

52. Elena L. Grigorenko, Ami Klin, and Fred Volkmar, "Annotation: Hyperlexia: Disability or Superability?," *Journal of Child Psychology and Psychiatry* 44, no. 8 (2003): 1079–91.

53. Bethany Good and Lin Fang, "Promoting Smart and Safe Internet Use among Children with Neurodevelopmental Disorders and Their Parents," *Clinical Social Work Journal* 43, no. 2 (2015): 179–88.

54. Sonia Livingstone and Mariya Stoilova, *The 4Cs: Classifying Online Risk to Children* (Hamburg: Leibniz-Institut für Medienforschung / Hans-Bredow-Institut (HBI) and CO:RE—Children Online: Research and Evidence, 2021).

55. Sonia Livingstone, "Children with Special Educational Needs and Disabilities More Likely to Encounter Harm Online, Say Parents," *Parenting for a Digital Future* (blog), February 4, 2019, https://blogs.lse.ac.uk/parenting4digitalfuture/2019/02/04/children -with-special-educational-needs-and-disabilities-more-likely-to-encounter-harm-online -parents-say/; Kirsty Macmillan et al., "Relating Autism to Online Safety, Child Well-being and Parental Risk Management," in *Proceedings of the 11th Nordic Conference on Human-Computer Interaction (NordiCHI)* (New York: ACM, 2020), 1–11; Kirsty MacMillan et al., "Online Safety Experiences of Autistic Young People: An Interpretative Phenom-enological Analysis," *Research in Autism Spectrum Disorders* 96 (August 2022), https:// www.sciencedirect.com/science/article/abs/pii/S1750946722000824?via%3Dihub.

56. Amelia Anderson and Abigail Phillips, "'Getting Basic Information Isn't as Help-ful as the Nuanced Advice We Can Give Each Other': Teens with Autism on Digital Citizenship Education," *Journal of Research on Libraries and Young Adults* 10, no. 3 (2019): 1–27; Sue Cramner, *Disabled Children and Digital Technologies: Learning in the Context of Inclusive Education* (London: Bloomsbury, 2021); Yonty Friesem, "Beyond Accessibility: How Media Literacy Education Addresses Issues of Disabilities," *Journal of Media Literacy Education* 9, no. 2 (2019): 1–16.

57. Christy Matte, "Baldi's Education in School 3D," Common Sense Media (n.d.), https://www.commonsensemedia.org/app-reviews/baldis-education-in-school-3d, accessed August 30, 2022.

58. "Is It Possible to Change a Username?," Scratch Wiki, February 6, 2022, https://en .scratch-wiki.info/wiki/Is_it_possible_to_change_a_username%3F. In its Privacy Policy (https://scratch.mit.edu/privacy_policy), Scratch encourages its users to refrain from including personal information.

59. Kathryn E. Ringland, "A Place to Play: The (Dis)Abled Embodied Experience for Autistic Children in Online Spaces," in *Proceedings of the 2019 CHI Conference on Human Factors in Computing Systems* (New York: ACM, 2019), 1–14.

60. Patricia M. Greenfield, "Technology and Informal Education: What Is Taught, What Is Learned," *Science* 323, no. 5910 (2009): 69–71.

61. John Dewey, *Democracy and Education: An Introduction to the Philosophy of Educa-tion* (New York: Macmillan, 1916).

62. Mizuko Ito et al., *The Connected Learning Research Network: Reflections on a Decade of Engaged Scholarship* (Irvine, CA: Connected Learning Alliance, 2020), 4.

63. Mizuko Ito et al., *Connected Learning: An Agenda for Research and Design* (Irvine, CA: Digital Media and Learning Research Hub, 2013).

64. Mizuko Ito et al., eds., *Hanging Out, Messing Around, and Geeking Out: Kids Living and Learning with New Media* (Cambridge, MA: MIT Press, 2010).

65. Karen Brennan, Andrés Monroy-Hernández, and Mitchel Resnick, "Making Projects, Making Friends: Online Community as Catalyst for Interactive Media Cre-ation," *New Directions for Youth Development* 2010, no. 128 (2010): 75–83.

66. It is estimated that 75 to 95 percent of autistic people have intense interests; Ami Klin et al., "Circumscribed Interests in Higher Functioning Individuals with Autism Spectrum Disorders: An Exploratory Study," *Research and Practice for Persons with Severe Disabilities* 32, no. 2 (2007): 89–100; Lauren M. Turner-Brown et al., "Phenomenology and Measurement of Circumscribed Interests in Autism Spectrum Disorders," *Autism* 15, no. 4 (2011): 437–56.

67. Mizuko Ito et al., *Living and Learning with New Media: Summary of Findings from the Digital Youth Project* (Cambridge, MA: MIT Press, 2009), 10.

68. Rebecca Wood, *Inclusive Education for Autistic Children: Helping Children and Young People to Learn and Flourish in the Classroom* (London: Jessica Kingsley, 2019).

69. Kristie Patten Koenig and Lauren Hough Williams, "Characterization and Utilization of Preferred Interests: A Survey of Adults on the Autism Spectrum," *Occupational Therapy in Mental Health* 33, no. 2 (2017): 129–40; Mary Ann Winter-Messiers et al., "How Far Can Brian Ride the Daylight 4449 Express? A Strength-Based Model of Asperger Syndrome Based on Special Interest Areas," *Focus on Autism and Other Developmental Disabilities* 22, no. 2 (2007): 67–79.

70. Kerri P. Nowell et al., "Characterization of Special Interests in Autism Spectrum Disorder: A Brief Review and Pilot Study Using the Special Interests Survey," *Journal of Autism and Developmental Disorders* 51, no. 8 (2021): 2711–24.

71. David Buckingham, *Beyond Technology: Children's Learning in the Age of Digital Culture* (Cambridge: Polity Press, 2007); Ellen Seiter, *The Internet Playground: Children's Access, Entertainment, and Mis-Education* (New York: Peter Lang, 2005).

72. Nowell et al., "Characterization of Special Interests."

73. Nowell et al.

74. Alyssa M. Alcorn, Helen Pain, and Judith Good, "Motivating Children's Initiations with Novelty and Surprise: Initial Design Recommendations for Autism," in *Proceedings of the 2014 Conference on Interaction Design and Children (IDC)* (New York: ACM, 2014), 225–28; Mirko Uljarević et al., "Toward Better Characterization of Restricted and Unusual Interests in Youth with Autism," *Autism* 26, no. 5 (November 24, 2021), https://journals.sagepub.com/doi/abs/10.1177/13623613211056720.

75. Nowell et al., "Characterization of Special Interests."

76. Ivy Y. K. Cho et al., "Circumscribed Interests in Adolescents with Autism Spectrum Disorder: A Look beyond Trains, Planes, and Clocks," *PLOS One* (2017): 1–21.

77. Kerry C. M. Gunn and Jonathan T. Delafield-Butt, "Teaching Children with Autism Spectrum Disorder with Restricted Interests: A Review of Evidence for Best Practice," *Review of Educational Research* 86, no. 2 (2016): 408–30; Robert L. Koegel et al., "Using Perseverative Interests to Improve Interactions between Adolescents with Autism and Their Typical Peers in School Settings," *Journal of Positive Behavior Interventions* 14, no. 3 (2012): 133–41.

78. Nowell et al., "Characterization of Special Interests," 2712.

79. Hailey R. Love and Margaret R. Beneke, "Pursuing Justice-Driven Inclusive Education Research: Disability Critical Race Theory (DisCrit) in Early Childhood," *Topics in Early Childhood Special Education* 41, no. 1 (2021): 31–44.

80. Jen White-Johnson, "Autistic Joy as an Act of Resistance," *Thinking Person's Guide to Autism* (blog), October 25, 2019, http://www.thinkingautismguide.com/2019/10/autistic-joy-as-act-of-resistance.html.

81. Dan Goodley and Katherine Runswick-Cole, "Emancipating Play: Dis/Abled Children, Development and Deconstruction," *Disability & Society* 25, no. 4 (2010): 499–512.

82. Ito et al., *Hanging Out, Messing Around, and Geeking Out.*

83. Carol A. Gray and Joy D. Garand, "Social Stories: Improving Responses of Students with Autism with Accurate Social Information," *Focus on Autistic Behavior* 8, no. 1 (1993): 1–10.

84. Naoki Higashida, *Fall Down 7 Times Get Up 8: A Young Man's Voice from the Silence of Autism*, trans. K. A. Yoshida and David Mitchell (New York: Random House, 2017), 185–86.

85. Kirstin B. Birtwell, Amanda K. Platner, and Lisa A. Nowinski, "Exploring the Use of Sidekicks! for Children with Autism Spectrum Disorder (ASD)," *Psychological Services* 16, no. 2 (2019): 266–70.

86. Seiter, "Practicing at Home."

87. Lareau, *Unequal Childhoods.*

88. Elizabeth Covay and William Carbonaro, "After the Bell: Participation in Extracurricular Activities, Classroom Behavior, and Academic Achievement," *Sociology of Education* 83, no. 1 (2010): 20–45; Kris D. Gutiérrez, Carolina Izquierdo, and Tamar Kremer-Sadlik, "Middle Class Working Families' Beliefs and Engagement in Children's Extra-curricular Activities: The Social Organization of Children's Futures," *International Journal of Learning* 17, no. 3 (2010): 633–56.

89. Sonia Livingstone and Julian Sefton-Green, *The Class: Living and Learning in the Digital Age* (New York: New York University Press, 2016).

90. Blum, *Raising Generation Rx.*

91. Morgan G. Ames and Jenna Burrell, "'Connected Learning' and the Equity Agenda: A Microsociology of Minecraft Play," in *Proceedings of the 2017 ACM Conference on Computer Supported Cooperative Work and Social Computing (CSCW)* (New York: ACM, 2017), 446–57; Jane Margolis et al., *Stuck in the Shallow End: Education, Race, and Computing* (Cambridge, MA: MIT Press, 2010); Cassidy Puckett and Jennifer L. Nelson, "The Geek Instinct: Theorizing Cultural Alignment in Disadvantaged Contexts," *Qualitative Sociology* 42, no. 1 (2019): 25–48.

92. Livingstone and Blum-Ross, *Parenting for a Digital Future*.

93. Nancy Baym, *Personal Connections in the Digital Age*, 2nd ed. (Cambridge: Polity Press, 2015).

94. Good and Fang, "Promoting Smart and Safe Internet Use"; Macmillan et al., "Relating Autism to Online Safety."

95. Meryl Alper, "Future Talk: Accounting for the Technological and Other Future Discourses in Daily Life," *International Journal of Communication* 13 (2019): 715–35; Livingstone and Blum-Ross, *Parenting for a Digital Future*.

96. Alper, "Future Talk."

CHAPTER 4

1. Digital technology serves multiple roles for transnational families, including maintaining emotional intimacy and relational continuity; Carmen Gonzalez and Vikki S. Katz, "Transnational Family Communication as a Driver of Technology Adoption," *International Journal of Communication* 10 (2016): 2683–703.

2. Melissa H. Kuo et al., "Media Use among Adolescents with Autism Spectrum Disorder," *Autism* 18, no. 8 (2014): 914–23.

3. Brenda Nally, Bob Houlton, and Sue Ralph, "Researches in Brief: The Management of Television and Video by Parents of Children with Autism," *Autism* 4, no. 3 (2000): 331–37.

4. Jennifer S. Singh, "Parenting Work and Autism Trajectories of Care," *Sociology of Health & Illness* 38, no. 7 (2016): 1106–20.

5. Amy C. Sousa, "From Refrigerator Mothers to Warrior-Heroes: The Cultural Identity Transformation of Mothers Raising Children with Intellectual Disabilities," *Symbolic Interaction* 34, no. 2 (2011): 220–43.

6. Ruth Schwartz Cowan, *More Work for Mother: The Ironies of Household Technology from the Open Hearth to the Microwave* (New York: Basic Books, 1983).

7. Ray H. Barsch, "Explanations Offered by Parents and Siblings of Brain-Damaged Children," *Exceptional Children* 27, no. 5 (1961): 286–91.

8. Thomas E. Jordan, "Research on the Handicapped Child and the Family," *Merrill-Palmer Quarterly of Behavior and Development* 8, no. 4 (1962): 225.

9. Jessica L. Greenlee, Marcia A. Winter, and Joshua John Diehl, "Family Level Processes Associated with Outcomes for Individuals with Autism Spectrum Disorder: A Scoping Review," *Research in Autism Spectrum Disorders* 53 (2018): 41–52.

10. Ami Tint and Jonathan A. Weiss, "Family Wellbeing of Individuals with Autism Spectrum Disorder: A Scoping Review," *Autism* 20, no. 3 (2016): 262–75. It is also important to note that not all autistic children live with their families full-time. Some parents place their children into short- or long-term respite and residential care

facilities to manage their child's physical and mental needs; Emma Cooke, Valerie Smith, and Maria Brenner, "Parents' Experiences of Accessing Respite Care for Children with Autism Spectrum Disorder (ASD) at the Acute and Primary Care Interface: A Systematic Review," *BMC Pediatrics* 20, no. 1 (2020): 1–12.

11. Martha J. Cox and Blair Paley, "Families as Systems," *Annual Review of Psychology* 48, no. 1 (1997): 243–67; Patricia Minuchin, "Families and Individual Development: Provocations from the Field of Family Therapy," *Child Development* 56 (1985): 289–302; Roy H. Rodgers and James M. White, "Family Development Theory," in *Sourcebook of Family Theories and Methods*, ed. Pauline Boss et al. (New York: Plenum, 1993), 225–54.

12. Lara S. Head and Leonard Abbeduto, "Recognizing the Role of Parents in Developmental Outcomes: A Systems Approach to Evaluating the Child with Developmental Disabilities," *Developmental Disabilities Research Reviews* 13, no. 4 (2007): 293–301; Sam B. Morgan, "The Autistic Child and Family Functioning: A Developmental-Family Systems Perspective," *Journal of Autism and Developmental Disorders* 18, no. 2 (1988): 263–80; Sarah L. Smith and Hannah B. McQuade, "Exploring the Health of Families with a Child with Autism," *Autism* 25, no. 5 (2021): 1203–15.

13. John J. Davies and Douglas A. Gentile, "Responses to Children's Media Use in Families with and without Siblings: A Family Development Perspective," *Family Relations* 61, no. 3 (2012): 410–25; Amy B. Jordan, "A Family Systems Approach to Examining the Role of the Internet in the Home," in *Children in the Digital Age: Influences of Electronic Media on Development*, ed. Sandra L. Calvert, Amy B. Jordan, and Rodney R. Cocking (Westport, CT: Prager, 2002), 231–47.

14. Kristen Harrison, "Media and the Family," *Journal of Children and Media* 9, no. 1 (2015): 1–4; Nancy Jennings, "Media and Families: Looking Ahead," *Journal of Family Communication* 17, no. 3 (2017): 203–7.

15. Sharon Hays, *The Cultural Contradictions of Motherhood* (New Haven, CT: Yale University Press, 1996).

16. Erica W. Austin, "Exploring the Effects of Active Parental Mediation of Television Content," *Journal of Broadcasting & Electronic Media* 37, no. 2 (1993): 147–58; Lynn Schofield Clark, "Parental Mediation Theory for the Digital Age," *Communication Theory* 21, no. 4 (2011): 323–43.

17. Galit Nimrod, Nelly Elias, and Dafna Lemish, "Measuring Mediation of Children's Media Use," *International Journal of Communication* 13 (2019): 342–58; Patti M. Valkenburg et al., "Developing a Scale to Assess Three Styles of Television Mediation: 'Instructive Mediation,' 'Restrictive Mediation,' and 'Social Coviewing,'" *Journal of Broadcasting & Electronic Media* 43 no. 1 (1999): 52–66. The concept of "joint media engagement" encompasses both active and social forms of parental mediation; Lori Takeuchi and Reed Stevens, *The New Coviewing: Designing for Learning through Joint Media Engagement* (New York: The Joan Ganz Cooney Center at Sesame Workshop, 2011), https://www.joanganzcooneycenter.org/wp-content/uploads/2011/12/jgc_coviewing_desktop.pdf.

18. Sonia Livingstone and Ellen Helsper, "Parental Mediation of Children's Internet Use," *Journal of Broadcasting & Electronic Media* 52, no. 4 (2008): 581–99; Nathalie Sonck, Peter Nikken, and Jos De Haan, "Determinants of Internet Mediation: A Comparison of the Reports by Dutch Parents and Children," *Journal of Children and Media* 7, no. 1 (2013): 96–113.

19. Ine Beyens, Patti M. Valkenburg, and Jessica T. Piotrowski, "Developmental Trajectories of Parental Mediation across Early and Middle Childhood," *Human Communication Research* 45, no. 2 (2019): 226–50.

20. Beyens, Valkenburg, and Piotrowski.

21. Beyens, Valkenburg, and Piotrowski.

22. Melissa H. Kuo, Joyce Magill-Evans, and Lonnie Zwaigenbaum, "Parental Mediation of Television Viewing and Videogaming of Adolescents with Autism Spectrum Disorder and Their Siblings," *Autism* 19, no. 6 (2015): 724–35.

23. Christopher R. Engelhardt & Micah O. Mazurek, "Video Game Access, Parental Rules, and Problem Behavior: A Study of Boys with Autism Spectrum Disorder," *Autism* 18, no. 5 (2014): 529–37. The authors were only able to assess the impact of the existence of these rules, not their enforcement.

24. Kuo et al., "Media Use among Adolescents with Autism Spectrum Disorder." It is unclear if this finding is causal (i.e., watching TV brings parents and autistic children closer), correlational (i.e., parents and autistic children with close relationships watch more TV together), or cyclical (i.e., relational closeness and TV viewing feed into each other).

25. Nally, Houlton, and Ralph, "Researches in Brief."

26. T. L. Taylor, *Watch Me Play: Twitch and the Rise of Game Live Streaming* (Princeton, NJ: Princeton University Press, 2018).

27. Nally, Houlton, and Ralph, "Researches in Brief."

28. Andrew R. Schrock, "Communicative Affordances of Mobile Media: Portability, Availability, Locatability, and Multimediality," *International Journal of Communication* 9 (2015): 1229–46.

29. Rebecca Lane and Jenny Radesky, "Digital Media and Autism Spectrum Disorders: Review of Evidence, Theoretical Concerns, and Opportunities for Intervention," *Journal of Developmental & Behavioral Pediatrics* 40, no. 5 (2019): 364–68; Margaret H. Laurie et al., "An International Survey of Parental Attitudes to Technology Use by Their Autistic Children at Home," *Journal of Autism and Developmental Disorders* 49, no. 4 (2019): 1517–30.

30. Murat Coskun et al., "Internet Use Habits, Parental Control and Psychiatric Comorbidity in Young Subjects with Asperger Syndrome," *Journal of Autism and Developmental Disorders* 50, no. 1 (2020): 171–79; Kuo, Magill-Evans, and Zwaigenbaum, "Parental Mediation of Television Viewing and Videogaming."

31. Rachel Dunifon, Paula Fomby, and Kelly Musick, "Siblings and Children's Time Use in the United States," *Demographic Research* 37 (2017): 1611–24; Susan M. McHale and Ann C. Crouter, "The Family Context of Children's Sibling Relationships," in *Sibling Relationships: Their Causes and Consequences*, ed. Gene H. Brody (Norwood, NJ: Ablex, 1996), 173–95.

32. Gene H. Brody, "Siblings' Direct and Indirect Contributions to Child Development," *Current Directions in Psychological Science* 13, no. 3 (2004): 124–26.

33. Davies and Gentile, "Responses to Children's Media Use."

34. Sarah E. Domoff et al., "A Naturalistic Study of Child and Family Screen Media and Mobile Device Use," *Journal of Child and Family Studies* 28, no. 2 (2019): 401–10; Marites F. Pinon, Aletha C. Huston, and John C. Wright, "Family Ecology and Child Characteristics That Predict Young Children's Educational Television Viewing," *Child Development* 60 (1989): 846–56.

35. Sarah M. Coyne et al., "*Super Mario* Brothers and Sisters: Associations between Coplaying Video Games and Sibling Conflict and Affection," *Journal of Adolescence* 47 (2016): 48–59.

36. Thomas J. Hoffmann et al., "Evidence of Reproductive Stoppage in Families with Autism Spectrum Disorder: A Large, Population-Based Cohort Study," *JAMA Psychiatry* 71, no. 8 (2014): 943–51.

37. Nicole M. McDonald et al., "Developmental Trajectories of Infants with Multiplex Family Risk for Autism: A Baby Siblings Research Consortium Study," *JAMA Neurology* 77, no. 1 (2020): 73–81; Sally Ozonoff et al., "Recurrence Risk for Autism Spectrum Disorders: A Baby Siblings Research Consortium Study," *Pediatrics* 128, no. 3 (2011): e488–95.

38. Kuo, Magill-Evans, and Zwaigenbaum, "Parental Mediation of Television Viewing and Videogaming"; Micah O. Mazurek and Colleen Wenstrup, "Television, Video Game and Social Media Use among Children with ASD and Typically Developing Siblings," *Journal of Autism and Developmental Disorders* 43, no. 6 (2013): 1258–71.

39. Common Sense Media and Survey Monkey, *Common Sense Media/SurveyMonkey YouTube Poll Topline* (San Francisco: Common Sense Media, 2018), https://www.commonsensemedia.org/sites/default/files/uploads/pdfs/commonsense-surveymonkey-youtube-topline.pdf.

40. Hannah Furfaro, "Sleep Problems in Autism, Explained," *Spectrum*, February 6, 2020, https://www.spectrumnews.org/news/sleep-problems-autism-explained/.

41. Amy I. Nathanson, "Parent and Child Perspectives on the Presence and Meaning of Parental Television Mediation," *Journal of Broadcasting & Electronic Media* 45, no. 2 (2001): 201–20.

42. Melissa Morgenlander, "Adult-Child Co-Viewing of Educational Television: Enhancing Preschoolers' Understanding of Mathematics Shown on *Sesame Street*" (PhD diss.,

Columbia University, 2010); Gabrielle A. Strouse, Katherine O'Doherty, and Georgene L. Troseth, "Effective Coviewing: Preschoolers' Learning from Video after a Dialogic Questioning Intervention," *Developmental Psychology* 49, no. 12 (2013): 2368–82.

43. Erik Linstead et al., "An Evaluation of the Effects of Intensity and Duration on Outcomes across Treatment Domains for Children with Autism Spectrum Disorder," *Translational Psychiatry* 7, no. 9 (2017): 1–6.

44. Patrick Kirkham, "'The Line between Intervention and Abuse'—Autism and Applied Behaviour Analysis," *History of the Human Sciences* 30, no. 2 (2017): 107–26.

45. Kristi S. Menear and James M. Ernest, "Comparison of Physical Activity, TV/Video Watching/Gaming, and Usage of a Portable Electronic Devices by Children with and without Autism Spectrum Disorder," *Maternal and Child Health Journal* 24, no. 12 (2020): 1464–72.

46. Susan L. Hyman et al., "Identification, Evaluation, and Management of Children with Autism Spectrum Disorder," *Pediatrics* 145, no. 1 (2020): e20193447.

47. Dan Goodley and Katherine Runswick-Cole, "Emancipating Play: Dis/Abled Children, Development and Deconstruction," *Disability & Society* 25, no. 4 (2010): 499–512.

48. Ellen Wartella et al., *Parenting in the Age of Digital Technology* (Evanston, IL: Center on Media and Human Development School of Communication, Northwestern University, 2013).

49. Arlie R. Hochschild, *The Second Shift: Working Parents and the Revolution at Home* (New York: Viking Penguin, 1989); Arlie R. Hochschild, "The Commercial Spirit of Intimate Life and the Abduction of Feminism: Signs from Women's Advice Books," *Theory, Culture & Society* 11, no. 2 (1994): 1–24.

50. Nelly Elias and Dafna Lemish, "Parents' Social Uses of Mobile Phones in Public Places: The Case of Eateries in Two National Contexts," *International Journal of Communication* 15 (2021): 2086–104.

51. Kristen Harrison, "Rude or Shrewd? Reframing Media Devices as Care Structures and Child Use as Accommodation," *Journal of Children and Media* 13, no. 3 (2019): 367–75; Jennifer A. Manganello, "Media Use for Children with Disabilities in the United States during COVID-19," *Journal of Children and Media* 15, no. 1 (2021): 29–32.

52. Nimrod, Elias, and Lemish, "Measuring Mediation of Children's Media Use."

53. Kuo, Magill-Evans, and Zwaigenbaum, "Parental Mediation of Television Viewing and Videogaming."

54. Susan L. Hyman and Suzannah Iadarola, "Simpler than Possible: Insurance Mandates for Autism Spectrum Disorders," *Pediatrics* 146, no. 4 (2020): e2020020396.

55. Elizabeth Devita-Raeburn, "The Controversy over Autism's Most Common Therapy," *Spectrum*, August 10, 2016, https://www.spectrumnews.org/features/deep-dive/controversy-autisms-common-therapy/.

56. Meryl Alper, "U.S. Parent Perspectives of Media Guidance from Pediatric Autism Professionals," *Journal of Children and Media* 15, no. 2 (2021): 165–82; Susan Mello, Meryl Alper, and Anna A. Allen, "Physician Mediation Theory and Pediatric Media Guidance in the Digital Age: A Survey of Autism Medical and Clinical Professionals," *Health Communication* 35, no. 8 (2020): 955–65.

57. Rebekah Willett, "'In Our Family, We Don't Watch Those Things': Parents' Discursive Constructions of Decision-Making Connected with Family Media Practices," *Journal of Family Studies* (in press).

58. Karen F. Heffler et al., "Association of Early-Life Social and Digital Media Experiences with Development of Autism Spectrum Disorder–Like Symptoms," *JAMA Pediatrics* 174, no. 7 (2020): 690–96. For a response, see Meryl Alper, "Improving Research on Screen Media, Autism, and Families of Young Children," *JAMA Pediatrics* 174, no. 12 (2020): 1223.

59. Leigh M. Vanderloo et al., "Applying Harm Reduction Principles to Address Screen Time in Young Children amidst the COVID-19 Pandemic," *Journal of Developmental & Behavioral Pediatrics* 41, no. 5 (2020): 335–36.

60. Google, "Supervised Experience on YouTube: Understand Your Choices as a Family," https://support.google.com/youtube/answer/10315420?hl=en&ref_topic=10314939, accessed August 30, 2022.

61. Benjamin Burroughs, "YouTube Kids: The App Economy and Mobile Parenting," *Social Media + Society* 3, no. 2 (2017): 1–8; Maarit Jaakkola, "From Vernacularized Commercialism to Kidbait: Toy Review Videos on YouTube and the Problematics of the Mash-Up Genre," *Journal of Children and Media* 14, no. 2 (2020): 237–54.

CHAPTER 5

1. Kevin Durkin, "Videogames and Young People with Developmental Disorders," *Review of General Psychology* 14, no. 2 (2010): 122–40.

2. William M. Bukowski, Andrew F. Newcomb, and Willard W. Hartup, "Friendship and Its Significance in Childhood and Adolescence: Introduction and Comment," in *The Company They Keep: Friendship in Childhood and Adolescence*, ed. William M. Bukowski, Andrew F. Newcomb, and Willard W. Hartup (Cambridge: Cambridge University Press, 1996), 1–19.

3. Andrew F. Newcomb and Catherine L. Bagwell, "Children's Friendship Relations: A Meta-Analytic Review," *Psychological Bulletin* 117, no. 2 (1995): 306–47.

4. Willard W. Hartup, "The Company They Keep: Friendships and Their Developmental Significance," *Child Development* 67, no. 1 (1996): 1–13.

5. Kenneth H. Rubin, William Bukowski, and Jeffrey G. Parker, "Peer Interactions, Relations, and Groups," in *Handbook of Child Psychology: Social, Emotional and Personality Development*, 5th ed., ed. Nancy Eisenberg (New York: Wiley, 1998), 619–700.

6. Patricia A. Adler and Peter Adler, *Peer Power: Preadolescent Culture and Identity* (New Brunswick, NJ: Rutgers University Press, 1998); Margarita Azmitia, Angela Ittel, and Kimberley Radmacher, "Narratives of Friendship and Self in Adolescence," *New Directions for Child and Adolescent Development* no. 107 (2005): 23–39.

7. Gary W. Ladd, *Children's Peer Relations and Social Competence: A Century of Progress* (New Haven, CT: Yale University Press, 2005).

8. Eleanor E. Maccoby, "Gender and Group Process: A Developmental Perspective," *Current Directions in Psychological Science* 11, no. 2 (2002): 54–58.

9. Sonia Livingstone, "From Family Television to Bedroom Culture: Young People's Media at Home," in *Media Studies: Key Issues and Debates*, ed. Eoin Devereux (Thousand Oaks, CA: Sage, 2007), 302–21; Patti M. Valkenburg and Jochen Peter, "Social Consequences of the Internet for Adolescents: A Decade of Research," *Current Directions in Psychological Science* 18, no. 1 (2009): 1–5.

10. Jackie Marsh, "Breaking the Ice: Play, Friendships, and Online Identities in Young Children's Use of Virtual Worlds," in *Children's Virtual Play Worlds: Culture, Learning, and Participation*, ed. Anne Burke and Jackie Marsh (New York: Peter Lang, 2013), 59–78.

11. Rebecca Dredge and Lara Schreurs, "Social Media Use and Offline Interpersonal Outcomes during Youth: A Systematic Literature Review," *Mass Communication and Society* 23, no. 6 (2020): 885–911; Emily Weinstein, "The Social Media See-Saw: Positive and Negative Influences on Adolescents' Affective Well-Being," *New Media & Society* 20, no. 10 (2018): 3597–623.

12. Victoria Rideout et al., *Common Sense Census: Media Use by Tweens and Teens, 2021* (San Francisco: Common Sense Media, 2021).

13. Monica Anderson and Jingjing Jiang, *Teens' Social Media Habits and Experiences* (Washington, DC: Pew Research Center, 2018).

14. Michelle Dean et al., "The Peer Relationships of Girls with ASD at School: Comparison to Boys and Girls with and without ASD," *Journal of Child Psychology and Psychiatry* 55, no. 11 (2014): 1218–25; Melissa H. Kuo et al., "Friendship Characteristics and Activity Patterns of Adolescents with an Autism Spectrum Disorder," *Autism* 17, no. 4 (2013): 481–500; Caitlin Malloy et al., "'They Can Even Make Waiting in Line Fun': A Quantitative Content Analysis of Autistic Children's Friendship Conceptualizations," *Psychology in the Schools* 57, no. 6 (2020): 973–89.

15. Neysa Petrina, Mark Carter, and Jennifer Stephenson, "The Nature of Friendship in Children with Autism Spectrum Disorders: A Systematic Review," *Research in Autism Spectrum Disorders* 8, no. 2 (2014): 111–26.

16. Elizabeth Fein, "'No One Has to Be Your Friend': Asperger's Syndrome and the Vicious Cycle of Social Disorder in Late Modern Identity Markers," *Ethos* 43, no. 1 (2015): 82–107; Neil Humphrey and Wendy Symes, "Peer Interaction Patterns among Adolescents with Autistic Spectrum Disorders (ASDs) in Mainstream School Settings," *Autism* 15, no. 4 (2011): 397–419.

17. Helen Tager-Flusberg and Connie Kasari, "Minimally Verbal School-Aged Children with Autism Spectrum Disorder: The Neglected End of the Spectrum," *Autism Research* 6, no. 6 (2013): 468–78.

18. Noah J. Sasson et al., "Neurotypical Peers Are Less Willing to Interact with Those with Autism Based on Thin Slice Judgments," *Scientific Reports* 7, no. 1 (2017): 1–10.

19. Kristen Bottema-Beutel and Zhushan Li, "Adolescent Judgments and Reasoning about the Failure to Include Peers with Social Disabilities," *Journal of Autism and Developmental Disorders* 45, no. 6 (2015): 1873–86; Connie Kasari et al., "Social Networks and Friendships at School: Comparing Children with and without ASD," *Journal of Autism and Developmental Disorders* 41, no. 5 (2011): 533–44.

20. Jill Locke et al., "Loneliness, Friendship Quality and the Social Networks of Adolescents with High-Functioning Autism in an Inclusive School Setting," *Journal of Research in Special Educational Needs* 10, no. 2 (2010): 74–81; Kate Simpson et al., "Investigating the Participation of Children on the Autism Spectrum across Home, School, and Community: A Longitudinal Study," *Child: Care, Health and Development* 45, no. 5 (2019): 681–87.

21. Rachel A. G. O'Connor et al., "Friendship Quality among Autistic and Non-Autistic (Pre-) Adolescents: Protective or Risk Factor for Mental Health?," *Autism*, January 22, 2022, https://doi.org/10.1177/13623613211073448.

22. Linda Beckman, Lisa Hellström, and Laura von Kobyletzki, "Cyber Bullying among Children with Neurodevelopmental Disorders: A Systematic Review," *Scandinavian Journal of Psychology* 61, no. 1 (2020): 54–67; Robin M. Kowalski and Cristin Fedina, "Cyber Bullying in ADHD and Asperger Syndrome Populations," *Research in Autism Spectrum Disorders* 5, no. 3 (2011): 1201–8; Robin M. Kowalski and Allison Toth, "Cyberbullying among Youth with and without Disabilities," *Journal of Child & Adolescent Trauma* 11, no. 1 (2018): 7–15; Eeske Van Roekel, Ron H. J. Scholte, and Robert Didden, "Bullying among Adolescents with Autism Spectrum Disorders: Prevalence and Perception," *Journal of Autism and Developmental Disorders* 40, no. 1 (2010): 63–73; Michelle F. Wright and Sebastian Wachs, "Does Peer Rejection Moderate the Associations among Cyberbullying Victimization, Depression, and Anxiety among Adolescents with Autism Spectrum Disorder?," *Children* 6, no. 3 (2019): 1–21.

23. Neysa Petrina et al., "Friendship Satisfaction in Children with Autism Spectrum Disorder and Nominated Friends," *Journal of Autism and Developmental Disorders* 47, no. 2 (2017): 384–92.

24. Lily Cresswell, Rebecca Hinch, and Eilidh Cage, "The Experiences of Peer Relationships amongst Autistic Adolescents: A Systematic Review of the Qualitative Evidence," *Research in Autism Spectrum Disorders* 61 (2019): 45–60.

25. Nirit Bauminger, Cory Shulman, and Galit Agam, "Peer Interaction and Loneliness in High-Functioning Children with Autism," *Journal of Autism and Developmental Disorders* 33, no. 5 (2003): 489–507; Locke et al., "Loneliness, Friendship Quality and the Social Networks."

26. Michelle F. Wright, "Parental Mediation, Cyber Victimization, Adjustment Difficulties, and Adolescents with Autism Spectrum Disorder," *Cyberpsychology: Journal of Psychosocial Research on Cyberspace* 11, no. 1 (2017): 6.

27. Nirir Bauminger and Connie Kasari, "Loneliness and Friendship in High-Functioning Children with Autism," *Child Development* 71, no. 2 (2000): 447–56; Michelle F. Wright, "Cyber Victimization and Depression among Adolescents with Autism Spectrum Disorder: The Buffering Effects of Parental Mediation and Social Support," *Journal of Child & Adolescent Trauma* 11, no. 1 (2018): 17–25.

28. Yu-Chien Chang et al., "Understanding the Characteristics of Friendship Quality, Activity Participation, and Emotional Well-Being in Taiwanese Adolescents with Autism Spectrum Disorder," *Scandinavian Journal of Occupational Therapy* 26, no. 6 (2018): 452–62; Motofumi Sumiya, Kazue Igarashi, and Motohide Miyahara, "Emotions Surrounding Friendships of Adolescents with Autism Spectrum Disorder in Japan: A Qualitative Interview Study," *PLOS One* 13, no. 2 (2018): 1–14.

29. Alexandra Sturrock et al., "In Their Own Words: The Impact of Subtle Language and Communication Difficulties as Described by Autistic Girls and Boys without Intellectual Disability," *Autism* 26, no, 2 (2022): 332–45.

30. Catherine Lord, Michael Rutter, and Ann Le Couteur, "Autism Diagnostic Interview-Revised: A Revised Version of a Diagnostic Interview for Caregivers of Individuals with Possible Pervasive Developmental Disorders," *Journal of Autism and Developmental Disorders* 24, no. 5 (1994): 659–85.

31. Elizabeth A. Laugeson and Fred Franke, *Social Skills for Teenagers with Developmental and Autism Spectrum Disorders: The PEERS Treatment Manual* (New York: Routledge, 2010); Michelle Garcia Winner, *Thinking about You Thinking about Me* (Santa Clara, CA: Think Social Publishing, 2002); Michelle Garcia Winner, *Inside Out: What Makes a Person with Social Cognitive Deficits Tick?* (Santa Clara, CA: Think Social Publishing, 2006).

32. Ari Ne'eman, "When Disability Is Defined by Behavior, Outcome Measures Should Not Promote 'Passing,'" *AMA Journal of Ethics* 23, no. 7 (2021): 569–75.

33. Kristen Bottema-Beutel, Haerin Park, and So Yoon Kim, "Commentary on Social Skills Training Curricula for Individuals with ASD: Social Interaction, Authenticity, and Stigma," *Journal of Autism and Developmental Disorders* 48, no. 3 (2018): 953–64.

34. Bottema-Beutel, Park, and Kim, "Commentary on Social Skills Training Curricula."

35. Fein, "'No One Has to Be Your Friend.'"

36. James Paul Gee, "Semiotic Social Spaces and Affinity Spaces: From the Age of Mythology to Today's Schools," in *Beyond Communities of Practice: Language, Power and Social Context*, ed. David Barton and Karin Tusting (Cambridge: Cambridge University Press, 2005), 214–32. See The Lab (https://thelab.org.au/), based in Australia, as one such example, which is geared toward autistic kids ages 10–16.

37. Kristen Bottema-Beutel et al., "Avoiding the 'Brick Wall of Awkward': Perspectives of Youth with Autism Spectrum Disorder on Social-Focused Intervention Practices," *Autism* 20, no. 2 (2016): 196–206; Leslie S. Daniel and Bonnie S. Billingsley, "What Boys with an Autism Spectrum Disorder Say about Establishing and Maintaining Friendships," *Focus on Autism and Other Developmental Disabilities* 25, no. 4 (2010): 220–29.

38. Hanna Bertilsdotter Rosqvist, Charlotte Brownlow, and Lindsay O'Dell, "'What's the Point of Having Friends?' Reformulating Notions of the Meaning of Friends and Friendship among Autistic People," *Disability Studies Quarterly* 35, no. 4 (2015); Dara V. Chan, Julie D. Doran, and Osly D. Galobardi, "Beyond Friendship: The Spectrum of Social Participation of Autistic Adults," *Journal of Autism and Developmental Disorders*, January 25, 2022, https://doi.org/10.1007/s10803-022-05441-1.

39. Charlotte Brownlow, Hanna Bertilsdotter Rosqvist, and Lindsay O'Dell, "Exploring the Potential for Social Networking among People with Autism: Challenging Dominant Ideas of 'Friendship,'" *Scandinavian Journal of Disability Research* 17, no. 2 (2015): 188–93.

40. Aviva Must et al., "Barriers to Physical Activity in Children with Autism Spectrum Disorders: Relationship to Physical Activity and Screen Time," *Journal of Physical Activity & Health* 12, no. 4 (2015): 529–34.

41. Kathryn E. Ringland, "A Place to Play: The (Dis)abled Embodied Experience for Autistic Children in Online Spaces," in *Proceedings of the 2019 ACM CHI Conference on Human Factors in Computing Systems* (New York: ACM, 2019), paper 288; Annuska Zolyomi and Marc Schmalz, "Mining for Social Skills: Minecraft in Home and Therapy for Neurodiverse Youth," in *Proceedings of the 50th Hawaii International Conference on System Sciences* (Honolulu: HICSS, 2017), 3391–440.

42. Michael F. Giangreco et al., "'Be Careful What You Wish For . . .': Five Reasons to be Concerned about the Assignment of Individual Paraprofessionals," *Teaching Exceptional Children* 37, no. 5 (2005): 28–34.

43. Allison Pugh, *Longing and Belonging: Parents, Children, and Consumer Culture* (Berkeley: University of California Press, 2009); Ellen Seiter, *Sold Separately: Children and Parents in Consumer Culture* (New Brunswick, NJ: Rutgers University Press, 1995).

44. Gwendolyn Kansen, "For Autistic Consumers, Pop Culture Can Be More than an Escape. It Can Be a Lifeline.," *Slate*, June 6, 2018, https://slate.com/culture/2018/06/autistic-consumers-can-use-pop-culture-for-social-skills.html.

45. Christian Ryan et al., "Perceptions of Friendship among Girls with Autism Spectrum Disorders," *European Journal of Special Needs Education* 36, no. 3 (2021): 393–407; Sturrock et al., "In Their Own Words."

46. Gerrit I. van Schalkwyk et al., "Social Media Use, Friendship Quality, and the Moderating Role of Anxiety in Adolescents with Autism Spectrum Disorder," *Journal of Autism and Developmental Disorders* 47, no. 9 (2017): 2805–13.

47. van Schalkwyk et al., "Social Media Use."

48. Ryan et al., "Perceptions of Friendship."

49. Jennifer Cook O'Toole, *The Asperkid's (Secret) Book of Social Rules: The Handbook of Not-So-Obvious Social Guidelines for Tweens and Teens with Asperger Syndrome* (London: Jessica Kingsley, 2012), 186–87.

50. Kuo et al., "Friendship Characteristics and Activity Patterns."

51. Rebecca S. Vine Foggo and Amanda A. Webster, "Understanding the Social Experiences of Adolescent Females on the Autism Spectrum," *Research in Autism Spectrum Disorders* 35 (2017): 74–85; Ryan et al., "Perceptions of Friendship."

52. Naseem Alhujaili et al., "Comparison of Social Media Use among Adolescents with Autism Spectrum Disorder and Non-ASD Adolescents," *Adolescent Health, Medicine and Therapeutics* 13 (2022): 15–21.

53. Sarah F. Rosaen and Jason L. Dibble, "Investigating the Relationships among Child's Age, Parasocial Interactions, and the Social Realism of Favorite Television Characters," *Communication Research Reports* 25, no. 2 (2008): 145–54.

54. Amanada N. Tolber and Kristin L. Drogos, "Tweens' Wishful Identification and Parasocial Relationships with YouTubers," *Frontiers in Psychology* 10 (2019): 1–15.

55. Kristin Harrison et al., "Sensory Curation: Theorizing Media Use for Sensory Regulation and Implications for Family Conflict," *Media Psychology* 22, no. 4 (2019): 653–88.

56. Elizabeth Fein, "Making Meaningful Worlds: Role-Playing Subcultures and the Autism Spectrum," *Culture, Medicine, and Psychiatry* 39, no. 2 (2015): 299–321.

57. Karen Louise Smith and Leslie Regan Shade, "Children's Digital Playgrounds as Data Assemblages: Problematics of Privacy, Personalization, and Promotional Culture," *Big Data & Society* 5, no. 2 (2018): 1–12.

58. Kathryn E. Ringland et al., "Making 'Safe': Community-Centered Practices in a Virtual World Dedicated to Children with Autism," in *Proceedings of the 2015 ACM International Conference on Computer Supported Collaborative Work (CSCW)* (New York: ACM, 2015), 1788–800.

59. Elizabeth K. Cridland et al., "Being a Girl in a Boys' World: Investigating the Experiences of Girls with Autism Spectrum Disorders during Adolescence," *Journal of Autism and Developmental Disorders* 44, no. 6 (2014): 1261–74; Siobhan Tierney, Jan Burns, and Elizabeth Kilbey, "Looking behind the Mask: Social Coping Strategies of Girls on the Autistic Spectrum," *Research in Autism Spectrum Disorders* 23 (2016): 73–83.

60. Claire K. Pescott, "'I Wish I Was Wearing a Filter Right Now': An Exploration of Identity Formation and Subjectivity of 10- and 11-Year Olds' Social Media Use," *Social Media + Society* 6, no. 4 (2020); Joanna C. Yau and Stephanie M. Reich, "'It's Just a Lot of Work': Adolescents' Self-Presentation Norms and Practices on Facebook and Instagram," *Journal of Research on Adolescence* 29, no. 1 (2018): 196–209.

61. Sara Grimes and Deborah Fields, *Kids Online: A New Research Agenda for Understanding Social Networking Forums* (New York: Joan Ganz Cooney Center at Sesame Workshop, 2012).

62. Katie Davis, "Friendship 2.0: Adolescents' Experiences of Belonging and Self-Disclosure Online," *Journal of Adolescence* 35, no. 6 (2012): 1527–36.

63. Jeffrey A. Hall, "When Is Social Media Use Social Interaction? Defining Mediated Social Interaction," *New Media & Society* 20, no. 1 (2018): 162–79.

64. Kathryn E. Ringland et al., "'Will I Always Be Not Social?' Re-conceptualizing Sociality in the Context of a Minecraft Community for Autism," in *Proceedings of the 2016 ACM CHI Conference on Human Factors in Computing Systems* (New York: ACM, 2016), 1256–69.

65. Ringland et al., "'Will I Always Be Not Social?'"

66. Julian Sefton-Green, "Introduction: Being Young in the Digital Age," in *Digital Diversions: Youth Culture in the Age of Multimedia*, ed. Julian Sefton-Green (London: University College London Press, 1998), 1.

67. Katie Davis, "Tensions of Identity in a Networked Era: Young People's Perspectives on the Risks and Rewards of Online Self-Expression," *New Media & Society* 14, no. 4 (2012): 634–51.

68. Karri Gillespie-Smith et al., "Using Social Media to Be 'Social': Perceptions of Social Media Benefits and Risk by Autistic Young People, and Parents," *Research in Developmental Disabilities* 118 (2021): 1–11.

69. Jessica N. Rocheleau and Sonia Chiasson, "Privacy and Safety on Social Networking Sites: Autistic and Non-autistic Teenagers' Attitudes and Behaviors," *ACM Transactions on Computer-Human Interaction* 29, no. 1 (2022): 1–39.

70. Paul Davarsi, "How Online Communities Lower Social Barriers for Kids across the Spectrum," *Connected Camps*, September 1, 2017, https://blog.connectedcamps .com/online-communities-lower-social-barriers-kids-across-spectrum/.

71. Marleena Mustola et al., "Reconsidering Passivity and Activity in Children's Digital Play," *New Media & Society* 20, no. 1 (2018): 237–54.

72. Margaret H. Laurie, Andrew Manches, and Sue Fletcher-Watson, "The Role of Robotic Toys in Shaping Play and Joint Engagement in Autistic Children: Implications for Future Design," *International Journal of Child-Computer Interaction* 32 (2022): 100384.

73. Emily Paige Ballou, Sharon daVanport, and Morénike Giwa Onaiwu, eds., *Sincerely, Your Autistic Child: What People on the Autism Spectrum Wish Their Parents Knew about Growing Up, Acceptance, and Identity* (Boston: Beacon Press, 2021).

74. Laurie, Manches, and Fletcher-Watson, "The Role of Robotic Toys."

75. Kathryn E. Ringland, "Playful Places in Online Playgrounds: An Ethnography of a Minecraft Virtual World for Children with Autism" (PhD diss., University of California, Irvine, 2018).

76. Louanne E. Boyd et al., "Evaluating a Collaborative iPad Game's Impact on Social Relationships for Children with Autism Spectrum Disorder," *ACM Transactions on Accessible Computing* 7, no. 1 (2015): 1–18.

77. Naoki Higashida, *Fall Down 7 Times Get Up 8: A Young Man's Voice from the Silence of Autism*, trans. K. A. Yoshida and David Mitchell (New York: Random House, 2017), 77.

CHAPTER 6

1. A. Jean Ayers and Jeff Robbins, *Sensory Integration and the Child: Understanding Hidden Sensory Challenges* (Los Angeles: Western Psychological Services, 2005).

2. Ben Belek, "Articulating Sensory Sensitivity: From Bodies with Autism to Autistic Bodies," *Medical Anthropology* 38, no. 1 (2019): 30–43.

3. Susan R. Leekam et al., "Describing the Sensory Abnormalities of Children and Adults with Autism," *Journal of Autism and Developmental Disorders* 37, no. 5 (2007): 894–910; Scott D. Tomchek and Winnie Dunn, "Sensory Processing in Children with and without Autism: A Comparative Study Using the Short Sensory Profile," *American Journal of Occupational Therapy* 61, no. 2 (2007): 190–200.

4. American Psychiatric Association, *Diagnostic and Statistical Manual of Mental Disorders: DSM-5* [5th ed.] (Washington, DC: American Psychiatric Association, 2013).

5. Donna Williams, *Autism and Sensing: The Unlost Instinct* (London: Jessica Kingsley, 1998).

6. Anne M. Donnellan, David A. Hill, and Martha R. Leary, "Rethinking Autism: Implications of Sensory and Movement Differences," *Disability Studies Quarterly* 30, no. 1 (2010): 18; Temple Grandin, *Thinking in Pictures: And Other Reports from My Life with Autism* (New York: Doubleday, 1995); Leekam et al., "Describing the Sensory Abnormalities"; Lillian N. Stiegler and Rebecca Davis, "Understanding Sound Sensitivity in Individuals with Autism Spectrum Disorders," *Focus on Autism and Other Developmental Disabilities* 25, no. 2 (2010): 67–75.

7. Ido Kedar, *Ido in Autismland: Climbing Out of Autism's Silent Prison* (n.p.: Sharon Kedar, 2012), 44.

8. Kristen Harrison et al., "Sensory Curation: Theorizing Media Use for Sensory Regulation and Implications for Family Media Conflict," *Media Psychology* 22, no. 4 (2019): 653–88; Sarah Pink, "Approaching Media through the Senses: Between Experience and Representation," *Media International Australia* 154, no. 1 (2015): 5–14.

9. Jason Nolan and Melanie McBride, "Embodied Semiosis: Autistic 'Stimming' as Sensory Praxis," in *International Handbook of Semiotics*, vol. 1, ed. Peter P. Trifonas (Dordrecht: Springer, 2015), 1069–78.

10. Katta Spiel et al., "Agency of Autistic Children in Technology Research—A Critical Literature Review," *ACM Transactions on Computer-Human Interaction* 26, no. 6 (2019): 1–40.

11. Howard C. Shane and Patti D. Albert, "Electronic Screen Media for Persons with Autism Spectrum Disorders: Results of a Survey," *Journal of Autism and Developmental Disorders* 38, no. 8 (2008): 1499–508.

12. Rebecca Lane and Jenny Radesky, "Digital Media and Autism Spectrum Disorders: Review of Evidence, Theoretical Concerns, and Opportunities for Intervention," *Journal of Developmental & Behavioral Pediatrics* 40, no. 5 (2019): 364–68; Kathryn E. Ringland et al., "Would You Be Mine: Appropriating Minecraft as an Assistive Technology for Youth with Autism," in *Proceedings of the 18th International ACM SIGACCESS Conference on Computers and Accessibility* (New York: ACM: 2016), 33–41.

13. This chapter is adapted from an earlier published piece, which focused on the methodological implications of this work; Meryl Alper, "Inclusive Sensory Ethnography: Studying New Media and Neurodiversity in Everyday Life," *New Media & Society* 20, no. 10 (2018): 3560–79, https://doi.org/10.1177/1461444818755394.

14. A. Jean Ayres, *Sensory Integration and the Child* (Los Angeles: Western Psychological Services, 1979); Winnie Dunn, "The Impact of Sensory Processing Abilities on the Daily Lives of Young Children and Their Families: A Conceptual Model," *Infants and Young Children* 9, no. 4 (1997): 23–35; Winnie Dunn, "The Sensations of Everyday Life: Empirical, Theoretical, and Pragmatic Considerations," *American Journal of Occupational Therapy* 55, no. 6 (2001): 608–20.

15. Ayers and Robbins, *Sensory Integration and the Child.*

16. Kathryn Lynn Geurts, "Senses," in *Keywords for Disability Studies*, ed. Rachel Adams, Benjamin Reiss, and David Serlin (New York: New York University Press, 2015), 161–63; Erving Goffman, *Stigma: Notes on the Management of Spoiled Identity* (New York: Simon & Schuster, 1963).

17. Sharon L. Snyder and David T. Mitchell, *Cultural Locations of Disability* (Chicago: University of Chicago Press, 2006).

18. Leah Lakshmi Piepzna-Samarasinha, *Care Work: Dreaming Disability Justice* (Vancouver, BC: Arsenal Pulp Press, 2018).

19. Donnellan, Hill, and Leary, "Rethinking Autism."

20. Julia Bascom, ed., *Loud Hands: Autistic People, Speaking* (Washington, DC: The Autistic Press, 2012).

21. James J. Gibson, "The Theory of Affordances," in *Perceiving, Acting, and Knowing: Toward an Ecological Psychology*, ed. Robert Shaw and John Bransford (Hillsdale, NJ: Lawrence Erlbaum Associates, 1977), 67–82; Maurice Merleau-Ponty, *Phenomenology of Perception* (London: Routledge & Kegan Paul, 1962).

22. Michael Bull et al., "Introducing Sensory Studies," *The Senses and Society* 1 (2006): 5–7.

23. Gili Hammer, "'This Is the Anthropologist, and She Is Sighted': Ethnographic Research with Blind Women," *Disability Studies Quarterly* 33, no 2 (2013): 1–23;

David Howes, *Sensual Relations: Engaging the Senses in Culture and Social Theory* (Ann Arbor: University of Michigan Press, 2003); Karen Nakamura, "Making Sense of Sensory Ethnography: The Sensual and the Multisensory," *American Anthropologist* 115, no. 1 (2013): 132–35; Georg Simmel, *The Sociology of Georg Simmel*, trans. Kurt H. Wolff (New York: Free Press, 1950); Olga Solomon, "Sense and the Senses: Anthropology and the Study of Autism," *Annual Review of Anthrolopogy* 39 (2010): 241–59; Phillip Vannini, Dennis Waskul, and Simon Gottschalk, *The Senses in Self, Society, and Culture: A Sociology of the Senses* (New York: Routledge, 2012).

24. Herbert Blumer, *Symbolic Interactionism: Perspective and Method* (Englewood Cliffs, NJ: Prentice-Hall, 1969); Norman K. Denzin, *Symbolic Interactionism and Cultural Studies: The Politics of Interpretation* (London: Blackwell, 1992).

25. Ingrid Richardson, "Faces, Interfaces, Screens: Relational Ontologies of Framing, Attention and Distraction," *Transformations: Journal of Media, Culture & Technology* 18 (2010); Ingrid Richardson and Larissa Hjorth, "Mobile Media, Domestic Play, and Haptic Ethnography," *New Media & Society* 19, no. 10 (2017): 1653–67.

26. Gibson, "The Theory of Affordances"; Donald Norman, "Affordances, Constraints and Design," *Interactions* 6 (1999): 38–43.

27. Peter Nagy and Gina Neff, "Imagined Affordance: Reconstructing a Keyword for Communication Theory," *Social Media + Society* 1, no. 2 (2015): 1–9.

28. Mark Paterson, *Senses of Touch: Haptics, Affects and Technologies* (Oxford: Berg, 2007).

29. Marshall McLuhan, *Understanding Media: The Extensions of Man* (1964; repr., Cambridge, MA: MIT Press, 1994), 316.

30. Marshall McLuhan, *The Medium Is the Message: An Inventory of Effects* (New York: Bantam Books, 1967); McLuhan, *Understanding Media*.

31. Donna Z. Davis and Tom Boellstorff, "Compulsive Creativity: Virtual Worlds, Disability, and Digital Capital," *International Journal of Communication* 10 (2016): 2096–118; Aimi Hamraie, *Building Access: Universal Design and the Politics of Disability* (Minneapolis: University of Minnesota Press, 2017).

32. Hamraie, *Building Access*.

33. Elizabeth Ellcessor, *Restricted Access: Media, Disability, and the Politics of Participation* (New York: New York University Press, 2016).

34. Gerard Goggin, "Disability and Haptic Mobile Media," *New Media & Society* 19, no. 10 (2017): 1563–80; Mark Paterson, "On Haptic Media and the Possibilities of a More Inclusive Interactivity," *New Media & Society* 19, no. 10 (2017): 1541–62.

35. Mara Mills, "On Disability and Cybernetics: Helen Keller, Norbert Wiener, and the Hearing Glove," *differences* 22 (2011): 74–111; Jonathan Sterne, *Diminished Faculties: A Political Phenomenology of Impairment* (Durham, NC: Duke University Press, 2022).

36. S. Lochlann Jain, "The Prosthetic Imagination: Enabling and Disabling the Prosthesis Trope," *Science, Technology, and Human Values* 24, no. 1 (1999): 31–54.

37. Jessica S. Rauchberg, "Imagining a Neuroqueer Technoscience," *Studies in Social Justice* 16, no. 2 (2022): 370–88.

38. Jaipreet Virdi, "Black Bars, White Text," *Literature and Medicine* 39, no. 1 (2021): 29–33, Project MUSE, https://muse.jhu.edu/article/796706.

39. Harrison et al., "Sensory Curation."

40. Mack Hagood, *Hush: Music and Sonic Self-Control* (Durham, NC: Duke University Press, 2019).

41. Apple, "Apple Previews Powerful Software Updates Designed for People with Disabilities," Apple, May 19, 2021, para. 2, https://www.apple.com/newsroom/2021/05/apple-previews-powerful-software-updates-designed-for-people-with-disabilities/.

42. Harrison et al., "Sensory Curation"; Kristin Harrison and Amelia Couture Bue, "Media Sensory Curation and Family Media Conflict: Replication and Validation of Short-Form Measures," *Media Psychology* 24, no. 4 (2021): 538–61.

43. Harrison et al., "Sensory Curation."

44. Wasan Nagib and Allison Williams, "Creating 'Therapeutic Landscapes' at Home: The Experiences of Families of Children with Autism," *Health & Place* 52 (2018): 46–54.

45. Nagib and Williams, "Creating 'Therapeutic Landscapes.'"

46. Olfactory sensory processing is excluded from this analysis based on the lack of relevant data collected.

47. Stephanie McNeal, "People Are Obsessed with This 'Mermaid Pillow" That You Can Change with A Swipe of Your Hand," BuzzFeed News, January 16, 2016, https://www.buzzfeed.com/stephaniemcneal/mermaid-pillow.

48. RIFGifts, "Custom Unicorn Pillow, Personalized Unicorn Pillow, Sensory Toy, Sensory Fidget, Unicorn Decor, Stress Toy, Cheer Gift, Reversible," Etsy, https://www.etsy.com/listing/562804224/custom-unicorn-pillow-personalized.

49. Meryl Alper, *Giving Voice: Mobile Communication, Disability, and Inequality* (Cambridge, MA: MIT Press, 2017).

50. Sharif Mowlabocus, "'Let's Get This Thing Open': The Pleasures of Unboxing Videos," *European Journal of Cultural Studies* 23, no. 4 (2020): 564–79.

51. Food aversions are a common occurrence among those on the spectrum; Sharon A. Cermak, Carol Curtin, and Linda G. Bandini, "Food Selectivity and Sensory Sensitivity in Children with Autism Spectrum Disorders," *Journal of the American Dietetic Association* 110, no. 2 (2010): 238–46.

52. Andrew R. Schrock, "Communicative Affordances of Mobile Media: Portability, Availability, Locatability, and Multimediality," *International Journal of Communication* 9 (2015): 1229–46.

53. Eli Clare, *Brilliant Imperfection: Grappling with Cure* (Durham, NC: Duke University Press, 2017).

54. Merleau-Ponty, *Phenomenology of Perception*.

55. Rosemarie Garland-Thomson, "Misfits: A Feminist Materialist Disability Concept," *Hypatia: A Journal of Feminist Philosophy* 26, no. 3 (2011): 591–609.

56. Nagib and Williams, "Creating 'Therapeutic Landscapes.'"

57. Brendan Hart, "Autism Parents & Neurodiversity: Radical Translation, Joint Embodiment and the Prosthetic Environment," *BioSocieties* 9, no. 3 (2014): 284–303.

58. Kristen Harrison, "Rude or Shrewd? Reframing Media Devices as Care Structures and Child Use as Accommodation," *Journal of Children and Media* 13, no. 3 (2019): 367–75.

59. Claire Martin, "Feel the Noise: Homemade Slime Becomes Big Business," *New York Times*, June 23, 2017, https://www.nytimes.com/2017/06/23/business/smallbusiness /homemade-slime-becomes-big-business.html.

60. Emma L. Barratt and Nick J. Davis, "Autonomous Sensory Meridian Response (ASMR): A Flowlike Mental State," *PeerJ* 3 (2015): 1–17.

61. Alper, *Giving Voice*; Ingunn Moser, "Disability and the Promises of Technology: Technology, Subjectivity, and Embodiment within an Order of the Normal," *Information, Communication, and Society* 9, no. 3 (2006): 373–95.

62. Aiyana Bailin, "What the Fidget Spinners Fad Reveals about Disability Discrimination," *Thinking Person's Guide to Autism*, May 20, 2017, http://www.thinkingau tismguide.com/2017/05/what-fidget-spinners-fad-reveals-about.html; Robert McRuer, *Crip Theory: Cultural Signs of Queerness and Disability* (New York: New York University Press, 2006).

63. This was tragically the case with Stephon Watts, a Black autistic 15-year-old killed by police in a Chicago suburb in 2012; Adrienne Hurst, "Black, Autistic, and Killed by Police," *Chicago Reader*, December 17, 2015, https://www.chicagoreader.com/chicago /stephon-watts-police-shooting-autism-death/Content?oid=20512018.

64. Mia Mingus, "Access Intimacy, Interdependence and Disability Justice," *Leaving Evidence* (blog), April 12, 2017, https://leavingevidence.wordpress.com/2017/04/12 /access-intimacy-interdependence-and-disability-justice/.

65. Aimi Hamraie and Kelly Fritsch, "Crip Technoscience Manifesto," *Catalyst: Feminism, Theory, Technoscience* 5, no. 1 (2019): 14.

66. Cynthia L. Bennett, Daniela K. Rosner, and Alex S. Taylor, "The Care Work of Access," in *Proceedings of the 2020 CHI Conference on Human Factors in Computing Systems* (New York: ACM, 2020), 1–15.

67. Piepzna-Samarasinha, *Care Work*.

68. Arseli Dokumaci, "People as Affordances: Building Disability Worlds through Care Intimacy," *Current Anthropology* 61, no. S21 (2020): S97–108.

69. Harrison, "Rude or Shrewd?"; Paddy Scannell, *Television and the Meaning of "Live": An Enquiry into the Human Situation* (Cambridge: Polity Press, 2014).

70. Estée Klar and Adam Wolfond, "Neurodiversity in Relation: Artistic Intraethno-graphic Practice," in *Centering Diverse Bodyminds in Critical Qualitative Inquiry*, ed. Jessica N. Lester and Emily A. Nusbaum (London: Routledge, 2021), 22–36.

71. Hart, "Autism Parents & Neurodiversity," 288.

72. Harrison et al., "Sensory Curation."

73. Lydia X. Z. Brown, "Disability Justice & Conference Space: Notes on Radical Access & Radical Inclusion," *Autistic Hoya* (blog), October 25, 2016, https://www.autistichoya.com/2016/10/disability-justice-conference-space-notes-on-radical-access-radical-inclusion.html.

74. Rebecca Lane and Jenny Radesky, "Digital Media and Autism Spectrum Disorders: Review of Evidence, Theoretical Concerns, and Opportunities for Intervention," *Journal of Developmental & Behavioral Pediatrics* 40, no. 5 (2019): 364–68.

CHAPTER 7

1. Dora M. Raymaker et al., "'Having All of Your Internal Resources Exhausted beyond Measure and Being Left with No Clean-Up Crew': Defining Autistic Burnout," *Autism in Adulthood* 2, no. 2 (2020): 132–43; Idalmis Santiesteban et al., "Individuals with Autism Share Others' Emotions: Evidence from the Continuous Affective Rating and Empathic Responses (CARER) Task," *Journal of Autism and Developmental Disorders* 51, no. 2 (2021): 391–404.

2. Dominic A. Trevisan et al., "How Do Adults and Teens with Self-Declared Autism Spectrum Disorder Experience Eye Contact? A Qualitative Analysis of First-Hand Accounts," *PLOS One* 12, no. 11 (2017): 1–22.

3. Rebecca Brewer et al., "Can Neurotypical Individuals Read Autistic Facial Expressions? Atypical Production of Emotional Facial Expressions in Autism Spectrum Disorders," *Autism Research* 9, no. 2 (2016): 262–71; Rosanna Edey et al., "Interaction Takes Two: Typical Adults Exhibit Mind-Blindness towards Those with Autism Spectrum Disorder," *Journal of Abnormal Psychology* 125, no. 7 (2016): 879–85; Elizabeth Sheppard et al., "How Easy Is It to Read the Minds of People with Autism Spectrum Disorder?," *Journal of Autism and Developmental Disorders* 46, no. 4 (2016): 1247–54.

4. Damian E. M. Milton, "On the Ontological Status of Autism: The 'Double Empathy Problem,'" *Disability & Society* 27, no. 6 (2012): 883–87.

5. Morénike Giwa Onaiwu, "'They Don't Know, Don't Show, or Don't Care': Autism's White Privilege Problem," *Autism in Adulthood* 4, no. 2 (2020): 270–72. For example, in November 2021, a 10-year-old Black autistic girl, Isabella "Izzy" Tichenor-Cox, tragically died by suicide after school officials ignored earlier calls by her mother, Brittany, to address harassment that she endured at the hands of her classmates and teacher; Courtney Tanner, "Community Mourns Utah 10-Year-Old Who Died by Suicide after Her Mom Says She Was Bullied for Being Black and Autistic," *Salt Lake Tribune,*

November 9, 2021, https://www.sltrib.com/news/education/2021/11/09/community -mourns-utah/.

6. Sami Schalk, *Bodyminds Reimagined: (Dis)ability, Race, and Gender in Black Women's Speculative Fiction* (Durham, NC: Duke University Press, 2018).

7. Yonty Friesem, "It's All about Control: How Giving Kids Control over Access, Content, and Format of Their Media Production Advances Social and Emotional Learning," *Media Practice and Education* 21, no. 4 (2020): 261–74.

8. Lisa F. Barrett, *How Emotions Are Made: The Secret Life of the Brain* (New York: Houghton Mifflin Harcourt, 2017).

9. Jack P. Shonkoff and Deborah A. Phillips, eds., *From Neurons to Neighborhoods: The Science of Early Childhood Development* (Washington, DC: National Academy Press, 2000).

10. Robert C. Solomon, *What Is an Emotion? Classic and Contemporary Readings* (Oxford: Oxford University Press, 2003).

11. Arlie R. Hochschild, "Emotion Work, Feeling Rules, and Social Structure," *American Journal of Sociology* 85, no. 3 (1979): 551–75.

12. Karen Caplovitz Barrett and Joseph J. Campos, "Perspectives on Emotional Development II: a Functionalist Approach to Emotions," in *Handbook of Infant Development*, 2nd ed., ed. Joy D. Osofsky (New York: Wiley, 1987), 555–78.

13. Paul Ekman, ed., *Emotion in the Human Face*, 2nd ed. (Los Altos, CA: Malor Books, 2013). See also Carroll E. Izard, *Human Emotions* (New York: Plenum, 1977).

14. Anna L. Hoffman and Luke Stark, "Hard Feelings—*Inside Out*, Silicon Valley, and Why Technologizing Emotion and Memory Is a Dangerous Idea," *Los Angeles Review of Books*, September 11, 2015, https://lareviewofbooks.org/article/hard -feelings-inside-out-silicon-valley-and-why-technologizing-emotion-and-memory-is -a-dangerous-idea/.

15. Carroll E. Izard et al., "Self-Organization of Discrete Emotions, Emotion Patterns, and Emotion-Cognition Relations," in *Emotion, Development, and Self-Organization*, ed. Marc D. Lewis and Isabela Granic (Cambridge: Cambridge University Press, 2000), 15–36.

16. Joseph J. Campos, Carl B. Frankel, and Linda Camras, "On the Nature of Emotion Regulation," *Child Development* 75, no. 2 (2004): 377–94.

17. Natasha H. Bailen, Lauren M. Green, and Renee J. Thompson, "Understanding Emotion in Adolescents: A Review of Emotional Frequency, Intensity, Instability, and Clarity," *Emotion Review* 11, no. 1 (2019): 63–73.

18. Barrett, *How Emotions Are Made*.

19. Eva Illouz, *Cold Intimacies: The Making of Emotional Capitalism* (Cambridge: Polity Press, 2007).

20. Patrick McDonagh, "Autism in an Age of Empathy: A Cautionary Critique," in *Worlds of Autism: Across the Spectrum of Neurological Difference*, ed. Joyce Davidson and Michael Orsini (Minneapolis: University of Minnesota Press, 2013), 31–51.

21. Anna Jaysane-Darr, "Enabling and Disabling Emotional Diversity: Negotiating Autism Spectrum Disorder in Therapeutic Encounters," *Children & Society* 34, no. 4 (2020): 261–75. See also Cara Roberts-Collins et al., "Emotion Awareness and Cognitive Behavioural Therapy in Young People with Autism Spectrum Disorder," *Autism* 22, no. 7 (2018): 837–44.

22. Victoria Pitts-Taylor, *The Brain's Body: Neuroscience and Corporeal Politics* (Durham, NC: Duke University Press, 2016).

23. Simon Baron-Cohen, *Mindblindness: An Essay on Autism and Theory of Mind* (Cambridge, MA: MIT Press, 1997); Simon Baron-Cohen, Alan M. Leslie, and Uta Frith, "Does the Autistic Child Have a 'Theory of Mind'?," *Cognition* 21, no. 1 (1985): 37–46.

24. Morton Ann Gernsbacher and M. Remi Yergeau, "Empirical Failures of the Claim That Autistic People Lack a Theory of Mind," *Archives of Scientific Psychology* 7, no. 1 (2019): 102–18. For more on dehumanization toward autistic people, see Eilidh Cage, Jessica Di Monaco, and Victoria Newell, "Understanding, Attitudes and Dehumanisation towards Autistic People," *Autism* 23, no. 6 (2019): 1373–83.

25. Kelly B. Beck et al., "Assessment and Treatment of Emotion Regulation Impairment in Autism Spectrum Disorder across the Life Span: Current State of the Science and Future Directions," *Child and Adolescent Psychiatric Clinics* 29, no. 3 (2020): 527–42; Ru Ying Kai et al., "Emotion Regulation in Autism Spectrum Disorder: Where We Are and Where We Need to Go," *Autism Research* 11, no. 7 (2018): 962–78; Andrea C. Samson et al., "Emotion Regulation in Children and Adolescents with Autism Spectrum Disorder," *Autism Research* 8, no. 1 (2015): 9–18. The large majority of work on emotion regulation and autism in kids is based on parent and teacher report rather than self-report from autistic kids. See Talia Burton et al., "Self-Reported Emotion Regulation in Children with Autism Spectrum Disorder, without Intellectual Disability," *Research in Autism Spectrum Disorders* 76 (2020): 1–10.

26. Judith A. Crowell, Jennifer Keluskar, and Amanda Gorecki, "Parenting Behavior and the Development of Children with Autism Spectrum Disorder," *Comprehensive Psychiatry* 90 (2019): 21–29; Lucinda B. C. Pouw et al., "The Link between Emotion Regulation, Social Functioning, and Depression in Boys with ASD," *Research in Autism Spectrum Disorders* 7, no. 4 (2013): 549–56.

27. Cáit Griffin, Michael V. Lombardo, and Bonnie Auyeung, "Alexithymia in Children with and without Autism Spectrum Disorders," *Autism Research* 9, no. 7 (2016): 773–80; Peter E. Sifneos, "The Prevalence of 'Alexithymic' Characteristics in Psychosomatic Patients," *Psychotherapy and Psychosomatics* 22, no. 2–6 (1973): 255–62.

28. Robert S. P. Jones, Andrew Zahl, and Jaci C. Huws, "First-Hand Accounts of Emotional Experiences in Autism: A Qualitative Analysis," *Disability & Society* 16, no. 3 (2001): 393–401.

29. Ido Kedar, *Ido in Autismland: Climbing Out of Autism's Silent Prison* (n.p.: Sharon Kedar, 2012), 73.

30. Lisa F. Barrett, "Are Emotions Natural Kinds?," *Perspectives on Psychological Science* 1, no. 1 (2006): 28–58; Lisa Barrett et al., "Emotional Expressions Reconsidered: Challenges to Inferring Emotion from Human Facial Movements," *Psychological Science in the Public Interest* 20, no. 1 (2019): 1–68.

31. Dominic A. Trevisan, Maureen Hoskyn, and Elina Birmingham, "Facial Expression Production in Autism: A Meta-Analysis," *Autism Research* 11, no. 12 (2018): 1586–601.

32. Connor T. Keating and Jennifer L. Cook, "Facial Expression Production and Recognition in Autism Spectrum Disorders: A Shifting Landscape," *Child & Adolescent Psychiatric Clinics* 29, no. 3 (2020): 557–71. A nonspeaking autistic child, for example, might emit a high-pitched scream when they are happy, a sound that a neurotypical individual would more likely associate with anguish.

33. Otniel E. Dror, "Counting the Affects: Discoursing in Numbers," *Social Research* 68, no. 2 (2001): 357–78; Phoebe Sengers et al., "The Disenchantment of Affect," *Personal and Ubiquitous Computing* 12, no. 5 (2008): 347–58; Luke Stark, "Affect and Emotion in DigitalSTS," in *DigitalSTS: A Field Guide for Science & Technology Studies*, ed. Janet Vertesi and David Ribes (Princeton, NJ: Princeton University Press, 2019), 117–35.

34. Rosalind W. Picard, *Affective Computing* (Cambridge, MA: MIT Press, 1997).

35. Mark Andrejevic and Neil Selwyn, "Facial Recognition Technology in Schools: Critical Questions and Concerns," *Learning, Media and Technology* 45, no. 2 (2020): 115–28; Andrew McStay, *Emotional AI: The Rise of Empathic Media* (Thousand Oaks, CA: Sage, 2018); Beth Semel, "Listening Like a Computer: Attentional Tensions and Mechanized Care in Psychiatric Digital Phenotyping," *Science, Technology, & Human Values* 47, no. 2 (2022): 266–90.

36. Oscar Schwartz, "Don't Look Now: Why You Should Be Worried about Machines Reading Your Emotions," *Guardian*, March 6, 2019, https://www.theguardian.com/technology/2019/mar/06/facial-recognition-software-emotional-science.

37. Meredith Whittaker et al., *Disability, Bias, and AI* (New York: AI Now Institute, 2019).

38. Sahil Chinoy, "The Racist History behind Facial Recognition," *New York Times*, July 10, 2019, https://www.nytimes.com/2019/07/10/opinion/facial-recognition-race.html.

39. Jack Gillum and Jeff Kao, "Aggression Detectors: The Unproven, Invasive Surveillance Technology Schools Are Using to Monitor Students," ProPublica, June 25, 2019, https://features.propublica.org/aggression-detector/the-unproven-invasive-surveillance-technology-schools-are-using-to-monitor-students/.

40. Os Keyes, "Automating Autism: Disability, Discourse, and Artificial Intelligence," *Journal of Sociotechnical Critique* 1, no. 1 (2020): 1–31; Jeff S. Nagy, "From 'Emotional

Hearing Aids' to 'Emotion as a Service': Psychometrics, Disability, and Emotional Big Data" (paper presented at the International Communication Association Conference, Communication History Division, Washington, DC, May 24, 2019), https://journals .sagepub.com/doi/full/10.1177/14614448221109550; Annuska Zolyomi and Jaime Snyder, "Social-Emotional-Sensory Design Map for Affective Computing Informed by Neurodivergent Experiences," *Proceedings of the ACM on Human-Computer Interaction* 5, no. CSCW1 (2021): 1–37, https://dl.acm.org/doi/abs/10.1145/3449151.

41. Rana El Kaliouby, "Q&A with Affectiva: Answers to Your Most Emotional Questions," Affectiva, March 3, 2017, para. 8, https://blog.affectiva.com/qa-with-affectiva -answers-to-your-most-emotional-questions.

42. Rana El Kaliouby, Rosalind W. Picard, and Simon Baron-Cohen, "Affective Computing and Autism," *Annals of the New York Academy of Sciences* 1093, no. 1 (2006): 228–48. Affectiva currently partners with Brain Power, a company that uses Google Glass and Affectiva's technology to commercialize its application for such therapeutic use; Cade Metz, "Google Glass May Have an Afterlife as a Device to Teach Autistic Children," *New York Times*, July 17, 2019, https://www.nytimes.com/2019/07/17 /technology/google-glass-device-treat-autism.html. For empirical and clinical critiques of wearable glass-based emotion-recognition applications for kids, see Hannah Furfaro, "Tech Firm's 'Superpower Glass' for Autism Not So Super, Experts Say," *Spectrum*, May 2, 2019, https://www.spectrumnews.org/news/tech-firms-superpower-glass-autism-not -super-experts-say/.

43. Raffi Khatchadourian, "We Know How You Feel," *New Yorker*, January 12, 2015, https://www.newyorker.com/magazine/2015/01/19/know-feel.

44. Mara Mills, "Deaf Jam: From Inscription to Reproduction to Information," *Social Text* 28, no. 1 (2010): 35–58.

45. Raymond Williams, *Marxism and Literature* (Oxford: Oxford University Press, 1977).

46. Luke Stark, "Algorithmic Psychometrics and the Scalable Subject," *Social Studies of Science* 48, no. 2 (2018): 204–31.

47. Luke Stark and Kate Crawford, "The Conservatism of Emoji: Affect, Work and Culture," *Social Media + Society* 1, no. 2 (2015): 1–11.

48. Andrew Begel et al., "Lessons Learned in Designing AI for Autistic Adults," in *Proceedings of the 2020 ACM SIGACCESS Conference on Computers and Accessibility* (New York: ACM, 2020), 1–6; Ezra Marcus, "Tone Is Hard to Grasp Online. Can Tone Indicators Help?," *New York Times*, December 9, 2020, https://www.nytimes.com /2020/12/09/style/tone-indicators-online.html.

49. Eli Clare, *Brilliant Imperfection: Grappling with Cure* (Durham, NC: Duke University Press, 2017).

50. Brent Malin, *Feeling Mediated: A History of Media Technology and Emotion in America* (New York: New York University Press, 2014), 21.

51. Sebastian Scherr et al., "Parents, Television, and Children's Emotional Expressions: A Cross-Cultural Multilevel Model," *Journal of Cross-Cultural Psychology* 50, no. 1 (2019): 22–46.

52. Nicole Martins, "Media and Emotional Development," in *The Routledge International Handbook of Children, Adolescents and Media*, ed. Dafna Lemish (New York: Routledge, 2015), 201–8.

53. Gerard Jones, *Killing Monsters: Our Children's Need for Fantasy, Heroism, and Make-Believe Violence* (New York: Basic Books, 2002).

54. Kathryn E. Ringland et al., "Would You Be Mine: Appropriating Minecraft as an Assistive Technology for Youth with Autism," in *Proceedings of the 18th International ACM SIGACCESS Conference on Computers and Accessibility* (New York: ACM: 2016), 33–41.

55. Rebecca Lane and Jenny Radesky, "Digital Media and Autism Spectrum Disorders: Review of Evidence, Theoretical Concerns, and Opportunities for Intervention," *Journal of Developmental & Behavioral Pediatrics* 40, no. 5 (2019): 364–68.

56. Melissa H. Kuo et al., "Media Use among Adolescents with Autism Spectrum Disorder," *Autism* 18, no. 8 (2014): 914–23.

57. Amy G. Halberstadt et al., "Racialized Emotion Recognition Accuracy and Anger Bias of Children's Faces," *Emotion* 22, no. 3 (2022): 403–17.

58. Morton Ann Gernsbacher, Emily M. Morson, and Elizabeth J. Grace, "Language and Speech in Autism," *Annual Review of Linguistics* 2 (2016): 413–25; Laura Sterponi, Kenton de Kirby, and Jennifer Shankey, "Rethinking Language in Autism," *Autism* 19, no. 5 (2015): 517–26.

59. *Daniel Tiger* added a Black autistic boy character named Max in 2021; Kate Hogan, "*Daniel Tiger's Neighborhood* Adds a New Character: Meet Max, Teacher Harriet's Nephew with Autism," *People*, March 12, 2021, https://people.com/parents/daniel-tigers-neighborhood-new-character-max/.

60. Wesley H. Dotson et al., "Evaluating the Ability of the PBS Children's Show *Daniel Tiger's Neighborhood* to Teach Skills to Two Young Children with Autism Spectrum Disorder," *Behavior Analysis in Practice* 10, no. 1 (2017): 67–71; Ofer Golan et al., "Enhancing Emotion Recognition in Children with Autism Spectrum Conditions: An Intervention Using Animated Vehicles with Real Emotional Faces," *Journal of Autism and Developmental Disorders* 40, no. 3 (2010): 269–79.

61. Meryl Alper, *Giving Voice: Mobile Communication, Disability, and Inequality* (Cambridge, MA: MIT Press, 2017).

62. Kristen Harrison et al., "Sensory Curation: Theorizing Media Use for Sensory Regulation and Implications for Family Media Conflict," *Media Psychology* 22, no. 4 (2019): 653–88.

63. Rachel Stonehouse, "Roblox: 'I Thought He Was Playing an Innocent Game,'" *BBC News*, May 30, 2019, https://www.bbc.com/news/technology-48450604; James

Clayton and Jasmin Dyer, "Roblox: The Children's Game with a Sex Problem," BBC News, February 15, 2022, https://www.bbc.com/news/technology-60314572.

64. Jessica L. Peterson et al., "Trauma and Autism Spectrum Disorder: Review, Proposed Treatment Adaptations and Future Directions," *Journal of Child & Adolescent Trauma* 12, no. 4 (2019): 529–47.

65. Lauren Bishop-Fitzpatrick and Amy J. H. Kind, "A Scoping Review of Health Disparities in Autism Spectrum Disorder," *Journal of Autism and Developmental Disorders* 47, no. 11 (2017): 3380–91; Jenna S. Eilenberg et al., "Disparities Based on Race, Ethnicity, and Socioeconomic Status over the Transition to Adulthood among Adolescents and Young Adults on the Autism Spectrum: A Systematic Review," *Current Psychiatry Reports* 21, no. 5 (2019): 1–16.

66. Meryl Alper, *Digital Youth with Disabilities* (Cambridge, MA: MIT Press, 2014).

67. Harrison et al., "Sensory Curation."

68. Yehuda Bar Lev and Nelly Elias, "Digital Parenting: Media Uses in Parenting Routines during the First Two Years of Life," *Studies in Media and Communication* 8, no. 2 (2020): 41–48; Lane and Radesky, "Digital Media and Autism Spectrum Disorders"; Jenny Radesky et al., "Use of Mobile Technology to Calm Upset Children: Associations with Socio-emotional Development," *JAMA Pediatrics* 170, no. 4 (2016): 397–99.

69. James Bridle, "How *Peppa Pig* Became a Video Nightmare for Children," *Guardian*, June 17, 2018, https://www.theguardian.com/technology/2018/jun/17/peppa-pig-youtube-weird-algorithms-automated-content.

70. Katya Borgos-Rodriguez, Kathryn E. Ringland, and Anne Marie Piper, "MyAutsomeFamilyLife: Analyzing Parents of Children with Developmental Disabilities on YouTube," in *Proceedings of the 2019 ACM International Conference on Computer Supported Collaborative Work (CSCW)* (New York: ACM, 2019), 1–26.

71. Embodied Inc., "Moxie," Embodied (n.d.), https://embodied.com/products/buy-moxie-robot.

72. Zolyomi and Snyder, "Social-Emotional-Sensory Design Map."

73. Andrew McStay, *Privacy and Philosophy: New Media and Affective Protocol* (New York: Peter Lang, 2014).

74. Nagy, "From 'Emotional Hearing Aids' to 'Emotion as a Service.'"

CHAPTER 8

1. Some of Caleb and Audrey's story appears in Meryl Alper, "The Silver Lining of Virtual School for Some Autistic Students," *Slate*, October 27, 2020, https://slate.com/technology/2020/10/virtual-school-autistic-students-social-life.html.

2. Pew Research Center, *The Internet and the Pandemic* (Washington, DC: Pew Research Center, 2021), https://www.pewresearch.org/internet/2021/09/01/the-internet-and-the-pandemic/.

3. Jaclyn Jeffrey-Wilensky, "'Flattening the Curve' May Pose Tough Challenge for Autistic People," *Spectrum*, April 1, 2020, https://www.spectrumnews.org/news/flattening-the
-curve-may-pose-tough-challenge-for-autistic-people/.

4. Itay Tokatly Latzer, Yael Leitner, and Orit Karnieli-Miller, "Core Experiences of Parents of Children with Autism during the COVID-19 Pandemic Lockdown," *Autism* 25, no. 4 (2021): 1047–59.

5. Philippa L. Howard and Felicity Sedgewick, "'Anything But the Phone!' Communication Mode Preferences in the Autism Community," *Autism* 25, no. 8 (2021): 2265–78.

6. Elizabeth Pellicano et al., "COVID-19, Social Isolation and the Mental Health of Autistic People and Their Families: A Qualitative Study," *Autism* 26, no. 4 (2022): 914–27.

7. Nicole Chung, "My Child Has a Disability. What Will Her Education Be Like This Year?," *New York Times Magazine*, September 15, 2020, https://www.nytimes
.com/interactive/2020/09/10/magazine/special-education-covid.html; Kristin Harrison, "Free, Appropriate, Public, and Educational? Screen-Schooling U.S. Children with Disabilities during the 2020 Pandemic," *Journal of Children and Media* 15, no. 1 (2021): 44–48.

8. Sarah Hurwitz, Blaine Garman-McClaine, and Kane Carlock, "Special Education for Students with Autism during the COVID-19 Pandemic: 'Each Day Brings New Challenges,'" *Autism* 26, no. 4 (2022): 889–99.

9. Scot Danforth and Srikala Naraian, "Use of the Machine Metaphor within Autism Research," *Journal of Developmental and Physical Disabilities* 19, no. 3 (2007): 273–90.

10. Nicholas Fearn, "Autistic Teenager Creates App to Help People on the Spectrum," *Forbes*, August 17, 2019, https://www.forbes.com/sites/nicholasfearn/2019
/08/17/autistic-teenager-creates-app-to-help-people-on-the-spectrum; Nathalie Fernback, "Autism App 'ASD and Me' Means Global Recognition for 12yo Townsville Developer," *ABC News* (Australian Broadcasting Corporation), October 3, 2017, https://www.abc.net.au/news/2017-10-04/austism-app-asd-and-me-means-global
-recognition-for-12yo/9014044.

11. Gareth Cook, "The Autism Advantage," *New York Times Magazine*, November 29, 2012, http://www.nytimes.com/2012/12/02/magazine/the-autism-advantage.html; Jordynn Jack, *Autism and Gender: From Refrigerator Mothers to Computer Geeks* (Urbana: University of Illinois Press, 2014).

12. Elizabeth Fein, "Making Meaningful Worlds: Role-Playing Subcultures and the Autism Spectrum," *Culture, Medicine, and Psychiatry* 39, no. 2 (2015): 299–321.

13. Megumi Kushima et al., "Association between Screen Time Exposure in Children at 1 Year of Age and Autism Spectrum Disorder at 3 Years of Age: The Japan Environment and Children's Study," *JAMA Pediatrics* 176, no. 4 (2022): 384–91; John Elder

Robison, "Is the Internet Making People a Little Bit Autistic?," *Psychology Today*, November 30, 2008, https://www.psychologytoday.com/us/blog/my-life-aspergers /200811/is-the-internet-making-people-little-bit-autistic.

14. Kristin Sainani, "Study Links Screen Time to Autism, But Problems Abound," *Spectrum*, February 1, 2022, https://www.spectrumnews.org/opinion/study-links-screen -time-to-autism-but-problems-abound/.

15. Cassidy Puckett and Jennifer L. Nelson, "The Geek Instinct: Theorizing Cultural Alignment in Disadvantaged Contexts," *Qualitative Sociology* 42, no. 1 (2019): 25–48.

16. Jessica A. Leveto, "Toward a Sociology of Autism and Neurodiversity," *Sociology Compass* 12, no. 12 (2018): 1–17; Majia H. Nadesan, *Constructing Autism: Unraveling the "Truth" and Understanding the Social* (New York: Routledge, 2005); Jessica S. Rauchberg, "Imagining a Neuroqueer Technoscience," *Studies in Social Justice* 16, no. 2 (2022): 370–88.

17. Meryl Alper, Vikki S. Katz, and Lynn Schofield Clark, "Researching Children, Intersectionality, and Diversity in the Digital Age," *Journal of Children and Media* 10, no. 1 (2016): 107–14.

18. Mizuko Ito et al., *Hanging Out, Messing Around, and Geeking Out: Kids Living and Learning with New Media* (Cambridge, MA: MIT Press, 2010).

19. Jason M. Nagata et al., "Screen Time Use among US Adolescents During the COVID-19 Pandemic: Findings from the Adolescent Brain Cognitive Development (ABCD) Study," *JAMA Pediatrics* 176, no. 1 (2022): 94–96.

20. For example: Sean Gregory, "Don't Feel Bad if Your Kids Are Gaming More than Ever. In Fact, Why Not Join Them?," *Time*, April 22, 2020, https://time.com /5825214/video-games-screen-time-parenting-coronavirus/.

21. Jessica N. Rocheleau and Sonia Chiasson, "Privacy and Safety on Social Networking Sites: Autistic and Non-autistic Teenagers' Attitudes and Behaviors," *ACM Transactions on Computer-Human Interaction* 29, no. 1 (2022): 1–39.

22. Meryl Alper, "Critical Media Access Studies: Deconstructing Power, Visibility, and Marginality in Mediated Space," *International Journal of Communication* 15 (2021): 840–61.

23. Rachel Dorsey, Hillary Crow, and Caroline Gaddy, "From My Perspective/Opinion: Putting Autistic Voices at the Forefront of Care," *ASHA LeaderLive*, October 1, 2020, https://leader.pubs.asha.org/do/10.1044/leader.FMP.25102020.8/full/.

24. Joshua K. Hartshorne et al., "Screen Time as an Index of Family Distress," *Current Research in Behavioral Sciences* 2 (2021): 1–9, para 3.

25. Meryl Alper, "U.S. Parent Perspectives of Media Guidance from Pediatric Autism Professionals," *Journal of Children and Media* 15, no. 2 (2021): 165–82.

26. Alper, Katz, and Clark, "Researching Children, Intersectionality, and Diversity."

27. Lisa Gerhardt and Jill Smith, "The Use of Minecraft in the Treatment of Trauma for a Child with Autism Spectrum Disorder," *Journal of Family Therapy* 42, no. 3 (2020): 365–84.

28. Elizabeth Fein, *Living on the Spectrum: Autism and Youth in Community* (New York: New York University Press, 2020).

29. I should note that I served as a consultant on *Hero Elementary* and provided some early advice on the development of one of the show's main protagonists, a Black autistic boy named AJ Gadgets, and gave story notes on a double episode intended to more explicitly discuss AJ's autism.

30. Katta Spiel et al., "Agency of Autistic Children in Technology Research—A Critical Literature Review," *ACM Transactions on Computer-Human Interaction* 26, no. 6 (2019): 1–40; Rua M. Williams and Juan E. Gilbert, "Perseverations of the Academy: A Survey of Wearable Technologies Applied to Autism Intervention," *International Journal of Human-Computer Studies* 143 (2020): 1–20.

31. Jung Won Kim et al., "Smartphone Apps for Autism Spectrum Disorder—Understanding the Evidence," *Journal of Technology in Behavioral Science* 3, no. 1 (2018): 1–4.

32. Inha Cha et al., "Exploring the Use of a Voice-Based Conversational Agent to Empower Adolescents with Autism Spectrum Disorder," in *Proceedings of the 2021 CHI Conference on Human Factors in Computing Systems* (New York: ACM, 2021), 1–15; Christopher Frauenberger, Katta Spiel, and Julia Makhaeva, "Thinking OutsideTheBox—Designing Smart Things with Autistic Children," *International Journal of Human-Computer Interaction* 35, no. 8 (2019): 666–78; Randy Zhu, Dianna Hardy, and Trina Myers, "Community Led Co-design of a Social Networking Platform with Adolescents with Autism Spectrum Disorder," *Journal of Autism and Developmental Disorders* 52 (2022): 38–51.

33. Meryl Alper and Gerard Goggin, "Digital Technology and Rights in the Lives of Children with Disabilities," *New Media & Society* 19, no. 5 (2017): 726–40.

34. Sharon Hays, *The Cultural Contradictions of Motherhood* (New Haven, CT: Yale University Press, 1996).

35. Lauren R. Strand, "Charting Relations between Intersectionality Theory and the Neurodiversity Paradigm," *Disability Studies Quarterly* 37, no. 2 (2017), https://dsq-sds.org/article/view/5374/4647.

36. James N. Gilmore, "Securing the Kids: Geofencing and Child Wearables," *Convergence* 25, no. 5–6 (2020): 1333–46; Amy Adele Hasinoff, "Where Are You? Location Tracking and the Promise of Child Safety," *Television & New Media* 18, no. 6 (2017): 496–512; Gary Marx and Valerie Steeves, "From the Beginning: Children as Subjects and Agents of Surveillance," *Surveillance & Society* 7, no. 3/4 (2010): 192–230; Margaret K. Nelson, *Parenting Out of Control: Anxious Parents in Uncertain Times* (New York: New York University Press, 2010).

37. Janice McLaughlin, Edmund Coleman-Fountain, and Emma Clavering, *Disabled Childhoods: Monitoring Differences and Emerging Identities* (London: Routledge, 2016).

38. Leon J. Hilton, "Avonte's Law: Autism, Wandering, and the Racial Surveillance of Neurological Difference," *African American Review* 50, no. 2 (2017): 221–35.

39. Brent Hayward, Fiona Ransley, and Rhiannon Memery, "GPS Devices for Elopement of People with Autism and Other Developmental Disabilities: A Review of the Published Literature," *Journal of Policy and Practice in Intellectual Disabilities* 13, no. 1 (2016): 69–74; Laura McLaughlin et al., "Wandering by Children with Autism Spectrum Disorders: Impact of Electronic Tracking Devices on Elopement Behavior and Quality of Life," *Journal of Developmental & Behavioral Pediatrics* 41, no. 7 (2020): 513–21.

40. Carolien Rieffe, Paul Oosterveld, and Mark Meerum Terwogt, "An Alexithymia Questionnaire for Children: Factorial and Concurrent Validation Results," *Personality and Individual Differences* 40, no. 1 (2006): 123–33.

41. Andrew J. Lampi, Vikram K. Jaswal, and Tanya M. Evans, "How Closely Related Are Parent and Child Reports of Child Alexithymia?," *Frontiers in Psychology* 11 (2021): 1–10.

42. Patti M. Valkenburg and Jessica T. Piotrowski, *Plugged In: How Media Attract and Affect Youth* (New Haven, CT: Yale University Press, 2017).

43. Anja Stiller and Thomas Mößle, "Media Use among Children and Adolescents with Autism Spectrum Disorder: A Systematic Review," *Review Journal of Autism and Developmental Disorders* 5, no. 3 (2018): 227–46.

44. Bryn Harris, Erin E. Barton, and Maryellen Brunson McClain, "Inclusion of Racially and Ethnically Diverse Populations in ASD Intervention Research," *Research in Autism Spectrum Disorders* 73 (2020): 1–6; Elizabeth A. West et al., "Racial and Ethnic Diversity of Participants in Research Supporting Evidence-Based Practices for Learners with Autism Spectrum Disorder," *Journal of Special Education* 50, no. 3 (2016): 151–63.

45. For example, see Karri Gillespie-Smith et al., "Using Social Media to Be 'Social': Perceptions of Social Media Benefits and Risk by Autistic Young People, and Parents," *Research in Developmental Disabilities* 118 (2021): 1–11; Rocheleau and Chiasson, "Privacy and Safety on Social Networking Sites."

46. Nicole Martins, Andy King, and Rebecca Beights, "Audiovisual Media Content Preferences of Children with Autism Spectrum Disorders: Insights from Parental Interviews," *Journal of Autism and Developmental Disorders* 50, no. 9 (2020): 3092–100.

47. Patrick Dwyer et al., "An Expert Roundtable Discussion on Experiences of Autistic Autism Researchers," *Autism in Adulthood* 3, no. 3 (2021): 209–20.

APPENDIX

1. Carmel Conn, *Autism and the Social World of Childhood: A Sociocultural Perspective on Theory and Practice* (New York: Routledge, 2014).

2. Leslie S. Daniel and Bonnie S. Billingsley, "What Boys with an Autism Spectrum Disorder Say about Establishing and Maintaining Friendships," *Focus on Autism and Other Developmental Disabilities* 25, no. 4 (2010): 220–29; Rackeb Tesfaye et al., "Assuming Ability of Youth with Autism: Synthesis of Methods Capturing the First-Person Perspectives of Children and Youth with Disabilities," *Autism* 23, no. 8 (2019): 1882–96.

3. Valérie Courchesne et al., "*Autism Voices*: A Novel Method to Access First-Person Perspective of Autistic Youth," *Autism* 26, no. 5, published online ahead of print, September 4, 2021, https://journals.sagepub.com/doi/full/10.1177/13623613211042128.

4. Lise Mogensen and Jan Mason, "The Meaning of a Label for Teenagers Negotiating Identity: Experiences with Autism Spectrum Disorder," *Sociology of Health & Illness* 37, no. 2 (2015): 255–69.

5. Michael Burawoy, "The Extended Case Method," *Sociological Theory* 16, no. 1 (1998): 4–33.

6. Victoria Reyes, "Ethnographic Toolkit: Strategic Positionality and Researchers' Visible and Invisible Tools in Field Research," *Ethnography* 21, no. 2 (2020): 220–40.

7. Carolyn Bridgemohan et al., "A Workforce Survey on Developmental-Behavioral Pediatrics," *Pediatrics* 141, no. 3 (2018): e20172164.

8. Meryl Alper, "Inclusive Sensory Ethnography: Studying New Media and Neurodiversity in Everyday Life," *New Media & Society* 20, no. 10 (2018): 3560–79.

9. Ann Swidler, "Culture in Action: Symbols and Strategies," *American Sociological Review* 51, no. 2 (1986): 273–86.

10. Michael Burawoy, "Revisits: An Outline of a Theory of Reflexive Ethnography," *American Sociological Review* 68, no. 5 (2003): 645–79; Paul Lichterman, "Interpretive Reflexivity in Ethnography," *Ethnography* 18, no. 1 (2017): 35–45.

11. Amy M. Daniels et al., "Verification of Parent-Report of Child Autism Spectrum Disorder Diagnosis to a Web-Based Autism Registry," *Journal of Autism and Developmental Disorders* 42, no. 2 (2012): 257–65.

12. Maarten van't Hof et al., "Age at Autism Spectrum Disorder Diagnosis: A Systematic Review and Meta-Analysis from 2012 to 2019," *Autism* 25, no. 4 (2021): 862–73.

13. US Department of Education, *A Guide to the Individualized Education Program* (Washington, DC: US Department of Education, 2019), https://www2.ed.gov/parents/needs/speced/iepguide/index.html.

14. Willard W. Hartup, "The Company They Keep: Friendships and Their Developmental Significance," *Child Development* 67, no. 1 (1996): 1–13.

15. Meryl Alper, *Giving Voice: Mobile Communication, Disability, and Inequality* (Cambridge, MA: MIT Press, 2017).

16. David Preece and Rita Jordan, "Obtaining the Views of Children and Young People with Autism Spectrum Disorders about Their Experience of Daily Life and Social Care Support," *British Journal of Learning Disabilities* 38, no. 1 (2010): 10–20.

17. Caitlin Harrington et al., "Engaging Young People with Autism Spectrum Disorder in Research Interviews," *British Journal of Learning Disabilities* 42, no. 2 (2014): 153–61.

18. Karen G. Sirota, "Narratives of Distinction: Personal Life Narrative as a Technology of the Self in the Everyday Lives and Relational Worlds of Children with Autism," *Ethos* 38, no. 1 (2010): 94.

19. Robert M. Emerson, Rachel I. Fretz, and Linda L. Shaw, *Writing Ethnographic Fieldnotes* (Chicago: University of Chicago Press, 2011).

20. Barney G. Glaser and Anselm L. Strauss, *The Discovery of Grounded Theory: Strategies for Qualitative Research* (New Brunswick, NJ: Aldine, 1967); Anselm L. Strauss and Juliet Corbin, *Basics of Qualitative Research: Techniques and Procedures for Developing Grounded Theory* (Thousand Oaks, CA: Sage, 1998).

21. Stephen J. Taylor and Robert Bogdan, *Introduction to Qualitative Research Methods*, 3rd ed. (New York: Wiley, 1998).

22. Johnny Saldaña, *The Coding Manual for Qualitative Researchers*, 3rd ed. (London: Sage, 2016).

23. Kathy Charmaz, "The Grounded Theory Method: An Explication and Interpretation," in *Contemporary Field Research*, ed. Robert M. Emerson (Boston: Little, Brown, 1983), 109–26.

24. Eric Garcia, *We're Not Broken: Changing the Autism Conversation* (New York: Houghton Mifflin Harcourt, 2021).

INDEX

Note: Page numbers in *italics* indicate figures.